WITHDRAWN

THE COLLECTED POETRY OF
Robinson Jeffers

Edited by Tim Hunt

VOLUME TWO

1928-1938

STANFORD UNIVERSITY PRESS   1989

Stanford, California

Stanford University Press, Stanford, California

Editorial matter © 1989 by the Board of Trustees of the Leland Stanford Junior University

Published with the assistance of the National Endowment for the Humanities; and of H. A. Klein, in memory of Mina Cooper Klein

Printed in the United States of America
CIP data appear at the end of the volume

CONTENTS

II

THURSO'S LANDING
1930-1931

III

GIVE YOUR HEART TO THE HAWKS
1931 - 1933

IV

SOLSTICE
1933 - 1935

V

SUCH COUNSELS YOU GAVE TO ME
1935 - 1938

EDITORIAL NOTE

SELECTION AND ARRANGEMENT

The Collected Poetry of Robinson Jeffers includes all of Jeffers' published poems from *Flagons and Apples* (1912) through *The Beginning and the End* (1963) and those manuscript poems Jeffers considered publishing. It excludes the poems from his undergraduate years at Occidental College and incomplete poems, even when, as with "The Alpine Christ" and the versions of "Point Alma Venus," these are of considerable length and of some critical interest.

The edition presents Jeffers' work chronologically. The length of the narrative poems and other commercial factors often meant poems planned for one volume were set aside for a later one. Several poems in *Dear Judas*, for instance, were to have appeared two volumes earlier in *The Women at Point Sur*; several of the longer pieces in *Give Your Heart to the Hawks* actually precede work from the previous collection, *Thurso's Landing*. Reproducing the accidents of the original publication sequence would be of little use to a contemporary reader, while a chronological arrangement helps clarify the actual shape of Jeffers' career.

Arranging Jeffers' work chronologically, however, raises the problem of where to begin. The earliest published work, the privately printed *Flagons and Apples*, is quite different from his mature work, which began to develop, as Jeffers himself noted, during the First World War and to coalesce about 1920 in such lyrics as "To the Stone-Cutters" and the narrative *Tamar*. A primary aim of this edition is to clarify what might be termed the "Jeffers canon," and, therefore, Volume One begins with the poems of 1920, postponing apprentice work until Volume Four. Volumes One to Three thus present a complete, chronological edition of the work on which Jeffers' reputation rests and will continue to rest—the work of 1920 to 1962. Volume Four includes the work of 1912–19, poems left in manuscript, documents such as Jeffers' "Fore-word" to *The Selected Poetry of Robinson Jeffers*, and the edition's editorial apparatus.

TEXTS

The primary textual issue with Jeffers' poems is punctuation. Particularly in his narratives, Jeffers let rhythmic and dramatic considerations, rather than grammatical ones, determine punctuation. His statements in various letters and the patterns of revision in his manuscripts show he did so knowingly. His publishers, though, at times adjusted his punctuation, typically by adding commas, presumably to bring it into accord with grammatical convention. As much as possible, the texts for this edition revert to Jeffers' own punctuation. In all cases the various published forms of the poems have been compared against each other and against all manuscript forms that can be located.

Unfortunately, in most cases Jeffers' final typescripts, used to set type for the original editions, were apparently discarded once the poems were published. The manuscripts used to prepare the final typescripts have typically survived but do not appear to include his final adjustments to punctuation, while the published forms typically show evidence of house styling. Study of the surviving galley and page proofs, the few surviving typescripts, and other textual evidence indicates that in most cases Jeffers' own manuscripts are closer to the missing typescripts than are the original published settings of the poems. In most cases, then, the manuscripts have been adopted as copy-text, and variant readings adopted from the published forms of the poems where the patterns suggested by the existing evidence indicate the published form likely follows the missing typescript. A full report of the edition's procedures, textual evidence, and adopted readings is included in Volume Four. In general, though, texts have been prepared following the guidelines developed by the Center for Editions of American Authors and its successor, the Committee on Scholarly Editions.

PRESENTATION

Jeffers' verse lines are often too long to be printed as a single line of type. In this edition, such lines are broken as close to the right margin as possible without breaking words (including Jeffers' hyphenated compounds); the remainder of the line is then indented and continued as a second line of type. Such lines should, though, be considered a single metrical unit.

Jeffers seldom utilized regular stanzas. However, he often divided his poems, both long and short, into a series of verse paragraphs. Jeffers used the traditional blank line to indicate a verse paragraph when the division occurs between two complete verse lines. At times, though, the sentence that begins the new verse paragraph occurs in the middle of a verse line rather than at the beginning. In such cases, Jeffers began the new verse paragraph on a separate line, indenting its first sentence to align with the end of the sentence concluding the preceding paragraph. The original settings of Jeffers' poems sometimes insert blank lines between such verse paragraphs and sometimes do not; this has given the impression that there may be a structural distinction between these two forms. Analysis of the manuscripts and typescripts suggest Jeffers intended no such distinction and that, as a general rule, either all verse paragraphs beginning mid-line should be preceded by a blank line or none should. The evidence further suggests that verse paragraphs occurring between completed verse lines and those beginning mid-line are also structurally equivalent. In this edition verse paragraphs are separated by a single blank line, unless unusual textual circumstances dictate otherwise. In Volume Two, the dramatic poems *Dear Judas*, *At the Fall of an Age*, and *At the Birth of an Age* are treated as exceptions, since this procedure would otherwise unnecessarily introduce blank lines between many of the speeches. These exceptions, along with the evidence for Jeffers' approach to verse paragraphing and structural divisions, are discussed more fully in the textual commentary in Volume Four.

For clarity's sake, in this edition no verse paragraphs occurring between completed lines have been allowed to coincide with page breaks. In some instances paragraphs that begin in the middle of a verse line do coincide with a page break; these instances are readily apparent. Those poems utilizing regular stanzas have been arranged on the page without regard to page breaks, since the set number of lines for each stanza allows the reader to judge easily when a page break coincides with a stanza break and when not.

Finally, one adjustment has been made to Jeffers' punctuation. Jeffers typically placed colons and semicolons inside concluding quotation marks. His publishers sometimes followed his texts on this point and sometimes moved the colons and semicolons outside the concluding mark. In this edition, semicolons and colons follow the concluding quotation mark.

ACKNOWLEDGMENTS

In addition to the help and support provided by those mentioned in Volume One, I should like to note and thank Allen Mears for his continued efforts on behalf of the scholar's grail, an error-free text, Joshua Welber for so ably playing the role of research assistant, Gerry Byrne for his kind help with the typescript for *Such Counsels You Gave to Me*, and Henrietta Bensussen and Jane's Secretarial Service for preparing computer files of poems. And I would like to thank Ellen F. Smith of Stanford University Press for her patience, attention to detail, and the errors she has saved me from, both in this volume and in Volume One. I would also like to recognize, belatedly, Elizabeth Witherell's work inspecting Volume One for the Committee on Scholarly Editions. Her good cheer and advice did much to improve the quality of the first volume and contributed, though indirectly, to this volume as well.

I would also like to thank the Tor House Foundation and its new president, Jean Ritter-Murray, for continued support and encouragement, along with the American Council for Learned Societies and the Texts Program of the NEH's Division of Research Programs for the grants that provided the time and resources to carry out the work of Volume Two. And my work would have been all but impossible were it not for the ongoing generosity of Tyrus Harmsen of the Occidental College Library, Steven Corey of the University of San Francisco's Gleeson Library, and Cathy Henderson, John Kirkpatrick, and Kenneth Craven of the University of Texas Humanities Research Center. Patricia C. Willis and Steve Jones of the Beinecke Library at Yale, Jean F. Preston of the Princeton University Library, and John P. Young of the William Jewell College Library were each kind enough to contribute their time. In addition, the following libraries provided material bearing on the texts for Volume Two: the Berg Collection of the New York Public Library; the Bancroft Library of the University of California, Berkeley; the Butler Library of Columbia University; the University of Houston Library; the Mills College Library; and the Stanford University Library.

Above all I wish to thank Susan, my wife, and John and Jessica. Too much of the time this work represents has been time that should have been theirs.

I

Dear Judas

1928-1929

HOODED NIGHT

At night, toward dawn, all the lights of the shore have died,
And a wind moves. Moves in the dark
The sleeping power of the ocean, no more beastlike than manlike,
Not to be compared; itself and itself.
Its breath blown shoreward huddles the world with a fog; no stars
Dance in heaven; no ship's light glances.
I see the heavy granite bodies of the rocks of the headland,
That were ancient here before Egypt had pyramids,
Bulk on the gray of the sky, and beyond them the jets of young trees
I planted the year of the Versailles peace.
But here is the final unridiculous peace. Before the first man
Here were the stones, the ocean, the cypresses,
And the pallid region in the stone-rough dome of fog where the moon
Falls on the west. Here is reality.
The other is a spectral episode; after the inquisitive animal's
Amusements are quiet: the dark glory.

EVENING EBB

The ocean has not been so quiet for a long while; five night-herons
Fly shorelong voiceless in the hush of the air
Over the calm of an ebb that almost mirrors their wings.
The sun has gone down, and the water has gone down
From the weed-clad rock, but the distant cloud-wall rises. The ebb
    whispers.
Great cloud-shadows float in the opal water.
Through rifts in the screen of the world pale gold gleams and the evening
Star suddenly glides like a flying torch.
As if we had not been meant to see her; rehearsing behind
The screen of the world for another audience.

HANDS

Inside a cave in a narrow canyon near Tassajara
The vault of rock is painted with hands,
A multitude of hands in the twilight, a cloud of men's palms, no more,
No other picture. There's no one to say
Whether the brown shy quiet people who are dead intended
Religion or magic, or made their tracings
In the idleness of art; but over the division of years these careful
Signs-manual are now like a sealed message
Saying: "Look: we also were human; we had hands, not paws. All hail
You people with the cleverer hands, our supplanters
In the beautiful country; enjoy her a season, her beauty, and come down
And be supplanted; for you also are human."

DEAR JUDAS—
or The Dreaming Dead

They have all died and their souls are extinguished; three remnant images
    of three passions too violent to vanish
Still haunt the garden; they are nearly unfleshed of time: but if they were
    they would be eternal: they are fading.

JESUS

Cypresses warped by the weight of many hundreds of years, these trees like
    columns of knobbed stone
Are not the same; remote seedlings of those; it is sure that nineteen
    hundred years have gone down,
Still I revisit my ancient garden, under the round white stone that shines in
    the gulf of sky
And in vain, being dead, aches for annihilation, whitening the night.

                                                    Now
    the torches come up to take me.
Dear Judas be comforted at last. The smoky red flares and the scared faces,
    the servants, the priests
Are all—and even the bit of money under your cloak—imaginary, Judas.
    You and I remain yet,
Re-dreaming under the moon our passions: but all this play is played out
    and all these people have been dead
A forest of years. The kiss comes next. What, must I prompt you?

JUDAS   I know

you are neither God nor God's son.
But you are *my* God.   *(He kisses him.)*

  *(The people with torches, and the other people imagined by the speakers, may be thought of as
  represented by a few maskers moving abstractedly in dumb show.)*

                          Take him, dog-priests. I have done the worst thing I
can imagine. Oh yes: for the money.

JESUS

His phantom face is like a flayed man's face. Dear Judas turn, dream rather the lion-colored hills

And soft shores of the lake. The locusts I think chirp in the storm of sunlight. No: it's a shepherd

Flutes in the shade under that rock.

JUDAS   The shepherd is happy: but O happy happy rock.

I think the burly shepherd when he knifes a lamb

Has no thought of its pain; or if he passes along the roadside the masts of crucified robbers

The Romans have caught, and some look down and cry to him, from rattling throats in the dry wind, straining

Their hands and feet, it is only a show to gape at. Yet sometime his own pain will possess him. O happy

Happy rock.

JESUS   Since you must dream, dream on from there.

JUDAS   Why, now, what luck have the fishermen drawn

From their blue glaze? A multitude runs to the bank to meet the boat. My eyes dazzle in the driving

Dust of the sun: Oh, that new prophet.

                    (He approaches Jesus again.)   I smell the green-fringed water across the dust and the smell

Of clothes and sweat.   *(He moves about as if struggling in a crowd.)*

                    No; I can never attain to him.

JESUS   Whoever is over-burdened, or hopeless, or wretched,

Or lies between the teeth of the world: let him come to me, I am able to save him.

JUDAS   Master: listen!

When I was a child, and ran errands for my father from my father's shop,

A little brown dog followed me home. I fed it and loved it for I was a
  lonely child, and found it
A nook under the counter to lie at nights. One day it trotted among the
  stalls of the butchers,
A cleaver was thrown, I carried it home bleeding in my arms. It could
  neither live nor die and I heard it
Moaning five days and I saw its eyes. Master I am neither sick nor poor nor
  heavy with sins,
But I am in prison of my pity; the moaning of men and beasts torments
  me; the pain is not my own pain
From which I come praying for deliverance.

JESUS   To other men I say *Be*
  merciful, to you alone
Be cruel. Life is not to be lived without some balance.

JUDAS   I knew that you had
  no power to save me.

JESUS   Come back,
For I have the power. Your name is Judas Iscariot, I have long known you.
  Dear Judas, does it make you glad
To see men joyful? To watch them feasting or laughing or fine with
  drunkenness?

JUDAS   Master: I don't know why,
But I am never joyful to see that. Certainly I'm not grieved; but the others'
  joy is not mine,
Only their pain. My heart is lonely; I groan for their pain.

JESUS   You have then
  only the night side of love.
Be with me Judas, and I will teach you to love by day and by night. Peter:
  this is Judas Iscariot.
John: this is Judas, he will be with us. He is not poor; and he is the son of
  a careful shopkeeper.

We need some one with wit to care for our pennies, they're always dripping
    away, and the little almsgivings,
So, Peter, give him the purse to carry. It is no burden. Come, children.
    Dear Judas, come.

*(Jesus and Judas walk together among the trees at the back of the garden. A woman of fifty, tall
and lean, with a passion-worn proud Jewish face, is entering. She does not see the others nor they
her.)*

THE WOMAN

Never look down, stone trees.
I am only a poor half-crazed old woman
That come and sit in the grove after dark,
Too old and poor for any one to do me harm.
It is true that I'm one
Who has known great and bitter occasions.
Oh garden that the glory from my body haunted,
The shining that came forth from between my thighs . . .
Is gone: past the flower and the fall
I sit and sing a cracked song.

(She sits on a stone in the white moonlight.)

I bid you fishermen mending brown nets
On the white sand,
I bid you beware of the net, fishermen.
You never can see it,
It flies through the white air and we all are snapped in it.
No, but look round you.
You see men walking and they seem to be free,
But look at the faces, they're caught.
There was never a man cut himself loose.
. . . . That's true but comfortless.

(She sits on the left; Jesus and Judas come forward on the right.)

Nor dead in their graves are not free,
The mistletoe root-threads

In the wood of the oak of the earth

Are a net, are a net.

JESUS

They're kind people in the quiet dwellings of Bethany. Their faces reflect
My Father's face.

JUDAS   Master. Master, we hear you sometimes say *our Father*;
     and at other times

You say *my Father*.

JESUS   *(trembling)*   Do you dare?

Who appointed Iscariot . . . I am not angry, I see that you ask in honor, I
     will not hide my glory

From those I love. It is trumpeted by ten thousand in heaven. Yet even
     from my own heart in my youth

This terrible dark and shining mystery was hidden.

I learned that the carpenter was not my father. Ah Judas, you're
     tender-hearted, you'd have pitied the torture

And dark and burning fire of my days then. What could I think? Not to
     impute against my own source

An impossible shame . . . I loathed my life, I was taken in a net. It drove
     me into the desert mountains,

Where, after I had fasted beyond the moon's ring, until my spirit was
     fluttering to leave the body, I then

Remembered the prophecies and heard voices from heaven. When I
     returned I asked her, *Was God my father?*

She wept and answered that He was my father. Also when John in Jordan
     baptized me a voice declared it

In thunder from the clear sky. It was heard by many, though now they are
     scattered. . . . I blame my mother.

She sinned, hoarding her knowledge in her heart's treasury. Truly the
     torment of those days of my ignorance

Never has healed.

JUDAS   Master, we know that you are God's son. Master, you
     are changed; the warm happiness
Seems not to radiate from your face as before.
JESUS   I feel my immeasurable
     height above men.
My heart is lonely. The sun has risen behind us; let us go on.
JUDAS   Our black
     shadows that move
Immeasurably stretched on the white road, they seem to reach even to
     Jerusalem, trouble my soul.
I wonder whether the evil that we reject from our hearts is not destroyed
     but goes blackening forth
To infest others?
JESUS   You are too scrupulous. Look how the city among the
     beautiful awakening hills
Shines by itself in the morning clearness, a jewel washed with new milk.
JUDAS   Son
     of God, let me go back.
I am not prepared. I dread the shining like the shining of paradise.
     (Jesus goes on; Judas returns and sees the woman. He takes a coin from the purse and drops it into
     her lap, and says:)   Why
     did you not cry out, mother,
To our Lord when he passed? He is altogether devoted to saving the
     helpless.
THE WOMAN   Eh? Do you still have saviors?
This one does wisely to walk at night. The surest-caught fish twists in the
     net and babbles to the others,
The cords cutting his gills, *I have come to save you.*
JUDAS   It is not night but the
     pearl of morning, and the Savior
Is the son of God.   *(The woman shudders and is silent.)*
                         I say that the living God is his father.

THE WOMAN   I have this
    comfort: we are caught in the net,
And the monsters of our sin are not our own monsters, but the cords
    drawing.
JUDAS   He has come to forgive sins,
    Though they were monstrous.
THE WOMAN   This is the night after the day; black and
    silver dream the stark trees;
And now that some other woman is damned is nothing to me.
JUDAS   As if this
    withered beggar-woman
    Were incarnate Night found sitting by the wayside, she throws . . . you
        throw magical darkness over my eyes
    So that I seem standing at midnight in a dreary garden. Good God if one
        remembers the future . . .
    That would be frightful.
THE WOMAN   Wee wanton brawler
    Pommeling the breast,
    Baby if it's shrunken,
    Whose lips but yours?
    I Night am your mother,
    Grow tall, wee bird,
    And watch your shadow
    Pointing you home.
                    Do you begin to remember the future? Then we
        must dream our dreams hastily.
    Life grows transparent: what's left us but to light the torches of violence, to
        line it visible with fire?
    But though you scream with pain, remember you're only a shadow.
                                (She peers up at his face.)   Stand
        into the moon. You are the one

Who wanted to be more merciful than mercy. Well, you shall go where the
    net draws you. I Night the Mother
Watching the bright abortions pour from my womb,
Gods, men, and the stars and Caesar,
Receive them with kindness when they stream home.
Listen, Judas, for this is your dream. Your Lord has raised
A dead man out of the grave, a man who'd begun rotting. Came up when
    he called. This witnessed miracle
Flying on all winds in the city and suburbs, his name begins at length to be
    known widely and the people
Believe, they flock to hear him, his innocent heart is exalted: so that he
    dreams more than a prophet's
Glory: a great king's. His wisdom's not of this world. He says in his heart,
    "The city fills for the passover,
The people know me, and I shall go up in triumph and the trumpets will
    blow. When all the folk as one man
Rise in the shining honor of righteousness: the Romans will be ashamed
    and respect them, and the prophet-killer
Herod will flee. The power of the people, sudden and erect and resolute, I
    trust my people."

JUDAS   Dear Master,
Too many have made rebellions before; they are drowned in blood.

THE WOMAN   He
    tells you that this one will not be blotted,
Not with one drop, Jew's nor Roman's nor a slave's; we are many, they few;
    we shall be merciful; a kingdom
Of peace and mercy.

JUDAS   *(turning from her, throwing out his hand to restrain some imaginary person whom he
    sees as present)*   No, Peter. No! That was too cruel.

THE WOMAN   His dream
    skips over to an easier pity.
He cannot bear this progress up to Jerusalem.

JUDAS   Peter has flung a stone and
  has broken the hawk's wing.
  The trustful hawk that perched in the fig-tree: now it will never again
    rejoice in the blowing air
  And blue spaces, but trail pain till it starves. Its wound saves many
    sparrows? I know it. Oh Simon
  Well called the Stone: what a net of cruelty
  Life gasps in, inextricably involved; so that I know not what to pray for but
    annihilation
  For a blessing on life. The bird's pain's nothing, though it grinds my heart;
    all the groaning world, Simon.
  Flogged slaves and tortured criminals, and bitter deaths of the innocent.
    Who created it? Who can endure it? Does no one,
  Not even our Lord, feel it but I alone? My soul is dark with images, and all
    are dreadful,
  Sword, scourge and javelin, and the Roman gibbet,
  Women dying horribly in hopeless birth-pangs, men dying of thirst and
    hunger, the miners dying in the mines
  Under the stinking torches, in summer by the Red Sea, consumed with
    labor in the metal darkness;
  And the ankles eaten with rust, and the blood-striped backs, of the oars in a
    thousand galleys; it would be salvation
  To think that I could willingly bear the suffering — if it were possible — for
    all that lives, I alone:
  I dare not think so.
THE WOMAN   (laughing)
                        But Simon says that if you've got a stone you wing
  the next bird, that's natural.
JUDAS
  Oh, hush. Our Lord is coming from the house.
  It's morning again, how the world bathes in light; and all the long clear
    shadows lying toward Jerusalem.

See there's the fig-tree . . . no, I'll forget my griefs . . . innumerably
   spreading his broad green hands
Sweet with their night-dew to the new day. O happy tree.

JESUS   *(coming in from the left, speaking to those imagined beside him)*   Keep back the
   people from me; I am faint
With the height within. Children, remember always that dreams are
   deceivers. No one's exempt from dreaming,
Not even I. But all's fraud: fragments of thought
Fitting themselves together without a mind. It seemed to me that I stood
   on a higher tower
Than any pier of those three that blot the tender blue above Herod's
   palace. Oh, beyond conception
Exalted over the hills and the seas. But the tower swayed—it means
   nothing: perhaps I slept
Having remembered the tower guilty of blood in Siloam—tottered and
   waved all its wild height,
I felt the rushes of the air and heard the stones crumbling . . . I will not
   cross my day of decision
With a dream's mind. Look how this fig-tree shakes his banners above me. I
   came fasting from the house
And now I am hungry, there will be fruit among the broad leaves. What,
   utterly barren? Let neither man
Nor bird henceforth eat of these boughs that have failed me.

JUDAS   Do you
   wish, Master, the beautiful tree were dead?

JESUS
What is that to you?

JUDAS   Oh Master. Master, your face is sorrowful, your
   eyes are bitter. Let us go back
To Galilee where the days were all glad.

JESUS   Faint-hearted, Ah brittle-hearted
   counsellor, must one build power

On the dry twigs and stubble of such friends as you? I tell you freely that
　　to-day will see done
What was determined before the rock was laid down under the towers of
　　the mountains. This jewel of time
Laid in my hand, rejected once would be lost forever. All greatness is a
　　wrestling with time,
And one who has got the grip of his gaunt opponent, if he lets go will not
　　thrive, not again, but go down
And the dust cover him, sheet over sheet above his forgotten face, century
　　on century. I feel
Signs in my soul and know my occasion. My soul is all towers.
That idle dream was the human part's rebellion against the divine: it is
　　dreadful for the frail flesh
Born of a woman to serve the triumphant occasions of God. The lightnings
　　and pinnacles of my spirit
Cry out and call me: my Father is my trumpet: and the people's eyes.
　　Indeed it is strange: I am now so lifted
Toward God that I seem to myself, among all these pressing
Faces and voices, rather to walk alone in an ancient garden, among dark
　　trunks of stone trees
And patches of moon; imagining these things.
I can shake it off.　　*(He addresses the imagined people.)*
　　　　　　　Listen and hear me. I have gone in the past privately up
　　to Jerusalem; but now
My sun has risen, the hour shines and beckons, my day has come up. It is
　　not forbidden you now to proclaim me
What your hearts know. I am called of my Father to lead this people; I
　　work my calling. It is not my desire
But even a bitterness to me to be called a king; yet to this purpose I was
　　born. What's kingdom to *me*?
To me that walked with God my Father before the foundation of the earth?
　　I ruled the angels in heaven:

And now I have come to a little place to save a lost people. What's kingdom to *me*? I seem to myself

Rather to walk alone in an old garden and watch the moon through the trees. You will proclaim me

King of the Jews in the city Jerusalem; and I must take and build up the throne of David, and shepherd

The flocks of God.

               (Friend, go to that man's house to whom you have spoken and fetch the colt he has ready;

I must now ride in triumph to the city.)

                        I will ride among you up to Jerusalem to be your King,

And all the streets and palaces will shout my coming. Yet listen and hear me. Herod will flee to Rome,

And Rome shall fall down, her discaptained soldiers

Run gaping and be flung on heaps: now I command you all to be utterly merciful in that high moment,

On the ridge of victory.

Let it be bloodless: let not one body be pierced, one soul made sorrowful. The people rise as one man,

And who shall stay them? but I am making a new thing in the world,

I am making a kingdom not built on blood, I am making a power weaponed with love not violence; a white

Dominion; a smokeless lamp; a pure light.

JUDAS   Alas my Master. Oh listen to me! He cannot hear me.

His ears are full of the foolish cries of these poor people. His eyes are utterly visionary,

His mind wild with its dream. He is leading them up to sudden bloody destruction.

JESUS   Farewell, farewell

Little friendly Bethany to which I shall never return

But crowned a king.

(He passes on, and approaches the far side of the scene.)

You narrow and envious and philacteried foreheads,
Ah generation of vipers,
I tell you that if these people should dare be silent the very stones of the
pavement would shout *Hosanna.*

(Jesus goes out, followed by Judas.)

THE WOMAN   *(She stands up and says:)*

I am very tired, and the sun is burning. I must have fallen on slumber while
I rested by the road,
I dreamed of hearing many people go shouting through a dark garden.
While I was the mother Night
Including them all. . . . But I am Mary, the wife of Joseph. I have come up
as fast as I could,
In hope to see my son at this time. My son is a great prophet among our
villages, and now
They tell me that even Jerusalem is crazy to hear him. I heard that he has
gone up more like a king . . .
I'm sure he'd never rise against government . . . the people threw down
their cloaks under the wheels of his chariot
To color the road with purple and softness, and long green palm-leaves. But
I come here with terror in my heart
To be near his triumph. Oh, while his fame flourishes I'll never intrude, I'll
see his face from far off,
And the dear masterful sweetness of his face. A few perhaps will know that
I am his mother, but no one
Will hear me claim him . . . though indeed I'm not a peasant, he needn't
be ashamed . . . but he's been lovely from boyhood,
Superior and born a leader, and such a power of discourse. I wouldn't,
however, go up to find him;

I'll visit here with his friends in Bethany.

(She stands at the edge of the scene, on the left.)   Oh: don't you know me? I am the mother of the man you love.

And you are Lazarus whom he raised from the dead. Your face has never changed since.

(She goes out of sight. The moon shines through the cypress-trees during a pause; and Judas comes in, from the right.)

JUDAS   (terribly agitated)

The glory is departed.

Oh, he has changed and changed. But I, what shall I do? His mind is dreadfully exalted and bitter,

And divided. I cannot understand what he suffers but I see what he does. He went up shining;

Whenever the people shouted the winning favor we used to adore was like a flame sweetened

With wine and honey in his face and motions. But when he had entered the city the people became silent,

Expecting something. Then we could see that he also expected something. —— That never came; and his face

Darkened. He then went up to the temple. But I and two others held close beside him, babbling like children

About the sights of the city, glad to be fools if we could divert the gloom of his mind. I showed him

The huge stones of the walls and terraces: he suddenly turned,

Stopped on the stair, and lifting his two clenched hands toward heaven, he screamed in a voice not like his own

To those below him, but like the lake gulls in Galilee over the full fishing-boats:

"They'll all be broken! Look at these stones that are as long as two men and the thickness of a man's height,

Not one shall stand but go down, the giants of old, not one be left on another. I destroy. I destroy.

The temple and the temple treasures, the priests and the gray rabbis. No
    man shall be saved but those that believe me

The son of God . . . What do I say," he shouted . . . "the son is the
    Father's equal. I, here, am God.

But keep it secret awhile." He looked at the people as though he hated
    them. We could do nothing. I remembered

How hard he has grown toward suffering lately, and careless of the poor.
    When the woman came and poured that perfume

Over his hair and his clothes, enough in value to have saved many from
    misery, he was pleased and praised her.

He is changed indeed.

He entered the temple: then those that vend pigeons to offer at the altar,
    and the poor hucksters that sell

The holy ribbons and trays of sweetmeats: the courts are crowded at
    passover-time: they seemed to enrage him.

He said, "Go forth. You are making the house of prayer a thieves' den." He
    twisted a whip out of hard cords

And drove them, and made a screaming riot in the temple. . . . So all the
    people were gathered to him again

To follow him, because they love destruction. He has found the dreadful
    key to their hearts. One poor old man

Had fallen and cut his forehead on the brass edge of the tray, and lay
    weeping among the crushed candies,

His white hair matted with watery blood.

We lifted him up. I cannot tell whether Jesus has gone mad, or has indeed
    grown

Too near the power that makes falcons and lions, earthquakes and Rome, as
    much as the corn in the fields

And the breasts of mothers, and the happier birds. He is terrible now. He
    has the shining power a few moments

And then stands brooding dumb, or suddenly through the old sweetness a
    jet of poison. I have begged and prayed to him,
On my knees, with tears, to return down from the city. He looked across
    me with haggard eyes and answered
That he was God, and would never go down. But then I heard that he has
    begun to despair, for he said
"The sacrifice has come to the temple: not a bull nor a goat; but God
Himself to God. Perhaps my kingdom is not of this world." Instantly he
    stretched his neck and shouted:
"This world is nothing. It is dust and spittle. All those that trust me inherit
    eternal life and eternal
Delight: all those that reject me shall scream
In fires a world with no end."
    *(Seeing one approaching from the right Judas moves toward the left and Jesus enters, addressing a
    crowd of people imagined about him.)*
JESUS   Ah Jerusalem, Jerusalem,
    How I'd have covered you with my wings and shielded you from my
        Father's anger. But now you shall see
    For the cold priests' sake and the lying scribes' sake and the mocking
        rabble's,
    The son of a woman but not a man come down like a mountain eagle
        above you cowering and strike
    The great stones of your walls asunder with his heel and crush your towers
        under the soles of his feet
    Until you are taught. If the people had been united the triumph would
        have been bloodless: but now, woe, woe,
    The mother city, the great stones on the ancient hill. The moon shall be
        blood and the sun darkened
    And the stars fall. I bring not peace but a sword; the brother shall hate the
        brother and the child his father.
    The old walls must be pulled down before the founding of the new, the
        field must be broken before the spring sowing,

The old wood must be cut before the young forest.   *(He goes out among the trees.)*

JUDAS   They gape and
     follow; he has found the dreadful key to their hearts.
     Now I see clearly my duty and destiny.
                                        . . . The passion is past, the
     bitter drop has been drained, the veins
In my hands and about my heart seem light and empty. I am like a ghost of
     one who did something
Ages ago, walking in a dead garden under the white of the moon.

THE WOMAN   *(coming in from the left)*   You
     happy traveller
Coming down from the crowded city: what news of the prophet Jesus?
     How do men hear him?

JUDAS   With fear
     And fascination, like birds charmed by a serpent.

THE WOMAN   Ah. Greatness never
     escaped envy. A few
Must hate the man whom all love. Go down: he is well rid of you.

JUDAS   I am
     one of those that love him more nearly
Than their own lives. He saved me from despair
The time when the cruelties that are done under the sky and all the
     oppressions trampled me to madness.
He has come perhaps nearer to God than any prophet before.

THE WOMAN   I, here,
     plain as I am,
Homely as I am, I am his mother.
            (Judas shudders and is silent.)   Oh why will you not look me in the
     eyes and why are you trembling?
Has evil come down? I know it is terrible to lead this people. But tell me
     quickly all the worst you have.

I shall endure it.   *(with pride)*   The mother of Jesus is not a weak woman.

JUDAS   He

is well. . . . Oh, he is well, mother. . . .

The people gather like sheep under the shadow of his boughs; against the
white burning noon, and death

On the dry hills. I have watched his white beauty

Above them like the mastlight over a boat, or the pilot of a boat sailing far
waters

Uncharted, no prow has furrowed before, the pale face flecked with foam of
danger and the constant eyes

Threading the rage of the storm, the hand among reefs unknown steady on
the helm.   *(miserably: to himself)*   That I am the reef

To wreck my captain! Should I tell her that!

(Jesus comes in and stands sorrowfully on the right of the scene.)

THE WOMAN   Oh happy friend: for he

must love you if you love him so well:

And maybe you've even touched him from day to day, serving his food or
the like: what does he aim at

Do you think? What can he reach and have rest?

JUDAS   Mother: those that

ascend the mountain toward God have none.

And whoever dares in the endless cross waves of time pilot the people,

Until misfortune wrecks him has none.

THE WOMAN   I thought . . . I believed you

loved him. What name are you called?

JUDAS   Judas.

THE WOMAN

Your face was like an uncovered grave when you said "misfortune." I will
send and . . . no, but go up myself

And warn him of you.

(She crosses over toward Jesus, walking wearily; but stops humbly at a little distance from him.)

JUDAS   Even before the fact my face is like a sepulchre in
    honest eyes
And my name is abominable. That's now . . . that's my calling.
I have seen dread in my life. I have seen a crucified man: I can't . . . He
    was a robber and murderer.
The black spread-eagle against the white cloud
Is cut in my mind past cure; strained basket ribs, and pale clay mouth
    opening and closing in the air.
If Jesus should persist in Jerusalem, preaching destruction, rousing the
    looting street-people: I see
The future as bitter clearly as the unendurable memory: the sudden Roman
    hand of suppression,
The machine squadrons, the screaming streets cleared:
And the Roman vengeance, all the roadside masted with moaning
    crucifixions, from the city to Bethany.
Oh Jesus, I also love men.
    (*Jesus on the extreme right of the scene speaks to those imagined about him. His mother stands
    waiting outside the circle.*)
JESUS   Whether you ought to pay tribute to Caesar?
    Whose name's on the coin? Caesar's?
JUDAS
    I think I have never been able in all the gray and futile years of my life
    To stop one tear or staunch one man's wound, but now I am able. I'll say to
        the priests "Quietness is all.
    Take him at night. I'm one of his men and I can lead you to his bed." What
        harm can they do him, but keep him
    Three or four days for the city peace and dismiss him?
    He has made no insurrection till now (from hour to hour he may do it—
        who knows his mind?—to captain
    A river of blood) they'll only keep him quiet and dismiss him home. There
        he'll not dream of towers,

But the sweet and passionate mind walk humbly. And he'll forgive me, he'll let me follow him, we'll walk together

In the white dust between the fig and the olive, as in the days that break my heart to remember.

(He stands rapt in thought.)

JESUS

. . . And to God the things that are God's. Some of you know

That God is here. God dreamed a dream yesterday for Israel but you were afraid. It is not you

That reject God, it is God rejecting this people. I dreamed a dream for the lion of Judah but the lion's

Dwindled to a dog; it will not lick the wounds of freedom and victory; it will lick the scab of its mange

And snuffle for a bone under Caesar's table. Therefore I have twitched the cloth of my kingdom out of your hands

To reach it westward: the Romans have courage and power and discipline and what have *you*? Hatred and memories.

They have no love in their hearts but you have mere hatred. See, while I speak you are ready to stone me. . . . Oh children,

Oh little sudden children, how can I help but love you? I am not turned

From one soul here. . . . But take up your sick: I'll heal none at this time. It is not easy to have seen

Hope die in rags, and be the fool of a city.

(to one who seems to speak to him privately) My mother? I have no mother. *(to the people)*

Go home to your places.

(Judas passes heavily across the scene to go out on the right.)

MARY

It is I, Jesus. I've come all the tired way from Nazareth.

JESUS You have not done wisely.

MARY   Look there: the man

    With the hollow face and the torn cloak: has turned against you, Judas his name, intends to betray you.

JESUS

    They all betray me. No one is able to betray me. You stood here listening,

    Did you not see me use them at pleasure? Sting them with words until the stones jumped in their hands,

    And show the other side of my heart and conquer them?

MARY   No man is great

    enough to stand where you stand.

    Kings have paid guards for the ebbs of favor; they buy faithfulness.

JESUS   No

    man. That is true. Poor withered rose,

    Does that which God has touched fade?

MARY   I am indeed so tired . . .

    (turning away from him: to herself)   Oh, if his confidence

    Lies there: then I am the one that betrays him, with the lie that covered my sin. Never forgiven.   *(to her son)*   Oh come home,

    Come home Jesus,

    From the fierce cowardly city and too many people. I watched their faces, their eyes are shallow and whetted

    Like the eyes of mice, and they have no faith. Their fathers murdered the prophets. The lake fishermen need you,

    The kindly villagers need you.

JESUS   I have not come up to return. The city is

    my Father's city.

MARY   Yes: David

    Throned here; but change . . .

JESUS   Why does your mind flee

    My Father's name as if it were a trap?

MARY   Oh, Oh, is it *not* a trap? It is this

    . . . it is this . . . belief,

Has lifted you up to over-dream nature, and scorn danger and wisdom. Oh,
    it is secret. Be a prophet
But not lay claim . . . Be a king if you can, but not to go mad.

JESUS   Woman,
    is it true or not, that the spirit
Of God shadowed you, and you were yet a virgin, and became my mother?

MARY   *(weeping)*   Oh,
    Oh, it is secret.

JESUS   I kept it
    Secret until I came to my power; I spoke of myself as the Son of Man, I
        told no one
Who was my Father, until this time was prepared of triumph.

MARY   Misery, to
    see your power and your ruin
Sprouting from the one root.

JESUS   *(beginning to tremble)*   You wept like this before when I asked you;
    your eyes hiding from mine.
    You'd almost persuade . . . I've not wholly
The clear faith that I had. . . . I am either a bastard or the son of God:
    who was my father?

MARY   *(sinking down before him, writhing with sobs, mutters:)*
                            Neither one!
The great stone on the road by Nazareth.   *(aloud)*   Oh God, God.
The most high God. . . . No sin, not to the end of the world, is ever
    forgiven.

JESUS   *(stands looking down at her and trembling, and says after a silence:)*
               It is enough.
Stand up. Whatever you'd answered, I'd not
Be weak enough to let go the faith that is the fountain of my life. As to the
    sin you weep at,
I'll not know what it is: it's wholly forgiven. The son of God has the power
    to forgive sins.

But go. Go quickly. I will never question you again, I will never see you
    again. Judas, your news was

Means to betray me: yes, truly: natural: I've loved him too. Mother, I hold
    the shining triumph

Here in my hand, the kingdom and the glory; I shall not fail but conquer.
    Leave me!   *(He turns from her with a violent gesture and she creeps away.)*   Out of this
    . . . weakness . . .

To go and let the mind sprawl from its throne, in the desert again, talking
    with demons in the morning

And counting the moonlights with white pebbles . . . there's a black one
    for you my mother . . . until this flesh

Falls off, to fall starving across a wind-furrow between the stone and the
    sand and find repose

This time in earnest, would be a weakness . . . not to return to . . .

The entertainments of demons

Between the flayed hills. "Look, I will give you all this glory." What glory?
    A few bones scoured by the sand-blast

After the desert birds have finished,

Because faith is dead.

Yet, Demon, I am the son of God. Not now in a desert, in a dark garden.
    Oh, as for these Jews,

They are taught from childhood to swallow absurd marvels

Without winking, what is that to me? They have no other glory now. The
    girls find a kind-hearted

Carpenter to patch the skiff with a scrap of marriage, or a cobbler to mend
    the leak in the shoe: common,

These years of the fall. The mystery remains though.

He must have been lovely . . . you daughters of Jerusalem that you stir not
    up nor awaken my love . . .

He is lovelier than the desert dawns. Three . . . four times in my life I
    have been one with our Father,

The night and the day, the dark seas and the little fountains, the sown and
the desert, the morning star
And the mountains against morning and the mountain cedars, the sheep
and the wolves, the Hebrews and the free nomads
That eat camels and worship a stone, and the sun cures them like salt into
the marrow in the bones;
All, all, and times future and past
The hanging leaves on one tree: there is not a word nor a dream nor any
way to declare his loveliness
Except to have felt and known, to have *been* the beauty. Even the cruelties
and agonies that my poor Judas
Chokes on: were there in the net, shining. The hawk shone like the dove.
Why, there it is! Exultation,
You stripped dupe? I have gathered my ruins.
Life after life, at the bottom of the pit comes exultation. I seem to
remember so many nights?
In the smell of old cypresses in the garden darkness. And the means of
power,
All clear and formed, like tangible symbols laid in my mind. Two thousand
years are laid in my hands
Like grains of corn. Not for the power: Oh, more than power, actual
possession. To be with my people,
In their very hearts, a part of their being, inseparable from those that love
me, more closely touching them
Than the cloth of the inner garment touches the flesh. That this is
tyrannous
I know, that it is love run to lust: but I will possess them. The hawk shines
like the dove. Oh, power
Bought at the price these hands and feet and all this body perishing in
torture will pay is holy.
Their minds love terror, their souls cry to be sacrificed for; pain's almost
the God

Of doubtful men, who tremble expecting to endure it. Their cruelty
    sublimed. And I think the brute cross itself,
Hewn down to a gibbet now, has been worshipped; it stands yet for an idol
    of life and power in the dreaming
Soul of the world and the waters under humanity, whence floating again
It will fly up heaven, and heavy with triumphant blood and renewal, the
    very nails and the beams alive.
I saw my future when I was with God; but now at length in a flashing
    moment the means: I frightfully
Lifted up drawing all men to my feet: I go a stranger passage to a greater
    dominion,
More tyrannous, more terrible, more true, than Caesar or any subduer of
    the earth before him has dared to dream of
In a dream in his bed, over the prostrate city, before the pale weary dawn
Creeps through his palace, through the purple fringes, between the polished
    agate pillars, to steal it away.

JUDAS   *(coming in and approaching him)*

Master, I have so longed to find you alone. I beseech you, Oh I adjure you,
    to come away from this city.

JESUS   You? Poor nerve of pity, is it so hard to do what you have to do?

JUDAS   For insurrection is blind madness, and would be punished
bloodily, lives upon lives. You have said that you love men: you go about to
destroy them. Oh, master, the poor drift of the street, with no weapons:
have you *seen* soldiers?

JESUS   I have seen the angels of God. When a handful of my followers
dares to lift up their hands against authority: that is the signal to call down
to our van the shining hosts of God.

JUDAS   Oh master. Oh our master, turn from this! . . . . I have been
spying for you: I come from mingling with the priests and the priests'
servants: they mean to arrest you. To imprison you: to-night perhaps. Ah,
my Lord. My savior in the past. I will call you my God: I beseech you to

leave this city to its own damnations. But do not you accept the guilt of the deaths of men. By torture: Rome nails them to crosses.

JESUS   You have always been without faith, and the sick fool of your pity.

JUDAS   *(falling on his knees, clutching at Jesus' cloak)*   You *teach* mercy: be merciful. All I ask is that you come away and not force destruction. To let the people alone is the mercy: all stirring is death to them.   *(He lets go the cloak.)*   I know by heart that agate inflexible look in his eyes. There is no hope in this merciless man: I must do my office.

JESUS

Needs must, poor Judas. But I am not merciless. Does brown agate

Being wrung flow drops like these? After you've done it, and seen the issue,
    Judas, you'll need consoling,

And find no comforter: but how can I comfort you now beforehand?

For if I could make you understand the death and the life your deed
    mothers, you'd never do it,

And twenty centuries to come go captainless, for lack of your deed. If it is
    required of you to die ignorant,

What is that to you? I tell you feelingly, it is the honor of all men living to
    be dupes of God

And serve not their own ends nor understandings but His, and so die. I that
    am more than a man

Know this and more, and serve and *am served*.

JUDAS   You are assuming the blood-guiltiness of perhaps a hundred lives forfeit in torment for rebellion; and not that alone: all the statutes and taxes screwed tighter afterwards on all the innocent. You that preached mercy! But I am able to prevent you. It is necessary for one man to be put under restraint, to save the people. . . . Oh my friend, my once master, my love forever: forgive me before the act!

JESUS

Listen to me now, Judas, and remember.

Because I know your scrupulous heart, and I don't wish you to die
    despairing. There is not one creature,

Neither yourself nor anyone, nor a fly nor flung stone, but does exactly and
   fatally the thing
That it needs must; neither less nor more. This is the roots of forgiveness.
   This is our secret, Judas.
For the people's hearts are not scrupulous like yours, and if they heard it
   they'd run on license and die,
In the falling and splitting world, now that the sword and civilization and
   exile will break the sureties
And ungroove the lives. . . . "I bid you beware of the net, fishermen.
You see men walking and they seem to be free but look at the faces, they're
   caught.
There was never a man cut himself loose." An old song, Judas, humming in
   my head, the woman my mother
Used to sing by the lake-shore: I fear now she's forgotten it. It meant the
   net of God's will. A song
That fountains power to the powerful, and to all, endurance. Suck on that
   when I'm gone.
   —But make haste my poor friend, see the priests and settle with them.
I warn you, the time runs short: to-morrow I intend to raise such a crested
wave of the people as will sweep me to my kingdom and drown resistance.
I shall draw all men to me: when I am *lifted up.*

   (*Judas goes, in haste, with a gesture of despair.*)

JESUS

   Now my heart is faint, even in the midst of its exultation. It is well for the
      Greek artist
   Shaping a stone to some form of beauty; he holds the plan in his mind and
      hews to it, and what falls off
   Is not hurt, nor the block moans at the mallet. But I that am cutting the
      world to a new shape
   And making a good and beautiful form, not of stone, unimagined before, a
      new age . . . Oh horrible, to carve

A child out of the shuddering breast and body of my mother! . . . Why do
    I dream that? Because I said
That those who do my will are my mother? She'll cry too, that unlucky
    mother of my body: but others
Have seen their sons killed, it is not uncommon. My poor Judas
I fear will die, or but linger maimed in the heart and self-tormenting: did I
    forget now to tell him
That his name shall ride with mine down forests of ages? but that's vanity.
    Oh, I'm not innocent. The chisel
Of *my* carving cuts flesh and bleeds.
    (*to the mutes who have entered*)
You are here, my faithful? Judas has fallen off from us, poor fellow, he has
gone over to lean on priests. Now keep watch for me to-night: did you
bring swords as I bade you? Two hacked old blades—Oh, it's enough. We
must always be ready to offer a form of resistance, for a signal to my
Father, who will send the angels.
    (*He withdraws from the mutes.*)
For mild submission might appease them and lose me the cross: without
    that
The fierce future world would never kneel down to slake its lusts at my
    fountain. Only a crucified
God can fill the wolf bowels of Rome; only a torture high up in the air, and
    crossed beams, hang sovereign
When the blond savages exalt their kings; when the north moves, and the
    hairy-breasted north is unbound,
And Caesar a mouse under the hooves of the horses. . . . Alas, poor
    dreamer,
Dreaming wildly because you must die. I know certainly the cross will
    conquer; but Rome to go down,
Or nations be born to colonize with new powers and peoples, and my
    gaunt pain erected in counterfeit,
The coasts of undreamed of oceans, is delirium.

(He returns to the mutes, who seem to be asleep.)

When I am bitterly troubled in spirit, could you not keep watch for me one
hour?

(He withdraws from the mutes.)

The long obscure future like a weeping cloud covers me with sadness. Dear
Judas, make haste!

Ere my heart fail and repent and renounce power. All power crushes its
object, there is none innocent.

Religion is the most tyrannous, worming its way through the ears and eyes
to the cup of spirit, overgrowing

The life in its pool with alien and stronger life, drugging the water at the
well-head: so I possess them

From inward: no man shall live

As if *I* had not lived. The hawk of my love is not left hungry. I sacrifice to
this end all the hopes

Of these good villagers who've come up from Galilee expecting kingdom;
and the woman my mother; and my own

Flesh to be tortured; and my poor Judas, who'll do his office and break; and
dreadful beyond these, unnumbered

Multitudes of souls from wombs unborn yet; the wasted valor of ten
thousand martyrs: Oh, my own people

Perhaps will stab each other in a sacred madness, disputing over some
chance word that my mouth made

While the mind slept. And men will imagine hells and go mad with terror,
for so I have feathered the arrows

Of persuasion with fire, and men will put out the eyes of their minds, lest
faith

Become impossible being looked at, and their souls perish.

                        . . . But what
are men *now*?

Are the bodies free, or the minds full of clear light, or the hearts fearless? I
having no foothold but slippery

Broken hearts and despairs, the world is so heaped against me, am yet
      lifting my peoples nearer
In emotion, and even at length in powers and perception, to the universal
      God than ever humanity
Has climbed before. . . . Dreams, dreams. Who can pick out the good
      from the evil? . . . It is likely that all these futures
Are only the raving mind of one about to be killed, myself and my poor
      Judas alone
Will bear the brunt; I shall go up and die and be presently forgotten. I have
      been deluded again,
Imagination my traitor, as often before. I am in the net, and this
      deliberately sought
Torture on the cross is the only real thing.
                                      Yonder the torches blink and
      dip among the black trunks.
They have lost the path, now they have found it again, and up the stone
      steps.
                  Dear Judas, it is God drives us.
It is not shameful to be duped by God. I have known his glory in my
      life-time, I have *been* his glory, I know
Beyond illusion the enormous beauty of the torch in which our agonies and
      all are particles of fire.
    (to his three or four companions, as the torches surround him:)
What, will you let them take me? Strike, Peter! He has missed the head
And cut a man's ear: save yourselves! Enough's done
To edge the required judgment.
    (to the others)
Let my friends go. I am the one. Tell them so, Judas.
    (His companions escape among the trees. Jesus is led out to the right, with Judas and the mutes of
    the other party. A pause, Mary comes in from the left.)

MARY

They have brought me words that shine like new stars. . . . Oh omnipotent
    God, with whom through delusion he is joined in truth,
How marvellously thou hast made my secret sin the glory of the world. I
    saw his triumph in his eyes
Before they told me. Without my sin he'd not have been born, nor yet
    without my falsehood have triumphed,
For that exalted his deceived heart to the height of his destiny. Now they
    have told me that to-day
Is the set day, and he enters his kingdom. He will appear with those calm
    shining eyes before Herod
And Herod will step down from his place and kneel down; and before
    Pontius Pilate the Roman governor,
Whose cold face will forget its pride. They both shall be dumb with shame,
    but Jesus will speak proudly
And kindly his decrees. I feared at first for awhile, remembering my sin, but
    now I am confident.
             (A mute passes.)   Oh traveller,
What news, what news? Oh, I knew it!
                                  My soul doth magnify the Lord,
    who maketh light out of darkness,
Honor out of shame, out of sin a shining. I knew from the first day, from
    the lips finding the breast,
From the day when the babe looked in my face and smiled.
His hand puts down the mighty and exalts the humble. All generations
    shall call me blessed.
             (A mute passes.)   Oh traveller,
What news, what news?
                        That is a lie, traveller. Lies glide about the city
    like fishes in a pool.
What the eyes have not seen is a lie. . . . Merciful God! whom I
    blasphemed in the bitter shame of his eyes:

But thou, Lord, knowest that my mind had gone wild with shame, and I
was myself deceived at first, being ignorant,

A child and a fool, and love had come to my soul in the holy evening, in
the field, in the flush of twilight,

And I knew nothing . . .

Will no one come from the city and tell me? . . . I wish the night of
darkness would cover me and I were asleep

Under deep waters, until the sandals of the man bearing true tidings be
heard in the dust.

*(She covers her eyes and sits erect, shuddering at moments, with her shawl drawn over her eyes. A
cross is set up, burdened with the form of a man, distantly visible at the back of the scene. A mute
passes in the foreground.)*

MARY

What news, Oh what news?

. . . You little gardens about Bethany, did
you hear this man? Oh mountains

And headlands of the north you have heard him; wide, ribbed and waterless
desert, Oh freedom of the Arab horsemen

And sunrise and the lions: for his words are true.

He tells me plainly that my son is exalted as on a hill, and uplifted on a
high place,

The people of the city flocking to his feet. They feed on the light of his
face; he is called their king; he beholds them.

You leap you mountains like flames, Oh Lebanon the forest shakes, you
little round hills like lambs of the flock

Dancing and butting with the curly foreheads: but as for me, I am stricken,
I can neither speak nor be glad,

I require nothing but death; I suffered too much, just now, while I was
quiet, while I sat waiting,

Joy is a sword, like a sharp sword.

*(She sits stonily erect, with open eyes and the lifted haggard features of ecstasy. A man with an
unchangeable bluish face enters and speaks without approaching Mary.)*

LAZARUS

I am Lazarus who lay dead four days; and having known death and the
dreams of corruption and lived afterwards

For several years, and again died, and rotted in the rock tomb, it is not
possible for me

To be deluded like others by any of the habits of death. I also am only a
shell and remainder

Like the other three ghosts that haunt the garden; but never subdued by
their dreams, and being incapable of pity,

Astonishment or fear or any other of the accidents of life, I am sent every
night at this time

To tell this woman not to rejoice; and that her son is condemned. It would
be better for these three

If they could sleep; but the great passions life was not wide enough for are
not so easily exhausted,

But echo in the wood for certain years or millenniums. As for myself, being
wholly released from pain

And pleasure, sleeping and waking are all one. . . . This woman is so
full-joyed at the false tidings her dream

Deludes her with, I would fain linger a little before I slay joy.

(He stands about the center of the scene, rigidly reposeful, and waits in silence.)

MARY   Lord God:

prayer-hearing Lord,

Oh beautiful and loving God, I have one thing left to implore. Bless thou
the traveller who passed but now

And brought me true word of my son's triumphs. His body and his soul,
his house and his sons, be happy forever.

Add nothing to me. The straining crystal spirit and the broken old
mother-body can hold no more

Happiness.

LAZARUS   Hail Mary, chosen for extremes. Remember that grief and
happiness are only shadows of a shadow.

A blade of grass is a thing but these are not things,

And sooner withered.

MARY   Not a thing but a fire: my happiness consumes me.

   Oh friend, you are not a stranger but Lazarus,

Whose guest I am; you have watched my son crowned king, and the

   winning favor of his ways when the people honored him.

Tell me nothing yet, for my heart is full.

LAZARUS   I would I might tell you

   nothing.

MARY   Oh why is your face not changed,

   Lazarus, Lazarus?

LAZARUS   Come into the house; for what I have to say ought not

   to be said by the road,

Where those that pass may see you and stare at you, a chosen woman.

MARY   I

   will not stir from this place.

LAZARUS   It is possible for

   Rumors not to be true.

MARY   Oh I know it, dear friend. I heard false tidings

   before the true came, and grieved

Before I was glad. . . . Your face not changed? I thought it would surely

   change when Jesus whom you love is glorified

In the favor of God and the great city. Yes, now I can see

Joy in your face.

LAZARUS   No, Mary, I am out of that net. I would to God that

   you were out of that net.

MARY

You have always been strange, they say, since you were called from the

   cavern, with the hands and the face wrapped in white cloths.

. . . . I am not so pierced with joy as I was: now you may tell me a little: a

   few of the words of Jesus

When he was praised; and whether he could keep from weeping. *I cannot.*
    The tears keep trickling, whatever I do.

LAZARUS

    He is not well.

MARY   Oh, I am sorry. It's one of the headaches he suffers after
    long days of sun.

    His spirit was always too hard a rider for the gentle body.

LAZARUS   Alas, the crown
    that they crowned him with

    Was painful; he endures anguish also in the hands

    And in the feet; there were red stripes on his back. I think he cannot live
    long.

MARY   How . . . stripes, Lazarus?

    God help you, it is not your will to bring me false news, but your mind is
    crazed

    Since the rock tomb.

LAZARUS   My thoughts were made straight there; and quieted,
    filled with the light of darkness. The minds are crazed

    That take joy at a penny's worth or pain at a penny's.

MARY   I have my joy, you
    shall not frighten it away.

LAZARUS

    But while you are clutching it, while you speak of it, you writhe with fear.
    Oh strong mother of one of the greatest

    Of torchlike men: there is only one pathway to peace for a great passion.
    Truth is the way, take the truth

    Against your breast and endure its horns. So life will at last be conquered.
    After some thousands of years

    The smoky unserviceable remainders of love and desire will be dissolved
    and be still. . . . Your son

Has chosen his tools and made his own death; he has chosen a painful
   death in order to become a God.

MARY

Ah poor flawed mind: you'd make me think my Jesus as wise as yourself,
   would you? . . . Listen, Lazarus . . .

you'll do well . . . go about the market-place singing riddles to people.
Have a boy with a drum and the half-caste Greeks will ring farthings on
the drum-skin. You'll be the best juggler . . . that blue-dead face will fetch
crowds, the resurrected man. . . .

Where is he now, in the temple?

LAZARUS   He is hanged on a cross on the hill
   Golgotha.

MARY   Fool. To dream I'd believe . . .

This is for my sin, this false terror; and his triumphs for my love. It is hard
   that I am so choked with sickness,

A stone in my throat, when I must walk to the city. Ai, God. Why do men
   lie?

JUDAS   (*Judas enters from the right, accompanied by several mutes. They are moving toward*
Lazarus and Mary.)
              . . . Telling my reasons.

I am Judas running like a snapping dog along the streets of Jerusalem,
   snapping my reasons.

I say to one man: (*He speaks to one of the mutes.*)
                Hear me, eyes! To get the firebrand locked up, to save
   the city. What we need is peace.

But who'd have dreamed they'd condemn him?

                                (*to another*)   Money money money.

Now mercy's been made a fool and pity is a murderer,

What won't a man do for the fat silver? A pity that I threw it back to
   them . . .

   (*to a third*)   I swear before God, friend,

I'm not the person that did it, I'm not . . . Let me go.

(to Mary)   Do y' see a brand, Madam,

On the mouth or brow? Am I marked? God marks them.

MARY   (to Lazarus)   What is this creature?

JUDAS   That means innocent murderers: but me:
The person that kills his . . .

(looking at Lazarus)   Bluebottle, don't I know you? And this
one's . . . Oh! . . . This old woman
Is the cave it came from.

(He falls on his knees before Mary, and tries to clutch the skirt of her garment.)
I loved him, mother.

MARY   (to Lazarus)   If it's a dog will you
keep it off me? The slaver's poisonous
When they go mad. Oh: dead man:
He'd never be warned: I warned him: I knew this hollow and vile
Face from the first, when it said "misfortune." But Jesus, because I warned
him of treachery, has walked into treachery.
I wish my mouth had been stopped with the seas of drowning.

(She strikes at Judas' head with her hand.)   I don't
believe. I don't believe. God's eyes
Are not put out yet, you are all liars. Oh! Oh! Oh!

LAZARUS   Cry out all your
heart, Mary,
Because you believe; me, and the ball of repentance moaning here at your
feet, and the witnesses here.

MARY
When my eyes see it I'll believe and die.

(looking up; triumphantly)   Look there where he comes,
freely striding, angrily. Oh faithless.

Oh fools. You *wished* him to be dead.

                             . . . It is not he; I am cheated.

JUDAS   I

remember my reason. Listen to me,

I have to tell you my reason: it was all for deliverance: I thought, by doing
the worst imaginable thing

I should be freed of tormenting pity. Wasn't that . . . No. No.

MARY   You

think, perhaps, kneeling there,

That I will curse you? Because you betrayed my son, because you are
infamous, because no viper is made

Venomous, nor reptile of the slime loathsome, to your measure? You think
I'll be troubled for that? I'll stand here and pray

God to fill up your hollow face with fire for a lantern in hell? To bathe the
long yellow fingers

In melted iron?

I will not curse you Judas, I will curse myself. I am the first that betrayed
him. The mothers, we do it:

Wolf-driven by love, or out of compliance, or fat convenience:

A child for Moloch. I am that woman: the giver of blood and milk to be
sacrificed. I'll never tell you,

Though worse follows, how else I betrayed again

My blood and my milk. I built it up and forced it up and adored it, and the
end's unbearable.

LAZARUS   Be silent.

Those inflamed rolling and desert eyes and the voice dragged through
sand-colored lips know nothing of the end.

You'd use a lonely and towered sorrow, and face the anguished core with
cut stone, if you could feel

Fixed on you out of the dark the yearning innumerable eyes of many
nations and an age of the world

Worshipping the mother of God, this palsied old woman. Your son has
  done what men are not able to do;
He has chosen and made his own fate. The Roman Caesar will call your
  son his master and his God; the floods
That wash away Caesar and divide the booty, shall worship your son. The
  unconjectured selvages
And closed orbits of the ocean-ends of the earth shall hear of him.

MARY   It was
  bitter enough when I was alone:
And now we are put into a pit to be stared at. I will go and find him.
  (She goes off toward the distantly seen cross.)

JUDAS   There,
  there, slowly the Mother
Night: but I can hurry and run home to her; I ache for darkness.

LAZARUS   You,
  Judas, cease trembling. You were his tool
And broke to serve him; the power that makes the future so consumes the
  present. Therefore your name shall couple
With his in men's minds for many centuries: you enter his kingdom with
  him, as the hawk's lice with the hawk
Climb the blue towers of the sky under the down of the feathers.

JUDAS   If
  blue-face were as cunning as he looks
He'd know what I hide under my coat: look here: a noosed cord. What's
  that for? Find one for yourself, Lazarus,
And undo the cruellest miracle man ever suffered. I am going a little
  distance into the wood
And buy myself an eternal peace for three minutes of breathlessness, never
  to see any more
The tortured nailed-up body in my mind, nor hear the useless and endless
  moaning of beasts and men.

LAZARUS

Let him go. He has done all he was made for; the rest's his own. Let him and the other at the poles of the wood,

Their pain drawn up to burning points and cut off, praise God after the monstrous manner of mankind.

While the white moon glides from this garden; the glory of darkness returns a moment, on the cliffs of dawn.

THE LOVING SHEPHERDESS

I

The little one-room schoolhouse among the redwoods
Opened its door, a dozen children ran out
And saw on the narrow road between the dense trees
A person—a girl by the long light-colored hair:
The torn brown cloak that she wore might be a man's
Or woman's either—walking hastily northward
Among a huddle of sheep. Her thin young face
Seemed joyful, and lighted from inside, and formed
Too finely to be so wind-burnt. As she went forward
One or another of the trotting sheep would turn
Its head to look at her face, and one would press
Its matted shoulder against her moving thigh.
The school-children stood laughing and shouting together.
"Who's that?" "Clare Walker," they said, "down from the hills.
She'd fifty sheep and now she's got eight, nine,
Ten: what have you done with all the others, Clare Walker?"
The joy that had lived in her face died, she yet
Went on as if she were deaf, with forward eyes
And lifted head, but the delicate lips moving.
The jeering children ran in behind her and the sheep
Drew nervously on before, except the old ram,
That close at her side dipped his coiled horns a little
But neither looked back nor edged forward. An urchin shouted
"You killed your daddy, why don't you kill your sheep?"
And a fat girl, "Oh where's your lover, Clare Walker?
He didn't want you after all."

                    The patriarch ram
That walked beside her wore a greasy brown bundle
Tied on his back with cords in the felt of wool,
And one of the little boys, running by, snatched at it
So that it fell. Clare bent to gather it fallen,
And tears dropped from her eyes. She offered no threat
With the bent staff of rosy-barked madrone-wood
That lay in her hand, but said "Oh please, Oh please,"
As meek as one of her ewes. An eight-year-old girl
Shrilled "Whistle for the dogs, make her run like a cat,
Call your dog, Charlie Geary!" But a brown-skinned
Spanish-Indian boy came forward and said
"You let her alone. They'll not hurt you, Clare Walker.
Don't cry, I'll walk beside you." She thanked him, still crying.
Four of the children, who lived southward, turned back;
The rest followed more quietly.

                    The black-haired boy
Said gently "Remember to keep in the road, Clare Walker.
There's enough grass. The ranchers will sick their dogs on you
If you go into the pastures, because their cows
Won't eat where the sheep have passed; but you can walk
Into the woods." She answered "You're kind, you're kind.
Oh yes, I always remember." The small road dipped
Under the river when they'd come down the hill,
A shallow mountain river that Clare skipped over
By stone after stone, the sheep wading beside her.
The friendly boy went south to the farm on the hill, "good-bye, good-bye,"
    and Clare with her little flock
Kept northward among great trees like towers in the river-valley. Her sheep
    sidled the path, sniffing

The bitter sorrel, lavender-flowering in shade, and the withered ferns.
    Toward evening they found a hollow
Of autumn grass.

II

                        Clare laughed and was glad, she undid the bundle from
    the ram's back
And found in the folds a battered metal cup and a broken loaf. She shared
    her bread with the sheep,
A morsel for each, and prettily laughing
Pushed down the reaching faces. "Piggies, eat grass. Leave me the crust,
    Tiny, I can't eat grass.
Nosie, keep off. Here Frannie, here Frannie." One of the ewes came close
    and stood to be milked, Clare stroked
The little udders and drank when the cup filled, and filled it again and
    drank, dividing her crust
With the milch ewe; the flock wandered the glade, nibbling white grass.
    There was only one lamb among them,
The others had died in the spring storm.

                        The light in the glade suddenly
    increased and changed, the hill
High eastward began to shine and be rosy-colored, and bathed in so clear a
    light that up the bare hill
Each clump of yucca stood like a star, bristling sharp rays; while westward
    the spires of the giant wood
Were strangely tall and intensely dark on the layered colors of the winter
    sundown; their blunt points touched
The high tender blue, their heads were backed by the amber, the
    thick-branched columns
Crossed flaming rose. Then Clare with the flush

Of the solemn and glad sky on her face went lightly down to the river to
  wash her cup; and the flock
Fed on a moment before they looked up and missed her. The ewe called
  Frannie had gone with Clare and the others
Heard Frannie's hooves on the crisp oak-leaves at the edge of the glade.
  They followed, bleating, and found their mistress
On the brink of the stream, in the clear gloom of the wood, and nipped the
  cresses from the water. Thence all returning
Lay down together in the glade, but Clare among them
Sat combing her hair, with a gap-toothed comb brought from the bundle.
  The evening deepened, the thick blond strands
Hissed in the comb and glimmered in the brown twilight, Clare began
  weeping, full of sorrow for no reason
As she had been full of happiness before. She braided her hair and pillowed
  her head on the bundle; she heard
The sheep breathing about her and felt the warmth of their bodies, through
  the heavy fleeces.

                    In the night she moaned
And bolted upright. "Oh come, come,
Come Fern, come Frannie, Leader and Saul and Tiny,
We have to go on," she whispered, sobbing with fear, and stood
With a glimmer in her hair among the sheep rising. The halved moon had
  arisen clear of the hill,
And touched her hair, and the hollow, in the mist from the river, was a lake
  of whiteness. Clare stood wreathed with her flock
And stared at the dark towers of the wood, the dream faded away from her
  mind, she sighed and fondled
The frightened foreheads. "Lie down, lie down darlings, we can't escape it."
  But after that they were restless
And heard noises in the night till dawn.

They rose in the quivering
Pale clearness before daylight, Clare milked her ewe,
The others feeding drifted across the glade
Like little clouds at sunrise wandering apart;
She lifted up the madrone-wood staff and called them.
"Fay, Fern, Oh Frannie. Come Saul.
Leader and Tiny and Nosie, we have to go on."
They went to the stream and then returned to the road
And very slowly went north, nibbling the margin
Bushes and grass, tracking the tender dust
With numberless prints of oblique crossings and driftings.
They came to Fogler's place and two ruffian dogs
Flew over the fence: Clare screaming "Oh, Oh, Oh, Oh,"
An inarticulate wild-bird cry, brandishing
The staff but never striking, stood out against them,
That dashed by her, and the packed and trembling ball
Of fleeces rolling into the wood was broken.
The sheep might have been torn there, some ewe or the lamb
Against the great foundations of the trees, but Fogler
Ran shouting over the road after his dogs
And drove them home. Clare gathered her flock, the sobbing
Throats and the tired eyes, "Fay, Fern, Oh Frannie,
Come Leader, come little Hornie, come Saul"; and Fogler:
"You ought to get a good dog to help take care of them."
He eyed curiously her thin young face,
Pale parted lips cracked by the sun and wind,
And then the thin bare ankles and broken shoes.
"Are you Clare Walker? I heard that you'd gone away:
But you're Clare Walker, aren't you?" "We had a dog,"
She said, "a long time ago but he went away.
There, Nosie. Poor Frannie. There. These poor things
Can find their food, but what could I keep a dog with?

But that was some years ago." He said, "Are these all?
They're all gathered? I heard you'd thirty or forty."
Then hastily, for he saw the long hazel eyes
Filling with tears, "Where are you going, Clare Walker?
Because I think it will rain in a week or two,
You can't sleep out then." She answered with a little shudder,
"Wherever I go this winter will be all right.
I'm going somewhere next April." Fogler stood rubbing
His short black beard, then dropped his hand to scratch
The ram's forehead by the horns but Saul drew away.
And Fogler said: "You're too young and too pretty
To wander around the country like this.
I'd ask you to come here when it rains, but my wife . . .
And how could I keep the sheep here?" "Ah, no," she answered,
"I couldn't come back." "Well, wait," he said, "for a minute,
Until I go to the house. Will you wait, Clare?
I'll tie up the dogs. I've got some biscuit and things . . ."
He returned with a sack of food, and two old shoes
A little better than Clare's. She sat on a root;
He knelt before her, fumbling the knotted laces
Of those she had on, and she felt his hands tremble.
His wife's shoes were too short for the slender feet. When the others
Had been replaced, Fogler bent suddenly and kissed
Clare's knee, where the coat had slipped back. He looked at her face,
His own burning, but in hers nor fear nor laughter,
Nor desire nor aversion showed. He said "good-bye,"
And hurried away.

        Clare travelled northward, and sometimes
Half running, more often loitering, and the sheep fed.
In the afternoon she led them into the willows,
And choosing a green pool of the shallow stream

Bathed, while the sheep bleated to her from the shoals.
They made a pleasant picture, the girl and her friends, in the green shade
Shafted with golden light falling through the alder branches. Her body, the
    scare-crow garments laid by,
Though hermit-ribbed and with boyishly flattened flanks hardly a woman's,
Was smooth and flowing, glazed with bright water, the shoulders and
    breasts beautiful, and moved with a rapid confidence
That contradicted her mind's abstractions. She laughed aloud and jetted
    handfuls of shining water
At the sheep on the bank; the old ram stood blinking with pleasure, shaking
    his horns. But after a time Clare's mood
Was changed, as if she thought happiness must end.
She shivered and moved heavily out of the stream
And wept on the shore, her hands clasping her ankles,
Her face bowed on her knees, her knotted-up coils
Of citron-colored hair loosening. The ewe
That she called Nosie approached behind her and pressed
Her chin on the wet shoulder; Clare turned then, moaning,
And drew the bony head against the soft breasts.
"Oh what will you do," she whispered laughing and sobbing,
"When all this comes to an end?"

                       She stood and stroked off
The drops of water, and dressed hastily. They went
On farther; now there was no more forest by the road,
But open fields. The river bent suddenly westward
And made a pond that shone like a red coal
Against the shore of the ocean, under the sundown
Sky, with a skeleton of sand-bar
Between the pond and the sea.

When deepening twilight
Made all things gray and made trespass safe, Clare entered
The seaward fields with her flock. They had fed scantly
In the redwood forest, and here in the dead grass
The cattle had cropped all summer they could not sleep.
She led them hour after hour under the still stars.
Once they ran down to the glimmering beach to avoid
The herd and the range bull; they returned, and wandered
The low last bluff, where sparse grass labors to live in the wind-heaped
   sand. Silently they pastured northward,
Gray file of shadows, between the glimmer and hushing moan of the ocean
   and the dark silence of the hills.
The erect one wore a pallor of starlight woven in her hair. Before moonrise
   they huddled together
In a hollow cup of old dune that opened seaward, but sheltered them from
   the nightwind and from morning eyes.

III

The bleating of sheep answered the barking of sea-lions and Clare awoke
Dazzled in the broad dawn. The land-wind lifted the light-spun manes of
   the waves, a drift of sea-lions
Swung in the surf and looked at the shore, sleek heads uplifted and great
   brown eyes with a glaze of blind
Blue sea-light in them. "You lovely creatures," she whispered.
She went to the verge and felt the foam at her ankles. "You lovely creatures
   come closer." The sheep followed her
And stopped in the sand with lonesome cries. Clare stood and trembled at
   the simple morning of the world; there was nothing
But hills and sea, not a tree on the shore nor a ship on the sea; an edge of
   the hill kindled with gold,

And the sun rose. Then Clare took home her soul from the world and went
    on. When she was wandering the flats
Of open pasture between the Sur Hill sea-face and the great separate
    sea-dome rock at Point Sur,
Forgetting, as often before, that she and her flock were trespassers
In cattle country: she looked and a young cowboy rode down from the east.
    "You'll have to get off this range.
Get out of this field," he said, "your tallow-hoofed mutton." "Oh," she
    answered trembling, "I'm going. I got lost in the night.
Don't drive them." "A woman?" he said. He jerked the reins and sat
    staring. "Where did *you* drop from?" She answered faintly,
With a favor-making smile, "From the south." "Who's with you?"
    "Nobody."
"Keep going, and get behind the hill if you can
Before Nick Miles the foreman looks down this way."
She said to the ram, "Oh Saul, Oh hurry. Come Leader.
Tiny and Frannie and Nosie, we have to go on.
Oh hurry Fern." They huddled bleating about her,
And she in the midst made haste; they pressed against her
And moved in silence. The young cowboy rode on the east
As hoping to hide the flock from Nick Miles his foreman,
Sidelong in the saddle, and gazed at Clare, at the twisting
Ripple of pale bright hair from her brown skin
Behind the temples. She felt that his looks were friendly,
She turned and timidly smiled. Then she could see
That he was not a man but a boy, sixteen
Or seventeen; she felt more courage. "What would your foreman
Do if he saw us?" "He'd be rough. But," he said,
"You'll soon be behind the hill. Where are you going?"
She made no answer. "To Monterey?" "Oh . . . to nowhere!"
She shivered and sought his face with her eyes. "To nowhere, I mean."
"Well," he said sulkily, "where did you sleep last night?

Somewhere?" She said with eagerness, "Ah, two miles back,
On the edge of the sand; we weren't really in the field."
He stared. "You're a queer one. Is that old coat
All you've got on?" "No, no, there's a dress under it.
But scrubbed so often," she said, "with sand and water
Because I had no soap, it's nothing but rags."
"You needn't hurry, no one can see you now.
 . . . My name's Will Brighton," he said. "Well, mine is Clare."
"Where do you live when you're at home, Clare?" "I haven't any."
They rounded the second spur of the hill. Gray lupine clothed the north
    flank, a herd of cattle stared down
From the pale slope of dead grass above the gray thicket. Rumps high, low
    quarters, they were part of the world's end sag,
The inverted arch from the Sur Hill height to the flat foreland and up the
    black lava rock of Point Sur;
In the open gap the mountain sea-wall of the world foam-footed went
    northward. Beyond the third spur Clare saw
A barn and a house up the wrinkled hill, oak-scrub and sycamores. The
    house built of squared logs, time-blackened,
Striped with white plaster between the black logs, a tall dead cube with a
    broken chimney, made her afraid;
Its indestructible crystalline shape. "Oh! There's a house.
They'll see us from there. I'll go back . . ." "Don't be afraid,"
He answered smiling, "that place has no eyes.
There you can turn your sheep in the old corral,
Or graze them under the buck-eyes until evening.
No one will come." She sighed, and then faintly:
"Nobody ever lives there, you're sure?" "Not for eight years.
You can go in," he said nervously; "maybe
You haven't been inside a house a good while?"
She looked up at his pleasant unformed young face,
It was blushing hot. "Oh, what's the matter with the house?"

"Nothing. Our owner bought the ranch, and the house
Stands empty, he didn't want it. They tell me an old man
Claiming to be God . . . a kind of a preacher boarded there,
And the family busted up." She said "I don't believe
Any such story." "Well, he was kind of a preacher.
They say his girl killed herself; he washed his hands
With fire and vanished." "Then she was crazy. What, spill
Her own one precious life," she said trembling,
"She'd nothing but that? Ah! no!
No matter how miserable, what goes in a moment,
You know . . . out . . ." Her head bowed, and her hand
Dug anxiously in the deep pads of wool
On the shoulder of the ram walking against her side;
When her face lifted again even the unwatchful boy
Took notice of tears.

                 They approached the house; the fence in front was
   broken but the windows and doors were whole,
The rose that grew over the rotted porch steps was dead; yet the sleep of
   the house seemed incorruptible,
It made Clare and the boy talk low. He dropped out of the saddle and
   made the bridle hang down
To serve for tether. "Come round by the back," he whispered, "this door is
   locked." "What for?" "To go in," he whispered.
"Ah no, I have to stay with my sheep. Why in the world should I go in to
   your dirty old house?"
His face now he'd dismounted was level with hers; she saw the
   straw-colored hairs on his lip, and freckles,
For he'd grown pale. "Hell," he said, narrowing his eyes, hoping to be
   manly and bully her: but the heart failed him,
He said sadly, "I hoped you'd come in." She breathed "Oh," her mouth
   twitching,

But whether with fear or laughter no one could tell,
And said, "You've been kind. Does nobody ever come here?
Because I'd have to leave my poor friends out-doors,
Someone might come and hurt them." "The sheep? Oh, nobody.
No one can see them. Oh, Clare, come on. Look here,"
He ran and opened a gate, "the corral fence
Is good as new and the grass hasn't been touched."
The small flock entered gladly and found green weeds
In the matted gray. Clare slowly returned. The boy
Catching her by the hand to draw her toward the house,
She saw his young strained face, and wondered. "Have you ever
Been, with a woman?" "Ah," he said proudly, "yes."
But the honesty of her gaze dissolving his confidence
He looked at the ground and said mournfully, "She wasn't white.
And I think she was quite old . . ." Clare in her turn
Reddened. "If it would make you happy," she said.
"I want to leave glad memories. And you'll not be sorry
After I'm gone?"

        The sheep, missing their mistress,
Bleated and moved uneasily, forgetting to feed,
While Clare walked in the house. She said, "Oh, not yet.
Let's look at the house. What was the man's name
Whose daughter . . . he said he was God and suddenly vanished?"
"A man named Barclay," he said, "kind of a preacher."
They spoke in whispers, peering about. At length Clare sighed,
And stripped off the long brown coat.

           When they returned out-doors,
Blinking in the sun, the boy bent his flushed face
Toward Clare's pale one and said "Dear, you can stay here
As long as you want, but I must go back to work."

She heard the sheep bleating, and said "Good-bye.
Good luck, Will Brighton." She hurried to her flock, while he
Mounted, but when he had ridden three strides of a canter
Clare was crying "Oh help. Oh help. Oo! Oo!" He returned,
And found her in the near corner of the corral
On hands and knees, her flock huddling about her,
Peering down a pit in the earth. Oak-scrub and leafless
Buck-eyes made a dark screen toward the hill, and Clare
Stood up against it, her white face and light hair
Shining against it, and cried "Oh help me, they've fallen,
Two have fallen." The pit was an old well;
The hand-pump had fallen in, and the timbers
That closed the mouth had crumbled to yellow meal.
Clare lay and moaned on the brink among the dark nettles,
Will Brighton brought the braided line that hung at his saddle
And made it fast and went down.

                                    The well-shaft was so filled up
With earth-fall and stones and rotting timbers, it was possible for the boy
    and girl to hoist up the fallen
Without other contrivance than the looped rope. The one came struggling
    and sobbing, Clare cried her name,
"Oh Fern, Fern, Fern." She stood and fell, and scrambled up to her feet,
    and plunged on three legs. The other
Came flaccid, it slipped in the rope and hung head downward, Clare made
    no cry. When it was laid by the well-brink
A slime of half-chewed leaves fell from its mouth. The boy climbed up.
    "While I was making your pleasure,"
Clare said, "this came. While I was lying there. What's punished is
    kindness." He touched the lifeless ewe with his foot,
Clare knelt against her and pushed him away. He said "It fell the first and
    its neck was broken." And Clare:

"This was the one that would nudge my hands
When I was quiet, she'd come behind me and touch me, I called her Nosie.
    One night we were all near frozen
And starved, I felt her friendly touches all night." She lifted the head. "Oh
    Nosie, I loved you best.
Fern's leg is broken. We'll all be like you in a little while." The boy ran and
    caught Fern, and said
"The bones are all right. A sprain I guess, a bad sprain. I'll come in the
    evening, Clare, if you're still here.
I'm sorry." She sat with the head on her lap, and he rode away. After a time
    she laid it on the earth.
She went and felt Fern's fore-leg and went slowly up the hill; her small flock
    followed.

IV

            Fern lagged and lagged,
Dibbling the dust with the mere points of the hoof
Of the hurt fore-leg, and rolling up to her shepherdess
The ache of reproachful eyes. "Oh Fern, Oh Fern,
What can I do? I'm not a man, to be able to carry you.
My father, he could have carried you." Tears from Clare's eyes
Fell in the roadway; she was always either joyful or weeping.
They climbed for half the day, only a steep mile
With many rests, and lay on the Sur Hill summit.
The sun and the ocean were far down below, like fire in a bowl;
The shadow of the hills lay slanting up a thin mist
Into the eastern sky, dark immense lines
Going out of the world.

            Clare slept wretchedly, for thirst
And anxious dreams and sorrow. She saw the lighthouse

Glow and flash all night under the hill;
The wind turned south, she smelled the river they had left,
Small flying clouds from the south crossed the weak stars.
In the morning Fern would not walk.

                                        Between noon and morning
A dark-skinned man on a tall hammer-headed
Flea-bitten gray horse rode north on the hill-crest.
Clare ran to meet him. "Please help me. One of my sheep
Has hurt her leg and can't walk. . . . Entiendes inglés?"
She faltered, seeing him Indian-Spanish, and the dark eyes
Gave no sign whether they understood, gazing through her with a blue
    light across them
Like the sea-lions' eyes. He answered easily in English, "What can I do?" in
    the gentle voice of his people;
And Clare: "I thought you might carry her down. We are very thirsty, the
    feed is all dry, here is no water,
And I've been gathering the withered grasses to feed her." He said, "We
    could tie her onto the horse." "Ah, no,
She'd be worse hurt. . . . She's light and little, she was born in the hills."
    The other sheep had followed their shepherdess
Into the road and sadly looked up, the man smiled and dismounted among
    them. "Where are you going?"
She answered "North. Oh come and see her. Unless you carry her
I don't know what we can do." "But it's two miles
Down to the river." The lame ewe, whether frightened
By the stranger and his horse, or rested at length,
Now rose and went quietly to Clare, the hurt fore-leg
Limping but serving. Clare laughed with pleasure. "Oh, now,
We can go down by ourselves. Come Fern, come Saul,
Fay, Frannie, Leader . . ." She was about to have called
The name of the one that died yesterday; her face

Changed and she walked in silence, Fern at her thigh.

The friendly stranger walked on the other side,

And his horse followed the sheep. He said: "I have seen

Many things, of this world and the others, but what are you?"

"My name's Clare Walker." "Well, I am Onorio Vasquez.

I meant, what are you doing? I think that I'd have seen you or heard of you

If you live near." "I'm doing? I'm taking care of my sheep." She looked at
his face to be sure of kindness,

And said, "I'm doing like most other people; take care of those that need
me and go on till I die.

But *I* know when it will be; that's the only. . . . I'm often afraid." Her look
went westward to the day moon,

Faint white shot bird in her wane, the wings bent downward, falling in the
clear over the ocean cloud-bank.

"Most people will see hundreds of moons: I shall see five.

When this one's finished." Vasquez looked intently at her thin young face,
turned sideways from him, the parted

Sun-scarred lips, the high bridge of the nose, dark eyes and light hair; she
was thin, but no sign of sickness; her eyes

Met his and he looked down and said nothing. When he looked down he
remembered chiefly the smooth brown throat

And the little hollow over the notch of the breast-bone. He said at length,
carefully, "You needn't be afraid.

I often," he murmured shyly, "have visions. I used to think they taught me
something, but I was a fool.

If you saw a vision, or you heard a voice from heaven, it is nothing." She
answered, "What I fear really's the pain.

The rest is only a kind of strangeness." Her eyes were full of tears and he
said anxiously, "Oh, never

Let visions nor voices fool you.

They are wonderful but we see them by chance; I think they mean
something in their own country but they mean

Nothing in this; they have nothing to do with our lives and deaths." She answered in so changed a voice that Vasquez

Stared; the tears were gone and her eyes were laughing. "Oh, no, it was nothing," she said, "in the way of that.

Visions? My trouble is a natural thing.

But tell me about those visions." He muttered to himself

With a shamed face and answered, "Not now." The south wind

That drove the dust of the little troop before them

Now increased and struck hard, where the road gained

A look-out point over the fork of the canyon

And the redwood forest below. The sheep were coughing

In the whirl of wind. At this point the lame ewe

Lay down and refused to rise, "Oh, now, now, now,"

Clare wrung her hands, "we're near the water too. We're all so thirsty.

Oh Fern!" Vasquez said sadly, "If she'd be quiet

Over my shoulders, but she won't." He heard a hoarse voice

Cry in the canyon, and Clare softly cried answer

And ran to the brink of the road. She stood there panting

Above the pitch and hollow of the gorge, her grotesque cloak

Blown up to her shoulders, flapping like wings

About the half nakedness of the slender body.

Vasquez looked down the way of her gaze, expecting

To see some tragical thing; he saw nothing but a wide heron

Laboring thwart wind from the shore over the heads of the redwoods. A heavy dark hawk balanced in the storm

And suddenly darted; the heron, the wings and long legs wavering in terror, fell, screaming, the long throat

Twisted under the body; Clare screamed in answer. The pirate death drove by and had missed, and circled

For a new strike, the poor frightened fisherman

Beat the air over the heads of the redwoods and labored upward. Again and again death struck, and the heron

Fell, with the same lost cry, and escaped; but the last fall
Was into the wood, the hawk followed, both passed from sight
Under the waving spires of the wood.

                              Clare Walker
Turned, striving with the gesture of a terrified child
To be quiet, her clenched fist pressed on her mouth,
Her teeth against the knuckles, and her blond hair
Wild on the wind. "Oh what can save him, can save him?
Oh how he cried at each fall!" She crouched in the wind
At the edge of the road, trembling; the ewe called Tiny
Crossed over and touched her, the others turned anxious looks
From sniffing the autumn-pinched leaves of the groundling blackberries.
When she was quieted Vasquez said, "You love
All creatures alike." She looked at his face inquiringly
With wide candid brown eyes, either not knowing
Or not thinking. He said, "It is now not far
Down to the running water; we'd better stretch her
Across the saddle" — he nodded toward the lame ewe —
"You hold her by the fore-legs and I by the hind ones,
She'll not be hurt." Clare's voice quieted the sheep
And Vasquez' the indignant horse. They came down at length
To dark water under gigantic trees.

V

She helped Fern drink before herself drooped eagerly
Her breast against the brown stones and kissed the cold stream.
She brought from the bundle what food remained, and shared it
With Vasquez and the munching sheep. There were three apples
From Fogler's trees, and a little jar of honey

And crumbled comb from his hives, and Clare drew a net
Of water-cress from the autumn-hushed water to freshen
The old bread and the broken biscuits. She was gay with delight
At having something to give. They sat on the bank, where century
After century of dropping redwood needles had made the earth, as if the
    dark trees were older
Than their own mother.

                       Clare answered Vasquez' question and said she
    had come from the coast mountains in the south;
She'd left her home a long time ago; and Fogler, the farmer by the Big Sur,
    had given her this food
Because he was sorry his dogs had worried the sheep. But yesterday she was
    passing Point Sur, and Fern
Had fallen into a well by the house. She said nothing of the other ewe, that
    had died; and Vasquez
Seemed to clench himself tight: "What were you doing at Point Sur, it's
    not on the road?" "The sheep were hungry,
And I wandered off the road in the dark. It was wicked of me to walk in the
    pasture, but a young cowboy
Helped me on the right way. We looked into the house." He said, "Let no
    one go back there, let its mice have it.
God lived there once and tried to make peace with the people; no peace
    was made." She stared in silence, and Vasquez:
"After that time I bawled for death, like a calf for the cow. There were no
    visions. My brothers watched me,
And held me under the hammers of food and sleep."
He ceased; then Clare in a troubled silence
Thought he was lying, for she thought certainly that no one
Ever had desired death. But, for he looked unhappy
And said nothing, she said Will Brighton had told her

Something about a man who claimed to be God,
"Whose daughter," she said, "died." Vasquez stood up
And said trembling, "In the ruin of San Antonio church
I saw an owl as big as one of your sheep
Sleeping above the little gilt Virgin above the altar.
That was no vision. I want to hear nothing
Of what there was at Point Sur." He went to his horse
That stood drooping against the stream-bank, and rode
The steep soft slope between the broad butts of trees.
But, leaving the undisturbed air of the wood
For the rough wind of the roadway, he stopped and went back.
"It will rain," he said. "You ought to think of yourself.
The wind is digging water since we came down.
My father's place is too far. There's an old empty cabin
A short ways on." She had been crouching again
Over the stream to drink, and rose with wet lips
But answered nothing. Vasquez felt inwardly dizzy
For no reason he knew, as if a gray bird
Turned in his breast and flirted half open wings
Like a wild pigeon bathing. He said "You'll see it
Above the creek on the right hand of the road
Only a little way north." He turned and rode back,
Hearing her call "Good-bye," into the wind on the road.

This man was that Onorio Vasquez
Who used to live on Palo Corona mountain
With his father and his six brothers, but now they lived
Up Mill Creek Canyon beside the abandoned lime-kiln
On land that was not their own. For yearly on this coast
Taxes increase, land grows harder to hold,
Poor people must move their places. Onorio had wealth
Of visions, but those are not coinable. A power in his mind

Was more than equal to the life he was born to,
But fear, or narrowing fortune, had kept it shut
From a larger life; the power wasted itself
In making purposeless visions, himself perceived them
To have no meaning relative to any known thing: but always
They made him different from his brothers; they gave him
A kind of freedom; they were the jewels and value of his life.
So that when once, at a critical time, they failed
And were not seen for a year, he'd hungered to die.
That was nine years ago; his mind was now quieter,
But still it found all its value in visions.
Between them, he hired out his hands to the coast farms,
Or delved the garden at home.

Clare Walker, when he was gone, forgot him at once.
She drank a third draught, then she dropped off her shoes
And washed the dust from her feet. Poor Fern was now hobbling
Among the others, and they'd found vines to feed on
At the near edge of the wood, so that Clare felt
Her shepherdess mind at peace, to throw off
The coat and the rags and bathe in the slender stream,
Flattening herself to find the finger's depth water.
The water and the air were cold now, she rubbed her body
Hastily dry with the bleached rags of her dress
And huddled the cloak about her, but hung the other
Over a branch to dry. Sadly she studied
The broken shoes and found them useless at last,
And flung them into the bushes. An hour later
She resumed the dress, she called her flock to go on
Northward. "Come Fern, come Frannie. Oh Saul.
Leader and Hornie and Tiny, we have to go on."

VI

The sky had blackened and the wind raised a dust
When they came up to the road from the closed quiet of the wood,
The sun was behind the hill but not down yet. Clare passed the
    lichen-plated abandoned cabin that Vasquez
Had wished her to use, because there was not a blade of pasture about it,
    nothing but the shafted jealousy
And foodless possession of the great redwoods. She saw the gray bed of the
    Little Sur like a dry bone
Through its winter willows, and on the left in the sudden
Sea-opening V of the canyon the sun streaming through a cloud, the lank
    striped ocean, and an arched film
Of sand blown from a dune at the stream's foot. The road ahead went over
    a bridge and up the bare hill
In lightning zigzags; a small black bead came down the lightning, flashing at
    the turns in the strained light,
A motor-car driven fast, Clare urged her flock into the ditch by the road,
    but the car turned
This side the bridge and glided down a steep driveway.
When Clare came and looked down she saw the farmhouse
Beside the creek, and a hundred bee-hives and a leafless orchard,
Crossed by the wheeling swords of the sun.
A man with a gray mustache covering his mouth
Stood by the road, Clare felt him stare at the sheep
And stare at her bare feet, though his eyes were hidden
In the dark of his face in the shadow of the turbid light.
She smiled and murmured "Good evening." He giggled to himself
Like a half-witted person and stared at her feet.
She passed, in the swirls of light and dust, the old man
Followed and called "Hey: Missy: where will you sleep?"
"Why, somewhere up there," she answered. He giggled, "Eh, Eh!

If I were you. Ho," he said joyfully,
"If I were in your *shoes*, I'd look for a roof.
It's big and bare, Serra Hill. You from the south?"
"I've been in the rain before," she answered. She laid
Her hand on a matted fleece. "I've got to find them
Some feeding-place, they're hungry, they've been in the hungry
Redwoods." He stopped and peered and giggled: "One's lame.
But," he said chuckling, "you could go on all night
And never muddy your shoes. Ho, ho! Listen, Missy.
You ain't a Mexican, I guess you've had bad luck.
I'll fix you up in the hay-shed and you'll sleep dry,
These fellows can feed all night." "The owner," she said,
"Wouldn't let me. They'd spoil the hay." "The owner.
Bless you, the poor old man's too busy to notice.
Paying his debts. That was his sharp son
Drove in just now. They hated the old man
But now they come like turkey-buzzards to watch him die."
"Oh! Is he dying?" "Why, fairly comfortable.
As well as you can expect." "I think, we'll go on,"
She murmured faintly. "Just as you like, Missy.
But nobody cares whether you spoil the hay.
There's plenty more in the barn, and all the stock
'll soon be cleared out. I don't work for his boys.
Ho, it's begun already." Some drops were flying, and the sun
Drowned in a cloud, or had set, suddenly the light was twilight. The old
    man waved his hand in the wind
Over the hives and the orchard. "This place," he giggled, "meant the world
    to old Warfield: Hey, watch them sell.
It means a shiny new car to each of the boys." He shot up the collar of his
    coat, and the huddling sheep
Tucked in their rumps; the rain on a burst of wind, small drops but many.
    The sheep looked up at their mistress,

Who said, feeling the drift like needles on her cheek, and cold drops
Run down by her shoulder, "If nobody minds, you think, about our lying
    in the hay." "Hell no, come in.
Only you'll have to be out in the gray to-morrow, before the sharp sons get
    up." He led her about
By the bridge, through the gapped fence, not to be seen from the house.
The hay-shed was well roofed, and walled southward
Against the usual drive of the rain. Clare saw in the twilight
Wealth of fodder and litter, and was glad, and the sheep
Entered and fed.

           After an hour the old man
Returned, with a smell of fried grease in the gray darkness.
Clare rose to meet him, she thought he was bringing food,
But the odor was but a relic of his own supper.
"It's raining," he said; as if she could fail to hear
The hissing drift on the roof; "you'd be cosy now
On Serra Hill." He paused and seemed deeply thoughtful,
And said, "But still you could walk all night and never
Get your shoes wet. Ho, ho! You're a fine girl,
How do you come to be on the road? Eh? Trouble?"
"I'm going north. You're kind," she said, "people are kind."
"Why yes, I'm a kind man. Well, now, sleep cosy."
He reached into the dark and touched her, she stood
Quietly and felt his hand. A dog was heard barking
Through the hiss of rain. He said "There's that damn' dog.
I tied him up after I let you in,
Now he'll be yelling all night." The old man stumped off
Into the rain, then Clare went back to her sheep
And burrowed in the hay amongst them.

                                        The old man returned
A second time; Clare was asleep and she felt
The sheep lifting their heads to stare at his lantern.
"Oh! What do you want?" "Company, company," he muttered.
"They've got an old hatchet-faced nurse in the house . . .
But he's been dying for a month, he makes me nervous.
The boys don't mind, but *I'm* nervous." He kicked
One of the sheep to make it rise and make room,
Clare murmured sadly "Don't hurt them." He sat in the hay
In heavy silence, holding the lantern on knee
As if it were a fretful baby. The fulvous glimmer
Through one of his hands showed the flesh red, and seemed
To etch the bones in it, the gnarled shafts of the fingers
And scaly lumps in the skin. Clare heard the chained dog howling,
And the rain had ceased. She reached in pitying tenderness
And touched the old man's illuminated hand and said
"How hard you have worked." "Akh," he groaned, "so has he.
And gets . . ." He moved his hand to let the warm light
Lie on her face, so that her face and his own were planets
To the lantern sun; hers smooth except the wind-blistered lips,
    pure-featured, pitying, with large dark eyes
The little sparkles of the reflected lantern had room to swim in; his bristly
    and wrinkled, and the eyes
Like sparks in a bush; the sheep uneasily below the faces moved formless,
    only Saul's watchful head
With the curled horns in the halo of light. The faint and farther rays of
    that sun touched falling spheres
Of water from the eaves at the open side of the shed, or lost themselves at
    the other in cobwebbed corners
And the dust of space. In the darkness beyond all stars the little river made
    a noise. The old man muttered,
"I heard him choking night before last and still he goes on.

It's a hell of a long ways to nothing. . . .
You know the best thing to do? Tip this in the straw,"
He tilted the lantern a little, "end in a minute,
In a blaze and yell." She said "No! no!" and he felt
The hay trembling beside him. The unconscious motion of her fear
Was not inward but toward the sheep. He observed
Nothing of that, but giggled to himself to feel
The hay trembling beside him. He dipped his hand
And caught her bare foot; clutching it with his fingers
He scratched the sole with his thumb, but Clare sat quiet
In pale terror of tipping the lantern. The old man
Groaned and stood up. "You wouldn't sit like a stone
If I were twenty years younger. Oh, damn you," he said,
"You think we get old? I'm the same fresh flame of youth still,
Stuck in an old wrinkled filthy rawhide
That soon'll rot and lie choking." She stammered "Ah, no, no,
You oughtn't to think so. You're well and strong. Or maybe
At last it'll come suddenly or while you sleep,
Never a pain." He swung up the lantern
Before his hairy and age-deformed face. "Look at me. Pfah!
And still it's April inside." He turned to go out,
Clare whispered, "Oh! Wait." She stood wringing her hands,
Warm light and darkness in waves flushing and veiling
Her perplexed face, the lantern in the old man's fist
Swinging beyond his body. "Oh, how can I tell?"
She said trembling. "You see: I'll never come back:
If anything I could do would give you some pleasure;
And you wouldn't be sorry after I'm gone." He turned,
Stamping his feet. "Heh?" He held up the lantern
And stared at her face and giggled. She heard the sheep
Nestling behind her and saw the old man's mouth
Open to speak, a black hole under the grizzled thatch,

And close again on round silence. "I'd like to make you
Happier," she faltered. "Heh?" He seemed to be trembling
Even more than Clare had trembled; he said at length,
"Was you in earnest?" "I had a great trouble,
So that now nothing seems hard . . .
That a shell broke and truly I love all people.
I'll . . . it's a little thing . . . my time is short."
He stood giggling and fidgeting. "Heh, heh! You be good.
I've got to get my sleep. I was just making the rounds.
He makes me nervous, that old man. It's his stomach
Won't hold nothing. You wouldn't play tricks to-night
And the old man puking his last? Now, you lie down.
Sleep cosy," he said. The lantern went slowly winking away,
And she was left among the warm sheep, and thoughts
Of death, and to hear the stream; and again the wind
Raved in the dark.

          She dreamed that a two-legged whiff of flame
Rose up from the house gable-peak crying, "Oh! Oh!"
And doubled in the middle and fled away on the wind
Like music above the bee-hives.

          At dawn a fresh burst of rain
Delayed her, and two of the sheep were coughing. She thought that no
    unfriendly person would come in the rain,
And hoped the old man might think to bring her some food, she was very
    hungry. The house-dog that all night long
Had yapped his chain's length, suddenly ran into the shed, then Clare
    leaped up in fear for the sheep, but this
Was a friendly dog, loving to fondle and be fondled, he shook his sides like
    a mill-wheel and remained amongst them.
The rain paused and returned, the sheep fed so contentedly

Clare let them rest all morning in the happy shelter, she dulled her own
    hunger with sleep. About noon
She lifted her long staff from the hay and stood up. "Come Saul, come
    little Hornie,
Fay, Fern and Frannie and Leader, we have to go on.
Tiny, Tiny, get up. Butt and Ben, come on":
These were the two old wethers: and she bade the dog
"Good-bye, good-bye." He followed however; but at length
Turned back from the crooked road up the open hill
When cold rain fell. Clare was glad of that, yet she wished
She'd had something to give him.

VII

                            She gained the blasty hill-top,
The unhappy sheep huddling against her thighs,
And so went northward barefoot in the gray rain,
Abstractedly, like a sleepwalker on the ridge
Of his inner necessity, or like
Some random immortal wish of the solitary hills.
If you had seen her you'd have thought that she always
Walked north in the rain on the ridge with the sheep about her.
Yet sometimes in the need of a little pleasure
To star the gray, she'd stop in the road and kiss
One of the wet foreheads: but then run quickly
A few steps on, as if loitering were dangerous,
You'd have pitied her to see her.

                        Over Mescal Creek
High on the hill, a brook in a rocky gulch, with no canyon,
Light-headed hunger and cold and the loneliness unlocked

Her troubled mind, she talked and sang as she went. "I can't eat the cold
   cress, but if there were acorns,
Bitter acorns. Ai chinita que si,
Ai que tu dami tu amor. Why did you
Have to go dry at the pinch, Frannie? Poor thing, no matter. Que venga
   con migo chinita
A donde vivo yo.
I gave them all my bread the poor shipwrecked people and they wanted
   more." She trembled and said "They're cruel,
But they were hungry. They'll never catch us I think.
Oh hurry, hurry." With songs learned from the shepherd she came to the
   fall of the road into Mill Creek Canyon.
Two of the sheep were sick and coughing, and Clare looked down. Flying
   bodies of fog, an unending fleet
Of formless gray ships in a file fled down the great canyon
Tearing their keels over the redwoods; Clare watched them and sang, "Oh
   golondrina, Oh darting swallow,"
And heard the ocean like the blood in her ears. The west-covered sun
   stared a wan light up-canyon
Against the cataract of little clouds.

                              The two coughing sheep
Brought her to a stand; then she opened their mouths and found
Their throats full of barbed seeds from the bad hay
Greedily eaten; and the gums about their teeth
Were quilled with the wicked spikes; which drawn, thin blood
Dripped from the jaw. The folds of the throat her fingers
Could not reach nor relieve; thereafter, when they coughed,
Clare shook with pain. Her pity poisoned her strength.

                                        Unhappy
   shepherdess,

Numbed feet and hands and the face
Turbid with fever:
You love, and that is no unhappy fate,
Not one person but all, does it warm your winter?
Walking with numbed and cut feet
Along the last ridge of migration
On the last coast above the not-to-be-colonized
Ocean, across the streams of the people
Drawing a faint pilgrimage
As if you were drawing a line at the end of the world
Under the columns of ancestral figures:
So many generations in Asia,
So many in Europe, so many in America:
To sum the whole. Poor Clare Walker, she already
Imagines what sum she will cast in April.

                                        She came by the farmhouse
At Mill Creek, then she wavered in the road and went to the door,
Leaving her sheep in the road; the day was draining
Toward twilight. Clare began to go around the house,
Then stopped and returned and knocked faintly at the door.
No answer; but when she was turning back to the road
The door was opened, by a pale slight young man
With no more chin than a bird, and Mongol-slanted
Eyes; he peered out, saying "What do you want?" Clare stood
Wringing the rain from her fingers. "Oh, Oh," she stammered,
"I don't know what. I have some sheep with me.
I don't know where we can stay." He stood in the door
And looked afraid. The sheep came stringing down
Through the gate Clare had left open. A gray-eyed man
With a white beard pushed by the boy and said
"What does she want? What, are you hungry? Take out your beasts,

We can't have sheep in the yard." Clare ran to the gate,
"Come Leader, come Saul." The old man returned in-doors
Saying, "Wait outside, I'll get you some bread." Clare waited
Leaning against the gate, it seemed a long while;
The old man came back with changed eyes and changed voice:
"We can't do anything for you. There isn't any bread.
Move on from here." She said through her chattering teeth,
"Come Saul, come Leader, come Frannie. We have to go on.
Poor Fern, come on." They drifted across the Mill Creek bridge
And up the road in the twilight. "The ground-squirrels," she said, "hide in
     their holes
All winter long, and the birds have perches but we have no place." They
     tried to huddle in the heart of a bush
Under a redwood, Clare crouched with the sheep about her, her thighs
     against her belly, her face on her knees,
Not sleeping, but in a twilight consciousness, while the night darkened.

                                                                    In
     an hour she thought she must move or die.
"Ah little Hornie," she said, feeling with shrivelled fingers the sprouts of
     the horns in the small arched forehead,
"Come Fern: are you there Leader? Come Saul, come Nosie . . . Ah no, I
     was dreaming. Oh dear," she whispered, "we're very
Miserable now." She crept out of the bush and the sheep followed; she
     couldn't count them, she heard them
Plunge in the bush and heard them coughing behind her. They came on
     the road
In the gray dark; there, though she'd meant to go north
She went back toward the farmhouse. Crossing the bridge
She smelled oak-smoke and thought of warmth. Grown reckless
Clare entered the farmhouse yard with her fleeced following,
But not daring enough to summon the door

Peered in a window. What she saw within

Mixed with her fever seemed fantastic and dreadful. It was nothing strange:

The weak-faced youth, the bearded old man, and two old women

Idle around a lamp on a table. They sat on their chairs in the warmth and
    streaming light and nothing

Moved their faces. But Clare felt dizzy at heart, she thought they were
    waiting for death: how could they sit

And not run and not cry? Perhaps they were dead already? Then, the old
    man's head

Turned, and the youth's fingers drummed on his chair. One of the blank
    old women was sewing and the other

Frowned and breathed. She lifted and spoke to white-beard, then the first
    old woman

Flashed eyes like rusty knives and sheathed them again

And sewed the cloth; they grew terribly quiet;

Only the white beard quivered. The young man stood up

And moved his mouth for a good while but no one

Of those in the room regarded him. He sighed and saw

Clare's face at the window. She leaped backward; the lamplight

Had fed her eyes with blindness toward the gray night,

She ran in a panic about the barren garden,

Unable to find the gate; the sheep catching her fear

Huddled and plunged, pricking the empty wet earth with numberless
    hoof-prints. But no one came out pursuing them,

The doors were not opened, the house was quiet. Clare found the gate

And stood by it, whispering "Dear Tiny. Ah, Fern, that's you. Come Saul,"
    she fumbled each head as it passed the gate-post,

To count the flock.

                    But all had not passed, a man on a horse

Came plodding the puddled road. Clare thought the world

Was all friendly except in that house, and she ran

To the road's crown. "Oh, Oh," she called; and Onorio
Vasquez answered, "I rode early in the morning
To find you and couldn't find you. I've been north and south.
I thought I could find the track of the sheep." She answered
Through chattering teeth, "I thought I could stand the rain.
I'm sick and the sheep are sick." He said gravely
"There's hardly a man on the coast wouldn't have helped you
Except in that house. There, I think they *need* help.
Well, come and we'll live the night." "How far?" she sighed
Faintly, and he said "Our place is away up-canyon,
You'll find it stiff travelling by day-light even.
To-night's a camp."

                    He led her to the bridge, and there
Found dry sticks up the bank, leavings of an old flood, under the spring of
    the timbers,
And made a fire against the creekside under the road for a roof. He
    stripped her of the dripping cloak
And clothed her in his, the oil-skin had kept it dry, and spread her the
    blanket from under his saddle to lie on.
The bridge with the tarred road-bed on it was a roof
Over their heads; the sheep, when Clare commanded them, lay down like
    dogs by the fire. The horse was tethered
To a clump of willow in the night outside.

                                   When her feet and her hands
    began to be warm he offered her food,
She ate three ravenous mouthfuls and ran from the fire and vomited. He
    heard her gasping in the night thicket
And a new rain. He went after while and dragged her
Back to the frugal fire and shelter of the bridge.

VIII

She lay and looked up at the great black timbers, the flapping fire-shadows,
And draggled cobwebs heavy with dirt and water;
While Vasquez watched the artery in the lit edge
Of her lean throat jiggle with its jet of blood
Like a slack harp-string plucked: a toneless trembling:
It made him grieve.

          After a time she exclaimed
"My sheep. My sheep. Count them." "What," he said, "they all
Are here beside you." "I never dreamed," she answered,
"That any were lost, Oh no! But my sight swam
When I looked at them in the bad light." He looked
And said "Are there not . . . ten?" "No, nine," she answered.
"Nosie has died. Count them and tell me the truth."
He stood, bowing down his head under the timbers,
And counted seven, then hastily the first two
A second time, and said "Nine." "I'm glad of that,"
She sighed, and was quiet, but her quill fingers working
The border of the saddle-blanket. He hoped she would soon
Sleep.

          The horse tethered outside the firelight
Snorted, and the sheep lifted their heads, a spot of white
Came down the dark slope. Vasquez laid his brown palm
Over Clare's wrists, "Lie still and rest. The old fellow from the house is
    coming.
Sleep if you can, I'll talk to him." "Is there a dog?" she whispered
    trembling. "No, no, the old man is alone."
Who peered under the heavy stringer of the bridge, his beard shone in the
    firelight. "Here," he shouted, "Hey!

Burn the road, would you? You want to make people stay home
And suck the sour bones in their own houses? Come out of that hole." But
    Vasquez: "Now, easy, old neighbor. She wanted
Fire and a roof, she's found what you wouldn't give." "By God, and a man
    to sleep with," he said, "that's lucky,
But the bridge, the bridge." "Don't trouble, I'm watching the fire. Fire's
    tame, this weather." The old man stood twitching and peering,
And heard the sheep coughing in their cave
Under the road. He squinted toward Clare, and muttered at length meekly,
    "Let me stay a few minutes.
To sit by the little road-fire of freedom. My wife and my sister have hated
    each other for thirty years,
And I between them. It makes the air of the house. I sometimes think I can
    see it boil up like smoke
When I look back at the house from the hill above." Vasquez said gravely
"I have often watched that." He answered "You haven't lived in it. They sit
    in the house and feed on their own poison
And live forever. I am now too feeble with age to escape." Clare Walker
    lifted her head, and faintly:
"Oh stay," she said, "I wish I could gather all that are unhappy
Before I die. But why do they hate each other?"
"Their nature," he answered, "old women." She sighed and lay down.
"I shan't grow old." "Young fellow," the old man said wearily
To Vasquez, "they all make that promise, they never keep it.
Life glides by and the bright loving creatures
Eat us in the evening. I'd have given this girl bread
And meat, but my hawks were watching me." He'd found a stone
On the edge of the creek, the other side of the fire, and squatted there, his
    two fists
Closing his eyes, the beard shimmering between the bent wrists. His voice
    being silent they heard the fire

Burst the tough bark of a wet branch; the wind turned north, then a gust of
    hail spattered in the willows
And checked at once, the air became suddenly cold. The old man lifted his
    face: "Ah can't you talk?
I thought you'd be gay or I'd not have stayed here, you too've grown old? I
    wish that a Power went through the world
And killed people at thirty when the ashes crust them. You, cowboy, die,
    your joints will begin to crackle,
You've had the best. Young bank-clerk you've had the best, grow fat and
    sorry and more dollars? Here, farmer, die,
You've spent the money: will bleed the mortgage
Fifty years more? You cunning pussy of the world, you've had the fun and
    the kissing, skip the diseases.
Oh you, you're an honest wife and you've made a baby: why should you
    watch him
Grow up and spoil, and dull like cut lead? I see, my dear, you'll never be
    filled till you grow poisonous
With eyes like rusty knives under the gray eye-brows. God bless you, die."
    He had risen from the stone, and trampled,
Each condemnation, some rosy coal fallen out at the fire's edge
Under his foot as if it had been a life. "Sharp at thirty," he said. Clare
    vaguely moaned
And turned her face to the outer darkness, then Vasquez
Misunderstanding her pain, thinking it stemmed
From the old man's folly: "Don't mind him, he's not in earnest.
These nothing-wishers of life are never in earnest;
Make mouths to scare you: if they meant it they'd do it
And not be alive to make mouths." She made no answer,
But lay and listened to her own rustling pulse-beat,
Her knees drawn up to her breast. White-beard knelt down and mended
    the fire,

And brushed his knees. "There's another law that I'd make: to burn the
   houses. Turn out the people on the roads,
And neither homes nor old women we'd be well off. All young, all gay, all
   moving, free larks and foolery
By gipsy fires." His voice fell sad: "It's bitter to be a reformer: with two
   commandments
I'd polish the world a-shining, make the sun ashamed."
Clare Walker stood up, then suddenly sought the dark night
To hide herself in the bushes; her bowels were loosened
With cold and fever. Vasquez half rose to follow her,
And he understood, and stayed by the fire. Then white-beard
Winking and nodding whispered: "Is she a good piece?
Hey, is she sick? I have to protect my son.
Where in hell did she get the sheep?" Vasquez said fiercely,
"You'd better get home, your wife'll be watching for you.
This girl is sick and half starved, I was unwilling
To let her die in the road." The old man stood up
As pricked with a pin at the thought of home. "What? We're free men,"
He said, lifting his feet in an anxious dance
About the low fire: "but it's devilish hard
To be the earthly jewel of two jealous women."
"Look," Vasquez said, "it seems to me that your house is afire.
I see rolls of tall smoke . . ." "By God," he answered,
"I wish it were," he trotted up to the road
While a new drift of hail hissed in the willows,
Softening to rain.

               When he was gone, Vasquez
Repaired the fire, and called "Clare! Come in to shelter.
Clare, come! The rain is dangerous for you. The old fool's gone home."
He stumbled in the dark along the strand of the creek
Calling "Clare, Clare!" then looking backward he saw

The huddle of firelit fleeces moving and rising,
And said "The sheep are scattering away to find you.
You ought to call them." She came then, and stood by the fire.
He heard the bleating cease, and looked back to see her
Quieting her friends, wringing the rain from her hair,
The fire had leaped up to a blaze. Vasquez returned
Under the bridge, then Clare with her lips flushed
And eyes brilliant with fever: "That poor old man, has he gone?
I'm sorry if he's gone.
My father was old, but after he'd plowed the hill-top I've seen him ride
The furrows at a dead run, sowing the grain with both hands, while he
    controlled the colt with his knees.
The time it fell at the furrow's end
In the fat clay, he was up first and laughing. He was kind and cruel." "Your
    father?" he said. She answered
"I can't remember my mother, she died to bear me, as I . . . We kept her
    picture, she looked like me,
And often my father said I was like her. — Oh what's become of the poor
    old man, has he gone home?
Here he was happy." "Yes, had to go home," he answered. "But you must
    sleep. I'll leave you alone if you like,
You promise to stay by the fire and sleep." "Oh I couldn't, truly. My mind's
    throwing all its wrecks on the shore
And I can't sleep. That was a shipwreck that drove us wandering. I
    remember all things. Your name's Onorio
Vasquez: I wish you had been my brother." He smiled and touched her
    cold hand. "For then," she said, "we could talk
Old troubles asleep: I haven't thought, thought,
For a long while, to-night I can't stop my thoughts. But we all must die?"
    "Spread out your hands to the fire,
Warm yourself, Clare." "No, no," she answered, her teeth chattering, "I'm
    hot.

My throat aches, yet you see I don't cough, it was Frannie coughing. — It
    was almost as if I killed my father,
To swear to the lies I told after he was killed, all to save Charlie. Do you
    think he'd care, after . . .
He was surely dead? You don't believe we have spirits? Nobody believes we
    have spirits." He began to answer,
And changed his words for caution. "Clare: all you are saying
Is hidden from me. It's like the visions I have,
That go from unknown to unknown." He said proudly,
"I've watched, the whole night of a full moon, an army of centaurs
Come out of the ocean, plunging on Sovranes reef
In wide splendors of silver water,
And swim with their broad hooves between the reef and the shore and go
    up
Over the mountain — I never knew why.
What you are saying is like that." "Oh, I'll tell you . . ." "To-morrow,"
He pleaded, remembering she'd eaten nothing and seeing
The pulse like a plucked harp-string jiggle in her throat;
He felt like a pain of his own the frail reserves of her body
Burn unreplenished. "Oh, but I'll tell you: so then
You'll know me, as if we'd been born in the same house,
You'll tell me not to be afraid: maybe I'll sleep
At the turn of night. Onorio — that's really your name?
How stately a name you have — lie down beside me.
I am now so changed: everyone's lovely in my eyes
Whether he's brown or white or that poor old man:
In those days nobody but Charlie Maurice
Seemed very dear, as if I'd been blind to all the others.
He lived on the next hill, two miles across a deep valley, and then it was
    five to the next neighbor
At Vicente Springs; people are so few there. We lived a long way south,
    where the hills fall straight to the sea,

And higher than these. He lived with his people. We used to meet near a
    madrone-tree, Charlie would kiss me
And put his hands on my breasts under my clothes. It was quite long before
    we learned the sweet way
That brings much joy to most living creatures, but brought us misery at
    last.

IX

      My father," she said,
"Had lived there for thirty years, but after he sold his cattle
And pastured sheep, to make more money, the neighbors
Were never our friends. Oh, they all feared my father;
Sometimes they threatened our shepherd, a Spanish man
Who looked like you, but was always laughing. He'd laugh
And say 'Guarda a Walker!' so then they'd leave him.
But we lived lonely.

                    One morning of great white clouds gliding from
    the sea
When I was with Charlie in the hollow near the madrones, I felt a pleasure
    like a sweet fire: for all
My joy before had been in *his* pleasure: but this was my own, it frightened
    me." She stopped speaking, for Vasquez
Stood up and left her; he went and sat by the fire. Then Clare:
"Why do you leave me, Onorio? Are you angry now?"
"I am afraid," he answered, "of this love.
My visions are the life of my life: if I let the pitcher
Break on the rock and the sun kill the stars,
Life would be emptier than death." Her mind went its own way,
Not understanding so strange a fear: "The clouds were as bright as stars
    and I could feel them," she said,

"Through the shut lids of my eyes while the sweet fire
Poured through my body: I knew that some dreadful pain would pay for
    such joy. I never slept after that
But dreamed of a laughing child and wakened with running tears. After I
    had trembled for days and nights
I asked Tia Livia—that was our shepherd's cousin, she helped me keep
    house—what sign tells women
When they have conceived: she told me the moon then ceases
To rule our blood. I counted the days then,
Not dreaming that Tia Livia would spy and talk.
Was that not strange? I think that she told the shepherd too,
And the shepherd had warned my lover: for Charlie failed
Our meeting time, but my father was there with a gray face.
In silence, he didn't accuse me, we went home together.

I met my lover in another place. 'Oh Charlie,
Why do you wear a revolver?' He said the mountain
Was full of rattlers, 'We've killed twenty in a week.
There never have been so many, step carefully sweetheart.'
Sweetheart he called me: you're listening Onorio?
'Step carefully by the loose stones.' We were too frightened that day
To play together the lovely way we had learned.

The next time that I saw him, he and my father
Met on a bare hill-top against a gray cloud.
I saw him turn back, but then I saw that he was ashamed
To seem afraid of a man on the ridge of earth,
With the hills and the ocean under his feet: and my father called him. —
    What was that moan?" She stopped, and Vasquez
Heard it far off, and heard the sap of a stick whistle in the fire. "Nothing,"
    he said, "low thunder

Far out the ocean, or the surf in the creek-mouth." " — I was running up
    the steep slope to reach them, the breath in my heart
Like saw-grass cut me, I had no power to cry out, the stones and the
    broken stubble flaked under my feet
So that I seemed running in one place, unable to go up. It was not because
    he hated my father,
But he was so frightened. They stood as if they were talking, a noise of
    smoke
Blew from between them, my father turned then and walked
Slowly along the cloud and sat on the hill-top
As if he were tired.
I said after a time, without thinking,
'Go home, Charlie. I'll say that he killed himself.
And give me the revolver, I'll say it was his.'
So Charlie did.
But when the men came up from Salinas I told my lie
So badly that they believed I was the murderer.
I smelled the jail a long while. I saw the day moon
Down the long street the morning I was taken to court,
As weary-looking and stained as if it were something of mine.
I remembered then, that since I came there my blood
Had never been moved when the moon filled: what Livia'd told me.
So then I told them my father took his own life
Because the sheep had a sickness and I was pregnant.
The shepherd and Livia swore that they saw him do it.
I'd have been let home:
But the fever I'd caught gathered to a bursting pain,
I had to be carried from the courthouse to the hospital
And for a time knew nothing.
When I began to see with my eyes again
The doctor said: 'The influenza that takes
Many lives has saved yours, you'll not have a child.

Listen,' he said, 'my girl if you're wise.
Your miscarriage is your luck. Your pelvis—the bones down there
Are so deformed that it's not possible for you
To bear a living baby: no life can pass there:
And yours would be lost. You'd better remember,
And try not to be reckless.' I remember so well, Onorio.
I have good reason to remember. You never could guess
What a good reason.

                    My little king was dead
And I was too weak to care. I have a new king.

When I got home," she said patiently,
"Everybody believed that I was a murderer;
And Charlie was gone. They left me so much alone
That often I myself believed it. I'd lead the sheep to that hill,
There were fifty left out of three hundred,
And pray for pardon."

                    Sleep and her fever confused her brain,
One heard phrases in the running babble, across a new burst of hail.
     "Forgive me, father, for I didn't
Know what I was doing." And, "Why have you forsaken me, father?" Her
     mind was living again the bare south hill-top
And the bitter penitence among the sheep. "The two men that I loved and
     the baby that I never saw,
All taken away."

                    Then Vasquez was calling her name to break the black
     memories; she turned on her side, the flame-light
Leaped, and he saw her face puckering with puzzled wonder. "Not all
     alone? But how can that be?"

She sighed and said "Oh Leader, don't stray for awhile. Dear Saul: can you
    keep them here on the hill around me
Without my watching? No one else helps me. I'll lie down here on the
    little grass in the windy sun
And think whether I can live. I have *you*, dear stragglers. Thoughts come
    and go back as lightly as deer on the hill,
But as hard to catch. . . . Not *all* alone. Oh. Not alone at *all*.
Indeed it is even stranger than I thought."

                          She laughed and sat up. "Oh
    sweet warm sun. . . .
Are you there, Onorio? But where's the poor old man
Who seemed to be so unhappy? I wish he hadn't gone home,
For now I remember what I ought to tell him. I'm sadly changed
Since that trouble and sickness, and though I'm happy
I hardly ever remember in the nick o' time
What ought to be said. You must tell him
That all our pain comes from restraint of love."
The hail had suddenly hushed, and all her words
Were clear but hurried. "I learned it easily, Onorio,
And never have thought about it again till now. The only wonder's
Not to've known always. The beetle beside my hand in the grass and the
    little brown bird tilted on a stone,
The short sad grass, burnt on the gable of the world with near sun and all
    winds: there was nothing there that I didn't
Love with my heart, yes the hill though drunk with dear blood: I looked far
    over the valley at the patch of oaks
At the head of a field, where Charlie's people had lived (they had moved
    away) and loved them, although they'd been
Always unfriendly I never thought of it." Then Vasquez, for the first time
    forgetting the person a moment

To regard the idea: "You were cut off from the natural objects of love, you
    turned toward others." "Ah," she answered
Eagerly, "I'd always been turned to all others,
And tired my poor strength confining the joy to few. But now I'd no more
    reason to confine it, I'd nothing
Left to lose nor keep back. — Has the poor old man gone?
He seemed to be truly unhappy.
Wasn't he afraid we'd burn the bridge: we ought surely
To have drowned our fire. I was sick, or I'd have done . . . anything.
But old men are so strange, to want and not want,
And then be angry."

                "He has gone," he answered.
"Now, Clare, if you could eat something, then sleep,
To fill the cup for to-morrow."
"I have to tell you the rest. — Why did he go?
Was he angry at me? — Oh, I feel better, Onorio,
But never more open-eyed.

                    There was one of those great owly hawks
That soar for hours, turning and turning below me along the bottom of the
    slope: I so loved it
I thought if it were hungry I'd give it my hand for meat.

                        Then winter
    came.
Then about Christmas time (because I'd counted the months and
    remembered Christmas) storm followed storm
Like frightened horses tethered to a tree, around and around. Three men
    came in the door without knocking,
Wherever they moved, water and black oil ran down. There'd been a
    shipwreck. I gave them the house, then one of them

Found the axe and began chopping firewood, another went back across wild
   rain to the fall of the hill
And shouted. He was so big, like a barrel walking, I ran in his shelter
And saw the great, black, masted thing almost on shore, lying on its side in
   the shadow of the hill,
And the flying steam of a fire they'd built on the beach. All that morning
   the people came up like ants,
Poor souls they were all so tired and cold, some hurt and some crying. I'd
   only," she said, "a few handfuls of flour
Left in the house." She trembled and lay down. "I can't remember any
   more."

            Vasquez made up the fire,
And went and drew up the blanket over Clare's shoulder.
He found her shuddering. "Now sleep. Now rest." She answered:
"They killed a sheep. They were hungry.
I'd grown to love so much the flock that was left.
Our shepherd, I think, had taken them away mostly
While I was kept in Salinas.
I heard her crying when they threw her down, she thought I could save her.
Her soft white throat.

That night I crept out in the thin rain at moonrise
And led them so far away, all that were left,
The house and the barn might hold a hundred hungry mouths
To hunt us all night and day and could never find us.
We hid in oak-woods. There was nothing to eat,
And never any dry place. We walked in the gray rain in the flowing gorges
   of canyons that no one
But the hawks have seen, and climbed wet stone and saw the storms racing
   below us, but still the thin rain

Sifted through the air as if it fell from the stars. I was then much stronger
Than ever since then.

                A man caught me at last, when I was too weak to
    run, and conquered my fear.
He was kind, he promised me not to hurt the poor flock,
But the half of them had been lost, I never could remember how. He lived
    alone; I was sick in his cabin
For many days, dreaming that a monkey nursed me: he looked so funny,
    he'd a frill of red hair
All around his face.

              When I grew better, he wanted to do like Charlie. I
    knew what the doctor had said,
But I was ashamed to speak of death: I was often ashamed in those days:
    he'd been so kind. Yet terror
Would come and cover my head like a cold wave.
I watched the moon, but at the full moon my fear
Flowed quietly away in the night.

The spring and summer were full of pleasure and happiness.
I'd no more fear of my friend, but we met seldom. I went in freedom
From mountain to mountain, wherever good pasture grew,
Watching the creeks grow quiet and color themselves
With cool green moss, and the green hills turn white.
The people at the few farms all knew me, and now
Their minds changed; they were kind. All the deer knew me;
They'd walk in my flock.

          In the midst of summer
When the moon filled, my blood failed to be moved,

The life that will make death began in my body.
I'd seen that moon when it was little as a chip
Over my left shoulder, from Palos ridge
By a purple cloud."

X

                "Oh, not till April," she said.
"All's quiet now, the bitterness is past, I have made peace
With death except in my dreams, those can't be ruled. But then, when I
    first
Began to believe and knew it had happened . . . I felt badly. I went back to
    my father's house,
Much was broken and chopped down, but I found
Little things that I'd loved when I was a child, hidden in corners. When I
    was drunk with crying
We hurried away. The lambs never seemed able to live, the mothers were
    glad to give me their milk,
We hid in the secret hills till it seemed desolate to die there. — Tell me,
    Onorio,
What month is this?"

              He answered, "Clare, Clare, fear nothing.
Death is as far away from you as from any one.
There was a girl (I've heard my brothers talking:
The road-overseer's daughter) was four or five months along
And went to a doctor: she had no trouble:
She's like a virgin again." Clare struck the earth with her hands
And raised her body, she stared through the red of the fire
With brilliant confused eyes. "Your face was like a devil's in the steamy
    glimmer:

But only because you don't understand. Why, Tia Livia herself . . . you are too innocent, Onorio,

Has done so . . . but women often have small round stones

Instead of hearts." "But," he answered, "if you're not able to bear it. Not even a priest would bid you die

For a child that couldn't be born alive. You've lived too much alone, bodiless fears have become

Giants in secret. I too am not able to think clearly to-night, in the stinging drift of the fire

And the strange place, to-morrow I'll tell you plainly. My mind is confused

As I have sometimes felt it before the clouds of the world

Were opened: but I know: for disease to refuse cure

Is self-murder, not virtue." She squatted upright

Wrapping the coat about her shoulders and knees,

And said, "Have you never seen in your visions

The golden country that our souls came from,

Before we looked at the moon and stars and knew

They are not perfect? We came from a purer peace

In a more perfect heaven; where there was nothing

But calm delight, no cold, no sickness, no sharp hail,

The haven of neither hunger nor sorrow,

But all-enfolding love and unchangeable joy

Near the heart of life." Vasquez turned from the fire

And stared at her lit face. "How did you learn

This wonder? It is true." "I remembered it,"

She answered, "when I was in trouble." "This is the bitter-sweet memory,"

He said, "that makes the breast of the earth bitter

After we are born and the dear sun ridiculous. We shall return there, we homesick."

"No," she answered. "The place was my mother's body before I was born. You may remember it a little but I've

Remembered plainly: and the wailing pain of entering this air. I've thought
    and thought and remembered. I found
A cave in a high cliff of white stone, when I was hiding from people: it was
    there I had the first memory.
There I'd have stayed in the safe darkness forever; the sheep were hungry
    and strayed out, so I couldn't stay.
I remembered again when I went home to our house and the door hung
    crazy
On a snapped hinge. You don't believe me, Onorio,
But after while you'll remember plainly, if some long trouble
Makes you want peace; or being handled has broken your shame. I have no
    shame now." He answered nothing
Because she seemed to speak from a frantic mind.
After a moment, "No matter," she said. "When I was in my worst trouble
I knew that the child was feeding on peace and happiness. I had happiness
    here in my body. It is not mine,
But I am its world and the sky around it, its loving God. It is having the
    prime and perfect of life,
The nine months that are better than the ninety years. I'd not steal one of
    its days to save my life.
I am like its God, how could I betray it? It has not moved yet
But feels its blessedness in its quietness; but soon I shall feel it move, Tia
    Livia said it will nestle
Down the warm nest and flutter like a winged creature. It shook her body,
    she said." But Vasquez, loathing
To hear these things, labored with the sick fire
In the steam of the wet wood, not listening, then Clare
Sighed and lay down. He heard her in a moment
Miserably sobbing, he went and touched her. "What is it?
Clare? Clare?" "Ai, when will morning come?
It is horrible to lie still," she said, "feeling

The black of April . . . it's nothing, it's nothing . . . like a cat
Tick tick on padded feet. Ah let me alone, will you?
Lying quiet does it: I'll have courage in my time."

A little later she asked for food, she ate,
And drank from the stream, and slept. She moved in her sleep
And tossed her arms, Vasquez would cover them again,
But the fever seemed quieted. He crossed the stream by the stones in the
    dull fire-glimmer
And fetched armfuls of flood-wood from under the opposite bridge-head.
    The fire revived; the earth turned past midnight;
Far eastward beyond the coasts of the continent morning troubled the
    Atlantic.

XI

            Vasquez crouched by the fire
And felt one of those revelations that were in his own regard the jewels and
    value of his life
Approach and begin. First passed — as always
Since Barclay was gone, whom he had taken for incarnate God — ancestral
    forms against the white cloud,
The high dark heads of Indian migrations, going south along the coast,
    drawn down from the hungry straits and from Asia,
The heads like worn coins and the high shoulders,
The brown-lipped patient mouths below vulture beaks, and burnished fall
    of black hair over slant foreheads,
Going up to the Mayan and the Aztec mountains, and sowing the coast.
    They swept the way and the cloud cleared,
The vision would come: came instead a strong pause.

A part of his mind
Wished to remember what the rest had forgotten,
And groping for it in the dark withstood the prepared
Pageant of dreams. He'd read in his curious boyhood
Of the child the mother is found incapable of bearing
Cut from the mother's belly. Both live; the wound
Heals: it was called the Caesarean section. But he, fearing
Whatever thought might threaten to infringe his careful
Chastity of mind, had quickly cancelled the memory;
That now sought a new birth; it might save Clare
If he could think of it.

That revived part
Made itself into the vision, all to no purpose,
His precious dreams were never to the point of life.
Only the imperial name, and the world's
Two-thousand-year and ten-thousand-miles-travelled
Caesarean memory appeared. He imagined at first that the voice
Cried "Ave Maria," but it cried "Ave Caesar."

He saw the firelight-gilded
Timbers of the bridge above; and one of the ewes lifted her head in the
    light beside Clare sleeping;
The smoke gathered its cloud into a floating globe and these were
    forgotten. On the globe of the earth
The aquiline-headed Roman, who summed in his one person the powers
    and ordered science of humanity,
Stood and possessed his orb of empire and looked at the stars. Then the
    voice cried
"The pride of the earth."

But Vasquez laughed aloud, for the earth was a grain of dust circling the fire,
And the fire itself but a spark, among innumerable sparks. The swarm of the points of light drifting
No path down darkness merged its pin-prick eyelets into one misty glimmer, a mill-stone in shape,
A coin in shape, a mere coin, a flipped luck-penny: but again Vasquez
Laughed out, for who was the spendthrift sowed them all over the sky, indistinguishable innumerable
Fish-scales of light? They drew together as they drifted away no path down the wild darkness; he saw
The webs of their rays made them one tissue, their rays that were their very substance and power filled wholly
The space they were in, so that each one touched all, there was no division between them, no emptiness, and each
Changed substance with all the others and became the others. It was dreadful to see
No space between them, no cave of peace nor no night of quietness, no blind spot nor no deaf heart, but the tides
Of power and substance flood every cranny; no annihilation, no escape but change: it must endure itself
Forever. It has the strength to endure itself. We others, being faintly made of the dust of a grain of dust
Have been permitted to fool our patience asleep by inventing death. A poor comfort, he thought,
Yet better than none, the imaginary cavern, how we all come clamoring
To the gates of our great invention after few years.
Though a cheat, it works.

The speckled tissue of universes
Drew into one formed and rounded light, and Vasquez
Worshipped the one light. One eye . . . what, an eye?

A dark mountain with an eye in its cliff? A coal-black stallion
Eyed with one burning eye in the mid-brow?
Night has an eye. The poor little vision-seer
Groaned, that he never had wit to understand visions.
See all and know nothing. The eye that makes its own light
And sees nothing but itself. "I am seeing Barclay again,"
He marvelled, as who should say "I am seeing God:
But what is God?" He continued gazing,
And beads of sweat spilled from his forehead into the fire-edge
Ashes. He saw at last, neither the eyed mountain
Nor the stallion, nor Barclay, but his own eye
In the darkness of his own face.

                          The circuit was closed;
"I can endure all things," he thought, "forever. I am he
Whom I have sought.

                     And Clare loves all things
Because all things are herself. She has killed her father
And inherited. Her old enormous father
Who rode the furrows full tilt, sowing with both hands
The high field above the hills and the ocean. We kill steers for meat, and
     God
To be atoned with him. But I remain from myself divided, gazing beyond
     the flaming walls,
Not fortunate enough, and too faint-hearted."

                                   He continued gazing
     across the wane of the fire at the dark
Vision of his own face turned sideways, the light of one eye. Clare turned
     in her place and awoke and said,
"How awfully little. Ooh, Ooh," in a dove's voice,

And then, "I forgot I wasn't alone, Onorio:
And here are the sheep. Have I slept a moment?
I did have a strange dream. I went out across the starlight
Knocking through flight after flight of the shiny balls
And got so far away that the sun and the great earth
And beautiful moon and all the stars were blended
Into one tiny light, Oh terribly little,
The flame of a pitiful little candle blown over
In the wind of darkness, in the fear of the night. It was so tiny
I wanted to be its comfort
And hold it and rock it on my breast. One wee flicker
In all the wild dark. What a dream." She turned anxiously
To touch the sheep, fondling their heads and naming them.
"Dear Fay, dear Fern. And here's Captain Saul. Ah bad little Hornie
Who taught you to be so bold?" Suddenly she cried
"Did Leader and Frannie go out—did two of the sheep
Go out lately?" But Vasquez, caught in his vision,
Answered "You also have broken
The fire-studded egg of heaven and we're together
In the world outside." "Ah Ah," she cried desolately,
"Did you lie when you counted them? When I was sick
And my eyes failed?" She ran into the darkness outside, calling their names;
The flock that remained stood up, in the edge of firelight, tremulously
    crying. Then Vasquez: "I hear a multitude
Of people crying, but why do you lament and cry? You particles of the eye
    of light, if some of you
Endure evil, the others endure good, the balance is perfect. The eye lives
    on mixed light and darkness,
Not either alone. And you are not many but one, the eye is not glad nor
    sorry, nor the dark face
Disquieted: be quiet, voices, and hear the real voice." Clare Walker came in
    from the dark with wide strained eyes,

In each iris the fire reflected made a red stain, and she cried:
"Onorio, for Christ's sake tell me, were they not with me?
Or have they slipped out?" He turned slowly an unanswering face
Of cool, dark and deaf stone, tempered to the mood
Of what he imagined . . . or perhaps perceived. And Clare:
"If I have slept and been dreaming while they're in danger
Or die in the dark: and they cried for me
In the dead night, while I slept and ate: I hope that all the miseries I ever
    feared for myself
Will come doubled, the rain on my hair be knives of ice, the sun whips of
    fire, the death I must die
Drawn out and dreadful like the dream of hell: Onorio, Oh come,
Help me to find them!" He rose, passively under command in the shrill of
    her voice, muttering: "I can't
Imagine what further's to find: yet I'll go along.
Is there another light or another darkness?"
"Oh," she answered, "it's black," and snatched the most eager brands
Out of the fire for a torch. He with deft fingers
Mimicking her act, but with a sleepwalker mindlessness,
Bound fire into a bundle of sallow twigs,
And calmly, twirling his torch to flame, followed
The red glow of her rod-ends. They ran on the bridge and wandered
Up the wet road, Clare calling her flock around her
And sobbing the names of the lost. The useless torches
Flared in the puddles and ruts of water, and ruddied
The plump backs of the sheep; so sanguine-outlined
The little ridiculous procession strayed up the road
In the lane of the trees, the great-trunked wood like storms
Of darkness on either hand. The torches died soon,
Then Clare stood still, desolately calling; weak dawn
Had washed all the world gray.

                    The heads of the little flock
Suddenly and all together were turned one way, then a limping ewe
Came out of the wood. Clare screamed with joy, and ran and dropped on
    her knees to embrace the lean neck. "Oh Leader!
Leader! She's safe, Onorio. Oh Leader where's Frannie?" But then the
    wound was discovered, the flap torn back
Red from the flank and hanging from the rump, and the blood-caked wool.
    Clare moaned awhile with no words, and said,
"When I forgot you because I was sick, when I forgot to call you and count
    you in the rain in the night:
I wish I had died. I have nothing but these
Onorio, to take care of, and lose and lose. She used to go first always, I
    called her Leader:
And now she's hurt." Onorio heard Clare's teeth clacking together in the
    thin cheeks, and her breath
Hissing between them, he answered calmly, still caught in his vision: "The
    five claws of a lion. Look, Clare.
But don't grieve, the great river of the blood of life is always bursting its
    banks, never runs dry,
Secret inexhaustible fountains feed it." She stared at his face and turned on
    the forest her desert eyes
And wrung her hands. "Leader is hurt; and Frannie I think has died."

                                                                They

    searched long; the fourth hour
Of daylight they found the half consumed body. The head was not
    mangled, Clare fell beside it
On the wet earth and kissed the half open eyes,
Weeping and self-reproachful, but yet she lamented
Less violently than Vasquez had feared. At length
He said, "If you wish, Clare, I will fetch tools
And bury it here." She answered faintly, "No matter.

She feels nothing to-day, darkness nor light,

Teeth nor the grave. Oh, I loved her well: but now, see,

She's not living any more. Onorio . . . isn't that your name?

What a stately name! . . . this is the one that fed me with milk

Long after the others were dry, she was like a mother to me, when I might
    have starved.

She loved me, I know.

But even the udders are torn. Her name, Onorio, was Frannie."

She turned and said, "Poor Leader. Can you come now?

Come Fern, come Fay, come Tiny, we have to go on.

Come Saul."

              Vasquez begged her to turn again

And stay at his father's place in the canyon

Until she was well. She had to go on, she answered.

And Vasquez: "My father is withered up with old age but he'd be kind; and
    my brothers

Would be your brothers. There's pasture for the sheep. We're only a sort of
    Indians but we can be kind. Come, Clare.

The place is pleasant and alone, up the deep canyon, beside the old quarry
    and the kilns where they burnt the lime.

A hundred laborers used to live there, but now the woods have grown back,
    the cabins are standing empty,

The roads are gone. I think the old masonry kilns are beautiful, standing
    like towers in the deep forest,

But cracked and leaning, and maidenhair fern grows from the cracks. The
    creek makes music below. Come, Clare.

It is deep with peace. When I have to go about and work on men's farms
    for wages I long for that place

Like someone thinking of water in deserts. Sometimes we hear the sea's
    thunder, far down the deep gorge.

The darkness under the trees in spring is starry with flowers, with redwood
    sorrel, colt's foot, wakerobin,
The slender-stemmed pale yellow violets,
And Solomon's-seal that makes intense islands of fragrance in April." "Oh,
    April," she said trembling,
"How exactly it follows. How could I rest? Ah, no,
Good-bye, good-bye, Onorio. Poor Leader, I am sure
We can go a little way before dark. Come, Saul, Saul."
She ran a few steps, panting hard.

                                    Vasquez perceived
No hope of staying her: "Then I'll go back to the bridge
And fetch my horse and my coat. I'll not leave you, Clare."
He went slowly, heavy and amazed. His horse
Had broken tether in the night, stung by the hail-stones.
Then Vasquez, still drunken with the dregs of his vision
To fatalist indifference, went hunting the horse
And found it late. He followed Clare the next morning,
But met another vision on the road, that waved
Impatient white hands against his passage, saying
"If I go up to Calvary ten million times: what is that to you?
Let me go up." Vasquez drew rein and sat staring.
He saw beyond the vision in the yellow mud
Prints of bare feet, dibbled about with many
Little crowding hoof-marks; he marvelled, feeling no sadness
But lonely thoughts.

XII

                        Clare Walker had crossed the ridge and gone down
To the mouth of Cawdor's Canyon. Japanese tenants
Now kept the house; short broad-faced men who planted

Lettuces in the garden against the creek-side
And beans on the hill. The barns were vacant, the cattle
Were vanished from the high pastures. The men were friendly,
Clare begged at their hands a little oil to soften
The bandage on Leader's wound; she'd torn her spent dress
In strips to bind it, and went now without clothing
But the long brown cloak.

                She went northward, and on a foreland
Found vacant cabins around a ruined saw-mill;
And finding sacks of dry straw with a worn blanket
In one of the cabins, slept well and awoke refreshed
To travel on slowly northward in the glad sunlight
And sparkle of the sea. But the next day was dark,
And one of the wethers died, she never knew why,
She wept and went on.

              Near Point Lobos, by a gate
Where Tamar Cauldwell used to lean from her white pony
To swing the bars, the lion-stricken ewe, Leader,
Groaned and lay down and died. Clare met much kindness there;
She was nursed in the house, helpless, for many days,
And the sheep were guarded and fed. The people clothed her
And calmed her wild mind; but she was not willing to tell them
Her griefs nor her cause of fear. They kept her by watchful force
Until she escaped, a great night of moonlight, and fled
With her small flock.

            Far up the Carmel Valley
The river became a brook, she watched a salmon
Row its worn body up-stream over the stones
And struck by a thwart current expose the bruised

White belly to the white of the sky, gashed with red wounds, but right
    itself
And wriggle up-stream, having that within it, spirit or desire,
Will spend all its dear flesh and all the power it has gathered, in the sweet
    salt pastures and fostering ocean,
To find the appointed high-place and perish. Clare Walker, in a bright
    moment's passage of anxious feeling,
Knowing nothing of its fate saw her own fate reflected. She drank, and the
    sheep drank; they went up the valley
And crossed, the next day, among the long-needled pines, the great thirsty
    sky-ridge.

            In the valley beyond
Clare journeyed northward again, anxiously avoiding
The travelled roads and hiding herself from people
In fear that someone's force or kindness might steal her
From the helpless flock; and later in habitual fear.

She was seen much later, heavily swollen
Toward child-birth, cowering from a thin April rain
By a little fire on the San Joaquin river-bank,
Sharing a camp of outcast men; no sheep
Remained with her, but when she moved in the morning
She called the names of many, Fern, Fay and Leader,
Nosie and Saul and little Hornie and the others,
"Dear Tiny, dear Frannie, come on, we have to go on."
The toothless tramp bandaging his foot by the fire
Looked up with a flicker of light in his slack face,
And the sickly sullen boy on the other side
Smiled without mockery. Clare had gone half a mile
And felt a grinding pang in her back, she clung to the fence
And saw the poplars planted along the road

Reach dreadfully away northward. When the pain ended
She went on northward; but after the second pain
She crept down to the river and hid her body
In a willow thicket. In the evening, between the rapid
Summits of agony before exhaustion, she called
The sheep about her and perceived that none came.

DESCENT TO THE DEAD
Poems Written in Ireland and Great Britain

SHANE O'NEILL'S CAIRN
to U. J.

When you and I on the Palos Verdes cliff
Found life more desperate than dear,
And when we hawked at it on the lake by Seattle,
In the west of the world, where hardly
Anything has died yet: we'd not have been sorry, Una,
But surprised, to foresee this gray
Coast in our days, the gray waters of the Moyle
Below us, and under our feet
The heavy black stones of the cairn of the lord of Ulster.
A man of blood who died bloodily
Four centuries ago: but death's nothing, and life,
From a high death-mark on a headland
Of this dim island of burials, is nothing either.
How beautiful are both these nothings.

OSSIAN'S GRAVE
Prehistoric monument near Cushendall, in Antrim

Steep up in Lubitavish townland stands
A ring of great stones like fangs, the shafts of the stones
Grown up with thousands of years of gradual turf,
The fangs of the stones still biting skyward; and hard
Against the stone ring, the oblong enclosure
Of an old grave guarded with erect slabs; gray rocks
Backed by broken thorn-trees, over the gorge of Glenaan;
It is called Ossian's Grave. Ossian rests high then,
Haughtily alone.
If there were any fame or burial or monument
For me to envy,
Warrior and poet they should be yours and yours.

For this is the pure fame, not caged in a poem,
Fabulous, a glory untroubled with works, a name in the north
Like a mountain in the mist, like Aura
Heavy with heather and the dark gray rocks, or Trostan
Dark purple in the cloud: happier than what the wings
And imperfections of work hover like vultures
Above the carcass.

              I also make a remembered name;
And I shall return home to the granite stones
On my cliff over the greatest ocean
To be blind ashes under the butts of the stones:
As you here under the fanged limestone columns
Are said to lie, over the narrow north straits
Toward Scotland, and the quick-tempered Moyle. But written reminders
Will blot for too long a year the bare sunlight

Above my rock-lair, heavy black birds
Over the field and the blood of the lost battle.

Oh but we lived splendidly
In the brief light of day
Who now twist in our graves.
You in the guard of the fanged
Erect stones; and the man-slayer
Shane O'Neill dreams yonder at Cushendun
Crushed under his cairn;
And Hugh McQuillan under his cairn
By his lost field in the bog on Aura;
And I a foreigner, one who has come to the country of the dead
Before I was called,
To eat the bitter dust of my ancestors;
And thousands on tens of thousands in the thronged earth
Under the rotting freestone tablets
At the bases of broken round-towers;
And the great Connaught queen on her mountain-summit
The high cloud hoods, it creeps through the eyes of the cairn.

We dead have our peculiar pleasures, of not
Doing, of not feeling, of not being.
Enough has been felt, enough done, Oh and surely
Enough of humanity has been. We lie under stones
Or drift through the endless northern twilights
And draw over our pale survivors the net of our dream.
All their lives are less
Substantial than one of our deaths, and they cut turf
Or stoop in the steep
Short furrows, or drive the red carts, like weeds waving
Under the glass of water in a locked bay,

Which neither the wind nor the wave nor their own will
Moves; when they seem to awake
It is only to madden in their dog-days for memories of dreams
That lost all meaning many centuries ago.

Oh but we lived splendidly
In the brief light of day,
You with hounds on the mountain
And princes in palaces,
I on the western cliff
In the rages of the sun:
Now you lie grandly under your stones
But I in a peasant's hut
Eat bread bitter with the dust of dead men;
The water I draw at the spring has been shed for tears
Ten thousand times,
Or wander through the endless northern twilights
From the rath to the cairn, through fields
Where every field-stone's been handled
Ten thousand times,
In a uterine country, soft
And wet and worn out, like an old womb
That I have returned to, being dead.

Oh but we lived splendidly
Who now twist in our graves.
The mountains are alive;
Tievebuilleagh lives, Trostan lives,
Lurigethan lives;
And Aura, the black-faced sheep in the belled heather;
And the swan-haunted loughs; but also a few of us dead
A life as inhuman and cold as those.

THE LOW SKY

No vulture is here, hardly a hawk,
Could long wings or great eyes fly
Under this low-lidded soft sky?

On the wide heather the curlew's whistle
Dies of its echo, it has no room
Under the low lid of this tomb.

But one to whom mind and imagination
Sometimes used to seem burdensome
Is glad to lie down awhile in the tomb.

Among stones and quietness
The mind dissolves without a sound,
The flesh drops into the ground.

THE BROADSTONE
near Finvoy, County Antrim

We climbed by the old quarries to the wide highland of heath,
On the slope of a swale a giant dolmen,
Three heavy basalt pillars upholding the enormous slab,
Towers and abides as if time were nothing.
The hard stones are hardly dusted with lichen in nobody knows
What ages of autumns in this high solitude
Since a recordless tribe of an unknown race lifted them up
To be the availing hero's memorial,
And temple of his power. They gathered their slighter dead from the biting
Winds of time in his lee, the wide moor
About him is swollen with barrows and breaks upon many stones,
Lean gray guardians of old urned ashes,
In waves on waves of purple heather and blithe spray of its bells.
Here lies the hero, more than half God,
And nobody knows his name nor his race, in the bee-bright necropolis,
With the stone circle and his tribe around him.
Sometimes perhaps (but who'd confess it?) in soft adolescence
We used to wonder at the world, and have wished
To hear some final harmony resolve the discords of life?
— Here they are all perfectly resolved.

THE GIANT'S RING
Ballylesson, near Belfast

Whoever is able will pursue the plainly

False immortality of not having lived in vain but leaving some mark in the
world.

Secretly mocking at his own insanity

He labors the same, he knows that no dead man's lip was ever curled in
self-scorn,

And immortality is for the dead.

Jesus and Caesar out of the bricks of man's weakness, Washington out of
the brittle

Bones of man's strength built their memorials,

This nameless chief of a knot of forgotten tribes in the Irish darkness used
faithfuller

Simpler materials: to diadem a hill-top

That sees the long loughs and the Mourne Mountains, with a ring of
enormous embankment, and to build

In the centre that great toad of a dolmen

Piled up of ponderous basalt that sheds the centuries like rain-drops. He
drove the labor,

And has ear-marked already some four millenniums.

His very presence is here, thick-bodied and brutish, a brutal and senseless
will-power.

Immortality? While Homer and Shakespeare are names,

Not of men but verses, and the elder has not lived nor the younger will
not, such treadings of time.

—Conclude that secular like Christian immortality's

Too cheap a bargain: the name, the work or the soul: glass beads are the
trade for savages.

IN THE HILL AT NEWGRANGE
One of the three great prehistoric burial-mounds on the River Boyne

"Who is it beside me, who is here beside me, in the hollow hill?"
A foreigner I am. "You've dug for nothing. The Danes were here
A thousand years before you and robbed me of my golden bracelets,
Stinking red-haired men from the sea, with torches and swords."
Dead king, you keep a better treasure than bracelets,
The peace of the dead is dearer than gold, no one can rob you.

What do you watch, old king, from the cave? "In the north the muddy
    chippers of flint on the Antrim coast,
Their chests covered with hair and filth, shrewd eyes under bushes of brow,
    clicking the flints together.
How we used to hate those hunters. One squats in a cave-mouth and makes
    an axe, one in a dune shapes bolt-heads."
They have all (and we too, old king) been dead for thousands of years. I see
    in the north a red-haired woman
Meeting her lover by Shane O'Neill's cairn, her peasant husband is drunk
    at home, she drifts up the hill
In the sleeve of twilight. "Mary Byrnes is that you?" "Ye may kiss a hure
    but not name her. Ah, lad, come down.
When I was a wee maid I used to be loving Jesus,
All helpless and bleeding on the big cross. I'd never have married my
    drunkard only the cart ran over him.
He lay helpless and bleeding in the black lane. Och, laddie, not here now.
Carry me up to the cairn: a man lies bloodily under the sharp black stones,
    I love that man."
Mary Byrnes, when her lover has done and finished, before he stands up
To button his clothes together, runs a knife in his throat. "Oh Shane
    O'Neill it's you I was loving,
Never one else. You helpless and bleeding under the stones.

Do ye weary of stretching quiet the four long centuries? Take this lad's
  blood to hearten you, it drops through the stones.
Drips, drops in the stones.
Drink, Shane; drink, dear: who cares if a hure is hanged? We kill each
  other in Ireland to pleasure the dead."

Great upright stones higher than the height of a man are our walls,
Huge overlapping stones are the summer clouds in our sky.
The hill of boulders is heaped over all. Each hundred years
One of the enormous stones will move an inch in the dark.
Each double century one of the oaks on the crown of the mound
Above us breaks in a wind, an oak or an ash grows.

"I see in the south Cloyne round-tower burning: the Christians have built a
  spire, the thieves from the sea have burnt it,
The happy flame streams roaring up the stone tube and breaks from the
  four windows below the stone roof
Like four bright banners.
The holy men scream in their praying, the golden reliquaries are melted,
  the bell falls clanging."
They have all (and we too, old king) been dead for a thousand years. I see
  on the island mountain Achill,
In the west where wave after wave of the beaten tribes ran up and starved,
  an old woman, her head
Covered with a shawl, sits on Slieve Mor. Two thin sharp tears like knives
  in the yellow grooves of her face,
"My cow has died," she says, "and my son forgets me." She crouches and
  starves, in the quivering Atlantic wind,
Among the great skulls of quartz on the Achill mountain.

What do you watch, old king, from the cave? "A cause of mighty laughter
  in the mound on the hill at Dundalk.

They piled the earth on the blood of one of their spitfire princes, their
    bold watch-dog of the Ulster border.
After two handfuls of centuries
One Bruce, a younger drinker of battles, bloodily ceasing to be king of
    Ireland was buried above him.
Now a rich merchant has built his house on the mound's head, a living
    man. The old capon perches there trembling,
The young men of Ireland are passionate again, it is bad for a man of peace
    to have built on the hill of battles,
Oh his dear skin, Oh the papers of his wealth.
Cuchulain looks up at Bruce and Bruce at the sweating merchant. By God
    if we dead that watch the living
Could open our mouths the earth would be split with laughter."

I hear like a hum in the ground the Boyne running through the aging
Fields forever, and one of our great blue spiral-cut stones
Settle in the dark a hair's breadth under the burden of the hill.
"We hear from cairn to cromlech all over Ireland the dead
Whisper and conspire, and whinnies of laughter tinkle in the raths.
The living dream but the dead are awake."

High in Donegal, in the bitter waste north, where miles on miles of black
    heather dwindle to the Bloody Foreland,
Walks an old priest, near crazy with solitude and his peasants like cattle, he
    has wrestled with his mental Satan
Half his lifetime, and endured and triumphed. He feels the reward
    suddenly await him, the churchyard wall
Looks light and faint, the slabs and mounds by the entrance. In the midst
    of mass the crucified image trembles
Above the altar, and favorably smiles. Then Father O'Donnel
Gabbles the Latin faster to an end and turns himself once more and says to
    the people, "Go home now.

Missa est." In the empty church he screams and spits on the Christ,

He strikes it with his hand. Well done, old priest. "Is the man on the cross
    his God, why does he strike his God?"

Because the tortured torturer is too long dying; because the strain in the
    wounded minds of men

Leaves them no peace; but here where life is worn out men should have
    peace. He desires nothing but unconsciousness,

To slip in the black bottomless lake and be still. Time for us also,

Old king, although no strain so many thousands of years has wounded our
    minds, time to have done

With vision, as in the world's youth with desire and deed. To lie in the dark
    in the hill until the stones crumble,

And the earth and the stars suck into nothing, the wheel slopes and returns,
    the beautiful burden is renewed.

For probably all the same things will be born and be beautiful again, but
    blessed is the night that has no glowworm.

ANTRIM

No spot of earth where men have so fiercely for ages of time
Fought and survived and cancelled each other,
Pict and Gael and Dane, McQuillan, Clandonnel, O'Neill,
Savages, the Scot, the Norman, the English,
Here in the narrow passage and the pitiless north, perpetual
Betrayals, relentless resultless fighting,
A random fury of dirks in the dark: a struggle for survival
Of hungry blind cells of life in the womb.
But now the womb has grown old, her strength has gone forth; a few red
    carts in a fog creak flax to the dubs,
And sheep in the high heather cry hungrily that life is hard; a plaintive
    peace; shepherds and peasants.

We have felt the blades meet in the flesh in a hundred ambushes
And the groaning blood bubble in the throat;
In a hundred battles the heavy axes bite the deep bone,
The mountain suddenly stagger and be darkened.
Generation on generation we have seen the blood of boys
And heard the moaning of women massacred,
The passionate flesh and nerves have flamed like pitch-pine and fallen
And lain in the earth softly dissolving.
I have lain and been humbled in all these graves, and mixed new flesh with
    the old and filled the hollow of my mouth
With maggots and rotten dust and ages of repose. I lie here and plot the
    agony of resurrection.

NO RESURRECTION

Friendship, when a friend meant a helping sword,
Faithfulness, when power and life were its fruits, hatred, when the hated
Held steel at your throat or had killed your children, were more than
   metaphors.
Life and the world were as bright as knives.

But now, if I should recall my ruins
From the grass-roots and build my body again in the heavy grave,
Twist myself naked up through the earth like a strong white worm,
Tip the great stone, gulp the white air,

And live once more after long ages
In the change of the world: I should find the old human affections
   hollowed.
Should I need a friend? No one will really stab me from behind,
The people in the land of the living walk weaponless.

Should I hate an enemy? The evil-doers
Are pitiable now. Or to whom be faithful? Of whom seek faith?
Who has eaten of the victor's feast and shared the fugitive silence
Of beaten men on the mountain: suffer

Resurrection to join this midge-dance
Of gutted and multiplied echoes of life in the latter sun?
Dead man, be quiet. A fool of a merchant, who'd sell good earth
And grass again to make modern flesh.

DELUSION OF SAINTS

The old pagan burials, uninscribed rock,
Secret-keeping mounds,
Have shed the feeble delusions that built them,
They stand inhumanly
Clean and massive; they have lost their priests.
But the cross-bearing stones
Still foot corruption, and their faces carved
With hopes and terrors
At length too savagely annulled to be left
Even ridiculous.
Long-suffering saints, flamelike aspirers,
You have won your reward:
You sleep now as easily as any dead murderer
Or worn-out lecher.
To have found your faith a liar is no thorn
In the narrow beds,
Nor laughter of unfriends nor rumor of the ruinous
Churches will reach you.
As at Clonmacnoise I saw them all ruined,
And at Cong, at Glendalough,
At Monasterboice; and at Kilmacduagh
All ruined, all roofless
But the great cyclopean-stoned spire
That leans toward its fall.
A place perfectly abandoned of life,
Except that we heard
One old horse neighing across the stone hedges
In the flooded fields.

IONA: THE GRAVES OF THE KINGS

I wish not to lie here.
There's hardly a plot of earth not blessed for burial, but here
One might dream badly.

In beautiful seas a beautiful
And sainted island, but the dark earth so shallow on the rock
Gorged with bad meat.

Kings buried in the lee of the saint,
Kings of fierce Norway, blood-boltered Scotland, bitterly dreaming
Treacherous Ireland.

Imagine what delusions of grandeur,
What suspicion-agonized eyes, what jellies of arrogance and terror
This earth has absorbed.

SHOOTING SEASON

in the north of Scotland

The whole countryside deployed on the hills of heather, an army with
    banners,
The beaters whoop the grouse to the butts.
Three gentlemen fling up their guns and the frightened covey is a few
    wings fewer;
Then grooms approach with the panniered horses.
The gray old moorland silence has closed like water and covered the
    gun-shots.
Wave on wave goes the moor to the great
Circle of the sky; the cairn on the slope names an old battle and beyond are
Broad gray rocks the grave-marks of clans.
Blond Celtic warriors lair in the sky-line barrows, down toward the sea
Stand the tall stones of the Danish captains.
We dead that handled weapons and hunted in earnest, we old dead have
    watched
Three little living gentlemen yonder
With a bitter flavor in the grin of amusement, uneasily remembering our
    own
Old sports and delights. It is better to be dust.

GHOSTS IN ENGLAND

At East Lulworth the dead were friendly and pitiful, I saw them peek
   from their ancient earth-works on the coast hills
At the camps of the living men in the valley, the army-mechanics' barracks,
   the roads where they try the tanks
And the armored cars: "We also," they say, "trembled in our time. We felt
   the world change in the rain,
Our people like yours were falling under the wheel. Great past and
   declining present are a pitiful burden
For living men; but failure is not the worm that worries the dead, you will
   not weep when you come,"
Said the soft mournful shadows on the Dorset shore. And those on the
   Rollright ridge by the time-eaten stone-circle
Said nothing and had no wish in the world, having blessedly aged out of
   humanity, stared with great eyes
White as the hollowed limestone, not caring but seeing, inhuman as the
   wind.

            But the other ghosts were not good,
But like a moon of jackals around a sick stag.
At Zennor in the tumbled granite chaos, at Marazion and the angel's
   Mount, from the hoar tide-lines:
"Be patient, dead men, the tides of their day have turned," from the stone
   rings of the dead huts on Dartmoor,
The prison town like a stain of dirt on the distant hill: "We not the last,"
   they said, "shall be hopeless,
We not alone hunger in the rain." From Avebury in the high heart of
   England, in the ancient temple,
When all the cottages darkened themselves to sleep: "Send it along the
   ridge-ways and say it on the hilltops
That the bone is broken and the meat will fall."

There was also a ghost
of a king, his cheeks hollow as the brows
Of an old horse, was paddling his hands in the reeds of Dozmare Pool, in
the shallow, in the rainy twilight,
Feeling for the hilt of a ruinous and rusted sword. But they said "Be patient
a little, you king of shadows,
But only wait, they will waste like snow." Then Arthur left hunting for the
lost sword, he grinned and stood up
Gaunt as a wolf; but soon resumed the old labor, shaking the reeds with his
hands.

Northeastward to Wantage
On the chalk downs the Saxon Alfred
Witlessly walks with his hands lamenting. "Who are the people and who
are the enemy?" He says bewildered,
"Who are the living, who are the dead?" The more ancient dead
Watch him from the wide earth-works on White Horse Hill, peer from the
Ridge-way barrows, goggle from the broken
Mound and the scattered stones in the oval wood above Ashbury. They
whisper and exult.

In the north also
I saw them, from the Picts' houses in the black Caithness heather to the
bleak stones on Culloden Moor,
The rags of lost races and beaten clans, nudging each other, the blue lips
cracking with joy, the fleshless
Anticipatory fingers jabbing at the south. And on the Welsh borders
Were dead men skipping and fleering behind all the hedges. An island of
ghosts. They seemed merry, and to feel
No pity for the great pillar of empire settling to a fall, the pride and the
power slowly dissolving.

INSCRIPTION FOR A GRAVESTONE

I am not dead, I have only become inhuman:
That is to say,
Undressed myself of laughable prides and infirmities,
But not as a man
Undresses to creep into bed, but like an athlete
Stripping for the race.
The delicate ravel of nerves that made me a measurer
Of certain fictions
Called good and evil; that made me contract with pain
And expand with pleasure;
Fussily adjusted like a little electroscope:
That's gone, it is true;
(I never miss it; if the universe does,
How easily replaced!)
But all the rest is heightened, widened, set free.
I admired the beauty
While I was human, now I am part of the beauty.
I wander in the air,
Being mostly gas and water, and flow in the ocean;
Touch you and Asia
At the same moment; have a hand in the sunrises
And the glow of this grass.
I left the light precipitate of ashes to earth
For a love-token.

SHAKESPEARE'S GRAVE

"Doggerel," he thought, "will do for churchwardens,
Poetry's precious enough not to be wasted,"
And rhymed it all out with a skew smile:
"Spare these stones. Curst be he that moves my bones—
Will hold the hands of masons and grave-diggers."
But why did the good man care? For he wanted quietness.
He had tasted enough life in his time
To stuff a thousand; he wanted not to swim wide
In waters, nor wander the enormous air,
Nor grow into grass, enter through the mouths of cattle
The bodies of lusty women and warriors,
But all be finished. He knew it feelingly; the game
Of the whirling circles had become tiresome.
"Annihilation's impossible, but insulated
In the church under the rhyming flagstone
Perhaps my passionate ruins may be kept off market
To the end of this age. Oh, a thousand years
Will hardly leach," he thought, "this dust of that fire."

THE DEAD TO CLEMENCEAU:
NOVEMBER 1929

Come (we say) Clemenceau.
Why should you live longer than others? The vacuum that sucked
Us down, and the former stars, draws at you also.

No wrench for a man near ninety.
They were younger who crowded us out of distinction the year you drove
   them
Like flies on a fire. We don't say it was wrong.

We don't say it was right.
These heavy choices are less than verbal, down here, to us dead.
Never a thorn in the crown of greatness down here.

Not even Wilson laments here
The cuckoo brood of design. This is the cave you conjectured;
Nothing in death, as nothing in life, surprises you.

You were not surprised when France
Put you aside, when the war was finished, as a sick man mending
Puts aside the strong poison that turned his fever.

You'd not be surprised to hear
Your enemies praising your name and the Paris cannon applaud you;
Not surprised, nor much pleased, nor envious of more.

Your negative straightness of mind—
And bleached like a drowned man's cast-up thigh-bone by eroding age—
Hardly required the clear corrections of death.

SUBJECTED EARTH

Walking in the flat Oxfordshire fields
Where the eye can find no rock to rest on but little flints
Speckle the soil, and the million-berried hedges
Tingle with birds at evening, I saw the somber
November day redden and go down; a flight of lapwings
Whirled in the hollow of the field, and half tame pheasants
Cried from the trees. I remembered impatiently
How the long bronze mountain of my own coast,
Where color is no account and pathos ridiculous, the sculpture is all,
Breaks the arrows of the setting sun
Over the enormous mounded eye-ball of ocean.

                                    The soft alien twilight
Worn and weak with too much humanity hooded my mind.
Poor flourishing earth, meek-smiling slave,
If sometime the swamps return and the heavy forest, black beech and
     oak-roots
Break up the paving of London streets;
And only, as long before, on the lifted ridge-ways
Few people shivering by little fires
Watch the night of the forest cover the land
And shiver to hear the wild dogs howling where the cities were,
Would you be glad to be free? I think you will never
Be glad again, so kneaded with human flesh, so humbled and changed.

Here all's down hill and passively goes to the grave,
Asks only a pinch of pleasure between the darknesses,
Contented to think that everything has been done

That's in the scope of the race: so should I also perhaps
Dream, under the empty angel of this twilight,
But the great memory of that unhumanized world,
With all its wave of good and evil to climb yet,
Its exorbitant power to match, its heartless passion to equal,
And all its music to make, beats on the grave-mound.

Notes to "Descent to the Dead"

It seems hardly necessary to stipulate that the elegiac tone of these verses reflects the writer's mood, and is not meant for economic or political opinion.

Shane O'Neill's cairn and the dateless monument called Ossian's Grave stand within a couple of miles of each other on the Antrim coast.

A dolmen is a prehistoric burial-house made of great stones set on end, roofed by a slab of stone. There are many still standing in Ireland and England.

Newgrange is one of three great artificial hills, on the Boyne west of Drogheda. Passages and cells were made of megalithic stonework, decorated with designs cut in the great stones, and the hills were heaped over them. No one assigns a reasonable date to these erections. Evidently they are burial mounds, like the pyramids.

The Irish round-towers are well known, of course, slender, tapering spires of stone and lime mortar, of mysterious origin, but probably belfries and towers of refuge, built between 600 and 1200 A.D. They are associated with the earliest Christian churches.

Antrim is the northeasternmost county of Ireland, only a few sea-miles from Scotland. Iona is the sacred island of the Hebrides.

Avebury is a little Wiltshire village inside a great prehistoric stone-circle and fosse. It was the religious and perhaps the political capital of southern England before Stonehenge was built, i.e. before 2000 B.C. probably. The circle and the remaining stones are greater than those at Stonehenge, but the stones were not hewn to shape. Most of them are gone now; broken up to build the village.

Dozmare Pool is in Cornwall, a little flat mere in a wide wilderness, said to be the water where the sword Excalibur was cast away when King Arthur died.

The ridge-ways are ancient grass-grown roads on the ridges of the hills, used by the pre-Celtic inhabitants of England, when the lowlands were impassable swamp and forest.

THE BED BY THE WINDOW

I chose the bed down-stairs by the sea-window for a good death-bed
When we built the house; it is ready waiting,
Unused unless by some guest in a twelvemonth, who hardly suspects
Its latter purpose. I often regard it,
With neither dislike nor desire: rather with both, so equalled
That they kill each other and a crystalline interest
Remains alone. We are safe to finish what we have to finish;
And then it will sound rather like music
When the patient daemon behind the screen of sea-rock and sky
Thumps with his staff, and calls thrice: "Come, Jeffers."

WINGED ROCK

The flesh of the house is heavy sea-orphaned stone, the imagination of
    the house
Is in those little clay kits of swallows
Hung in the eaves, bright wings flash and return, the heavy rock walls
    commercing
With harbors of the far hills and the high
Rills of water, the river-meadow and the sea-cloud. You have also, O sleepy
    stones,
The red, the white and the marbled pigeons
To beat the blue air over the pinewood and back again in a moment; and
    the bush-hidden
Killdeer-nest against the west wall-foot,
That is fed from many strange ebbs; besides the woodful of finches, the
    shoring gulls,
The sudden attentive passages of hawks.

SECOND-BEST

A Celtic spearman forcing the cromlech-builder's brown daughter;
A blond Saxon, a slayer of Britons,
Building his farm outside the village he'd burned; a Norse
Voyager, wielder of oars and a sword,
Thridding the rocks at the fjord sea-end, hungry as a hawk;
A hungry Gaelic chiefling in Ulster,
Whose blood with the Norseman's rotted in the rain on a heather hill:
These by the world's time were very recent
Forefathers of yours. And you are a maker of verses. The pallid
Pursuit of the world's beauty on paper,
Unless a tall angel comes to require it, is a pitiful pastime.
If, burnished new from God's eyes, an angel:
And the ardors of the simple blood showing clearly a little ridiculous
In this changed world: — write and be quiet.

II

Thurso's Landing

1930-1931

RESURRECTION

George hadn't gone down to the canyon mouth for a whole week and so
he brought home

Six newspapers and two advertising letters, and one for his wife. There was
also a sack of sugar

He'd sent for, to feed the starving bees, for the flowers had failed. He gave
Hildis the letter: as usual

There was nothing in it. One thing there was. Her mother'd been up to
San Francisco, and "On Market Street

I passed a man that I thought was Carson Pierce. I turned around but he'd
gone, then I remembered

That Carson's been dead five years next April. That's a good thing. I nearly
spoke to him." Hildis reading

Hated her mother a moment without a reason. She folded and opened
again the letter, and looked

At Estie playing on the floor with Bobbie, unrolling the papers. Estie so
restless with life and pleasure

It seemed impossible she was the dead man's child. And Bobbie was a dead
woman's: no strangeness in that,

Although his cheeks were as bright as Esther's. What a good life they
enjoyed. And Hildis herself; a good life;

However perfectly cut off on the coast mountain from most of the things
that seemed of value to her.

Security was good. She'd felt and she quite remembered the pinch of the
world's dog-teeth.

                    Light from the westward
Window distinguished her face when she stood up. It lacked color and
        would have been stony white
Except the sun and the wind had stained it; in its matt pallor of a mask the
        eyes
Were the strange light: not for expressiveness:
Blank lights they seemed, with nothing to express and little to hide; the
        pupils unapparent; color, or you'd say
Default of color made their distinction; pearl gray in a pale face they were
        whiter than the face; they gathered
All the light and changed it. For the rest, the face
Was well-made oval, under thick pale-brown hair, its bones a little too
        heavy perhaps for symmetry;
The body well outlined through the light clothing, wide-shouldered,
        formed for vitality, but cold and passive in action
As if the fine lamp were never lighted with fire.

                                        In the evening after she
        washed the supper dishes,
The children tousling each other at bed-time, Hildis would often quietly
        go out in the cool darkness
And climb a stone's throw from the back door of the house toward the
        black oaks at the hill-top; she rather disliked
The dark steep space and depth and the night-wind, the wildness of stars,
        but here she could feel and gather herself,
Be cold and freed, enjoy the motions and smoothness of her own body. She
        sometimes unfastened her dress
And felt with her hand the firm round sensitive breasts her months of
        nursing Esther had not deformed,
The rippled wall of muscle below them, and the smooth of her shoulders.

                                                    Once
     in five or ten minutes the ocean—
Calm nights, when a surf ran—would slap a crash like thunder on the
     creek-mouth sand-beach; one heard the shock
Beat inland for miles up the winding canyon and the off-set gorges. One
     saw through vast gray air the black Y-tailed
Serpent of redwood forest in the pit of the canyon; high eastward one saw
     the under face of a cloud
Brushed with strange light every half minute, she'd wondered at that; of all
     the gleams and rhythms of the mountain
That light alone attracted her eyes and mind. An air-beacon, she believed,
     to guide the night fliers
Far away beyond the shaggy insensate mountain, above the long valley
     inland, where little cities
Were strung like jewels. King City, Soledad, Gonzales, Chualar, Salinas,
     the lights and the shining: Oh lovely
To look down on, out of the wild high darkness. But neither Hildis herself
     nor the man her mother had named
Ever could see them: Carson was dead and buried in France and she in this
     mountain.

               She went down to the house,
And found the two children quarrelling and put them to bed. Herself soon
     followed. George was deep in the newspapers.
Whenever he read the Bible she had to take his embrace; though he seemed
     old for that, he was fifty,
But luckily either herself or George was now barren, so it didn't matter.
     She nestled down in the bed
And felt on her cheek the air from the window, and saw the lamplight
     under the door like a slant bar
Of dazzle on the dark. It glimmered in the lashes of her eyes closing, and
     the lids annulled it. She saw the floating

Echoes and purple images of it, then the usual procession of changing faces
  of people
Caricatured more and more wildly-faintly
Appeared on the blank wall of her mind and she fell asleep. Her dream
  seemed to be placed in the orchard
She used to play in when she was a little child, when her father was living.
  At least the dog was her father's
Old collie; she hardly even remembered him. The grass was mounded
  upward as if by a giant mole,
The fibrous grass-roots cracked and parted, the dog came up from the
  burrow, his hide matted with earth,
And cold wind blew; the dream faded at the end. George had brought in
  the lamp; she awoke and lay still;
George had drawn down the covers to her ankles, the night-dress was
  crumpled up to her arms, he stood and smiled
Lovingly under his gray mustache, holding the lamp in his hand. Hildis lay
  still, with closed eyes,
Her anger mixing into a kind of enjoyment; she thought that her body was
  beautiful, and even George's
Attention pleased her, because she'd not been tired nor asleep heavily. She
  feigned sleep, and could feel
In the visualizing habit of her mind, exactly the disposition of her body in
  the amber lamplight,
The supple feline curve of her back and shoulders, she lay gathered, on her
  side, the shining rounded
Height of the hip-bone, from which the long clear thigh sloped to the bent
  white knees that carefully lay
The one on the other though her feet were parted. At length she groaned
  impatiently, her mouth in the pillow, "I'm cold.
Ah let me alone."

His antics did not appear absurd nor hateful; she liked
   him and she was his wife;
She kept herself as much as possible asleep. Her thoughts were wakened
   however and vaguely wandered:
She thought of the road to the foot of the canyon and to Monterey, on the
   way north one passed on a bank
Three old graves with painted wooden head-boards, suppose the buried
   people revived and pushed up the earth,
It would be mounded upward as if by great moles, the net of grass-roots
   would crackle and part and the people
Stand gasping, staring like mad, their feet in the broken pits. "It will not be
   long," she thought patiently,
"Then I can turn on my side and sleep." She moved her body mechanically
   and began to hope
In spite of past disillusionment to share his pleasure. A thought swept
   through her mind of all the graves breaking
All over the world, marble monuments toppling,
The rock tombs in the mountains unplugged, the graves by rivers and in
   muddy valleys and under pyramids
Pouring their people upward into the air. The multitudinous agitation and
   the eyes
Of captives released, the erected arms and the croaking voices, the cheeks
   of the earth pitted like small-pox
With broken graves.

         George pressed himself against her and ceased; but
   the strangeness of that imagination troubled her mind
So that she found it hard to go back to sleep. What if so vivid a fancy, and
   felt like a physical
Thrill at that particular moment, meant impregnation? She remembered
   the superstition of women

Who think they feel it. What an annoyance! This fear returned at
    moments, the following days, until time
Proved it unreal.

        Next month one of the local earthquakes
Moved in the mountain. It was afternoon, and Hildis was down at the
    garden below the house, with the children.
She heard the thunder of the hidden rock and felt the soil of the hillside
    quiver; when she looked up
The little house seemed to be dancing by itself, the dark mane of oaks
On the spine of the hill nodded above: then instantly she felt the whole
    mountain lifted a little,
And waver and fall, as if some power in the rock weighed it on bloody
    shoulders, struggling to rise.
Then the earth was quiet; Hildis looked wildly about at the slopes of
    mountain. Nothing was changed. She went up
Thinking that all the cups and saucers were broken, but nothing was
    broken except a hanging mirror
In which she liked to see her own face, had drawn its nail from the wall and
    fallen and splintered: that scared
And pleased her, so that the strange pallor of her eyes big with delight
Burned like silent summer lightning on George come up from the barn.
    "Look here. It's lucky we're not
Superstitious: the old women would say we're in for it. Think of it
    choosing
The mirror to break! not a dish is broken." He said: "The horses knew it
    was coming, they've been in terror
Since morning; and the cat ran off; it's queer how the beasts know." "They
    don't," she answered. "All superstition.
Aren't you afraid? I felt a thing moving under the ground
Will some day break all its coverings and come to sunlight. A rock-splitter,
    my dear. Even Estie felt it; she said

It felt like somebody under the mountain trying to get up." Then Estie,
    who had said nothing, looked up
And shook her head but said nothing.

                        Hildis remembered the gesture,
        and some days later,
"Come here," she said, "Estie, I've something to show you. Bobbie can
    come." She led them the path to the well,
But turned and went down below it, below the wild laurel thicket. There
    the steep clay had never grown grass
Since George cleared it; it was now baked hard at the end of summer and
    rifted across with a long crack
The earthquake had made; this crack had wet lips; a little spring had been
    freed there; strange fleshy and discolored outbreaks
Of fungus pushed up between the gray lips. "I told you that there was
    something under the ground, Estie,
Trying to get up. They look like dead people's hands." — So foolishly the
    directionless life in her body
Imputed to the earth what it was afraid to feel in itself; and wished to
    frighten the children in lack
Of better hope in a wish. She had lived too bitterly awhile before
To dare wish much.

                        The seasons turned before their time that year: came
        early showers; in October
The south wind bent its shining rods on the mountain, the angel of rain,
    racing in the blaze of the sun,
The mountains breaking its crystal river into many rapids. Over Long
    Ridge it made a great arch
Of steady violence; in the rock traps of the gorges it darted
Like the strokes of a hurt snake among its tormentors; in Palo Colorado in
    the redwood forest

Above the sacred silence at the trees' bases it was like a lion in their boughs,
  and here at the head
Of Palo Colorado it poured so fiercely by the little house on the steep
  slope that Hildis
Dared not let the children out-doors.

                        George had not plowed his field
  yet, when the first racing cloud
Covered the sun and slid over he hurried away. At noon Hildis took up a
  basket of food
To the high field. The storm struck down against her climbing, and her
  heart sang though her head was bent,
Her months of wishing change, half wishing catastrophe, seemed beyond
  hope resolved in the rush of storm.
Rain in floods would come down, the stale white summer was over; the
  power that she'd feared straining in the earth
Was nothing evil, but the hope of the feeding fields, and the dark roots that
  raise the green fire of grass,
Straining to live: she did not think these things but felt them: and stooping
  her face out of the wind
Saw sticks and bits of quartz race in the path, the rock-dust run like a
  stream. At last, on the height,
The wheel-track doubled around a hissing oak-bush to enter the field. She
  leaning back on the wind
Lifted her eyes; she saw the flying smoke of red dust and the horses in it
  like heavy shadows,
The dust from the hill-top field like a flag over the hollow of the canyon,
  the plowman strode in the clear
Behind the long banner, the plow and his foot-prints smoking; a wave of
  dark gray stubble and of hot red earth
Ran and curled before him, heaved from the blade of the plow. Here was
  that power breaking the earth

For a good purpose, the giant mole she'd imagined, cracking the
    grass-roots. Her pale eyes widened and shone
Like the eyes of one made free for a moment, but then that carefully
    guarded watchfulness covered their light;
Her husband returned down the next furrow, in the smoke of the hill. She
    gazed about her at the great hills;
There was one stood higher and the rest below, and the strange liquid light
    of the world now the sky had clouded.
The wind's urgence was little seen from that height in the wide web of
    branching valleys far down,
Though the wan light that filled them was coppery with dust it was full of
    clearness. On Mescal Ridge crept a red
Serpent of flame, burning brush to make pasture, a far hill eastward was
    domed with delicate smoke,
And northward a plume, calked by the wind in a crack of mountain. West
    lay the low sea like a snake's back
Striped and speckled.

           Toward evening a veil of rain limited the fires.
    When it failed they revived. At twilight
Rain came and killed them; the red twigs blackened; little gray serpents of
    ash and water ran down the black slopes;
Then night and the rain covered the coast.

                 Hildis was doing the supper
    dishes and George well tired
Slept in his chair; the noise of wind and rain became a motion at the door;
    a knocking began;
Hildis thought *"Now,"* and called "George." He groaned and awoke. She
    dried her hands, repeating—because it appeared
Impossible—they'd no visitors, and certainly

Not at night in the storm — "Someone knocked at the door." "Well, open
  it then," he said blinking,
She went and opened. While the man entered she heard the wind in the
  eaves and the little winter brook
Gurgle in the crease of the slope, the revived world shudder in the dark.
  She closed the door on the wind,
The lamp-flame, that had flared up in a passion, shone quietly again in its
  blackened glass. The stranger was tall;
And failed to speak. She looked for his face but the light after the darkness
  disturbed her eyes. Then George
Stood up and said, "Eh. What do you want? Come in" — as if the man were
  outside — "Where have *you* come from?"
The stranger, wrinkling his brows in the lamplight, and looking now at the
  two children, who sat on the floor
Staring: "This Ramsay's place?" He looked at Hildis again. "My car's stuck
  in the road below.
I can't get on. I saw your light and came up." Hildis when she heard his
  voice retreated from him
And stood by the wall; George answered: "Well, brother, you're out of
  luck. No help to-night. My horses and I
Have worked all day and we're done." The stranger laughed: "I wouldn't
  drive your wagon-track higher in the dark
And water if you'd give me the mountain. Don't worry, old man." "Hm,"
  he said, "what do you want?" The stranger
Looked at Hildis; she stood with her back to the wall with her hands
  against it; and pale, the great light gray eyes
Wide open at last. "A night's lodging, most likely. What did you think, an
  umbrella?" "No. Can't be done.
We've no spare bed; no room . . ." "Oh, I can pay for it. I'll sleep on the
  floor, there in the corner: I've slept
In worse places, at home and abroad. It's pretty certain you'll not turn me
  out-doors to-night

Without a tussle." George grumbled and yielded sullenly. "Take his coat
     and hat to the kitchen, Hildis;
He'll have to stay; hang them by the stove." Hildis remained by the wall
     and without answer; both men
Gazed at her then and saw the shudder of her breast as the breath ran
     between the parted white lips,
Below the ice-colored eyes. The stranger stripped off his overcoat and
     handed it to her; she took passively
The heavy thick garment, dull olive color, blackened by the rain, and
     holding it not to touch her, went out
To the next room. The children hastily followed, but walking backward to
     stare at the stranger. Then George:
"Sit down. How did you know my name was Ramsay, you're a stranger
     here." "I asked directions," he answered,
"At the canyon foot." "You're bound for up higher?" He shook his head
     and then smiled. "Not to-night." "There's only one place
Up higher, and you can't make it with a car." The stranger said nothing; his
     head bent forward, his gaze on the floor
Where Hildis had passed. George studied his face with distrust in silence.
     It was long, high-featured and somewhat handsome,
And sallow like a sunless plant; the nose a straight bar of bone between the
     blue eyes, broadest above.
Perhaps he was thirty.

                    One of the children was heard
Through the plank wall, shrilly complaining "Not bed-time, mother, not
     yet, mother." The stranger looked up
And said, "A boy and a girl. Are they both hers?" George made a noise in
     his throat that meant nothing;
And after a moment: "You haven't told me your name. Mine's Ramsay."
     "It's a good thing," said the other, "the women
To have lots of babies. So many lives

Went out in the war: leaves a . . . vacuum, you see . . ." George frowned
and said, "That's a good while ago.
It's over. Were *you* in the war?" "Oh, yes," he answered, as if surprised to
remember, "for a time I was.
Then I've been out for a time. . . . What is she doing?" he said more
loudly. "Putting the children to bed?
Won't she come back?" George rose and answered with anger, "What's that
to you, brother? Here in the country
We work hard and sleep early, whatever you're used to at home. I'll bring
your blankets." The other stood up;
He was tall, his opaque blue eyes higher than the farmer's forehead, who
turned and said the more angrily: "Sit down.
You can make your bed after I get the blankets." "Yes, but I've something
to tell" — he paused — "Hildis,"
He said more loudly, looking above the farmer's head at the door. "I have
to see her to-night.
I've come far and paid high for it." "By God but you make yourself at
home here. — Who is this fellow?" George said
Raging, for Hildis came to the door, but she did not answer. She stood
with her face dark in the shadow
The lamp-shade cast, and her eyes like white stones. The stranger: "Pierce
is my name." "It's you, Carson," she answered,
Lifting her left hand clenched and twitching to her mouth, and walked
stiffly across the room to a chair;
There were three chairs in the room; she chose the one farthest from him.
"I was dead," he answered, "and I have come back.
I had no peace." That imagination of all the graves opening
Stood in her mind, and blown above it like a banner of dust across the
domed furrows on the hill the visible
Red voice of trumpets crying to the dead to live: she laughed and
trembled. "We read your name in the lists:

And everybody in Greenfield knew you were dead: it was all a mistake."
George passed between them, his puckered

Eyes and thrust chin disparaging his guest, who answered Hildis, "It was
not a mistake, I was killed all right.

And lay for some days under the flies, and they came and buried me. I lay
for some years under the heavy

Foreign soil." She sighed and looked at her hands. "I used to see the gold
star in your mother's window.

I am very sorry it was all a mistake." "Well, you're sorry.

That will not stop me." "What *really* happened?" she said, "and where have
you been?" "What I tell you. I have been buried

With a thousand others, and all the bodies but mine were quiet, quietly
made earth. I made earth too;

With poison in it; never a moment, not a moment of peace; but straining
in the heavy darkness

Like a smothered seed planted too deep." Hildis, perplexed by all those
recent dreams of a power

Straining to lift itself from the earth, covered the memories of them under
sane thoughts, and said

Carefully and clearly aloud: "He was wounded no doubt in the head and
lost his mind, and has lost his memory

Of several years that he was kept in some hospital. They're probably
looking for him; he's probably escaped.

I'm very sorry to see him alive. — Why did you come here?" she said
fiercely, "I hated you enough

Before . . ." "Will you listen a little," he answered. "What does it matter
whether you hate me? We do what we have to

In spite of feelings: I learned that much in the earthy darkness
remembering myself: you'll do what you have to

Because I am here. Do you think, Hildis,

That anyone who has passed the hard edge of death, and safe in the peace
on the other side, *wants*

To crawl back and live? Not such fools as that. Ha, fuss with clothes, eat
   and drink and make dung, take pain
As it comes, and age, and suffer again the comical animal fear of dying that
   chills live flesh
In spite of reasons? Change peace for filth and fire, music for noise? I tell
   you I had perfect happiness
At first; knew nothing, wanted nothing, feared nothing,
Like a happy drunkard; the darkness down there was like a soft light. But
   when it began to reflect your face
My dream turned bad."

                    George, who'd stood by his chair in a kind of
   suspended anger, now for some reason
Chuckled to himself and sat down; then Hildis moved with her eyes but
   not her body; her pale eyes returned
And watched the young man continue speaking. "I began to be conscious
   of my lost body dissolving to dirt
Down there in the busy darkness where it never freezes, falling from power
   like a stone dropped in a well . . .
I wanted you so . . . away from your face. I knew there was nothing to do
   and no chance. . . . The little shadows
Under your cheek-bones, the pale, flame-pale, insane-colored gray eyes and
   the light thick hair; the breasts
With never a shadow of brown 'round their pink flowers; there's not
   enough of pigment in all your body
To stain a match-end. As white as a stone.
You haunted me there, the living haunted the dead, you like a dream of
   water to a man dying
Of thirst in the sand: there I was shut down: until I'd have bitten the
   stinking earth like a trapped mad-dog
But nothing would move, the half liquid morsels of my own flesh gone out
   of my power crawled in the dark

Not by my will, dripping in the dark. Listen, Hildis:

In the other dead the consciousness followed the fragments—Oh, you can't
    understand!—it had stopped being human

And slipped in separate particles into the dreaming soul of the earth. Mine
    was blocked up and crystallized

Around the image and memory and eyes and face. It couldn't flow out.
    There I was caught and tortured

For not having known you in the good time. Not enough known you. I
    remember everything. I forgot to tell you,

The night before the dawn of my death, I was cut off in a shell-hole; I'd led
    some night strokes before;

Our luck ran out that evening and left me stranded. The others were killed,
    mostly. I could have crawled back

After a time, but got to thinking what good was it all. I was damn' tired of
    killing and dodging,

And sick of the food, and baseball behind the lines, and the yellow French
    girls. It seemed to me that all life

Was dirt and skinny women; I forgot you, Hildis. I was hiding under a
    fellow

That had no face; it was all of a pulp. I never thought of you, all night
    long. When sunrise came

I stood straight up on the edge and took all they sent me. That was how it
    was."

    Hildis again shifted

The pale stones of her eyes toward George, to see what he thought. He was
    empty of thought: some show of contempt

Below the mustache, but the eyes more puzzled than anything. He was very
    tired. Then back to Carson, continuing:

"So I was cheated, the change was all bad.

A thousand around me laid in ridiculous rows enjoyed the deep freedom
    beyond desire

While I lay damned. My very flesh that slid and fell off was full of you, the
    slime that it made burned.
The bared bones were flutes blown with your name. Like a prisoner
    scraping the end of a broken bolt
Against a stone, for weeks, without any hope at all, but willing to grind it
    to a sharp point
To pick the cement from the bearings of the barred window, I lay, but for
    years, in the dark sharpening desire,
In the quiet place where no one wants anything. Like a lantern of pain
    among the good graves. Like a growing cancer
In the body of death. For I began to get power. I think now that there's
    nothing can keep you quiet
If you *want* enough."

                    Hildis grew suddenly afraid of her dreams of the
    power
Straining under the ground, so that she cried trembling: "Ah for shame,
    keep still. There's not a true word
In all this talk. An escaped lunatic's talk or a common liar's. Ah. Ah." Both
    George and Carson
Looked steadfastly at her face and saw it turn whiter than pale. Then
    Carson went on unchanged: "It is better
Not to want. The fear of death's nothing
Against the fear and disgust and pain of returning life. I felt the tides draw
    inward again,
The waters of conscious power turning in the ebb, lapping around your
    image in the sucking emptiness
That I had become. We were like two sucking monsters of emptiness, death
And I: our desires: two monsters in the earth: but I was the emptier." He
    smiled painfully and Hildis saw
His tongue glitter in the lamplight, moistening his lips. "I got my own
    back," he said. "More than my own;

The tides were turned for fair, and the powers

Of much perished humanity came pouring in, not only the dead around
    me: the older dead:

That ground's charged like a mine: multitudes of strength, many forms of
    memory. I gathered my forlorn fragments

Like grains of gold under the grass-roots, with a hundred hands; each atom
    came shining with pain like fiery

Wires into place. Then sometime I broke the earth and swam in the
    embracing earth and came up and stood

Naked with the straining ribs of a man strangled,

And dirt in my mouth. The white sun half stunned me. I saw the
    grave-mark knocked over in the broken pit, and I staggered

Gasping and drunk between the silly rows of white standard crosses."

                                                                    Hildis
        drummed her clenched fists

The one on the other, stammering: "I saw that! I saw that!" but after a
    moment, "Oh, what a liar!" and sat

Wringing her hands between parted knees, while — not with conscious
    purpose but certainly to clear herself

From hearing the man — she pictured the night out-doors and the dark
    mountains in her mind, the enormous pool

Of night and thin rain filling the gape of the canyon; the forests of pointed
    redwoods far down, the rain

In all their spires; the drifts of thin black rain on the bare faces of the
    mountain; the wind drawing mournfully

Through the high wet darkness and the hushing night. Her mind coiled
    like a serpent around that egg of visionary

Space and the dark.

        She heard her husband speak angrily and Carson
    answer, "Why, yes.

I have come for that." "By God, so you sneaked in . . ." George rose and
    she saw him trembling. "You'd better sneak out.

Time for you now to get out." But Carson shook his head vaguely, not
    rising from the chair, looking at Hildis,

Who felt her mind coil closer on the hollow egg of darkness; after a
    moment she lifted both hands

To her mouth, and laughed like one in shrill pain,

Though suffering nothing. At that, George set his hand roughly on the
    young man's shoulder, who caught it by the wrist

Without rising, and wrenched it so that George reeled

Before him, and stumbled backward being freed; stood twitching a moment;
    then turned and snatched his hunting-rifle

From its rests in the wall. But Carson leaped and struck twice before he
    could face from the wall. George fell. Hildis

Ran and knelt down and lifted his head. He was not much hurt but half
    stunned. Carson before she reached him

Had taken the rifle; he went and opened the door and pitched it the
    muzzle foremost into the darkness

Down the deep slope. "Ah," she said, "your courage.

You dared to hit an old man from behind. I saw your face: your face was
    crazy with fear." "Do you think,"

Carson answered, the terror she'd seen indeed still hollowing his eyes, "I
    can risk getting killed again

Before I've had you, and to writhe in the quicklime of another grave?" She
    answered: "Are you better, George? This coward

Struck you from behind." She helped him, and placed his chair, then
    turned toward Carson: "I hated you enough when I thought

You were safely dead: when I saw you alive it came up to loathing: what
    cloudy mountain do you think it's grown to

Now? So you broke the fingers of death to come and play the bully in a
    little house in the hills,

And seeing it's a distant and unneighbored place

You've dared to hit an old man and frighten a woman. The perfect picture
  of a coward: look at him, George:
His eyes, ringed white and black like marks in the Bay Street
  shooting-galleries. Say booh and he'll run." The young man
Sighed and said dully, "You've changed a little. No matter, Hildis.
  Although I remember you cried and clung to me
At our parting-time. You wanted me still to wait and be drafted; but I was
  a fool. And once I remember
You took off all your clothes to show yourself to me, among the wild lilacs
  above your mother's house,
Because you were jealous. Without that memory
I might have found peace in death. Or if there'd been a blotch of black
  hair, or a mole, or one brown stain
On the stone-white form." Hildis looked hastily down at her husband but
  he was still dulled; he sat bent over,
Handling the back of his neck where the blows had struck. "Oh George
  you ought to have shot him at the very first.
You waited too long. He'd never be asked for. We'd have had such
  happiness,
Day after day, rolling the mountain stones on the grave; we'd have made a
  heap that would hold him down
If he were God. But now we're helpless it seems; he's got the power in the
  house; now, because he burned
In the dirty grave with the dreams of rotting flesh, we have to obey him."
  She listened and said, "Estie's
Crying in the dark: I can't let her cry."

                                    She went in quickly, then Carson
  began to follow her; he stopped,
Remembering the rifle, and turned to regard George. The old man had
  looked up, but the sick face and passive

Red eyes had no action in them; yet Carson went to the outer door and
 locked it and drew the key,
Then followed Hildis. She seemed to have stayed in the kitchen, he heard
 her go just ahead of him through the dark room
To the room beyond, where a child was sobbing. He struck a match in the
 second doorway and saw Hildis
Bending above the bed in which the two children lay; one slept, and the
 other with scared blue eyes
Winked at the light. "Hush," Hildis whispered, "I'll come back in a
 minute. — Why, Estie," she said, "what woke you?
You heard our voices? We've found that this man is an old friend, isn't that
 strange? He was away,
And now he's come back we didn't at first remember him." The match
 burned out; Hildis quietly continued:
"Sleep soundly, Bobbie's asleep beside you like a woolly lambkin. Father
 and mother must talk for awhile
About old times, then all go to sleep. Good-night, dear Estie."

                                                                    Carson
        could hear her kissing the child,
For now the rain and the wind had fallen on silence. Feeling his way back
 to the light he heard
Her breathing behind him like a tired runner, and foot-steps that kept no
 rhythm, hurrying and pausing. He saw
George still quiet in the chair. Hildis came in and she had dark eyes, the
 pupils enlarged with darkness,
But after the lamplight touched them they whitened. "Estie's pitiful," she
 said; "I'd heard her crying a good while,
As if she knew. Did nothing move in you, Carson, when you heard her
 crying? Perhaps the father feels nothing,
Especially when he's been dead a good while. This is the child, Carson,
 while you were fooling in France

I bore in sorrow. And later, when you were beginning to tire of the skinny
   French girls, I got a job
In a restaurant, to earn the dimes for her milk, and my mother kept her.
   But after the war was over
I couldn't get work. We lived a bad time. . . . I managed, while you were
   burning and dreaming in the dirty grave
I peddled myself in the streets——she was kept supplied. You see, Carson,
   those pleasures
That set you dreaming and burning in the dirty grave
Have been useful too." He answered thickly in his throat: "No matter. It's
   very likely. Why talk about it?"
"To let you know that what you eyed so hotly among the wild lilacs
Is less white than it was." He answered, "Have you hurt your hand? Why
   do you keep it hidden?" But George
Suddenly stood up, shaking and reddened: "You'd better get out. You
   harlot get out," he said choking.
"I knew you'd done it for love, you never told me, for dollars . . ." "That's
   another thing," she said gravely,
Not looking at him. "I got clean work at last in a store in Monterey. I was
   there when George
Married me; he didn't have to ask twice. Since then, while you were
   dreaming and burning in the dirty grave
He's kept us happy and secure, both me and Esther. I owe him some loving
   thoughts, Carson; and you—
Some less than loving. I owe you . . . I hoped he'd have gone and got back
   the rifle
While you and I were away. I left that for him to do, but he was afraid. I
   am very lucky
Between such a husband and such a lover." "He locked the door," George
   muttered. "But the windows were left. . . . Well:
Except the knife I got from the kitchen drawer and hide in my hand, this
   dead man has all the power

Under this roof. Perhaps he'll begin to bully us again. You see it's not one
    of those bendy knives,
But bright thick steel; a hunting-knife really;
George often kills deer in season, he's not afraid to kill *deer*." Carson said
    slowly: "You've the courage, Hildis,
Though not the strength. But this is greater than death; it will not be
    changed. I'd come again; though it might be
In a worse body, the reek of the grave about it; or only a blank spirit,
    bodiless desire
Blowing to your bed in the dark; but neither you nor I can escape." "Why,"
    she answered, "that's worse than bullying,
That's lying. I've got my power of choice in my hand; I found it in the
    kitchen drawer. Whatever I do
I shall do freely." "What will you do?" "Go with you," she answered. And
    said, "Our Estie's crying again.
Oh, George, George, I can't take her; she'll have to cry. This man's from
    the grave; he'll turn black and untouchable
When his love's fed. There's no security nor hope for any human creature
    in the way that I go.
— Your knife, George: I thought all the while that I'd never need it. — We'll
    be going, Carson."

                    They went out together,
And down the gross darkness of the night mountain. They were rather like
    one star than two people, for that night at least,
So love had joined them to burn a moment for each other, no other star
    was needed in all the black world.
But love or hatred
Or good or evil are hardly
A hair's weight here in the balance.
One being risen from the dead,
The irrational mind revives,
All things are possible again.

THE PLACE FOR NO STORY

The coast hills at Sovranes Creek;
No trees, but dark scant pasture drawn thin
Over rock shaped like flame;
The old ocean at the land's foot, the vast
Gray extension beyond the long white violence;
A herd of cows and the bull
Far distant, hardly apparent up the dark slope;
And the gray air haunted with hawks:
This place is the noblest thing I have ever seen. No imaginable
Human presence here could do anything
But dilute the lonely self-watchful passion.

NEW MEXICAN MOUNTAIN

I watch the Indians dancing to help the young corn at Taos pueblo. The
old men squat in a ring
And make the song, the young women with fat bare arms, and a few
shame-faced young men, shuffle the dance.

The lean-muscled young men are naked to the narrow loins, their breasts
and backs daubed with white clay,
Two eagle-feathers plume the black heads. They dance with reluctance, they
are growing civilized; the old men persuade them.

Only the drum is confident, it thinks the world has not changed; the
beating heart, the simplest of rhythms,
It thinks the world has not changed at all; it is only a dreamer, a brainless
heart, the drum has no eyes.

These tourists have eyes, the hundred watching the dance, white Americans,
hungrily too, with reverence, not laughter;
Pilgrims from civilization, anxiously seeking beauty, religion, poetry;
pilgrims from the vacuum.

People from cities, anxious to be human again. Poor show how they suck
you empty! The Indians are emptied,
And certainly there was never religion enough, nor beauty nor poetry here
. . . to fill Americans.

Only the drum is confident, it thinks the world has not changed.
Apparently only myself and the strong
Tribal drum, and the rock-head of Taos mountain, remember that
civilization is a transient sickness.

NOVEMBER SURF

Some lucky day each November great waves awake and are drawn
Like smoking mountains bright from the west
And come and cover the cliff with white violent cleanness: then suddenly
The old granite forgets half a year's filth:
The orange-peel, egg-shells, papers, pieces of clothing, the clots
Of dung in corners of the rock, and used
Sheaths that make light love safe in the evenings: all the droppings of the
    summer
Idlers washed off in a winter ecstasy:
I think this cumbered continent envies its cliff then. . . . But all seasons
The earth, in her childlike prophetic sleep,
Keeps dreaming of the bath of a storm that prepares up the long coast
Of the future to scour more than her sea-lines:
The cities gone down, the people fewer and the hawks more numerous,
The rivers mouth to source pure; when the two-footed
Mammal, being someways one of the nobler animals, regains
The dignity of room, the value of rareness.

MARGRAVE

On the small marble-paved platform
On the turret on the head of the tower
Watching the night deepen.
I feel the rock-edge of the continent
Reel eastward with me below the broad stars,
I lean on the broad worn stones of the parapet-top
And the stones and my hands that touch them reel eastward.
The inland mountains go down and new lights
Glow over the sinking east rim of the earth.
The dark ocean comes up,
And reddens the western stars with its fog-breath
And hides them with its mounded darkness.

The earth was the world and man was its measure, but our minds have
    looked
Through the little mock-dome of heaven the telescope-slotted observatory
    eye-ball, there space and multitude came in
And the earth is a particle of dust by a sand-grain sun, lost in a nameless
    cove of the shores of a continent.
Galaxy on galaxy, innumerable swirls of innumerable stars, endured as it
    were forever and humanity
Came into being, its two or three million years are a moment, in a moment
    it will certainly cease out from being
And galaxy on galaxy endure after that as it were forever . . . But man is
    conscious,
He brings the world to focus in a feeling brain,
In a net of nerves catches the splendor of things,
Breaks the somnambulism of nature . . . His distinction perhaps,
Hardly his advantage. To slaver for contemptible pleasures
And scream with pain, are hardly an advantage.

Consciousness? The learned astronomer
Analyzing the light of most remote star-swirls
Has found them—or a trick of distance deludes his prism—
All at incredible speeds fleeing outward from ours.
I thought, no doubt they are fleeing the contagion
Of consciousness that infects this corner of space.

For often I have heard the hard rocks I handled
Groan, because lichen and time and water dissolve them,
And they have to travel down the strange falling scale
Of soil and plants and the flesh of beasts to become
The bodies of men; they murmur at their fate
In the hollows of windless nights, they'd rather be anything
Than human flesh played on by pain and joy,
They pray for annihilation sooner, but annihilation's
Not in the book yet.

                    So, I thought, the rumor
Of human consciousness has gone abroad in the world,
The sane uninfected far-outer universes
Flee it in a panic of escape, as men flee the plague
Taking a city: for look at the fruits of consciousness:
As in young Walter Margrave when he'd been sentenced for murder: he was
      thinking when they brought him back
To the cell in jail, "I've only a moment to arrange my thoughts, I must
      think quickly, I must think clearly,
And settle the world in my mind before I kick off," but to feel the curious
      eyes of his fellow-prisoners
And the wry-mouthed guard's and so forth torment him through the steel
      bars put his mind in a stupor, he could only
Sit frowning, ostentatiously unafraid. "But I can control my mind, their
      eyes can't touch my will.

One against all. What use is will at this end of everything? A kind of
    nausea is the chief feeling . . .
In my stomach and throat . . . but in my head pride: I fought a good fight
    and they can't break me; alone, unbroken,
Against a hundred and twenty-three million people. They are going to kill
    the best brain perhaps in the world,
That might have made such discoveries in science
As would set the world centuries ahead, for I had the mind and the power.
    Boo, it's their loss. Blind fools,
Killing their best." When his mind forgot the eyes it made rapid capricious
    pictures instead of words,
But not of the medical school and the laboratories, its late intense interest;
    not at all of his crime; glimpses
Of the coast-range at home; the V of a westward canyon with the vibrating
Blue line of the ocean strung sharp across it; that domed hill up the valley,
    two cows like specks on the summit
And a beautiful-colored jungle of poison-oak at the foot; his sister half
    naked washing her hair,
"My dirty sister," whose example and her lovers had kept him chaste by
    revulsion; the reed-grown mouth of the river
And the sand-bar against the stinging splendor of the sea . . . and anguish
    behind all the pictures
(He began to consider his own mind again) "like a wall they hang on."
    Hang. The anguish came forward, an actual
Knife between two heart-beats, the organ stopped and then raced. He
    experimented awhile with his heart,
Making in his mind a picture of a man hanged, pretending to himself it was
    to happen next moment,
Trying to observe whether the beat suspended — "suspended," he
    thought — in systole or in diastole.
The effect soon failed; the anguish remained. "Ah my slack lawyer, damn
    him, let slip chance after chance.

Scared traitor." Then broken pictures of the scenes in court, the jury, the
    judge, the idlers, and not one face
But bleak with hatred. "But I met their eyes, one against all." Suddenly his
    mind became incapable
Of making pictures or words, but still wildly active, striking in all
    directions like a snake in a fire,
Finding nothing but the fiery element of its own anguish. He got up and
    felt the guard's eyes and sat down,
Turned side-face, resting his chin on his fist, frowning and trembling. He
    saw clearly in his mind the little
Adrenal glands perched on the red-brown kidneys, as if all his doomed
    tissues became transparent,
Pouring in these passions their violent secretion
Into his blood-stream, raising the tension unbearably. And the thyroids:
    tension, tension. A long course of that
Should work grave changes. "If they tortured a man like a laboratory dog
    for discovery: there'd be value gained: but by process
Of law for vengeance, because his glands and his brain have made him act
    in another than common manner:
You incredible breed of asses!" He smiled self-consciously in open scorn of
    the people, the guard at the door
To observe that smile — "my God, do I care about the turn-key's
    opinion?" — suddenly his mind again
Was lashing like a burnt snake. Then it was torpid for a while. This
    continued for months.

His father had come to visit him, he saw the ruinous white-haired head
Through two steel wickets under the bluish electric light that seemed to
    peel the skin from the face.
Walter said cheerfully too loudly, "Hullo. You look like a skull." The
    shaven sunk jaws in answer chewed

Inaudible words. Walter with an edge of pleasure thought "Once he was stronger than I! I used to admire

This poor old man's strength when I was a child," and said "Buck up, old fellow, it will soon be over. Here's nothing

To cry for. Do you think I'm afraid to die? It's good people that fear death, people with the soft streak

Of goodness in them fear death: but I, you know, am a monster, don't you read the papers? Caught at last:

I fought a hundred and twenty-three million people. How's Hazel? How's the farm? I could get out of this scrape

By playing dementia, but I refuse to, there's not an alienist living

Could catch me out. I'm the king of Spain dying for the world. I've been persecuted since I was born

By a secret sect, they stuck pins into me

And fed me regular doses of poison for a certain reason. Why do you pretend that you're my father?

God is. . . . Believe me, I could get by with it.

But I refuse."

Old Margrave looked timidly at the two guards listening, and drew his brown tremulous hand

Across his eyes below the white hair. "I thought of going to try to see the governor, Walter."

"That's it!" "Don't hope for anything, Walter, they tell me that there's no hope. They say that I shan't even

Be allowed to see him." "By God," the young man said trembling, "you can if you want to. Never believe that lawyer.

If I'd had Dorking: but you couldn't afford him. Poor men have no right to breed sons. I'd not be here

If you'd had money to put me through college. Tell the governor

I know he won't pardon, but he can commute the sentence to life imprisonment. Then I can read and study,

I can help the penitentiary doctor, I can do something to help humanity.
    Tell him it's madness
To throw such a brain as mine into the garbage. Don't deny my guilt but
    tell him my reasons.
I kidnapped the little girl to get money to finish my medical education.
    What's one child's life
Against a career like mine that might have saved
Thousands of children? Say I'd isolated the organism of infantile paralysis:
    I'd have done more:
But that alone would save thousands of children. I was merciful; she died
    quietly; tell him that.
It was only pithing a little white frog.
Don't you think you can make him understand? I'm not a criminal: I judge
    differently from others. I wasn't
Afraid to think for myself. All I did
Was for money for my education, to help humanity. And tell him if I've
    done wrong—what's wrong?—I've paid for it
With frightful suffering: the more developed the brain the greater the
    agony. He won't admit that. Oh God,
These brains the size of a pea! To be juried
And strangled by a hundred and twenty-three million peas. Go down on
    your knees to him. You owe me that: you'd no right
To breed, you're poor.
But you itched for a woman, you had to fetch me out of the happy hill of
    not-being. Pfah, to hug a woman
And make this I. That's the evil in the world, that letter. I—I—Tell the
    governor
That I'm not afraid of dying, that I laugh at death. No, no, we'll laugh in
    private. Tell him I'm crazy.
I've come to that: after being the only sane mind among a hundred and
    twenty-three million peas.
Anything, anything . . ."

He had let his nerves go wild on purpose, to
   edge on the old man to action, now at last
Escaping utterly out of control they stumbled into a bog of thick sobs. The
   guards pulled him up
And walked him away as if he were half insensible. He was not insensible,
   but more acutely aware
Than ever in his life before of all that touched him, and of shame and
   anguish.

      You would be wise, you far stars,
To flee with the speed of light this infection.
For here the good sane invulnerable material
And nature of things more and more grows alive and cries.
The rock and water grow human, the bitter weed
Of consciousness catches the sun, it clings to the near stars,
Even the nearer portion of the universal God
Seems to become conscious, yearns and rejoices
And suffers: I believe this hurt will be healed
Some age of time after mankind has died,
Then the sun will say "What ailed me a moment?" and resume
The old soulless triumph, and the iron and stone earth
With confident inorganic glory obliterate
Her ruins and fossils, like that incredible unfading red rose
Of desert in Arizona glowing life to scorn,
And grind the chalky emptied seed-shells of consciousness
The bare skulls of the dead to powder; after some million
Courses around the sun her sadness may pass:
But why should you worlds of the virgin distance
Endure to survive what it were better to escape?

I also am not innocent
Of contagion, but have spread my spirit on the deep world.

I have gotten sons and sent the fire wider.
I have planted trees, they also feel while they live.
I have humanized the ancient sea-sculptured cliff
And the ocean's wreckage of rock
Into a house and a tower,
Hastening the sure decay of granite with my hammer,
Its hard dust will make soft flesh;
And have widened in my idleness
The disastrous personality of life with poems,
That are pleasant enough in the breeding but go bitterly at last
To envy oblivion and the early deaths of nobler
Verse, and much nobler flesh;
And I have projected my spirit
Behind the superb sufficient forehead of nature
To gift the inhuman God with this rankling consciousness.

But who is our judge? It is likely the enormous
Beauty of the world requires for completion our ghostly increment,
It has to dream, and dream badly, a moment of its night.

On the little stone-belted platform
On the turret on the head of the tower,
Between the stars and the earth
And the ocean and the continent.
One ship's light shines and eclipses
Very far out, behind the high waves on the hill of water.
In the east under the Hyades and rising Orion
Are many cities and multitudes of people,
But westward a long ways they are few enough.
It is fortunate to look westward as to look upward.
In the south the dark river-mouth pool mirrors a star

That stands over Margrave's farmhouse. The old man has lost it, he isn't
    there any more. He went down to the river-mouth
Last December, when recent rains had opened the stream and the salmon
    were running. Fishermen very solemnly
Stood all along the low sand like herons, and sea-lions off-shore in the
    rolling waves with deep wet voices
Coughed at each other; the sea-air is hoarse with their voices that time of
    year. Margrave had rambled since noon
Among the little folds of the seaward field that he had forgotten to plow
    and was trying to sell
Though he used to love it, but everything was lost now. He lay awhile on
    his face in the rotting stubble and random
Unsown green blades, then he got up and drifted over the ridge to the
    river-mouth sands, unaimed,
Pale and gap-eyed, as the day moon a clear morning, opposite the sun. He
    noticed with surprise the many
Fishermen like herons in the shallows and along the sands; and then that his
    girl Hazel was with him: who'd feared
What he might do to himself and had come to watch him when he lay face
    down in the field. "I know what they're doing,"
He said slyly, "Hazel, they're fishing! I guess they don't know,"
He whispered, "about our trouble. Oh no, don't tell them." She said,
    "Don't go down father, your face would tell them.
Sit here on the edge of grass, watch the brown river meet the blue sea. Do
    look: that boy's caught something.
How the line cuts the water and the small wheel sings." "If I'd been rich,"
Old Margrave answered, "they'd have fixed the hook for . . . Walter . . .
    with some other bait. It sticks in my mind that . . . Walter
Blames me too much." "Look," Hazel said, "he's landing it now. Oh, it's a
    big one." "I dreamed about fishing,
Some time ago," he answered, "but we were the fish. I saw the people all
    running reaching for prizes

That dangled on long lines from the sky. A lovely girl or a sack of money
    or a case of whiskey,
Or fake things like reputation, hackle-feathers and a hook. A man would
    reach up and grab and the line
Jerked, then you knew by his face that the hook was in him, wherever he
    went. Often they're played for half
A life-time before they're landed: others, like . . . my son . . . pulled up
    short. Oh, Oh,
It's not a dream." He said gently, "He wanted money for his education, but
    you poor girl
Wanted boy friends, now you've got a round belly. That's the hook. I
    wanted children and got
Walter and you. Hm? Hooked twice is too much. Let's walk." "Not that
    way: let's go up home, daddy.
It makes you unhappy to see them fishing." "No," he answered, "nothing
    can. I have it in my pocket." She walked behind him,
Hiding herself, ashamed of her visible pregnancy and her brother's fate; but
    when the old man stumbled
And wavered on the slope she went beside him to support him, her right
    hand under his elbow, and wreathed his body
With the other arm.

                The clear brown river ran eagerly through the
    sand-hill, undercutting its banks,
That slid in masses; tall waves walked very slowly up-stream from the sea,
    and stood
Stationary in the throat of the channel before they dissolved. The rock the
    children call Red-cap stood
High and naked among the fishermen, the orange lichen on its head. At the
    sea-end of the sand
Two boys and a man had rifles instead of rods, they meant to punish the
    salmon-devouring sea-lions

Because the fish were fewer than last year; whenever a sleek brown head
    with the big questioning eyes
Broke sea they fired. Margrave had heard the shots but taken no notice, but
    when he walked by the stream
He saw a swimmer look up from the water and its round dark eye
Suddenly burst red blood before it went down. He cried out and twisted
    himself from Hazel's hand
And ran like a squirrel along the stream-bank. "I'll not allow it!" He
    snatched at a rifle. "Why should my lad
Be hanged for killing and all you others go free?" He wrestled feebly to
    gain the rifle, the sand-bank
Slid under his feet, he slipped and lay face down in the running stream and
    was hauled astrand. Then Hazel
Came running heavily, and when he was able to walk she led him away. The
    sea-beast, blinded but a painful
Vain gleam, starved long before it could die; old Margrave still lives.
    Death's like a little gay child that runs
The world around with the keys of salvation in his foolish fingers, lends
    them at random where they're not wanted,
But often withholds them where most required.

                                    Margrave's son at this
    time
Had only four days to wait, but death now appeared so dreadful to him
    that to speak of his thoughts and the abject
Horror, would be to insult humanity more than it deserves. At last the
    jerked hemp snapped the neck sideways
And bruised the cable of nerves that threads the bone rings; the intolerably
    strained consciousness in a moment changed.
It was strangely cut in two parts at the noose, the head's
Consciousness from the body's; both were set free and flamed; the head's
    with flashing paradisal light

Like the wild birth of a star, but crying in bewilderment and suddenly
    extinguished; the body's with a sharp emotion
Of satisfied love, a wave of hard warmth and joy, that ebbed cold on
    darkness. After a time of darkness
The dreams that follow upon death came and subsided, like fibrillar
    twitchings
Of the nerves unorganizing themselves; and some of the small dreams were
    delightful and some slight miseries,
But nothing intense; then consciousness wandered home from the cell to
    the molecule, was utterly dissolved and changed;
Peace was the end of the play, so far as concerns humanity. Oh beautiful
    capricious little savior,
Death, the gay child with the gipsy eyes, to avoid you for a time I think is
    virtuous, to fear you is insane.

On the little stone-girdled platform
Over the earth and the ocean
I seem to have stood a long time and watched the stars pass.
They also shall perish I believe.
Here to-day, gone to-morrow, desperate wee galaxies
Scattering themselves and shining their substance away
Like a passionate thought. It is very well ordered.

AN IRISH HEADLAND

Fair Head in Antrim, long dark waves of wet heather to the black lips of
    the height
Where the old McDonnel war-chief three days of grief and madness raged
    like a storm on the precipice-head
Watching the massacre that came to Rathlin on ships, helplessly seeing
Unavengeable things across the thin sleeve of sea. The old man's anguish
    and burning anger were not
Even in the moment of blood and smoke
Ponderable against the tough and sombre passion of the headland; they
    were nothing; not a gannet-feather's
Weight on the rock; the mood of this black basalt has never turned since it
    cooled.

            The most beautiful woman
Of the northern world made landfall under this cliff when she came to the
    bitter end that makes the life shine,
But the black towers of the rock were more beautiful than Deirdre.
Weep for the pity of lovers and the beauty of bereaved men, the beauty of
    the earth is too great to weep for.

EDISON
(October 1931)

A great toy-maker, light-bringer, patient
Finder of powers that were promptly applied to foolish and mean
Purposes; a man full of benevolence,
Eager for knowledge, has dropped his tools and forgotten contrivance.
Why must the careful gifts of good men
Narrow the lives and erode the souls of people, as trader's
Whiskey unravels a run of savages?

FIRE ON THE HILLS

The deer were bounding like blown leaves
Under the smoke in front of the roaring wave of the brushfire;
I thought of the smaller lives that were caught.
Beauty is not always lovely; the fire was beautiful, the terror
Of the deer was beautiful; and when I returned
Down the black slopes after the fire had gone by, an eagle
Was perched on the jag of a burnt pine,
Insolent and gorged, cloaked in the folded storms of his shoulders.
He had come from far off for the good hunting
With fire for his beater to drive the game; the sky was merciless
Blue, and the hills merciless black,
The sombre-feathered great bird sleepily merciless between them.
I thought, painfully, but the whole mind,
The destruction that brings an eagle from heaven is better than mercy.

THURSO'S LANDING

I

The coast-road was being straightened and repaired again,
A group of men labored at the steep curve
Where it falls from the north to Mill Creek. They scattered and hid
Behind cut banks, except one blond young man
Who stooped over the rock and strolled away smiling
As if he shared a secret joke with the dynamite;
It waited until he had passed back of a boulder,
Then split its rock cage; a yellowish torrent
Of fragments rose up the air and the echoes bumped
From mountain to mountain. The men returned slowly
And took up their dropped tools, while a banner of dust
Waved over the gorge on the northwest wind, very high
Above the heads of the forest.

                         Some distance west of the road,
On the promontory above the triangle
Of glittering ocean that fills the gorge-mouth,
A woman and a lame man from the farm below
Had been watching, and turned to go down the hill. The young woman
    looked back,
Widening her violet eyes under the shade of her hand. "I think they'll blast
    again in a minute."
And the man: "I wish they'd let the poor old road be. I don't like
    improvements." "Why not?" "They bring in the world;
We're well without it." His lameness gave him some look of age but he was
    young too; tall and thin-faced,
With a high wavering nose. "Isn't he amusing," she said, "that boy Rick
    Armstrong, the dynamite man,

How slowly he walks away after he lights the fuse. He loves to show off.
    Reave likes him too,"
She added; and they clambered down the path in the rock-face, little dark
    specks
Between the great headland rock and the bright blue sea.

II

                                                                    The
    road-workers had made their camp
North of this headland, where the sea-cliff was broken down and sloped to
    a cove. The violet-eyed woman's husband,
Reave Thurso, rode down the slope to the camp in the gorgeous autumn
    sundown, his hired man Johnny Luna
Riding behind him. The road-men had just quit work and four or five were
    bathing in the purple surf-edge,
The others talked by the tents; blue smoke fragrant with food and
    oak-wood drifted from the cabin stove-pipe
And slowly went fainting up the vast hill.

                                        Thurso drew rein by a group of
    men at a tent door
And frowned at them without speaking, square-shouldered and
    heavy-jawed, too heavy with strength for so young a man,
He chose one of the men with his eyes. "You're Danny Woodruff, aren't
    you, that drives the tractor." Who smiled
And answered "Maybe. What then?" "Why, nothing, except you broke my
    fence and you've got to fix it." "You don't say,"
He said laughing. "Did somebody break your fence? Well, that's too bad."
    "My man here saw you do it.
He warned you out of the field." "Oh, was I warned?" He turned to Luna:
    "What did I say to you, cowboy?"

"You say, you say," Luna's dark face flushed black, "you say 'Go to hell.' "
    Woodruff gravely, to Thurso:
"That's what I say." The farmer had a whip in his hand, a hotter man might
    have struck, but he carefully
Hung it on the saddle-horn by the thong at the butt, dismounted, and said,
    "You'll fix it though." He was somewhat
Short-coupled, but so broad in the chest and throat, and obviously all oak,
    that Woodruff recoiled a step,
Saying "If you've got a claim for damages, take it to the county." "I'm
    taking it nearer hand.
You'll fix the fence." Woodruff's companions
Began to come in between, and one said "Wait for him
Until he fixes it, your cows will be down the road."
Thurso shook his head slightly and bored forward
Toward his one object; who felt the persecuting
Pale eyes under dark brows dazzle resistance.
He was glad the bathers came up the shore to ask
What the dispute was, their presence released his mind
A moment from the obstinate eyes. The blithe young firer
Of dynamite blasts, Rick Armstrong, came in foremost,
Naked and very beautiful, all his blond body
Gleaming from the sea; he'd been one or two evenings
A guest at the farmhouse, and now took Thurso's part
So gracefully that the tractor-driver, already
Unnerved by that leaden doggedness, was glad to yield.
He'd mend the fence in the morning: Oh, sure, he wanted
To do the right thing: but Thurso's manner
Had put him off.

              The group dissolved apart, having made for a moment
  its unconscious beauty

In the vast landscape above the ocean in the colored evening; the naked
   bodies of the young bathers
Polished with light, against the brown and blue denim core of the rest; and
   the ponies, one brown, one piebald,
Compacted into the group, the Spanish-Indian horseman dark bronze
   above them, under broad red
Heavens leaning to the lonely mountain.

III

In the moonlight two hours before Sunday dawn
Rick Armstrong went on foot over the hill
Toward the farmhouse in the deep gorge, where it was dark
And he smelled the stream. Thurso had invited him
To go deer-hunting with them, seeing lights in the house
He hurried down, not to make his friends wait.
He passed under a lonely noise in the sky
And wondered at it, and remembered the great cable
That spanned the gorge from the hill, with a rusted iron skip
Hanging from it like a stuck black moon; relics,
With other engines on the headland, of ancient lime-kilns
High up the canyon, from which they shot the lime
To the promontory along the airy cable-way
To be shipped by sea. The works had failed; the iron skip
Stuck on its rusted pulleys would never move again
Until it fell, but to make a desolate creaking
In the mountain east wind that poured down the gorge
Every clear night. He looked for it and could not find it
Against the white sky, but stumbled over a root
And hurried down to the house.

There were layered smells of horses and
   leather
About the porch; the door stood half open, in the yellow slot
Of lamplight appeared two faces, Johnny Luna's dark hollow Egyptian
   profile and Helen Thurso's
Very white beyond, her wide-parted violet eyes looked black and her lips
   moved. Her husband's wide chest
Eclipsed the doorway. "Here you are. I was afraid you wouldn't wake up.
   Come in," Thurso said,
"Coffee and bacon, it will be long to lunch." A fourth in the room was the
   lame man, Reave Thurso's brother,
Who said at parting, "Take care of Helen, won't you, Reave,
Don't tire her out." He was not of the party but had risen to see them off.
   She answered from the porch, laughing,
The light from the door gilding her cheek, "I'll not be the tired one, Mark,
   by evening. Pity the others."
"Let the men do the shooting, Helen, spare yourself. Killing's against your
   nature, it would hurt with unhappy thought
Some later time." "Ah," she answered, "not so gentle as you think.
   Good-bye, brother."
They mounted the drooping horses and rode up canyon
Between black trees, under that lonely creaking in the sky, and turned
   southward
Along the coast-road to enter a darker canyon.
The horses jerked at the bridle-hands,
Nosing out a way for the stammering hooves
Along the rocks of a ribbed creek-bed; thence a path upward
To the height of a ridge; in that clear the red moonset
Appeared between murky hills, like a burning ship
On the world's verge.

Thurso and Luna stealthily dismounted.

They stole two ways down the starry-glimmering slope like assassins, above the black fur of forest, and vanished

In the shifty gray. The two others remained, Armstrong looked wistfully

Toward his companion through the high reddish gloom, and saw the swell of her breast and droop of her throat

Darkling against the low moon-scarred west. She whispered and said, "The poor thing may drive up hill toward us:

And I'll not fire, do you want to trade rifles with me? The old one that Reave has lent you is little use."

He answered, "I guess one gun's as good as another, you can't see the bead, you can't see the notch." "Oh: well.

The light will grow." They were silent a time, sitting and holding the horses, the red moon on the sea-line

Suddenly foundered; still the east had nothing.

                                    "We'd better take ourselves

Out of the sky, and tie up the horses." She began to move, down the way lately climbed, the cowboy's

Pony trailing behind her, Armstrong led Reave's. He saw her white shirt below him gleam in the starlight

Like bare shoulders above the shadow. They unbridled the horses and tethered them to buckthorn bushes, and went back

Into the sky; but lay close against the ridge to be hidden, for a cloud whitened. Orion and Sirius

Stood southward in the mid heaven, and Armstrong said

"They're strange at dawn, see, they're not autumn stars,

They belong to last March." "Maybe *next* March," she answered

Without looking. "Tell me how you've charmed Reave

To make him love you? He never has cared for a friend before,

Cold and lonely by nature. He seems to love you."

"Why: nothing. If he lacks friends perhaps it's only
Because this country has been too vacant for him
To make choices from." "No," she answered, "he's cold,
And all alone in himself. Well. His goodness is strength.
He's never set his mind on anything yet
But got it with a strong hand. His brother, you met this morning,
Is very different, a weak man of course,
But kindly and full of pity toward every creature, but really at heart
As cold as Reave. I never loved hunting, and he's
Persuaded me to hate it. Let him persuade
Reave if he could!" Armstrong said, "Why did you come then?"
"Ah? To watch things be killed."

                                   They heard the wind
Flustering below, and felt the sallow increase of clearness
On grass-blades, and the girl's face, and the far sea,
A light of visions, faint and a virgin. One rifle-shot
Snapped the still dawn; Armstrong cradled his gun
But nothing came up the hill. The cloud-line eastward
Suddenly flushed with rose-color flame, and standing
Rays of transparent purple shadow appeared
Behind the fired fleece. Helen Thurso sighed and stood up,
"Let's see if we can't lead one of the horses down,
Now light has come, to bring up the corpse." "The . . . for what?"
"The meat," she said impatiently, "the killed thing. It's a hard climb."
"You think they got it?" "Couldn't fail; but other years
They've taken two in that trap." Nearly straight down,
At the edge of the wood, in the pool of blue shade in the cleft hill,
The two men were seen, one burdened, like mites in a bowl; and Helen
    with a kind of triumph: "Look down there:

What size Reave Thurso is really: one of those little dirty black ants that
    come to dead things could carry him
With the deer added."

                    They drove a horse down the headlong pitch; the
    sun came up like a man shouting
While they climbed back, then Helen halted for breath. Thurso tightened
    the lashings under the saddle,
That held his booty on the pony's back, and said to Armstrong, "That tree
    that stands alone on the spur,
It looks like a match: its trunk's twenty feet through. The biggest redwoods
    left on the coast are there,
The lumber-men couldn't reach them."

                                Johnny Luna, when they reached
    the ridge,
Was sent home leading his horse, with the buck mounted. The others rode
    east, the two men ahead, and Helen
Regarding their heads and shoulders against the sharp sky or the sides of
    hills; they left the redwood canyons
And rode a long while among interminable gray ranges bushed on the north
    with oak and lupin;
Farther they wandered among flayed bison-shaped hills, and rode at noon
    under sparse bull-pines,
And so returned, having seen no life at all
Except high up the sun the black vultures,
Some hawks hunting the gorges, and a far coyote.
In the afternoon, nearing toward home, it was Helen
Who saw five deer strung on a ridge. "Oh. Look.
So I've betrayed them," she said bitterly. Reave said to Armstrong,
"Your shot: the buck to the north," and while he spoke fired, but the other
Had raised his cheek from the rifle-stock to look

At Helen angrily laughing, her face brilliant
In the hard sunlight, with lakes of deep shade
Under the brows and the chin; when he looked back
The ridge was cleared. "Why didn't you let him have it?
You'd such an easy shot," Thurso said,
"Against the cloud, mine was among the bushes,
I saw him fall and roll over." "Be very happy,"
Helen said. "He was hard hit, for he ran down hill.
That makes you shine."

                    They labored across the gorge
And climbed up to the ridge. A spongy scarlet thing
Was found at the foot of a green oak-bush and Helen
Came and saw it. "He was hit in the lung," Reave said,
"Coughed up a froth of blood and ran down hill.
I have to get him." "It looks like a red toadstool:
Red scum on rotten wood. Does it make you sick?
Not a bit: it makes you happy." "Why do you come hunting, Helen,
If you hate hunting? Keep still at least. As for being happy:
Look where I have to go down." He showed her the foamy spots of blood,
    on the earth and the small leaves,
Going down a steep thicket that seemed impassable. She answered, "Let
    the poor thing die in peace." "It would seem a pity,"
He answered, "to let him suffer; besides the waste." Armstrong looked
    down and said, "He'll be in the creek-bed.
I'll go down there and work up the gulch, if you go down here." "You'd
    never find him without the blood-trail,"
Reave answered. Then Helen suddenly went back and touched the foam of
    blood on the ground, dipping four fingers,
And returned and said, "I was afraid to do it, so I did it. Now I'm no better
    than you. Don't go down.

Please, Reave. Let's hurry and go home. I'm tired." Reave said to
    Armstrong, "That would be best, if you'd take her home.
It's only a mile and a half, help her with the horses, won't you? Take mine
    too. I'll hang the buck in a tree
Near where I find him, and come fetch him to-morrow." "If you want,"
    Armstrong said. Helen clenched
Her blood-tipped fingers and felt them stick to the palm. "All right. I'll do
What, you've chosen," she said with smoothed lips. "Mark wins, he said I'd
    be tired. But he was wrong,"
Opening her hand, regarding the red-lined nails,
"To think me all milk and kindness." Thurso went down
The thicket; and Helen: "Nothing could turn him back.
He's never set his mind on anything yet
But snuffled like a bloodhound to the bitter end." They heard the branches
Breaking below, and returned by the open slope
To the horses across the creek.

                        They rode softly
Down the canyon; Helen said, "I'm not tired.
Do you ever think about death? I've seen you play with it,
Strolling away while the fuse fizzed in the rock."
"Hell no, that was all settled when they made the hills."
"Did you notice how high he held his bright head
And the branched horns, keen with happiness? Nothing told him
That all would break in a moment and the blood choke his throat. I hope
    that poor stag
Had many loves in his life." He looked curiously,
A little moved, at her face; too pale, like a white flame
That has form but no brilliance in the light of day;
The wide violet eyes hollowed with points of craving darkness
Under the long dark lashes; and the charcoal mark
Across her slightly hollowed cheek, where a twig had crossed it

When they rode the burnt hillside. He said: "I ought
To've gone with Reave, it doesn't seem fair to let him
Sweat alone in that jungle." "He *enjoys* toil.
You don't know him yet. Give him a blood-trail to follow,
That's all he wants for Christmas. What he's got's nothing to him,
His game's the getting. But slow, slow: be hours yet.
From here we can choose ways, and though it's a good deal longer,
There's daylight left, we'll go by the head of the hill: up there you can see the whole coast
And a thousand hills. Look," she said laughing,
"What the crooked bushes have done," showing her light shirt
Torn at the breast, and a long red scratch
Under the bright smooth breast. He felt in his mind
A moving dizziness, and shifted his body backward
From the saddle-horn.

                    A curl of sea-cloud stood on the head of the hill
Like a wave breaking against the wind; but when they reached it, windows of clearness in it were passing
From the northwest, through which the mountain sea-wall looked abrupt as dreams, from Lobos like a hand on the sea
To the offshore giant at Point Sur southward. Straight down through the coursing mists like a crack in the mountain sea-root,
Mill Creek Canyon, like a crack in the naked root of a dead pine when the bark peels off. The bottom
Of the fissure was black with redwood, and lower
Green with alders; between the black and the green the painted roof of the farmhouse, like a dropped seed,
Thurso's house, like a grain of corn in the crack of a plank, where the hens can't reach it.

Cloud steered between;
Helen Thurso said "What if the rut is a rock canyon,
Look how I'm stuck in a rut: do I have to live there?
And Reave's old mother's like a white-headed hawk.
Your job here's nearly finished, where will you go?"
"I haven't thought: all places are like each other:
Maybe Nevada in the spring.
There's work all over." "I," she said trembling; "it seems cold up here.
I hate the sea-fog. Now let's look east." They had tied
The horses to the highest bushes on the north slope,
And walked on the open dome of the hill, they crossed it
And the east was clear; the beautiful desolate inhuman range beyond range
    of summits all seen at once,
Dry bright and quiet and their huge blue shadows. Helen said faintly,
"He's down there somewhere. It's that deer's blood.
It made me drunk, it was too red I thought.
Life is so tiny little, and if it shoots
Into the darkness without ever once flashing?"
They turned back to the dome-top under the cloud.
"You're tired, Helen." "I'll not let the days of my life
Hang like a string of naughts between two nothings.
Wear a necklace of round zeros for pearls;
I'm not made that way. Think what you please. Shall we go down now?"
"The cloud has come all around us," he answered, seeing the distilled drops
    of the cloud like seed-pearls
Hung in her hair and on the dark lashes. He turned to go down to the
    horses, she said "I have seen dawn with you,
The red moonset and white dawn,
And starlight on the mountain, and noon on burnt hills where there was no
    shadow but a vulture's, and that stag's blood: I've lived with you
A long day like a lifetime, at last I've drawn something

In the string of blanks." She lifted her face against his shoulder and said
  "Good-bye." He said "I'm Reave's friend,"
And kissed her good-bye seeing she desired it, her breasts burrowed against
  him and friendship forgot his mind,
With such brief wooing they stirred the deep wells of pleasure.

                                                            She lay
    but half quieted, still hotly longing,
Her eyes morbidly shuttered like the sleep of fever showed threads of the
  white and faint arcs of the crystalline
Violet irises, barred across by the strong dark lashes; the night of the lids
  covered the pupils,
Behind them, and under the thick brown hair and under the cunning
  sutures of the hollow bone the nerve-cells
With locking fibrils made their own world and light, the multitude of small
  rayed animals of one descent
That make one mind, imagined a mountain
Higher than the scope of nature, predominant over all these edges of the
  earth, on its head a sacrifice
Half naked, all flaming, her hair blown like a fire through the level skies; for
  she had to believe this passion
Not the wild heat of nature, but the superstitiously worshipped spirit of
  love, that is thought to burn
All its acts righteous.

              While Helen adorned the deed with the dream it
    needed, her lover meanwhile
Explored with hands and eyes the moulded smoothness through the open
  clothing, reviving his spent desire
Until they were joined in longer-lasting delight; her nerve-cells intermitted
  their human dream;

The happy automatism of life, inhuman as the sucking heart of the
    whirlwind, usurped the whole person,
Aping pain, crying out and writing like torture.

                                    They rose and went
    down to the horses;
The light had changed in the sea-cloud, the sun must be near setting.
    When they were half way down the mountain
The whole cloud began to glow with color like a huge rose, a forest of
    transparent pale-crimson petals
Blowing all about them; slowly the glory
Flared up the slope and faded in the high air.

IV

                                    They rode through pale
    twilight
And whispered at the farmhouse door inarticulate leave-takings.
Helen went in; Armstrong unsaddled the horses
And walked heavily up canyon and crossed the hill.

Helen said, "Reave went after a wounded deer
And sent me home. He hasn't come home yet?"
Reave's mother said "We've not seen him," steadily watching her
Across the lamplight with eyes like an old hawk's,
Red-brown and indomitable, and tired. But if she was hawklike
As Helen fancied, it was not in the snatching look
But the alienation and tamelessness and sullied splendor
Of a crippled hawk in a cage. She was worn at fifty
To thin old age; the attritions of time and toil and arthritis
That wear old women to likeness had whetted this one

To difference, as if they had bitten on a bronze hawk
Under the eroded flesh.

                    Helen avoided her eyes
And said to the other in the room, "Ah, Mark, you guessed right.
I'm tired to death, must creep up to bed now." The old woman:
"So you came home alone? That young Armstrong
Stayed with Reave." Helen faltered an instant and said,
"No, for Reave sent him with me, wishing his horse
To be taken home. Mr. Armstrong stopped
By the corral, he was unsaddling the horses I think,
But I was too tired to help him. My rifle, Mark,
Is clean: I minded your words."

                         An hour later the heavy tread of a man
    was heard on the steps
And the fall of a fleshy bulk by the door, crossed by the click of hooves or
    antlers, and Reave came in,
His shirt blood-stained on the breast and shoulders. "I got him," he said.
    "It seemed for awhile I'd be out all night.
By luck I found him, at twilight in a buck-eye bush. Where's Helen, gone
    to bed?" "She seemed flurried with thoughts,"
His mother answered, and going to the door that led to the kitchen she
    called, "Olvidia:
Bring in the supper." "Well yes," Reave said. "I must first hang up the
    carcass and wash my hands." "Olvidia,"
His mother called to the kitchen, "will you tell Johnny: is Johnny there?
    Tell him to fetch the meat
From the door-step and hang it up with the other." Mark said, "How far,
    Reave, did you carry it?" "Two miles or so.

Rough country at first; I held it in front of me to butt the brush with."
  "Why, what does it weigh?" "Oh," he said, "a young buck.
About Helen's weight." "You are strong," his mother said, "that's good; but
  a fool." "Well, mother, I might have hung it
In a tree and gone up with a horse to-morrow; I shouldered it to save
  time."

          Mark, enviously:
"You've seen many green canyons and the clouds on a hundred hills.
My mind has better mountains than these in it,
And bloodless ones." The dark Spanish-Indian woman
Olvidia took Reave's empty plate and the dish,
And Mrs. Thurso said, "Reave, you've big arms,
And ribs like a rain-barrel, what do they amount to
If the mind inside is a baby? Our white-face bull's
Bigger and wiser." "What have I done?" "I'll never say
Your young Helen's worth keeping, but while you have her
Don't turn her out to pasture on the mountain
With the yellow-haired young man. Those heavy blue eyes
Came home all enriched." Reave laughed and Mark said bitterly, "Mother,
  that's mean.
You know her too well for that. Helen is as clear as the crystal sky, don't
  breathe on her." "You," she answered fondly.
Reave smiled, "I trust Rick Armstrong as I do my own hand." "It shames
  my time of life,"
She answered, "to have milky-new sons. What has he done for you
To be your angel?" "Why," he said, "I like him." "That's generous,
And rare in you. How old is he?" "My age. Twenty-four."
"Oh, that's a better reason to trust him." "Hm?" "You're the same age."
"That's no reason." "No," she answered.

V

Toward noon the next day
Helen was ironing linen by the kitchen stove,
A gunshot was heard quite near the house, she dropped the iron
And ran out-doors and met Mark. "What was that shot?" "Don't go up
   there, Helen." "Why not why not," she stammered,
"Why not," the flush of the stove-heat graying on her cheek. "Reave has
   put poor old Bones out of pain." "Oh, that!"
Laughing and trembling, "your funeral face. I thought something had
   happened to someone. Let the old dog sleep."
She went up hill to the screen of seawind-stunted laurel and oak, where
   Reave was already spading
Dust into the gape of a small grave. "You've done for poor old Bones, have
   you? You knew I loved him,
So you took him off." "A pity you came just now, Helen. He died in a
   moment. If we'd used this mercy
Two or three months ago we'd have saved pain." She answered quivering
   with anger, "You do it on the sly
And call it mercy. Ah, killing's your pleasure, your secret vice." "I'll wish
   you sunnier pleasures: and a little
Sense in your head: he was made of miseries: you've seen him plead
To be helped, and wonder at us when the pain stayed.
I've helped him now." "Will you do as much for yourself
When life dirties and darkens? Your father did."
"No, I will not," he said, shovelling the dust.
"What's that said for? For spite?" "No, Reave.
I was wondering. For I think it's reasonable.
When the flower and fruit are gone, nothing but sour rind,
Why suck the shell? I think your father was right."
"Drop a little silence on him," Reave answered.
"We may help out the beasts, but a man mustn't be beaten.

That was a little too easy, to pop himself off because he went broke.
I was ten years old, I tried not to despise the soft stuff
That ran away to the dark from a touch of trouble:
Because the lime-kilns failed and the lumber-mill
Ran out of redwood.
My mother took up his ruins and made a farm;
She wouldn't run away, to death or charity. Mark and I helped.
We lost most of the land but we saved enough."
"Think of one man owning so many canyons:
Sovranes, Granite," she counted on her fingers, "Garapatas, Palo Colorado,
Rocky Creek, and this Mill Creek." "Oh, that was nothing, the land was worth nothing
In those days, only for lime and redwood." She answered,
"You needn't despise him, Reave. *My* dad never owned anything.
While I worked in a laundry and while I crated fruit
He ate my wages and lived as long as he could
And died crying." "We're proud of our fathers, hm?
Well, he was sick a long time," Reave said, patting
The back of the spade on the filled grave; "but courage might live
While the lungs rot. I think it might. You never
Saw him again, did you?" "How saw him?" "We used to see mine
Often in the evenings." "What do you mean, Reave?" "Why: in the evenings.
Coming back to stare at his unfinished things.
Mother still often sees him." Helen's face brightening
With happy interest, "Oh where?" she said. "On the paths;
Looking up at that thing, with his mouth open."
Reave waved his hand toward the great brown iron skip
Hanging on its cable in the canyon sky,
That used to carry the lime from the hill, but now
Stuck on dead pulleys in the sky. "It ought to be taken down
Before it falls. I'll do it when we've done the plowing."

Helen said, "Does he ever speak?" "Too ashamed of himself. I spoke to
    him once:
I was carrying firewood into the house, my arms were full. He worked a
    smile on his face and pointed
At the trolley up there." "Do you really believe," she said, "that your
    father's ghost?" "Certainly not. Some stain
Stagnates here in the hollow canyon air, or sticks in our minds. How could
    too weak to live
Show after it died?" "I knew," she answered, blanching again with
    capricious anger, "you'd no mercy in you,
But only sudden judgment for any weak thing;
And neither loving nor passionate; dull, cold and scornful. I used to keep a
    gay heart in my worst days
And laugh a little: how can I live
Where nothing except poor Mark is even half human, you like a stone,
    hard and joyless, dark inside,
And your mother like an old hawk, and even dirty Olvidia and Johnny
    Luna, dark and hollow
As the hearts of jugs. The dog here in the ground—Oh but how carefully
    you scrape the blood-lake—
Had loving brown eyes: so you killed him: he was sometimes joyful: it
    wouldn't do. You killed him for that." He answered,
Staring, "Were you born a fool? What's the matter, Helen?" "If I had to
    stay here
I'd turn stone too: cold and dark: I'd give a dollar
For a mirror now, and show you that square face of yours
Taken to pieces with amazement: you never guessed
Helen's a shrew. Oh, what do you want her for?
Let her go." She left him; and when he came in at noon
Spoke meekly, she seemed to have wept.

VI

                                        In the evening, in Helen's

   presence,
Reave's mother said, "Did that sand-haired young man
Find you, Reave, when he came this afternoon?
He didn't come to the house." "Who?" "That road-worker,
Arnfield." "Rick Armstrong?" "Most likely: the one I warned you
Not to pasture your heifer with." "He was here?" "No,
Not here. I saw him come down the hill, and Helen
Went out to meet him." Mark Thurso looked up
From the book he'd been reading, and watched his mother
As a pigeon on a rock watches a falcon quartering
The field beyond the next fence; but Helen suddenly:
"Now listen, Mark. I'm to be framed, ah?
I think so. I never liked her." The old woman said,
"Did you say something?" "Not yet," she answered. Reave made a mocking
Noise in his throat and said, "Let them alone.
No peace between women.
This morning I sent Luna over the hill
With one of the bucks we killed, no doubt my friend came over
At quitting-time to say thank you: why he didn't find me's
Less clear, but watch the women build it between them
To a big darkness." "Not I," Helen said,
And dipped her needle two or three careful stitches
In the cloth she was mending, then looked up suddenly
To see who watched her. "If I'd seen him," she said, "I'd have spoken to
   him.
I am not sick with jealousy of your new friend. But he was probably not
   here; the old eyes that make
A dead man's phantom can imagine a live one's." The old woman: "When
   you saw him you ran to meet him; I sent Olvidia

To see if the speckled hen had stolen a nest in the willows. She walked
  down there, what she saw amazed her.
I've not allowed her to tell me though she bubbles with it. Your business,
  Reave: ask her. Not mine: I'm only
The slow man's mother." Helen stood up, trembling a little and smiling,
  she held the needle and the spool
And folded the cloth, saying "Your mother, Reave,
Loves you well: too well: you and I honor her for that. She has hated me
  from the day she heard of me,
But that was jealousy, the shadow that shows love's real: nothing to resent.
  But now you seem very friendly
With that young man too: she can't bear to yield you again, it cracks the
  string of her mind. No one can fancy
What she's plotted with the kitchen-woman . . ." Mark Thurso said with
  lips that suddenly whitened: "*I* met
Armstrong. I told him you'd ridden up the high pasture, for so I believed.
  He asked me to thank you warmly
For the buck you sent: I forgot to tell you. I was with him while he was
  here, and when he went back I hobbled
Some ways up hill." The old woman moved her lips but said nothing; but
  Reave: "Here: what's the matter,
Brother? You were with me constantly all afternoon." "But an hour," Mark
  said. "Hm? Five minutes." Then Helen,
Looking from the one to the other: "If I am hated, I think I am loved too.
  I'd something to say . . .
Oh: yes: will you promise, Reave, promise Olvidia
You'll give her, for telling the perfect truth, whatever your mother has
  promised her for telling lies: then I'm safe.
Call her and ask her." He answered, "She'll sleep in hell first. Here's
  enough stories
Without hers in the egg-basket. Do you think it was Armstrong you saw,
  mother? I trust Rick Armstrong

From the bright point to the handle." Helen said, "Ah, Mark,
You'd never imagine I'd be satisfied with that.
I have to be satisfied with that." "Why not?" Reave said.
And she: "If it was nothing worse than killing to fear
I'd confess. All kinds of lies. I fear you so much
I'd confess . . . all kinds of lies . . . to get it over with,"
She said, making a clicking noise in her throat
Like one who has drunk too much and hiccoughs, "only
To get it over with: only, I haven't done anything.
This terror, Mark, has no reason,
Reave never struck nor threatened me, yet well I know
That while I've lived here I've always been sick with fear
As that woman is with jealousy. Deep in me, a black lake
His eyes drill to, it spurts. Sometime he'll drill to my heart
And that's the nut of courage hidden in the lake.
Then we'll see. I don't mean anything bad, you know: I'm very innocent,
And wish to think high, like Mark. Olvidia of course is a hollow liar. May I
   go now? I'm trembling-tired:
If you'll allow me to go up to bed? But indeed I dare not
While you sit judging." She looked at Mark and slightly
Reached both her hands toward him, smiled and went out.
But in the little dark hallway under the stair,
When she hastened through it in the sudden darkness,
The door being neither open nor shut passed edgewise
Between her two groping hands, her cheek and brow
Struck hard on the edge.

           Her moan was heard in the room of lamplight;
Where they had been sitting silent while she went out,
And when she had gone Mark Thurso had said, "Mother:
You've done an infamous thing." "They might play Jack and queen
All they please," she answered, "but not my son

For the fool card in the deck," the shock of struck wood was heard,
And Helen's hushed groan: Mark, dragging his lameness, reeled
Swiftly across the room saying "What has she done?"
He groped in the passage and spoke tenderly, then Reave
Went and brought Helen to the lamplight; a little blood
Ran through her left eye to her lips from the cut eye-brow.
The implacable old woman said "She's not hurt.
Will you make a fuss?" Helen said, "The wood of your house
Is like your mother, Reave, hits in the dark.
This will wash off." She went to the kitchen and met
Olvidia who'd been listening against the door,
Then Helen, moaning "I'm ringed with my enemies," turned
To flee, and turned back. "I will take it now. My husband, Olvidia,
Is ready to kill me, you see. I have been kind to you
Two or three times. Have you seen any unusual
Or wicked meeting to-day?" The Indian woman,
Dreading Reave's anger and seeing the blood, but hardly
Understanding the words, blanked her dark face
And wagged her head. "Don't know. What you mean, wicked?
I better keep out of this." "A dish of water, Olvidia.
Be near me, Mark. Reave: will you ask her now?"
He said "Wash and be quiet." Helen said, "Oh Olvidia,
Someone has made him angry at you and me.
Look in my eyes. Tell no bad stories . . . lies, that is . . .
Did you see anything when you looked for eggs
In the willows along the creek?" Olvidia folded
Her lips together and stepped backward, then Helen
Sighed, dabbling her cheek with water. "It hurts. I think
It will turn black." Reave suddenly shouted "Answer."
Olvidia, retreating farther: "What you want of me?
I find no eggs." Mark said, "Come, Helen, Oh come. I've watched
    innocence tormented

And can no more. Go up and sleep if you can, I'll speak for you, to-morrow all this black cloud of wrong
    Will be melted quite away in the morning." Reave said, "Don't fawn on her, you make me mad. Women will do it.
But why praise 'em for it?" Helen, meekly: "I am very tired and helpless and driven to the edge. Think kindly of me,
Mark, I believe I shall be much hated. Your mother . . .
This is all. Light me a candle." At the foot of the stair
She closed the door, and silently tiptoed through
The passage and the other room to the door of the house,
There pinched the wick, and praying for no wind
To make a stir in the house, carefully opened
The outer door and latched it behind her.

                                        She traversed the hill,
And at the road-men's camp, plucking at the fly
Of a lit tent, thought momently it was curious
She stood among so many unrestrained men
Without fear, yet feared Reave. "I must see Rick Armstrong
This moment: which tent?" They laid their hands of cards
Carefully face down on the packing-box.
"Why, ma'am, I can't say exactly," but she had run off
To another lamp of shining canvas and found him.
"Let me stand into the light." She showed her cut brow
A little bleeding again with hurry in the dark,
And the purpling bruise. "What Reave did. Your friend Reave.
His mother spied and told on us. What will you do?"
"By God!" "Oh," she said, "that's no good.
How could you keep me *here*? Borrow a car,
There are cars here." He said "I'll take care of you." She shuddered,
Beating her fists together, breathed long and said:
"If you choose to stand here and talk among the men listening

It is not my fault. I say if you and these men could stop him when he
    comes—
You can't—to-night, to-night, in an hour—nothing can stop him: he'd call
    the sheriff to-morrow and have me
Like a stolen cow, nothing but ridiculous, a mark for children to hoot at,
    crying in my hair, probably
Led on a rope. Don't you know him? *I* do. Oh my lover
Take me to the worst hut at the world's end and kill me there, but take me
    from here before Reave comes.
I'd go so gladly. And how could you bear to face him, he thought you his
    faithful friend, for shame even?
Oh hurry, hurry!"

VII

                    In the desert at the foot of sun-rotted hills
A row of wooden cabins flanks a gaunt building
Squatted on marbly terraces of its own excrement,
Digested rock from which the metal has been sucked,
Drying in the rage of the sun. Reave Thurso stopped
At the first cabin, a woman came out and pointed;
He went to the farthest cabin, knocked, and went in.
"Well, Helen. You found a real sunny place." Opening the door
She'd been a violet-eyed girl, a little slatternly
But rich with life; she stood back from the door
Sallow, with pinched nostrils and dwindled eyes,
As if she had lost a fountain of blood, and faintly
Whispering "I knew you." Reave looked about him like one
Attentively learning the place, and Helen said
"I never hoped that you wouldn't come at last,
It seemed a kind of blood-trail for you to follow.
And then I knew you were tardy and cold of course and at last

You'd come at last, you never give up anything,

How did you track us at last?" "Oh," he laughed, "time and I.

He's at work?" "Yes." "If you wanted to hide

You'd have got him to change his name." "I begged him to," she answered

Suddenly weeping, "so many times." "Don't cry, don't cry.

You know that I'll never hurt you. Mark loves you too, he's been very

    lonely. He wanted me to let you go,

But that was nonsense. He's been sick since you went away. Do you

    remember the rose-bush you made me buy

That time in Salinas? Mark's watered it for you, sick or well,

Every day, limping around the house with a pail of water spilling on his

    poor ankle-joint,

He'll be glad to see you again. Well, pack your things." She gathered

Her blanked face to some show of life. "Look around at this country. Oh

    Reave. Reave. Look. I let him

Take me here at last. And he hasn't been always perfectly kind: but since

    I've been living with him I love him . . .

My heart would break if I tried to tell you how much. I'm not ashamed.

    There was something in me that didn't

Know about love until I was living with him. I kissed him, when he went

    back to work this noon.

I didn't know you were coming; forgot you were coming sometime. See

    how it is. No: I understand:

You won't take me." He, astonished: "Not take you! After hunting you a

    whole year? You dream too much, Helen.

It makes you lovely in a way, but it clouds your mind. You must

    distinguish. All this misfortune of yours

Probably . . ." "Oh God," she said shuddering,

"Will you preach too? First listen to me: I tell you all the other joys I've

    ever known in my life

Were dust to this . . . misfortune; the desert sun out there is a crow's wing

    against the brightness of this . . .

Misfortune: Oh I didn't mean, dear,

To make you angry." She was suddenly kneeling to him and pressed her
 face

On his hard thigh: "I know I've been wicked, Reave.

You must leave me in the dirt for a bad woman: the women here

See the marks of it, look sidelings at me.

I'll still believe you used to love me a little,

But now of course

You wouldn't want for a wife . . . a handkerchief

You lost and another man picked me up and

Wiped his mouth. Oh there may have been many

Other men. In a year: you can't tell.

Your mother is strong and always rightly despised me.

She'd spit on me if she saw me now. So now

You'll simply cast me off; you're strong, like your mother,

And when you see that a thing's perfectly worthless

You can pick it out of your thoughts. Don't forgive me. I only

Pray you to hate me. Say 'She's no good. To hell with her,'

That's the mercy I pray you for." He said hastily, "Get up,

This is no theater. I intend to take you back, Helen,

I never was very angry at you, remembering

That a woman's more like a child, besides you were muddled

With imaginations and foolish reading. So we'll shut this bad year

In a box of silence and drown it out of our minds." She stood away from
 him toward the farther wall

With a sharp white face, like a knife-blade worn thin and hollow with too
 much whetting, and said, turning her face

Toward the window, "How do I know that he can compel me? He can
 torment us, but there's no law

To give me to him. You can't take me against my will. No: I won't go. Do
 you think you're God,

And we have to do what you want?" He said, "You'll go all right." She,
    laughing, "At last you've struck something
Stiffer than you. Reave, that stubborn will
Is not strength but disease, I've always known it, like the slow limey
    sickness
You hear about, that turns a man's flesh to bone,
The willing muscles and fibres little by little
Grow hard and helpless, at last you can't dent them, nothing will move,
He lands in a tent beside the circus, with a painting of him
Over the door and people pay ten cents
To see the petrified man: that's your stubbornness,
Your mind sets and can't change, you don't go on
Because you want to but because you have to, I pity you,
But here you're stopped." Suddenly she trembled and shrank little again. "*If
    you could take me*
I'd stab you in bed sleeping." "You know," he answered,
"You're talking foolishness. I have to see Armstrong before we go,
When he quits work, I guess there's a couple of hours, but you'd best get
    ready." "Why must you see . . . Rick?"
Reave made no answer, Helen covertly watched him, slowly the metal
    temper failed from her face.
"I'll go," she said faintly, "and tell him." "You'll stay here." "Reave?
Reave. You said you weren't angry." "Not at you. If I'd anyone
To help me, I'd send you off first. Walked around like a man,
Was a male bitch . . ." "I led him, I called him, I did it.
It's all mine." "What?" "The blame, the blame, the blame,
I planned it, all mine, I did it, Reave." A white speck glittered
At the commissure of his lips, he licked his lips
As if he were thirsty and said difficultly, "I've had a
Year to think about it: have to have relief, you're
Let off, keep still." She felt his eyes

Craftily avoiding hers, and something monstrous in him moulding the mass
of his body to a coarsened
More apelike form, that a moment appeared and then was cramped back to
human: her image-making mind beheld
Her lover go under the hammers of this coarse power, his face running
thick blood turn up at last
Like a drowning man's, before he went down the darkness, all his gay
bravery crushed made horrible submission:
With any warning or whatever weapons he'd be like a bird in a dog's
mouth, Reave had all the strength,
Would fight foul with all means and no mercy: "Oh, Oh, take me with you
If you want me, but now. Before he comes.
How could I look at him again if I'm going to leave him? You understand
That's too much to ask me, to stand between you
Like a cow between the brown bull and the white one.
In spite of all I'm not so . . . . shameless as . . .
You think." He made a questioning noise, "Hm?" and she thinking
He'd failed to hear: "I'll go and live with you
If you'll take me now. I can't face Rick, not wait for Rick,"
She said weaving and parting the fingers
Of her two supplicant hands. She essayed more words,
But only the lips and no voice made them, then again
Breath filled the words, "I've done, wickedly, I'm sorry.
I will obey you now." His eyes were hidden
While he considered, all at once he said joyfully
"Pack then." "Me, not my things: there's nothing." "Then come."
She followed him; suddenly in the doorway she dropped
And kissed the threshold.

        Thurso watched and said nothing;
She got up and walked at his side in the hot white dust by the row of small
cabins,

The wood of their doors and walls was worn to the look of sea-drift by the
    desert sand-scour. Suddenly Helen
Laughed like the bitter crying of a killdeer when someone walks near the
    nest, "My God, Reave, have you come for me
In the old wreck of a farm-truck, will it still run?" "What else? We haven't
    got rich, we haven't bought cars
While I've been away from home hunting you." "The pigs and I," she cried
    shrilly. Reave nodded, and went to the door
Of the last cabin, and said to the woman to whom he had spoken before:
    "I'm taking my wife home.
This woman's my wife. When Armstrong comes, tell that bastard
We're going west. He's got a car." Helen cried, "Oh cheat, cheat,
Will you tole him after you?" He said heavily "What do you mean?
Come on," and so holding her wrist that the bones ached
Drew her to the car. She had yielded and was subject to him,
She could imagine no recourse, her mind palsied
Like the wrist-clenched hand.

VIII

                           After twenty miles he turned
The carbureter-connection, slyly regarding
His seat-mate, she fogged with misery observed nothing.
The engine went lame. "What's the matter?" he said, turning
The carbureter-connection; the engine stalled.
He lifted the hood and made the motions of helplessness,
Looking up sometimes at Helen, who sat in the dust on the high seat on
    the folded blanket,
Her face in her hands. "We're stuck here," Thurso said. "Well, we have
    water." She dropped her hands from her face
And stared at the road ahead; then she began to see the desert about them,
    the unending incandescent

Plain of white dust, stippled with exact placing of small gray plants, each
    tuft a painfully measured
Far distance from every other and so apparently forever, all wavering under
    the rage of the sun,
A perfect arena for the man's cruelty; but now she was helpless.
Still Armstrong failed to come; Helen awoke again
From blind misery, and watched Reave's nerves
Growing brittle while the sun sailed west. He babbled childlike
About cattle and pastures, things unreal, unimaginable,
In the white anguish here; his hands quivered,
And the sun sank.

        In the night Helen revived
Enough to make action appear possible again.
She crept stealthily away in the starry darkness
Thinking Reave slept; when he spoke she tried to run,
Her thighs and calves were like hollow water, he followed
And brought her back through the vast unnatural pallor of the night,
Rough-handed, but only saying "You're too restless." She writhed her
    hands together like bitter flames and lay down
On the spread blanket. After while she lay face upward. Those
    foam-bubbles on the stale water of night
Were floating stars, what did it matter, which of two men? Yesterday the
    one had been lovely and the other
Came in like ugly death, but difference had died. Rick Armstrong must
    have made some ridiculous plan
For heading them off or else he'd have come. Perhaps he thought she went
    willingly. Why not? "I go with you willingly,"
She said aloud, "dear, do you hear me? I've shot my load of feeling, there's
    nothing left in the world
Worth thinking twice. We'll crawl home to our hole."

He answered, "I can't believe he's a coward: he'll come in the morning." "I
dread death
More than your mother's eyes," she answered. "I'm the coward or I'd kill
myself. Dear, I fear death
More than I hate this dishwater broth of life. A bowlful a day, Oh God!
Do the stars look
Like lonely and pretty sparkles when you look up?
They look to me like bubbles of grease on cold
Dishwater." He said, "Sleep, you'll feel better." He heard her sighing
And twisting her body on the sand while the night waned.
He got up and stood beside her and said anxiously,
"I was to blame too, Helen. Part of the blame
Is mine, Helen. I didn't show enough love,
Nor do often enough
What women want. Maybe it made your life
Seem empty. It seems . . . it seems to me it wouldn't be decent
To do it just now: but I'll remember and be
Better when we get home." She said, "Oh God! Fool, fool,
A spoonful a night. Your mother was lying to you.
She knows better."

                    In the morning
Thurso waited two hours from sunrise;
They had nothing to eat; Helen endured her headache, and the shameless
sun
Blared from the east. Reave greased the joints of the truck.
When one of those long gray desert lizards that run
With heads raised high, scudded through the white sand,
He flung the wrench suddenly and broke its back
And said "He won't come then. My God, Helen,
Was he tired of you? He won't come." She watched her husband
Pick up the wrench and batter that broken life,

Still lifting up its head at him, into the sand. He saw the yellow
Grains of fat in the red flesh and said,
"Come here, Helen. Yellow you see, yellow you see.
Your friend makes us all vile." She understood
That "yellow" meant cowardly, and that this was Armstrong
Battered to a cake of blood.

IX

They drove west
Through the white land; the heat and the light increased,
At length around a ridge of ancient black lava
Appeared a place of dust where food could be bought, but Helen
Would eat nothing. In the evening they came
Among fantastic Joshua-trees to a neat
Framed square of cabins at the foot of a mountain
Like a skeleton; seeing Helen so white and sick,
And the motor misfiring, Reave chose to lodge at this camp.
He'd tinker the engine while there was daylight. He found the timer
Choked up with drift of the desert; having washed it with gasoline and
    heard the cylinders
Roar cheerfully again, he returned to Helen.

She was not in the cabin,
But sat with chance companions on a painted bench under the boughs of
    one of those reptilian trees
Near the camp entrance; no longer white and morose, her face was flushed,
    her eyes sparkling with darkness
In the purple evening that washed the mountain. Before he came she was
    saying, "My husband just doesn't care
What anyone thinks: he said, all right, if I wanted to see the desert, but he
    wouldn't take either one

Of our new cars to be spoiled, he'd drive the old farm-truck . . ." Seeing
    Reave approaching, greased black to the elbows, "Oh, Oh,
What's he been doing? Oh: it's black, I think? Dear, I felt better
When the sun went down." He, staring at her companions: "That's good."
    "They call it desert fever," she stammered,
"The heat's the cause." She stood up, giggling and swaying. "Was nearly
    exhausted, they gave me a little medicine.
Nice people." "What did you give her?" "She begged for a table-spoonful,"
    the old woman answered, "Texas corn-whiskey.
Are you going west?" Helen said gravely, "A spoonful a night: Oh God!"
    "She's eaten nothing," Reave said,
"Since yesterday. Come and lie down, Helen." She obeyed, walking
    unsteadily beside him, with terrified eyes.
"Dear, please don't touch me, your hands are terrible," she said. "They
    think you killed him."
He made her lie down on the bed while he washed himself.
She wept and said, "I always make friends easily.
I used to be full of joy. Now my wishes
Or your own soul will destroy you when you get home.
I'd give my life to save you." He groaned angrily,
But she was unable to be silent and said:
"I think you're even worse hurt than I am. Were you ever on a ship?
This place is like a ship, everything smells
In spite of neatness, and I am desert-sick.
Oh Reave I never dreamed that you'd be deep-wounded.
Forgive me dear." He violently: "Lick your own sores.
The man was my friend and that degrades me: but you've
Slept with him. You couldn't help but have learned him
In a year's familiar life and I've been thinking
That whores you, because no woman can love a coward,
And still you stayed . . ." "For his money, for his money you know,"
She answered through chattering teeth, "and the fine house

You found me in among the rich gardens, the jewels and furs,

Necklaces of pearls like round zeroes, all these hangings of gold

That make me heavy . . ." "Ah," he said, "be quiet." He went out, and
    returning after a time with a tray of food

Lighted the lamp and cut meat in small bites and forced her to eat. "Dear,"
    she mourned, "I can't swallow

Though I chew and chew. The rocking of the ship and the hot smell close
    up my throat. Oh be patient with me.

When we land I'll feel better," her deep-colored eyes moving in sickly
    rhythm to the roll of the ship,

He said "You're in the desert: an auto-camp by the road. Wake up and
    eat." She sat up on the bed

And looked anxiously about the bleak lamplight, then took the tray

And obeyed his will. "I thought you were my dad.

Once we travelled on a boat from the south

To San Francisco. I expect I saw from the deck the Mill Creek mountains
    and never

Guessed," she said shuddering. While she ate she began to fear

That people who were going to die dreamed of a ship

The night before. The truck would be overturned

And crush her body in the sand like that lizard's,

A tire would have burst.

                    Against the black horror of death

All living miseries looked sweet; in a moment of aimless

Wild anguish she was unable not to cry out, and said:

"Ah Ah what have you done, tearing me from him? I love him you know.

Maybe he's cowardly or maybe he's only tired of me, but if he's yellow to
    the bones, if he's yellower than gold,

I love him you know.

If I were crushed in the sand like that lizard you killed, to a cake of
    blood—why not? for I think you'll

Do it sometime — the sun would dry me and my dust would blow to his
  feet: if I were dead in the desert
And he drowned in the middle ocean toward Asia, yet something and
  something from us would climb like white
Fires up the sky and twine high shining wings in the hollow sky: while you
  in your grave lie stuck
Like a stone in a ditch." He, frowning: "Have you finished?" He took the
  tray and said, "Have you had enough?"
"Never enough. Dear, give me back to him. I can't think yet
That you understand," she said slyly and trembling.
"Don't you care, that he and I have made love together
In the mountains and in the city and in the desert,
And once at a Navajo shepherd's camp in the desert in a storm of lightnings
Playing through the cracks of the shed: can you wink and swallow
All that?" "I can't help it. You've played the beast.
But you are my goods and you'll be guarded, your filthy time
Has closed. Now keep still."

                              She was silent and restless for a good while.
He said, "You'll be sleeping soon, and you need sleep.
I'll go outside while you get ready for bed."
"Let me speak, just a little," she said humbly.
"Please, Reave, won't you leave me here in the morning, I'll manage
  somehow.
You're too strong for us, but dear, be merciful.
I think you don't greatly want me: what you love really
Is something to track down: your mountains are full of deer:
Oh, hunt some bleeding doe. I truly love you.
I always thought of you as a dear, dear friend
When even we were hiding from you." He was astonished
To see her undress while she was speaking to him,
She seemed to regard him as a mere object, a keeper,

But nothing human. "And Rick Armstrong," she said,
"I can't be sure that I love him; dear, I don't know
That I'll go back to him; but I must have freedom, I must have freedom
If only to die in, it comes too late . . ."
She turned her back and slipped off the under-garment
And glided into the bed. She was beautiful still,
The smooth fluted back and lovely long tapering legs not changed,
Nor the supple motions; nor that recklessness
Of what Thurso called modesty was any change;
She never tried to conceal her body from him
Since they were married, but always thoughtless and natural;
And nestled her head in the pillow when she lay down
With little nods, the tender way he remembered:
So that a wave of compassionate love
Dissolved his heart: he thought, "Dearest, I've done
Brutally: I'll not keep you against your will.
But you must promise to write to me for help
When you leave that cur." He made the words in his mind
And began to say: "Dearest . . ." but nothing further
Had meaning in it, mere jargon of mutterings, the mouth's refusal
Of the mind's surrender; and his mind flung up a memory
Of that poor dead man his father, with the sad beaten face
When the lime-kilns failed: that man yielded and was beaten,
A man mustn't be beaten. But Helen hearing
The "dearest," and the changed voice, wishfully
Lifted her head, and the great violet eyes
Sucked at Reave's face. "No," he said. He blew out the lamp,
Resolved to make this night a new marriage-night
And undo their separation. She bitterly submitted;
"I can bear this: it doesn't matter: I'll never tell him.
I feel the ship sailing to a bad place. Reave, I'm so tired
That I shall die. If my wrist were broken

You wouldn't take my hand and arm in your hands
And wriggle the bones for pleasure? You're doing that
With a worse wound." Her mind had many layers;
The vocal one was busy with anguish, and others
Finding a satisfaction in martyrdom
Enjoyed its outcry; the mass of her mind
Remained apparently quite neutral, under a familiar
Embrace without sting, without savor, without significance,
Except that this breast was hairier.

X

They drove through the two deserts
and arrived home. Helen went in
With whetted nerves for the war with Reave's mother, resolving
Not to be humble at least; but instead of the sharp old woman a little
creature
With yellow hair and pleated excess of clothing stood up in the room; and
blushed and whitened, anxiously
Gazing, clasping thin hands together. Reave said, "It's Hester Clark." And
to Hester Clark: "Tell Olvidia
To count two more for supper; my wife and I have come home." She
answered, "Oh yes," fleeing. Then Helen:
"What's this little thing? Why does it wear my dress?" "She's only hemmed
it over," he said, "at the edges.
Have it again if you want, I had to find something for her." His mother was
heard on the stair, and entering
Looked hard at Helen and went and kissed Reave. Who said, "I shall stay
at home now, mother: Helen's come home."
"Yes. How do you do." Her red-brown eyes brushed Helen's body from the
neck to the ankles, "I'll have them heat

Bathwater." Helen trembled and said, "How kind. There are showers in all
    the camps: if you mean anything else:
Reave seems content." "Very well. He's easily of course contented. He
    picks up things by the road: one of them
I've allowed to live here: to speak honestly
In hope to keep his mind off another woman: but that cramps and can't
    change." "If I knew what I want!"
Helen cried suddenly. "The girl is a servant here," Reave said. "I hate the
    spitefulness of women. The housework
Needed help when you were not here." Then Helen: "She's quite sick I
    think: she'll have to clear out I think.
Yet something in me felt kindly toward that little wax face
On my old clothes. I came home against my will. Why isn't Mark here?"
    The far door opened for Olvidia,
Unable to imagine any pretext for entrance, but unable to bridle her need
Of coming, to stare and smile from flat black eyes. Behind her
Johnny Luna was seen peering, but dared not enter.
Then Helen wondered, where was that thin little thing?
Crying somewhere? And Reave's mother said: "Now you'll cut down
The old cable, as you promised, Reave. We're tired of seeing it.
You'll have time now." He answered, "Where's Mark, mother?
Helen just asked you." "I heard her." "I heard her.
Sitting under a bush on the hill, probably. Your wife's, adventures,
Stick in his throat." Then Helen, trembling, and the words marred
By sudden twitchings of her lips: "I'm not ashamed. No reason to be. I
    tried to take myself out of here
And am brought back by threats and by force, to a gray place like a jail,
    where the sea-fog blows up and down
From the hill to the rock, around a house where no one ever loved or was
    glad. But your spite's nothing,
Pour it out, I'll swim in it: and fear Reave but not you, and maybe after
    while . . . That's all. Reave, I'll go up

And change my dress before supper, if your . . . if little wax-face you know
   . . . has left me any
Clothes in the closet."

                              She went up-stairs; the others were silent,
Until the old woman: "Ah why, why," she said, "Reave,
Did you have to bring back. . . . I know. You had to. Your mind
Sticks in its own iron: when you've said 'I will'
Then you're insane, the cold madness begins.
It's better than weakness."
He answered with shamefast look shunning her eyes, "I must tell you,
   mother,
Though it may seem strange: I love her, you know. Some accident,
Or my neglect, changed her; I'll change her over
And bring the gold back." "You talk like poor Mark. Oh, worse.
Mark at least feels disgust. A woman that can't it seems
Even have babies . . . About the old cable:
He's been seeing lately . . . your father: the man who's dead . . .
Pitifully staring up at it in the evenings.
He broods on that. The shock of your disgrace I believe
Started his mind swarming, and he hobbles out
In the starlight. I wish you to keep your promise
And cut that ruin from our sky. It's bad for Mark
To remember his father; and I've a feeling
The memory slacks us all, something unlucky will clear
When that cord's cut. Don't you hate seeing it?" "Oh, yes,
Like anything else that's no use. It'd fall by itself
Some winter. I'll cut it down. There are trees under it
That have to be saved. Mother, I won't ask you
To make friends with my wife: you're not to fuss either.
And don't prod her with Hester. We'll have some peace in the house,
Or I'll growl too."

XI

Mark's lameness appeared more painful than formerly;
Helen from the window seeing him
Limping across the dooryard, she went and followed. He stood by the
sycamore, under great yellowing leaves,
And Helen: "You hardly spoke to me last night, though a year had passed.
Have I lost your love, my brother? I valued it.
I need it more than in happier times." "That . . ." he answered,
"Oh Helen!" "Because I could hardly think how to live here," she said,
"without it." "I have no color of words
To say how dearly . . . when I seem dark: you must think of me as a
foolish day-dreamer
Whose indulgence turns and clouds him, so that he sees a dead man
Walk on the deck and feels the ship sailing
Through darkness to a bad place." She, astonished with memory:
"The ship, the ship?" "You see. My foolish dreams
Twine into my common talk. Maybe it's my hearing at night
The watery noises and hoarse whisper of the shore that sets me
Into that dream, I feel the see-sawing keel, my mind tries darkly ahead
under the stars
What destiny we're driving toward . . . Do you think, Helen, a dead man's
Soul can flit back to his scene long afterwards?" "Your father you mean?
But I was lying in the scrawny desert
A thousand miles from any noise of the shore. It scared me because I seem
to remember hearing
That to dream of a ship means death . . ." "If that's all," he smiled
meagrely:
"If we both dream it. I, for one, shan't trouble
My survivors with any starlight returns, but stick to peace
Like a hungry tick." "Oh," she said eagerly, "hush.
It's wicked to talk like that." He was silent, then said,

"Did you love him, Helen?" She clenched her hands, and turning

Her head from him, "I thought you'd ask that. What's love?"

And laid her hand on the leaning pillar of the tree

To turn herself back to his face, to study no higher

Than the lean jaw and strained mouth, lower than the eyes,

And carefully said, "Of course I loved him; but I believe

My shining terror of Reave was the cause.

For now that desert stalk's cut, the old root of fear

Seems aching to a new flowering. Why do I fear him? I know for certain

He'll neither kill me nor beat me, I've proved it: and I even tricked him out

    of his vengeance, you know, he came home

With nothing but me. . . . Where did he get that Hester? No, tell me after

    while . . . Listen. I used to think

That the only good thing is a good time: I've got past that . . .

Into the dark. I need something, I can't know what it is." She thought in

    her heart: "I know.

To humble your strong man, that's what I need." And said: "To be free. He

    called me a harlot, Mark. I am a

Harlot of a rare nature. The flesh is only a symbol. Oh, can't you see me

Beaten back and forth between the two poles, between you and Reave?"

She watched, that his lips moved like a plucked string,

So that she thought "It can be done," and said,

"The one pole's power, that I tried to escape: that strong man, you know:

And have been . . . retrieved, and can't tell whether I hate him

Or what. The second, you can name better than I:

The power behind power, that *makes* what the other can only

Direct or destroy. See how wise I've grown. Dear: in the desert

I cried a good deal at night: it wasn't for Reave,

Nor for his mother! my eyelids rained in the dusty

Country where rain's not natural. I'd look up the night

And see the sharp dry stars like great bubbles

Blown up and swollen, full of most bitter rainbows,

Float on the wave of the world: it was for you
My tears ran down."

　　　　　　　　　　　She watched his mouth, in the thought
That if she stretched romance to laughter, or his doubting point,
She'd be warned by his lips: but Mark perhaps had not even heard her; he
　　　said, "I used to thank God
Whatever it is that's coming, Helen's not here. If even she's crying in the
　　　night somewhere: she's flown
Like a bird out of the hands of *our* catcher. Now you've come home! . . .
　　　Oh, at better times
I think my fears are only a flaw of the mind;
Or else that the dark ship driving to its drowning
Is only my own poor life: *that* might go down
Without a bubble." She angrily: "Reave at least
Is something solid to fear . . . You and your shadows!
I was going to make love to you, Mark,
All to spite Reave and because he bores me, but your nonsense
Has run mine out of breath. You've missed something.
Tell me about this . . . what's her name? Reave's wisp,
All eyes and hair." Mark failed to answer; she looked
And saw his face fixed and anxious. "What's the matter now?"
"Is that Reave?" he whispered. "Exactly. What's in Reave
To make you dome out your eyes like a caught fish?"
"He's staring up at the cable, Helen! The old man stands in
That same place and stares up at the cable
Every night." "Soon to miss his amusement, poor ghost.
Reave's planning to take it down. Be sure when Reave looks up
He has a purpose."

　　　　　　　　　　　He approached and said, "To-morrow morning
We'll cut it down. But the best trees in the canyon

Stand in the shadow of its fall.
I've planned a way to tie the cut end with rope
And steer it west in its fall, and I hope clear them.
They must take their chance." He looked at Mark and said, "We'll feel
   better
After the old advertisement of failure's down.
It's cobwebbed the canyon for twenty years." He looked at Helen:
"We'll start a new life to-morrow." She marvelled secretly
At the reasonless anger that ran through her dry nerves like a summer
   grass-fire, and shrilly, "You and I?" she answered,
"Or you and your . . . . little floosie, that whittled match?" He frowned,
   his temples darkened with the heavy muscle
Setting the jaw, he said in a moment: "I've given Hester notice to go. She's
   going to-morrow.
You're staying. So rest your mind." "Ah, Ah," she said, "be proud of
   strength while you can. Cut the cable
And forget your father. Whatever fails, cut it down. Whatever gets old or
   weakens. Send Hester packing
Because a bigger woman's brought home. If a dog or a horse have been
   faithful, kill them on the shore of age
Before they slacken. See to keep everything around you as strong and
   stupid
As Reave Thurso." And turning suddenly:
"Oh, Mark, tell me what's good, I don't know which way to turn. Is there
   anything good? Whisper, whisper.
That mould of hard beef and bone never asks,
He never wonders, took it ready-made when he was a baby, never changes,
   can't change. You and I
Have to wonder at the world and stand between choices. That's why we're
   weak and ruled. If we could ever
Find out what's good, we'd do it. He'd be surprised.
What a rebellion!" She changed and said, "Reave?

Let that girl stay a week; you might need her yet.
In any case I'd like to know her a little.
She keeps out of my way, I haven't had time.
A week or two." He, staring: "That's a sickly thing
For a man's wife to want. No. She's going
At the set time. If you can't tell what's good:
It's lucky I have a compass and can steer the ship."
"Oh, Oh. That ship again?" she cried laughing,
"Maybe there's something in it, if even Reave . . .
Can you feel it straining through the dark night? Mark: you heard him:
He's a dreamer too. You'd never imagine it,
To see him stand there so fleshy, shaking his head
Like a bull in fly-time: if he dreams he'll fall yet. We'll try."
She turned and went toward the house.

                              Reave said, "What was all that?
There was a time when I'd have stared at myself
For bringing home . . . and letting it talk and talk
As if it had rights in the world. It's her colored abounding life
That makes her lovely." "She's tied to you," Mark answered,
"Like a falcon tied up short to a stone, a fierce one
Fluttering and striking in ten inches of air. I believe deeply
You're precious to each other." "Hm. I bear clawing
As well as anyone." Mark, earnestly: "Oh be good to her,
Not to let her be hurt in the coming time."
"No more of that, Mark. You know these forebodings
Date from our time in France and the muddy splinter
That wrecked your ankle. You must make allowances." He answered,
   "You'd think
This rocked-in gorge would be the last place in the world to bear the
   brunt: but it's not so: they told me
This is the prow and plunging cutwater,

This rock shore here, bound to strike first, and the world behind will watch
    us endure prophetical things
And learn its fate from our ends." "Booh. We'll end well," he answered,
    laughing, "the world won't watch.
When you and I toast long white beards and old freckled hands, and Helen
Like a little shrivelled apple by the fire between us
Still faintly glows, in the late evenings of life,
We'll have the fun that old people know, guessing
Which of us three will die first. I dare say the world
Will be quite changed then." "You're very hopeful. But even you
I think feel the steep time build like a wave, towering to break,
Higher and higher; and they've trimmed the ship top-heavy.
. . . Do you take it down to-morrow?" "Ah? The cable you mean?
I told you: in the morning. You must all come and watch.
The fall will be grand. Those things have weight."

XII

                              Helen had gone
As if she carried news in her mind through the house to the kitchen; there
    dark Olvidia
Stood big and ominous in a steam of beef boiling. "Where's your helper,
    Olvidia, the little mop
That pares potatoes?" She answered sadly, "Is cabbage too." "I say where's
    the elf-child,
The inch with the yellow hair? Ought to be helping you."
"Oh, that? She going away." "To-morrow, maybe.
Where is she now?" The Indian rolled her dun eyes
Toward the open door of the laundry, and Helen passing
Looked all about among piled tubs and behind
An old desk of Reave's father's; the girl she sought
Stood up in a corner. "What enormous eyes you have.

Why were you hiding?" Helen said. "Oh no. I'd done my work,"
She answered plaintively, "I was just thinking here.
I have to go away to-morrow." "Wearing my dress," Helen said.
"Did you come here without any clothes at all?" "He . . . Mr. Thurso . . .
    mine were worn out,
He burned them up." "A handkerchief would cover you, though.
I don't believe you weigh ninety pounds
Without the weight of my clothes. Oh, you're welcome.
I think I'll take the prettiest one in the closet
And cut it to fit you like finch's feathers.
Is your name Hester? How can you bear Reave's weight,
Your body's the width of my arm?" The girl trembled
And twisted herself sidewise. "Aren't you angry at me?"
"Oh no," Helen said; and anxiously: "I don't know. I'm lost.
Oh why should I be angry, nothing is worth . . .
Nothing, I believe.
Do you want to stay here? Don't you hate Reave? *I* do.
Madly." The other with a begging whine: "I'd work.
You are so kind." And whispered, "I might do all
The old Spanish woman's work, you could let her go."
Then Helen suddenly, her lips withering
From the white teeth: "Olvidia, come here. This scrap
Wants us to fire you: she wants to be with my husband:
Take both our places, how's that for treachery? Because she's nothing
    earthly but a stack of hair and enormous
Gray eyes, thinks I'll stand anything. . . . Wives hate your trade, don't you
    know that?" "I . . . didn't understand. I thought you
Meant me to stay. I never felt safe before, but here I had my own room and
    was warm enough,
And Mr. Thurso was never drunk." "Oh, that was something.
Where did you come from?" She looked at Olvidia's dark expressionless
    face, and sidling a little nearer

To Helen for shelter: "Hymettus, Nebraska: I lived with my aunt
    Margaret, she was always punishing me
Because my uncle wouldn't let me alone. She was big and thin.
I ran away with a boy but he soon left me.
I tried to get rides west, people would keep me awhile
And turn me out. I think I was going to die
When Mr. Thurso saw me beside the road."
"And loaded you into the farm-truck, ah?
Go on." "He gave me some bread and got some coffee
At the next place. I've been happy here. Oh,
What will become of me now?" "I can't guess," Helen said. "My husband
Can't change his mind: so you'll have to go, whatever you and I want. It
    jams in the slot; nothing
Will budge it after that, not with a crow-bar. What will he be at fifty, ah?
    How old are you, Hester?"
"Eighteen . . . nineteen." "I expect it's true: that stack of hair, Olvidia,
    took time to grow." Olvidia
Scowled and said darkly to Hester: "You set the table.
It's time for dinner." The girl moved quickly to obey, but Helen: "Stay
    here."

                She stood then in white anxiety
Between the two, and suddenly began to weep.
Helen went near her and said, "I want awfully
To know you, Hester. There's deep strangeness in your
Wanting to stay in this place. . . . Olvidia, I'm still your mistress:
Make us two sandwiches: set the table yourself.
Sandwiches: meat between bread." She said to Hester:
"You're not false, I think. Helpless; perfectly;
A person without any will: mine's only hiding.
If I could just imagine what's good, or even
What's bad, you'd see the machine move like a ship.

You mustn't fear Reave, either.

He has a great will, frittered away on trifles,

Farm things, and you and me. And unable to strike a woman:

So we needn't fear to take food in our hands

And go and play on the shore. Yes, I command you.

That makes it easy."

They walked under the alders that pave the gorge,
   and Helen: "Does it taste mouldy,

The meat of this house? But you must eat and not waste it or you'll be
   sorry, for freedom, Hester, that's coming,

Is a hungry condition. . . . Where will you go to?" "He says I must go to
   San Francisco." Helen looked, and laughed

To see tears in her eyes. "You're crazy to cry about that. You wouldn't stay
   in this wretched crack

Between two rocks? Come along, walk faster. Hester: that first time,

When you ran away with a boy: did you want a boy,

Or only you didn't dare go alone? Ah? I think that's

What makes you cry. It keeps grinding in my mind

That maybe I too . . . just to break jail . . .

It would be a dirty discovery."

The creekbank path

Straightened a moment, so that a great aisle of bright breathing ocean

Stood clear ahead, and Helen: "Hester! do you know what?

I'm going with you. I'll cut my hair to the bone

And borrow Johnny Luna's greasy black hat,

We'll fly away. I'll work for you, beg if we have to,

We'll try all the roads in America

And never quarrel; no disgust and no bullying. . . . Dear, it won't do.

You'd obey orders, we know: but look at these hips

And breasts of mine: these bulges in a man's blue-jeans

Would bulge the laws of nature, ah? My affections
Go with my build, we're talking froth, dear,
Only to poultice the inner bitterness: taste *me* and you'd call
Quinine honey."

                Suddenly emerging at the creek-mouth beach they
   breathed and stood still. The narrow crescent
Of dark gravel, sundered away from the world by its walls of cliff, smoked
   in a burst of sun
And murmured in the high tide through its polished pebbles. The surf
   broke dazzling on fins of rock far out
And foam flowed on the ankles of the precipice. Helen looked up, cliff over
   cliff, the great naked hill
All of one rifted rock covering the northwest sky; and said: "It's called
   Thurso's Landing. That's something,
To have the standing sea-cliffs named after you. His father used to swing
   down the barrels of lime
From the head of that to the hulls of ships. The old wrecks of rusting
   engines are still to be seen up there
And the great concrete block that anchors the cable. I hope you'll stay
To see it come down. He said, in the morning. You'll ride the mail-stage, I
   think:
Passes at noon. . . . Will you have the willow or the rock, Hester,
To undress beside?" "What . . . what is it?" "For a swim.
Didn't they have a swimming-pool in Nebraska?
Here's ours." "I can't. Oh, Oh." "You can duck up and down
In the long waves," Helen said laughing. "Undress.
What do you think we came down for, to see cormorants?"
"The cold will kill me." She answered, "You by this rock
And I by that one. I've been ruled with dull iron,
Now I'll rule *you* at least."

THURSO'S LANDING   223

She went, and returned
In a moment clean of clothing, but her small companion
Stood shivering in a worn cotton under-shift
And quavered, "I'll go down like this." Helen suddenly
Anxious and haggard, standing far off, with a screaming voice:
"I told you I want to see you: if I die of it.
Nothing can be worse than what I imagine.
Take off that rag." She sobbing and obedient
Dropped it to the ankles and stepped out and stood
Furled like a sail to the mast, the straw-thin arms
Crossed on her breast, the hands hugging the tiny
Bones of her crooked shoulders in the golden under-spray
Of coiled-up hair. Helen stared and sighed, "Nothing
But a white bony doll"; and turning to the sea: "We're all monstrous
Under the skins, but nothing is real I think
Even if you *can't* see it. Come on, poor thing, let's be launched; the
    foam-ripple's
Like running cream and the clouds gather."

                              She went down and Hester
    followed helplessly a few sad steps,
But when the steel chill of the wave ached in her feet stood still, whining
    between hammering teeth, then Helen
Caught her by the hand and dragged her thigh-deep, still keeping her face
    averse from her victim, like one compelled
To handle a loathsome thing she made her dance in the waves. "Don't you
    love it, Hester, isn't this cold
More noble than the heat of a sleeping man? Here comes a foamhead. I
    hate the man, yet I can hardly
Keep back my hands from holding you down and drowning you: why's that,
    why's that?" while Hester childlike lamenting

Danced up and down as the seas deepened. Helen said, "He killed my
   friend
In the bitter desert, a beautiful youth
Yellow-haired like you, like you a wanderer. He flung a hammer,"
She said, seeing in her mind the running lizard
That Reave had killed, "my dear friend fell, and that man
Who seems so quiet and controlled wallowed like a boar
Gnashing and trampling. There was no help anywhere
In all the abominable flat lifeless plain. When Reave stood up
A crooked red stump that had no eyes was dying in the sand, instead of the
   blond beautiful body
I had often hugged in my arms. I heard it die. We travelled on, blinded
   with thirst and sun,
And left it blackening; there are no tears in the desert,
Water's too precious there."

                        A greater wave came, gathering
The mottled lit blue water in a bladed heap, then Helen braced well apart
Her straight white legs, and lifted her little nearly fainting companion over
   the comb of the wave,
So that the face was clear and the yellow hair felt but the spray. In the
   trough behind the white wave
Helen shook her dark head, the water sluiced from her shoulders
And rose-tipped breasts. "Fear nothing, Hester, I'm strong enough.
That deadly secret I told you: if you should dare
To tell it again, think what might happen: a hanging.
I might be freed. . . . Look up: there he comes now: can't live without us."
   She jeered, "Look at him,
Stolid on the wild colt." They were looking shoreward and a wave covered
   them,
Then Helen drew her companion from the roaring foam and carried her
   ashore.

Thurso's half-broken mount

Danced on the sea's edge in beaten terror, the thin black whip streaked the
brown flanks; and Helen Thurso

Like a myth of dawn born in the west for once, glowing rose through white
all her smooth streaming body

Came through the foam, and dragged beside her for a morning star fainting
and dull in the rose of dawn

That wisp of silver flesh and the water-darkened burden of hair;

She stood panting, unable to speak, and Thurso

Felt through his under-consciousness something morbid and menacing

In blue-shadowed silver foiled upon glowing rose, against the livid

Foam, the tongues of cobalt water, and the shark-fin gray

Rocks of the inlet, for now the sun was clouded

All colors found their significance: then Helen wrestling for breath:

"Ah Reave. Here, Reave.

I knew you'd come, I left word with Olvidia.

Here's your wet honey: without my dress to pad her life-size

Compare us two." His face wried and dark red

He twitched the whip in his hand, choking with anger, and Helen:

"That's for your colt: not me you daren't. You haven't the courage, simply
you haven't the courage. This peeled thing—"

She held Hester by the wrist not to escape—"this peeled and breastless
willow-twig here feared you

Until I told her . . . Strike, strike. Let her see you." He shuddered and
blackened, laboring for words, and groaned "Go home.

Get on your clothes." "Now I've learned something," she answered, "that
even a thin slip like this is a better lover

Than any . . . strike *me*, not her!" She let Hester go, who vanished
instantly, and Helen raised both round arms

To unguard her smooth flanks and said writhing, "That whip of yours

Might do what no love nor strength . . . you've never let yourself go,

You've never . . . I always bitterly feared you:

Give me cause, cause. I could bear much, I'd not move nor scream
While you wrote the red stripes:
But there's no nature in you, nothing but . . . noble . . .
Nothing but . . . one of those predestined stone men
For women to respect and cheat . . ." She was suddenly weeping
And shivering; she leaned her face toward his knee
And the horse danced sidewise, with a dull clashing sound
Of unshod hooves in the pebbles, curving its body
Away from her and against the whip; she stood back,
Saying, "He thinks I'm a monster out of the sea.
I'm not like . . . what you think. I'd have kissed your stirrup:
But that's not sense either." She limped like an old woman
Across the gravel toward her clothing, bent over,
Stroking the sea-water off.

XIII

It is certain that too violent
Self-control is unlucky, it attracts hard events
As height does lightning; so Thurso rode up the canyon with a little death
    in himself,
Seeing in his mind Helen's naked body like a red bird-cage
Welted with whip-stripes; and having refused the precious relief of
    brutality, and being by chance or trick
Cheated of revenge on her desert lover, he endured small deaths in his
    mind, atrophied spots, like mouse-holes
For the casual malice of things to creep in uncountered: so shortened by
    refusal of a fair act, Thurso
Rode up from the shore in the frown of fortune. The cress-paved pools of
    the stream, the fortifying beauty on the north
Of the rock rampart, and toward the south of the forested slope, and the
    brave clouds with flashing bellies

Crossing the gorge like a fleet of salmon, were as nothing to him. Once he
  jerked back the colt's
Bit-spread jaws to its breast and half turned back
To the shore again, but sat bewildered a moment
And snapped his teeth together and rode on, imagining
Some work to do.

He tied the colt by the house-door
And went through the house to a closet where hunting-gear,
Guns, traps and vermin-poisons were kept, he fetched some pounds of
  bitter barley in the butt of a sack
To abate the pest ground-squirrels. Returning through the still rooms
He met his mother and said, "I've been to the beach, where they were
  bathing. I'm going to the upper field
With squirrel-poison." She said, "In October?" "Nobody else
Seems to have kept them down, in my absences.
Without some killing they'll breed armies in spring."
"Mark isn't able to kill, Luna's too lazy:
I ought to have driven him: I didn't think of it, Reave,
Not being often in the fields." He sighed and said,
"I wish it would rain. Mother, you have been right
To dislike that woman. I guess you're right." She turned
Her reddish flint eyes from his face to the window,
Thinking "What now has she done?" and saying, "Nobody
Can praise your choices. Soft pliable men have the luck in love.
Maybe you can get rid of her without much trouble."
He answered fiercely, "Why did you let Luna
Bridle the brown colt while I was away?
He broke it with a whip: it was gentle-natured.
Don't speak, mother, of Helen.
I never will let her go until she is dead."
The old woman, sharply eyeing him again: "If you could stand her

Under the iron skip when you cut the cable
To-morrow morning." He looked down at the flat
White hair on the gray forehead and laughed doubtfully
Without knowing why. "Our ship sails when I cut the cable.
He ought to be whipped himself: Johnny a horse-breaker!
The colt is spoilt. . . . I must ask you, mother,
Not to interfere between mine and me.
Whatever you say about the stock or the fields
I'll see to very patiently: my wife is my own concern,
You must not meddle." "I have no desire to: as you know clearly, Reave,
In your mind's quiet time." "What does that mean, that I seem excited:
    drunk, hm? Wrong, mother, quite wrong.
I've noticed in other autumns, when the earth bakes brittle and the rains
    lag, I become gloomy and quarrelsome,
But not this year. Cheerful. Squirrel-poison's
What I came in for,
To sow it in the fields above: they increased out of all bounds in my
    absences."

                    He left the house
And rode up the hill to the gray stubble-field, where many ground-squirrels
    scampered away before him, or erected
Like pegs on mounds of dug earth before their house-doors barked shrill
    warning to each other in the sunny air,
While Thurso, leading his horse about the borders of the field, laid at the
    mouth of each burrow and carefully
In the little trackways light treacherous gifts; he mounted and rode to the
    lower plowland. From thence returning
Above the path of dazzle on the burnished sea, he heard one of his vermin
    singing its terror
In the first pain of death; its chirping voice was muffled in the earth; and
    Thurso likewise went down

Out of the tension of the sun to the shadowed canyon. Where the path
  from the hill
Joined one that wound into the redwoods, he saw his brother
Cross hastily and glance toward him, and labor down
Like a hobbled horse, the plunge and drag of lame haste.
Reave overtook him. Mark said, "Look. Now he stands.
I was talking to him until he drifted away
As if a wind had come up. Reave, I beg you
Ride some way around, or he'll glide off again
And never tell me the rest." Reave leaned in the saddle
And took his brother by the shoulder: "Come up from dreams, old fellow.
This won't do, you'll be sick again. These fancies
Are nothing if you don't yield." "Keep your hand off me,"
He said angrily. "If you can't see him clear
Against the dark leaves of laurel: blindness is all.
He's wearing a different coat, and his tie-pin's
A small jade mask I never noticed before.
Ss: quiet: he's coming toward us . . . You told me, father . . .
Ah, Ah." The deranged man's trembling excitement
Infected the ill-tamed colt, it sweat and shuddered
Between Reave's knees, with hard breathings
Cupping its ears toward the image that Mark imagined,
But the bit and the knees held it.

                              Mark, mournfully: "Then death's
No nearer peace. No dreamlessness. That's bad." He listened again,
And shrewdly answered, "Harmonized: happier, happier?
I do wish to have faith: but your voice, father,
Sounds flat of happiness, and all the woes of the world
Seem hosting behind your smile. For God's sake tell me
The honest truth." He listened, and said painfully,
"Make me sure of it. For if the blind tugging here

And self-contempt continue, and death's no peace,
It would be better to live forever . . . . but best, best,
Never've been born." He listened again and said,
"I'll try . . ." Then turning to Reave; who sat like bronze,
Half his mind grieving to hear his brother's madness, and half
Busied with its own bitterness: "He says to warn you,
Let his work stand. He says *honor your father*
That your days may . . . I have it wrong. Shortened?
Shortened? Because death's better, I suppose.
. . . Not to pull down his work." Reave laughed impatiently,
Saying, "Tell that imagination I honor as much
As I can see of him: that's nothing. A perfect ground-squirrel,
Pop out of life for the first dog that barked
Into the shady earth. Come down to the house
And rest, brother. We owe him no duties
If he were really in the wind here." He laid his hand again on Mark's
    shoulder,
Whose loaded nerves suddenly discharging at the touch of restraint struck
    his clenched bony fist
To the neck of the colt; that flew a leap sidewise and three forward in the
    crackling brushwood, then breathed itself
With vertical flights and humped bone-rigid landings. Reave hurt it with
    whip and bridle, he squeezed it tame
Between his two knees and angrily returned.

                                    Mark meanwhile, following
    his vision,
With no mind for this world, questioned it hard
About that other, he ate its fallacious answers
Together with his own doubts, like a starved man gulping
The meal with the weevils. "Life's all a dream," it said,
"And death is a better more vivid immortal dream,

THURSO'S LANDING   231

But love is real; both are made out of love,
That's never perfect in life, and the voids in it
Are the pains of life; but when our ungainly loads
Of blood and bone are thrown down, then the voids close,
Love becomes perfect, all's favor and immediate joy,
For then we are what we love." So the false prophet
Sang sweetly, Mark was drunken with the easy ecstasy,
But while he listened his eyes kept wavering down
From the face to the throat of his vision, to that tie-pin
Tipped with white jade: that also had a face, carved
In the bright waxy stone, and was grown bigger,
The face was Helen's. The spectre sang that love
Must become conscious of itself and claim its own,
Mark's gaze drifting again to the stone at its throat
Found a cleft whiteness, for the carving reversed
Was now the beautiful fork of female thighs,
And the little hill: because the seer was virgin,
Knowing only pictures of women, he saw smooth white
What's rough in nature; but very smooth was too rough
For that intolerant sick mind. He fled back in terror,
Crying shrilly, "I can't. I can't. Oh Reave, the cunning devil
Was making traps to take me, and I have conceived
A monstrous thing, poisoning the soul with flesh.
Either our dead hate us or the living devil
Was here instead." Reave followed him and coaxed him home,
Where Helen stood in the room. They nodded to her
Like two effigies.

          In the night Reave dreamed that Helen
Lay with him in the deep grave, he awoke loathing her,
But when the weak moment between sleep and waking
Was past, his need of her and his judgment of her

Knew their suspended duel; and he heard her breathing,
Irregularly, gently in the dark.

XIV

To save the redwoods under it, a rope was drawn
From the old cable, near the end to be cut,
To an oak a little higher than the cable-anchorage
And fifty yards to the west; so in their falling
The heavy steel serpent and the hanging iron skip
Should be deflected enough to miss those highest
And best-grown trees; the cable would be swung west
Before the inch rope should take the whole weight and snap,
Or, holding, be cut at leisure.

                         Reave had brought up a hack-saw,
But the blades broke on the strained steel; he wedged a wood block
In the rusty angle between the black cable and the brown concrete, and
    worked against it with a slim file
Until four strands were gored through and his palm bleeding; he pried the
    wires back and put Luna to work,
Himself walking aside, testing the guide-rope's tautness, and somewhat
    wondering
What engines his father used to sling so great weight so high: a man
    capable of that, blow out
In the first draught of bad luck like a poor candle!
In the open, in the fresh morning, high up the precipitous hill, his spirit
    mounted to a kind of cheerfulness;
He had work to do; and now the sea-wind began, the wool-white fog on
    the ocean detached clouds
Flying up the gorge of the gulf underfoot, so Thurso felt for a moment a
    little laughably godlike,

Above the cloud-stream, hewing an old failure from the face of nature.
    Down in the gorge, from the house dooryard
The cable and the skip could be seen high up the east, the rapid
    mist-wreaths flowing in the sky below them
Like ice-cakes under a spidery bridge. Mark and his mother stood on the
    path to the porch, she'd brought him
Out of his bed-room to watch the cable go down, hoping it might cure sick
    thoughts. Hester and Olvidia
Stood, each alone, at some distance; but Helen came down from among the
    trees. Then Mark remembering
His lawless vision trembled at her approach.
She came and said, "Reave left the gate open,
And the horses were coming out when I happened past.
I never knew him to be forgetful before.
What was he thinking of?" They looked at her, Mark with eyes
That mutely implored pardon and fled away,
His mother made a carefully disinterested
Stare, and no answer. Helen stood wilfully near them,
And said, "How long has it hung?" After a moment
Mark answered hoarsely. And Helen: "Not more? eighteen?
I thought it had always hung on these hills. I've seen it myself
Through an earthquake and some big winds, and that brushfire
Three years ago. When *Reave* tackles it,
Down it shall come. Not the mountain-backed earth bucking like a bad
    horse, nor fire's
Red foxtail on the hills at midnight, nor the mad southeasters: nothing can
    do it
But Reave Thurso, ah? That's the man we're measured against."
The old woman considered her once more, smiled, and to Mark:
"An inch to the mile. Dear, are you tired standing?
Surely it will not be long now." Mark whispered to her,
"Do you think he cares?" "Who?" "Father: his old work

Falling from the air at last." "We'll credit the dead
With a little more intelligence than to be troubled
About old iron." Helen overheard her,
And out of the uneasy malice of unhappiness: "Why credit them?
Very likely their minds like their spoiled bodies
Decay and go down the scale, through childish mutterings
To poisonous imbecility, and things that seem
Worthless to us might be to them like playthings
Precious to children, worth spite, all they've got left . . ." "You—"
The old woman felt Mark's anguish, and pushing by him
Stood against Helen—"weren't asked. When we're dull and want laughter
We'll ask you to tell us your thoughts." Helen retreated
With looks of startled innocence, "Oh, how have I made you angry? I was
    praising your son, the other one,
A man who masters earthquake, storm and bad horses, and has no fear of
    the dead, and can drive a truck
With his wife in it; never reached out his hand for anything yet but down it
    came. Look up: he's there
By the oak-tree, your strong man of this hollow, his feet on a cloud. He'd
    never falter if a thousand ghosts
Were camped against him: but look at the size of the man: one of those
    tiny
Black ants that come to dead things could carry him
With the oak too. Mark, you hate cruelty and killers: do you know that he
    spent yesterday
Poisoning squirrels? Olvidia told me.
Poor little dusty monkeys whipped for my sins
Dying in agony." Mark answered hollow and slow,
"It has to be done, I suppose. Once he told me,
No poison no farms. He said that strychnin's
What civilized California: there'd still be grizzlies
And timber-wolves." "So all your sweet starts of mercy

Tune down to that meek end. Well, Mark: sometime
San Francisco and New York and Chicago will fall
On the heads of their ghosts, so will that cable."

                                        A small bright falcon,
Invisible from the floor of the gorge, but Reave saw it
Above the cloud-stream, shot down the shiny sky
And lighted on the long cable above the skip,
Folded its wings, and veered its vizarded face
With sharp looks north and south. Reave thought, "All the birds
Count on this ironware for as fixed as mountains,
It was here before they were hatched in the high nests,
Now I'll surprise him." He said "Hand me the axe,"
For all the weight was hanging on a few cords
Of twisted wire. He lifted the dinted axe,
An old one for rough work. "Stand clear, Johnny," but the wires
Were not chewed deep enough yet; the edge nicked and bent them
Into the block, the whole cable like a hive of bees
Hummed over the gulf in the hanging air, and the hawk flew,
But the wires held. Reave looked at the bright crescent
Chipped in the brown axe-edge. "The old man's tough;
But wait a minute." An instant thought of Helen
Ran like a string of ants over his mind,
No danger of Helen standing under the skip
As his mother wished in her spite, but Mark's mind
Was not secure, better look down. The trees in the canyon
Hid the dooryard from here, and Reave went seaward
Some twenty paces along the steep of the hill
Through pale oak-leaves and russet ferns to see Mark standing
By his mother, Helen beside them, foreshortened specks
On the foot-worn patch of earth from the dark redwoods
And the globular golden puff of the sycamore

236 THURSO'S LANDING

To the painted roofs of the house. Light mist flew over them,
Helen lifted the pin-point white of her face,
She looked like an incredibly small flower-stock
Suddenly flowering.

Johnny Luna
Stood by the cable with a file, and looking down
Saw the wires move like a scarred twist of worms
In the wood they were dented into, the all but invisible
Kinks printed in them by the steel edge straightening,
A nicked strand broke, then all parted at once
Very smoothly and instantly. He saw the scything rope
That ran from the cable to the oak-tree go west
And strike Reave standing, he was bent at the loins backward
And flung on the face of the hill.

Helen also saw,
But the others watched the great cable and the skip fall,
Obliquely in the draw of the rope, and the high oak-tree
Rush down the hill, the arched balks and crooked thighs
Of root in the scant soil on the near rock
Channelled with dry-rot, proving less masterful
Than one inch twist of hemp: so avalanchelike
The whole tree went down to the gorge, from its great yellow furrow in the
    face of the hill
A long track of dust blew east, above and below
The racing clouds.

Thus the long trough and the covering sky
Of Mill Creek Canyon were cleared of that old cobweb,
The black moon over the gorge was down, and the mountain lips
Wiped clean. Helen Thurso ran up

Under the trees, through the oak-thicket, up the glacis
Of gray dead grass to the wreck of the oak-tree,
And up by the long furrow of the slide to Reave's
Body on its edge, dragged down and flung aside,
Like a red root cut by the plow and pitched
Forth of the furrow. He was not dead but crawling,
His belly and legs flat to the ground, his head
Lifted, like that lizard in the desert, and Helen saw the red ropes of muscle
Labor in his great shoulder, the shirt and the skin flayed off them.

                                        Luna

     came down from above, then Helen's
Face frightened him more than his master's body, it was white as lightning,
     eyed and mouthed with darkness, and the strained breath
Whined from the pit of her lungs like a bat's cries. She stood
Wavering, Reave crawled at her feet, the gorge glimmered below. "God
     evens things. My lover in the desert,"
She gasped, "crawled in the sand like that after Reave struck him. A bushel
     for a bushel says God exactly.
What can we do?" Luna stood mute and helpless, the color of his Indian
     skin like pale blue slate.
Reave crawled down hill between them; they watched the corded strips of
     flesh in his shoulder reddening and paling,
And when he began to speak they were terrified. "Must 'a' been holes in my
     mind. Everything wrong. Won't die."
Helen cried shrilly, "How can we get you down, where can I touch you?"
     "Hell," he said, "you'll wash." "For your pain!"
She cried shrilly. He raised up his gray face, fantastically grown smaller,
     hewn thin and focussed
On resistance, like a flint chip: "Can't worsen it, fool. I won't die. Drag."
     They dragged him a little way

Down the hill and his mother came: in a flash Helen understood whose
    face it was
That Reave's in pain resembled identically, and felt toward his old mother
Her heart move in a jet of loving compassion
Wild and lost like peering down a precipice,
She cried "Oh mother!" The old woman went to Reave's head
And carried it against her breast. Helen and Luna
Carried his body, so they went tottering down;
His legs dragged in the feather-gray sage until Olvidia
And Hester came. On the steep of the slope came Mark
Hitching up on hands and knees for his lameness.
Helen thought, "Both her sons crawling!" and cried shrilly,
"Get out of the way will you. He's met somebody
Stronger than himself. Now I forgive him, now I forgive him.
I'd die for him." The old woman glanced at her
With astonished hatred across Reave's head. "You forgive him!"

XV

Winter had begun and Reave was brought home from the hospital
In Monterey. Luna drove and Helen crouched
Beside Reave's mattress in the open body of the farm-truck.
She thought they all came by turns to ride in it: pigs and calves to the
    butcher, Hester Clark from Nevada,
Herself from her lover and the desert mine, and again Reave Thurso. All
    compelled; all unhappy; all helpless.
Clouds with dragging keels came in from the ocean, over Mal Paso bridge a
    thin rain began,
Helen drew up the oil-skin over the blanket and said, "I know that you
    suffer pain day and night,
And now the jolting of the road is torture." He was silent a time; his face
    looked like his mother's. "What of it?"

He said suddenly. "Not to hide it from me, hidden pain's worse. If you
    trusted me . . ." "Do you think rat-gnawings
Mean much to a man who never any more . . . all the endless rest of his
    life lie flat like a cut tree . . .
Something to think about, ah? Have food brought and be wiped, grow fat
    between a tray and a bed-pan,
While every shiftless and wavering fool in the world
Has walking legs. Never waste pity: the cramps and the stabbing are my
    best diversion: if they ever ended
I'd have to lie and burn my fingers with matches. Well: day by day." She
    watched the small rain-drops
Beading his rough eye-brows and hair, and said "I'd willingly die for you: I
    have not one grain of comfort
To answer with."

                At Sovranes Creek he began to peer about and look up
    the mountain, but dimly
To be seen through leaning pillars of rain. "You throw off the oil-cloth.
    What are you looking at, dear?" "Pasture.
Pasture for cows." Helen saw mist-green veils tapering up the iron folds to
    the mountain-head,
The noble slopes and the crowning pyramid, and suddenly began to weep
    aloud. He said, "I can't help it.
You promised lightly to take the worse with the better. This is the worse.
I never will let you go until you are dead.
When you played the chippy I went and fetched you back;
You'll never try it again." His focussed will
Forgot to control the outthrows of bodily pain,
He ended groaning, with convulsed lips. Helen answered,
"I wasn't crying. I wasn't crying for myself. I will not be
At last contemptible." And lifting her white throat
Against the blue hills and rain: "Nothing can break you,

It was only bones and nerves broke, nothing can change you.
Now I've begun to know good from bad
I can be straight too." "Hell," he said, "changed enough.
Dead legs and a back strapped in plaster. You'll never
Be as straight as this." Helen shivered in the rain and said,
"What kind of a doctor was that, who leaves you suffering."
"An honest old man. He told me plainly that the nerves of pain
Might live, and the nerves of motion were lost. He told me,
When I asked him, that I shall never ride, walk, nor even
Be able to stand." She answered suddenly, "I'll never leave you
In life or death." He smiled and his lips whitened with pain. He said,
    "How's Mark?" "Stark mad: all his gentleness
Gone into vengeful broodings. He thinks a dead man tore up an oak on the
    mountain . . ." Reave frowned and said,
"Exactly. With my imbecility to spring the trap. Our fathers build and
    cowardly slip out and we
Catch the fall. Not so crazy as you think. Do you think there's anything
    beyond death, Helen?" "Yes," she answered.
"Worms." "And sleep, without pain or waking. Don't worry, I'll never ease
    myself out by hand. The old dog
Stinks in that alley."

            Luna drove fast; Helen leaned on her hands for
    balance in the swirling turn
Around the cape of the road over Garapatas and said, "How did he kill
    himself? I never knew."
Reave sharply between tight lips of suffering: "Leave that." She answered,
    "He acted cowardly and you despise him,
But perfect courage might call death like a servant at the proper time, not
    shamefully but proudly." His mind
At civil war in the darkness forgot to control the animal tokens of pain, he
    groaned and answered:

"Means your freedom, ah?" "You are right," Helen said, "to expect vileness
    in me: I will show you before the end
That I am changed." "I didn't mean that. Blind bitterness. But I mean to
    stick it out, you know, and there's tempting
Too sweet to be patient with. I say damn quitters."

                          The little farm-truck,
    with its dull-smouldering sparks of sad life,
Ran swiftly on south the wavering and twisted road on the steep foot of the
    mountain sea-wall. No life
Ought to be thought important in the weave of the world, whatever it may
    show of courage or endured pain;
It owns no other manner of shining, in the broad gray eye of the ocean, at
    the foot of the beauty of the mountains
And skies, but to bear pain; for pleasure is too little, our inhuman God is
    too great, thought is too lost.
It drove above the long crescent beach toward Palo Colorado,
That is lined with lonely splendor of standing wind-carven rocks, like a
    chariot-racetrack adorned with images,
Watched by the waving crowds and clamor of the sea, but there are no
    chariots. Thurso's Landing
Stood heavy-shouldered in the south beyond.

XVI

After some days and nights Reave called for Luna.
Helen fetched him, Reave instructed him to choose two fence-rails
And whittle handles on the ends, and nail cross-pieces
To make a stretcher. An old tarpaulin was cut
For canvas, which Helen sewed over and bound with fish-line
Between the two rails. Reave had thought carefully,
There was no reason for being jailed in the house,

There were things he was bound to bear, that was not one of them.
Helen and Olvidia each holding a handle,
And Luna at the other end, carried him forth
Heavily, of fantastic shape and weight
With the plaster girdle about his loins: like a stone man,
Petrified man, was echoing in Helen's mind
While she labored with the weight, "Does everything I dream come true?"
They laid him on a low bank near the corral,
Where he could turn his head and at times
See horses in the muddy enclosure. Or see tall redwoods,
And if he wished, the long narrow canyon sky,
Reminding him what its clearance had cost.

                                        One day that Helen
Was bringing his lunch from the house, she saw Mark
Waiting in her path; she went about him to avoid him,
Feeling unable at length to hear his troublesome
Mysteries with patience, and approached Reave
An unusual way unseen and silently, on the new grass
Around a thicket. She saw the whitened knuckles
Of his heavy-boned hands over his breast,
One clutching the other, and then the fists beaten together
Like stones, and heard a high helpless moaning. She stole back
And broke through branches into her accustomed path,
To go to him lying quiet and watching stolidly
While she came near. She trembled and set the tray on the ground,
And said, "May I shift the pillows under you?" He answered, rolling his
    head,
"I can shift them. Look here." The bluish bruised look of his face
    darkened, that the gray eyes
Looked white in it, his thick neck swelled; he was raising himself upward
    with prodigious pain and effort by the thrust

Of his elbows backward against the earth, saying harshly, "I am not
   helpless." He clutched his hands in the soil
And slowly with immobile face and no groan lay down. She felt in her
   breast like the rush of a big bird
Flying from a covert and the threshing wings: "If I'd never been here," she
   said, "nothing would have been the same."
She knew that she ought to be silent, she could not cease, crying
   uncontrollably,
"You'd not be hurt, you'd be riding on the hill. I wish I had died in misery
   before you saw me,
I wish you had seen me first lying five days dead in the jagged mountain,
   blackening on a white rock
In a dry place, the vultures had dipped their white beaks in my eyes, their
   red heads in my side,
You'd make them raise the great wings and soar, you'd see my bowels
   drawn out of my body and the rock stained under me
And the soil of death, I was lying black-mouthed in the filth of death.
   You'd not have wanted me then, and nothing
Would be as it is, but you'd be lucky and I quiet." He looked in her eyes
   and smiled, with that bruised look,
Not hearing, bent inward on his own pain; but after a time he seemed to
   remember that she spoke of death
And said angrily: "Have you death for sale, you talk like a salesman.
Every fool knows it's pleasant to rot in peace
After long pain but that's not the question.
I saw a nigger boxer in Monterey one night
Cut all to pieces
Sail on up the wind of fists, beaten and blinded,
Vomiting blood: he needed only let down
His knees onto the canvas and be at peace,
He wouldn't do it. I say I cared for that man;
He was better than a better fighter."

XVII

Reave's doctor came to break the cast from his body; Helen helped, and
washed the ill-smelling
Long-enclosed flesh. Afterwards while Reave rested she spoke with his
mother in another room. "You saw him.
The giant shoulders and the pitiful part below. I know that he has hoped
secretly to live again . . .
Ride a horse . . . he'll never sit up in bed. What can we do?" She answered
with a like contorted face,
But not twitching like Helen's: "There were two oaks broken that morning.
What can you do? Run away.
Follow that Hester. You and she are out of employment
When a man's withered from the waist down." She answered, "Yet I was
thinking there's . . . . another kindness
That I could do for him. Another that his mother can't." "What?" she said
fiercely. "Nothing, nothing, nothing,"
Helen faintly answered. "However, I'll never leave him. I promised him
never to leave him and I've grown faithful
At last." She felt the old woman's eyes like flints press on her own, she
shuddered and said, "I know
You hate me: let our spites lie, we're both unhappy. Tell me something, if
you know, what's all this troublesome
Affair of living, and people being troubled and the sun rising and setting:
what's it all about, what's it for?
I've seen you go on bitterly year after year, living, planning, working: do
you know something
That's hidden from the weak like me? Or it's only
Gloomy stubbornness like Reave's blind . . . or else perhaps we live for no
other reason than because our parents
Enjoyed their pleasure and we dread to die? *I* dread it," she said with her
hands at her throat, "so . . . I can't bear it,

THURSO'S LANDING   245

But Reave's too proud. I mean, if the pain ceases, if his pain ceases at last
    . . . then I can't imagine.
But if the pain keeps up I must do it." "What can you do
But run away off? You're not the make. I wish
He could see your slobbered face, Helen, he'd hardly
Have hunted into Arizona to fetch it home.
Do what then?" Her mouth shuddered and tautened, she answered,
"I cannot tell." "I believe you," she answered scornfully.
Helen stood moving her sad lips in silence
Like one casting a sum of numbers, and said,
"I must have read it somewhere: a hundred and twenty-three
Millions in this one country of the world, besides the animals. Far more in
    Asia. How can it be sacred
Being so common? I've never hated you back for hating me; I've called you
    Mother; now if you'd help me
To know what's right I'd be grateful." The old woman with eyes like a
    hawk's watching
A bush of sparrows: "Tell me then." "For now it seems to me that all the
    billion and a half of our lives on earth,
And the more that died long ago, and the things that happened and will
    happen again, and all the beacons of time
Up to this time look very senseless, a roadless forest full of cries and
    ignorance. But is life precious
At the worst you know? I used to wish for round jewels and a fur cloak: I
    could love opals,
Born in October: and a set of gay laughing friends to fool with, and one of
    those long low stream-lined cars
That glide quietly and shine like satin: so I can't say, whether life maybe
    might 'a' been precious
At the best. And death's awful. . . . We're too closed-in here." "If you
    think of killing yourself": she laughed,
Lifting her shoulders. Helen looked down and said,

"How did . . . Reave's dad do it?" "In the forehead, poor fool,
And was long dying." "In the heart would have been better?"
"You must find out for yourself." "I wasn't thinking of myself;
I'm faithful now." "To the death? Ah?
A new color for you, worn strangely."

                                             She went through the house
To her son's room. Helen followed saying, "Go quietly,
And listen." They tiptoed down to hear a thin moaning
Increase and break off; then hands beat on the bed
In the room behind the shut door; a silence followed,
And again the moaning. The old woman rolled her gray head
And whispered, "I'll not awake him." But Helen: "If that is sleep,
Then life's a dream." She touched the door-handle
And the room was full of silence; they entered, Reave lay
Stolid and strong, meeting them with calm eyes
Blood-shot around the gray-blue. Helen said faintly,
"May I turn you now?" He said "What meanness in you
Is always making me out worse than I am? Helpless enough,
But not to that point." The old woman went to the window and looked
   down the canyon; then turning: "Helen talks strangely.
She says that she's now faithful. What does that mean, do you think?"
   Reave answered, "I know she is, and I pay it
With cross impatiences: I'm sorry, Helen." "Oh, but you'd never guess,"
   the mother said furiously,
"How far that reaches, this kind of faithfulness. She's likely had word
From the yellow-haired man, because . . ." Helen said sharply,
"That man is dead." Reave strained up his head, groaning,
"Who told you? Everything slips away. I was hopeful still
To touch him with my hands. He might have come near me
Sometime to mock my ruin . . ." The old woman said,

"How could she hear? She's lying, I watched her mouth." "Reave killed
    him,"
Helen said patiently; "only by waiting for him and he didn't come, beat
    him to corrupt earth,
Dust and a wind. Oh Reave, be at peace
For anything you owed there." "She was lying again,"
The mother said, "but a moment ago in the other room
Her truth came out. This white, violet-eyed thing
Would if she dared murder you: Oh, from high motives,
All mercy and good will like a lamp in a window, but mostly wondering
Whether a dutiful wife will shoot her man
In the head or the heart." Helen had cried out to speak,
But checked herself and watched Reave; he answered heavily,
His light eyes withstanding his mother's dark ones: "We've talked it over.
But I have forbidden her." Then Helen cried, "Don't send me away.
I believe you will never need me: but God's not moderate enough to trust,
    and when he turns bad, no one
Can bear him to the end." He answered, "That's cowardly said; there's
    nothing a man can't bear. Push my bed
To the window and let me look out westward." They moved his bed; in the
    mouth of the gorge the evening sea-cloud
Hung heavy black, leoparded all over with sanguine fire-spots; he muttered
    wearily, "We're too closed-in here.
I lie like a felled log in a gully and women wrangle above me. I have no
    power and no use
And no comfort left and I cannot sleep. I have my own law
That I will keep, and not die despising myself."

                                        The stormy twilight

    closed over and filled the canyon

And drowned the house, and the ocean made a great noise in the dark,
   crying up the canyon; with between the cries
Noises like trespassers breaking fences, or the cattle running.

                                 Helen slept
   in a room by herself,
For Thurso wanted no witness to hear his nights of endured pain, and had
   sent her from the low couch
Beside his bed, to use the little room that Hester Clark had been glad of.
She fell asleep for a moment and lay an hour
Terribly awake, and went down the stair, having a candle
In both her hands, the right hooding the flame
That etched red lines between the dark fingers,
The left holding the shaft, and the white grease
Dripped hot films on it. She went barefoot and silently
With the one piece of linen about her, hearing
The stairs groan like a man, and stole through the house
To a distant closet where vermin-traps and squirrel-poison,
Hunting-gear and a smell of leather were kept. She sought her own rifle
In that close place, meaning to hide it in her bed
Between the springs and the mattress, knowing that no one
Commands life without the tools of death
Readily hid in the background. She loaded in
New cartridges with glittering brass jackets, for oil
Or time might have damped the old; and turned to the door.
Mark stood in the door.
But Helen thought that the strain in her mind had bred a phantom,
And waited for it to fade.

                    He said, "A thready light
Pricked into my room through the cracked panel.
I think my mind has been roiled, when I lie wakeful

Blades of strange light. Are you going hunting?
Dear Helen let the deer feed. Life's bad for people,
But the clean deer, that leap on the high hills
And feed by the hollow streams, there's not one of them
Lame nor a fool." She answered in her mind, "Nothing
Is very serious," and said, "Ah, there's one hurt one,
Would thank me kindly, if it had a man's brain,
For death, that great fallen stag." "Where is it? I'll feed it
With tender grass." "It fell on the mountain and its broken bones
Have caught the nerves in their hard lumps of healing,
So that it's in pain forever: I hate . . . love him too.
Love him, I said." "If you kill any living
Creature, the happiness of your heart is troubled
In quiet times afterwards." "What's that to me?
I shall have no quiet time after this hunting;
But brief and violent. Let me go now." He answered,
"I know what love is, I saw it in the devil's tie-pin.
How dared you come down undressed?" She saw him shaking
In the candle-light, and thought with a thread ravelled
From her mind's gathering fire-mist, "You poor good fool,
Is it there with you?" He said, "Horrible dreams of love
Like splintered glass in my bed cut me all night, like a splintered mirror.
Reave betrayed you with that pale bright doll." He came from the doorway
    toward her, then Helen laughed and dipped
Her hand in a half sack of barley on the shelf, and felt the kernels light and
    luxuriously
Lie in her fingers, and said through white lips: "Is this the poison-soaked
    grain? that makes the squirrels cry
In the quiet of their little caves, that bitter death?" "Let it alone. Oh, this
    place crawls with death,
Traps, guns, knives, poisons: but no one sleeps near, no one can hear us.
    There's a bright wanting beast in me:

Hunt that, Helen. Kill that. I thought love

Was kindness, it's a blind burning beast. Oh, wait: because I heard voices
    and answered them, saw spirits and feared them,

You and the rest were whispering that I was crazy. Why, that was nothing.
    But now, when I burn to tear

That last white rag from you, and do—how can I say it?—striking the
    obscene parts of our flesh together—

This is the real thing, this is the madness." She laughed and ran her fingers
    through the deadly barley and answered:

"Yours is a common trouble, we'd manage you a kind cure

If I were liberal; but you'd loathe me for it, and my winter's come. I wish to
    leave my poor spotted memory

A little lonely and distinct at this bitter end. Is it nearly morning?" "Do
    you think . . ." he answered, and suddenly

The pallor of his face gleamed with a film of sweat, he said "I've fooled
    myself out of life for fancy

Feelings and second-hand noble dreams. Kill all the deer on the mountain,
    what's that to me? I've seen them

Go to it like dogs in the bushes outside the cantonment: wise soldiers: did
    you think you could come naked

And not be mauled?" She said furiously,

"You fool," and heard him hiss when he touched her breast and cry:

"The lids of your eyes are swollen, your eyes are knives.

This is it. Yes." His teeth clattered together so that she thought of a
    crooked stone the returning

Wave sucks, and the stone rolls over and over, clashing on the pebbles. He
    wiped his forehead with his hand and shook

The fingers as if blood hung on them, saying, "That Hester's gone. I might
    have had a second-hand . . .

Noble thought very likely.

Tell the audience for all those cat-calls there's not one of them

But's more or less in my manner

Done out of his dear life by scrupulous cowardices.
Men ought to ravage: then down comes the black curtain,
We died like old empty priests." But Helen seeing him
All shrunken again, "Believe me," she said in pity,
"These rosy toys you've missed make a bad bargain
At the time of the end. I could be very envious
Of virgins and a quiet life." "The two you've had
Are nothing," he answered, "take two hundred. But only
Beware not to make a baby, we know what life is:
That mercy's weakness, and honesty
The simple fear of detection; and beauty, paint;
And love, a furious longing to join the sewers of two bodies.
That's how God made us and the next wars
Will swallow up all. . . . Helen, I'm very tired
With cloudy thoughts, and have been fearful at times
Of falling into some unclearness of mind.
That would be bad: lunacy's worse than death.
If I should consider taking a certain remedy
While I'm still sane, to scour the rancid bowl
Back to its first brightness, who could be blamed?
You've always been kind beyond words."

                                        He went, and Helen
At once forgot him, all her energy reverting
To its old preoccupation like a freed spring,
She took the rifle to hide it below her mattress
And barefoot stilly went up through the house.

                                        She passed Reave's door,
And returned again to listen whether he moaned
Or slept. No sound appeared, but wind or the ocean
Whispering high over the house. In that silence

Her intention flowered; she became calm, convinced
That time had come to cut all the knots at once
And lead the agonies of strain to a sharp end.
Mark's outcry, though she forgot him, had tired her,
The resistances of a drained spirit faint
Before the power does, she had lost the strength not to act
And stealthily unlatched the door. It seemed clear, plain
And reasonable, to seal that heavy sleep
From ever waking to worse; but having planted
The candle upon the chest by the door, and drawing
Down the steel barrel the three points to one line,
She met his eyes wide open, broad and inhuman, like the universal eyes of
    night, judging
And damning her act, with remote absolute merciless comprehension. She
    was like a touched sleepwalker,
Unnerved and annihilated: what contemptible
Distraction had made the reasons of her dream? and Reave:
"Come closer. You'd botch it from there, and I'd be days
Dying or not, cursing you for a fool."
She leaned and shuffled toward him.

                    She felt her neck
Wrenched by the buffet, and lukewarm blood wandering
From her mouth down the left side of her throat and tasted
The thick salt sweetness, and Reave saying furiously, "Sneak in behind me
Fighting on my last inch? I never struck you before, you earned it enough."
    She mumbled,
"It doesn't hurt . . ." "Trust you," he said, "to side with my enemy." His
    great hands, and the white knuckles
Like peaks among the black hairs, blazed in the lit center of the orbital
    darknesses that hooded her eyes.

His hands had her little rifle and were strained to break it, but the great
    strength that she believed could do anything
Failed after all. Snapping and whining with pain like a wounded dog he
    shifted over on his elbows
And thrust the barrel under the board of the bedside, drew up against his
    own weight, and the splitting stock
Ripped from the steel. "That's yours," he said gasping. "Go call Luna." She
    felt the pain of her lip swelling,
Cut on the dog-tooth edge, and the blood on her throat, and muttered, "It
    doesn't hurt." "You red and white
Barber's-pole," he said, "fetch Johnny Luna.
We'll have a disarmament here." "What?" "Light the lamp and take
Your light and fetch him." "What? Oh, Oh!" she cowered and knelt down
    against the bedside, "don't send me away.
I'll promise never . . . I promise . . ." "You'll not be sent away, I'll not let
    you go." "How could I sleep,"
She prayed, not hearing him, "or lie down, or *live*, in another place, not
    knowing
How you were, and never see you nor touch you?" "You lie," he groaned,
    "or you're changed.
Be sure I'll not let you go. I am not changed."
She clenched a fold of the coverlet and stammered, "*I* am not changed.
I was only ignorant. When the idiot body and perverse
Imagination went whoring . . . then still whatever it is
That loves, was weeping here."

                  Reave's old mother
Stood in the door, her corded bare throat thrust
From the fold of a brown cloak, and dull-white wisps
Starring her head; the noise of the broken gun-stock
Had beckoned her from a dream. "Praying is she? Religion's
Their last trick . . ." She saw the blood-streak, and blazing

Went and dragged up Helen's face, one hand in the hair,
One at her throat, saying "What have you done, you . . .
It's your own is it? That's better." Reave said, "Let her alone.
I called and she came running asleep, in the dark,
She struck her face." The old woman looked down the candle-light
At the rifle-barrel and the splintered stock, and said,
"You are still strong." "But can't run my own errands.
Wash yourself," he said to Helen; "light the lamp;
Go and call Johnny."

               When Helen was gone, the old mother:
"Tell me what she was doing." He rolled his shoulders
And groaned, striking his hand down at his thigh.
"Would you believe this fixed and passive flesh
Has red-hot wire in it? What nights." "Why have you sent for Luna
At midnight?" "To amuse me awhile. Get to bed, mother,
Before the aching night strikes to your bones.
I had an inflamed throat
After that fall of rain, all my discomforts
Turned fiery then. . . . Oh, if you need, I'll tell you.
We've rifles and a shot-gun, but nobody
Will ever go hunting from here again, and to save oiling
He's to break the guns. They call it disarmament. I dreamed
The old dog that was your husband and my father
Stood in a cave-mouth calling; and, to speak exactly,
I'll not be tempted."

XVIII

              The house in the deep gorge
Had been darkened again. One of those night-birds that cry in quickening
   rhythm like the rattle of a spun plate falling

Cried, then the silver streak southeast loosed a slight moon. A few of the
    house-windows feebly glittered
Back its horned light; the massed black obelisks of redwood utterly ignored
    it, but the leafless leaning sycamore
Shone like a trunked and branched moon on the dark wood, a tree made
    wholly of luminous lunar material,
Except one long hanging shadow. The clouds took the moon again, the
    sycamore vanished, the dream in the eyes
Of the house died; and imperceptibly a twilight began to exist, without
    wind or color, or foam
Of a formal cloud, but misty rain fell. A faintly more curded mist-wreath
    flowed from a chimney and down
The house-roof valleys, it spread earthling dissolving, and sensitive wild
    nostrils up the great gorge
Tasted the oak-smoke and coffee fragrance of a waking house. The world
    lightened, the rain increased.
A broad brown face peered from a window, a woman whose blood had
    known this coast for ten thousand years
Perceived a strangeness of shape in that moony sycamore. She had work in
    hand, but an hour later she poured
Coffee for Mark Thurso, who'd not come down yet, and set it with his egg
    back of the stove and went
To empty the grounds into the willows. She hooded her head against the
    rain with an apron, but returning
Saw the sycamore framed in the apron-fold
And it looked dreadful. She approached and found Mark hanging
Long-necked, very wet with rain. She stood at some distance,
Mournfully, with the coffee-pot in her hand,
Thinking the grounds were bad for chickens, but this
Rainy morning she might have mixed them with the other leavings,
Not gone out, and seen nothing. She went and washed plates and cups,
Wishing for Johnny, but he was busy in the barn.

The rain fell on the barn roof, the rain fell . . . . everywhere . . . .
And no one could sleep: smashing rifles all night.
Old Mrs. Thurso went in and out; Olvidia
Trembled each time, but after going to the privy
Was more composed in her mind.

                              The soft beneficent rain hung on the
      hills without flowing down
And filled the soil to the rock, all it could hold; it lay on the shore, it
      sweetened the bitter sea,
It dripped from every bough of the forest, and from the feet of the dead
      man and his hands and his chin,
It glazed his pale-blue face, and glazed the great seaward rock-face of
      Thurso's Landing, and each green leaf
And grass-blade south by the coast to Point Conception; and north into
      Oregon; so long an island of cloud,
Blinding white above, dark and dove-purple below, rained on a thousand
      miles of the continent's edge;
The old savage brood-mare, the earth, drank strength and forgot her
      deserts. Helen Thurso
Walked in Reave's room and looked out the window, and the ivory tree
Seemed to have borne in the rain enormous fruit.
She covered her mouth, through incredulous fear feeling
The bulge of her bruised lip, and left the room
Silently; she met Reave's mother carrying a white
Bundle of linen that glimmered down the dark passage,
And said, "Have you seen Mark?" She answered jealously
"What do you want?" "Oh, Oh. If he's in his room.
I was thinking about the rain, I haven't seen him this morning . . .
My eyes are sick." She passed and felt the smell
Of the freshly ironed linen mix with her fear,
And came to Olvidia in the hot kitchen

Stroking the iron on the board. "Come to the door

For God's sake, for the windows are blind with rain.

In the sycamore tree?" The Indian hung back, mumbling

"Might 'a' been a mountain-lion or a big hawk," and Helen

Dragged her by the wrist, but the old mother

Had followed and heard, and when they came to the door

She was at the foot of the tree. They heard her cry

Three times, a dry scream more goshawk's than woman's.

Helen breathed and said "Reave has heard that. I . . . .

Get a knife." She ran to the tree; where Mark's mother

Stood stiffly quiet by the grotesque legs

And said, "I can't reach. He is the one I loved."

Helen began to clamber at the tree, her knees

Slipping on the wet bark and her fingers

On the ivory bough, the old woman said harshly, "Make no show of
   yourself.

He's been long dead and will not admire you. This one is mine, my
   servants will help me. Stand off, you."

Helen looked back at her face and saw Olvidia and Luna coming; she
   looked at the dead man's face

And said, "Oh good-bye," and looked down quickly. "I will go to Reave,"
   she said trembling.

                    She went to his room.

The bed-covers were trailed on the floor and he at the window

Hung like a broken snake, his hands on the sill lifting his head to the glass.
   He turned toward her,

Wrinkled like a fighting mastiff with rage and pain, saying "That dead
   dog." She shivering and shrill cried out

"No!" but he said, "The dead dog that walks in the wood, that he used to
   talk to, has done this: too shot with cowardice

To live, and too envious to let his sons. Praising death. Oh my poor
    brother,
If you lived in the hell of pain and impotence
That I inhabit, yet you oughtn't to have yielded. It was something to see
    the envy slaver with hunger
And not be fed." Then Helen said faintly, half borne into belief by Reave's
    passion, "Oh, have you seen him?"
The great strained shoulders began to fail, the hooked fingers to slip on the
    painted sill, "Felt him," he said,
Angularly falling.

                    Unable to lift his weight, she dragged it
To the side of the bed, and heaved up the dead half
Of his body, and he the living. She fell over against him
In the strain of lifting, his violent hands held her
Like a lover's, hurting her breasts against his ribs, she felt a ghastliness in
    him
But forced her charged nerves to make no resistance
And kissed his cheek with her bruised mouth, the hardening
Muscles of his jaw hurt that. "Fool," he said hoarsely.
"Have you forgotten? You'll have to learn to endure
A starved life for a hot woman." She stood up
And saw his lips bluish and compressed and his eyes blunted. "Our loves
    now,
Ah," he said, "a little too heavy. A wrench of pain
For the consummation.
Pain is the solidest thing in the world, it has hard edges,
I think it has a shape and might be handled,
Like a rock worn with flat sides and edges, harder than rock, but
Like love it can hardly last more than fifty years.
Mark is dead. He'd not have yielded in his right mind.
Go help my mother." Helen said, "She drove me away.

THURSO'S LANDING   259

He was always faithful and kind. Oh, Oh, what shore
Are we sailing toward, with such wrecks for the sea-marks?
Dear, you didn't dream I meant to outlive you? Our poor brother
Did very wisely though I wish . . . I can hardly remember
The time when death used to seem terrible to me:
I've worse fears now. But if the whole world should be burned alive.
Our brother, whom we loved well, is safe."

XIX

Reave sighed,

And said, "Go and tell her to send Luna.
He'll have to ride to Lobos, there's no telephone
Nearer. To let the coroner know. Oh God, why bother?
I used to have legs and do my own business.
Do you believe in a God?" "I didn't use to."
"Well? Now do you?" "We've less reason to. Yes.
There's not a tinge of goodness in the whole world,
But war in my mind and agony in yours, and darkness
Over the sea and the heights and all bright spirits
Forsake the earth. We've excellent cause
To know there's none: but there is." "Go to church then.
A torturer then." He wiped his forehead and said,
"Another dead dog to bite us. What, that sits calmly
Above the stars, and sees the old woman lose both her sons for nothing,
    one in a dirty noose
And the other like a broken stick on a dung-hill; then smiles over the sea to
    China on a million people
Dying of hunger, the lucky ones sold their children for tufts of grass and
    die with green teeth, God pats
His baby hands together and looks down pleasantly. No, the world's not so
    comic as that: I'll tell you

What the world's like: like a stone for no reason falling in the night from a
    cliff in the hills, that makes a lonely
Noise and a spark in the hollow darkness, and nobody sees and nobody
    cares. There's nothing good in it
Except the courage in us not to be beaten. It can't make us
Cringe or say please." "Dear," she answered,
"Where would the weakness be in kicking off a random and senseless
Darkness like that? Strength doesn't suffer for nothing,
Strength would refuse to suffer for nothing, but choose its times
To live or die." "Listen," he said; "there's a silver spoon
With my initials on it in a drawer somewhere.
When I was five years old I saw my father
Use it in his mouth: I never would touch it again.
No doubt it stinks." Tenderly she answered,
"You have great hands: I love you: kill me first,
And then eat with *my* spoon. It would be wine and honey,
Oh sweet, sweet, after this life." He laughed angrily
And moaned and said, "Let's talk sense if we talk.
I'll not have him buried here and put him forever
In the black dog's power: superstitious as you:
To Monterey, some old graveyard
Where decent people are lying beside each other
And a rose turns from the sea.

                                . . . Mother," he said,
She entering the room, "your loss is hard.
There's nothing. We must take our pain and live in it." Her eyes
More like dry flints than ever, "Can you read this,"
She said, holding a rag of sodden paper,
"My sight fails, and the rain has washed it, pinned to his coat."
She gave it to Reave, he holding it against the light
Said wearily, "Read it, Helen." Sick pencil-marks

On death-cold paper: she read in a brittle voice:
"I fear insanity. Forgive this ugly sight,
Dribbling and screeching would be an uglier sight,
Or to do something worse. Oh why did you go away,
Why did you come back?
My only cause for this act is fear of madness.
That must be stated clearly. No other cause. Dear love
Come soon, this room is purer." Helen's voice fainted on the final words.
She fixed her eyes on the old mother's and said,
"It was written to *you*." Who answered harshly, "*I* did not go away nor
    come back. Her tricks of nature
Have made their misery again. I never hated her enough." Helen, without
    moving: "How could I care
Who hates me or not, when I think about him writing that in the night?
    He often made notes for thoughts
With a stub pencil," she bit her lip not to weep, and suddenly the tears
    rained down. The old mother: "Ah, Reave?
We have to face it: she fished for *him* too. If I'd married a stronger man my
    sons might have outlived me,
But a woman from nowhere comes and burns you like wax. Give me that
    paper." Helen gave it and the wet slip
Tore in the taking. Reave said, "Snatch, sea-gull. Be a little quiet over my
    head, pain's worn me thin,
And Mark's dead in the house. We're sorry for you,
Mother. As for that message, it has no meaning but the pity in it." The old
    woman looked young, with the angry
Color on her cheek-bones; Helen looked aged and pale, saying "Very likely
    it is quite true that I brought
Misery in both my hands, unwillingly. I am much to be blamed for all our
    miseries. I can bear it.
But while the night darkens, and God closes his hand on this house, and
    there's no help, I might do well at last

What you can't do. After that I'll submit meekly, whether you wish to
    punish me or please to say
Some merciful thing."

                    Reave opened his eyes and said,
"Mark's not to be buried here, this is the dog's ditch.
He'd 'a' lived long if he hadn't walked in the woods.
If you have to sell horses to buy a grave to the north, there's a little colt
That has no name, I'm fond of him, I rode him before the fall." His
    mother stared, saying "Who buys horses?"
He answered, "He's not for sale, I'll not have it. I hunted the desert for him
When he strayed, and brought him back. Are you all ganged against me
With the devil in the woods?" The old woman touched him and said,
"Reave. Nobody will sell your horses. There's no buyer.
You're tired." He answered, "Not tired: but to say it plainly:
In hell, in hell. . . . I have talked foolishness.
I can bear twice as much. Go back to Mark, mother.
He needs . . . I remember." The women stood side by side
Gazing at his locked face, the mother weaving
Her thin hands together, having that rainy paper
Crushed between the two palms, but Helen stone still; then Reave
Drew down the lids over his staring eyes
And made a thin careful smile. The old woman suddenly
Sighed and went out.

                    Reave drew loud breath and his eyes
Opened, fastened on Helen's: "Don't let her come in again.
I'd hate to tell her. She's much to be pitied too. Never let her know," he
    said craftily,
"That she's the cause. She lay with my enemy, all springs from that. I
    believe you'd never dream it, to look at her,

She'd do such things. Has it cleared?" She stammered "What—what?" "Go
    to the window," he said, "and look out, and see
Whether the rain has stopped yet." She went and said, "No." "It is clearing
    eastward?" "All dark. Some wind moves
The sky-ridge trees." "Rain or not"; and after a moment, "Did you notice
    anything," he said, "Helen, disordered
In what I said lately?" "I know you suffer
Overpowering pain at times." "Hm? Not a bit. Firm as a rock . . . Listen,
    Helen:
My pride and I have agreed: I can bear this punishment,
But I don't have to." She thought he had yielded and was willing to die;
That he was beaten seemed to be breaking her heart, that he would die
    terrified her, that his useless pain
Would find its goal in peace was a great sheaf of good; so three ways
    stricken, white and faint: and the undertow
Unconscious enmity that never died from her mind tearing her too with its
    exultation: "Oh,"
She whispered, "what change?" "Why should I refuse the means to relieve
    it?"
He said defiantly. "I'm like in the sea's gut here,
Weighed down with tons of green thick water: while above the air's
Clean and alive. We're too closed-in here." He paused,
His eyes glassed and hands clenched. "A twinge. Don't imagine
I'm running from the dead dog: we'll make a bonfire
Of his platforms on the rock head some night.
That's my one point in life now: to clean out
Trace and shape and smell of him and leave the canyon
Virgin if fire and dynamite can do it.
In summer when the ground hardens we'll slash
A driveway up to the kilns and blow them clean
By the foundations. Have you told him yet?" "What?" she asked.
"What!—bring it to the door." "Dear, I'm dull with sadness,

I can't see to your mind." "Have I not told you
Three times already? The truck, the truck, the motor-truck.
The thing that runs on four wheels. Tell him—tell Luna
To bring it to the door and help you load on your cripple,
So I'll taste air to-day." "Where?" "Where it's widest,
And the ocean and hills are clear to be seen,
On the Landing: the rock head: up there." "Oh, Oh, that's in the sky.
That's well thought." She trembled violently and said,
"I'll do my part. It's noon:
First you must eat, though Mark's dead in the house.
Then we'll go up to the rock. It seems long
Since morning." He said, "To-morrow they'll need the motor
To take my brother . . . who has died, as you say. Akh, do quickly."

XX

"You'll need the jack and a shovel, Johnny Luna,
For the ground's rotten with rain; and an axe
For brushwood no doubt has grown up in the old road.
Yet another thing:
There was a man named Rick Armstrong: do you remember?
He's dead quite lately. *He* died too. The world's
Full of that kind of thing." She pressed her hand
On the reeling pulse in her throat and said, "I'll tell you.
He drove too fast at the Salinas River bridge,
Suddenly his sins came on him and swerved the wheel
Over the concrete, he rolled with his car
And got his life bumped out in the willow-bushes.
Do you understand? It will please my husband,
For he was his bitter enemy: but if *I* told him
I might not be believed.
I am very anxious to make him feel . . . contentment

Before he . . . sleeps, because he suffers great pain
And has no joy nor hope. Johnny, you'll help me
For love of him, and I'll give you this ring besides.
I wore it through all my ventures, bought long ago
With money I earned. I paid twelve dollars for it,
You can get three no doubt: the stone's nothing,
But the hoop's gold. Take it please.
I've nothing else of any priceable value
Except my marriage-ring: I'll die in that,
Though stained, some acid. What you must do is, tell him
About Rick Armstrong's death, as I told it to you,
To make him happier; but say the Vasquez boys
Told you, not I. Everyone's talking about it,
He was well known on the coast; he worked, you know,
With the road-builders. Mind the jack and the spade,
And the hand-axe: he's half mad with pain
Or he'd not want to go up. Why, the rain's stopped,"
She said, and sobbed once and smiled. "That's a grand sign.
Ah don't forget how Rick Armstrong died."

XXI

Reave's mother heard
The motor stammer to the house-door, and spin and stop. She stood up
   beside her own bed,
On which she had had her dearest laid down, and had never ceased to
   arrange the body, to make it seem
Happily asleep if she could; having dried it with a warm towel and washed
   the rain-stains, and dressed her son
In clean night-clothes, covering the throat: she looked at the bed with
   unmoistened eyes like a mother falcon,

And went down-stairs to the door; Luna was entering. "Who ordered this?
    Take it back to the shed.
He will stay in my house with me to-night: if we go to-morrow
To another place, *I* will tell you, not that woman." Helen came while she
    spoke, and Luna
Looked from her face to hers, as a boatman
From the rock shore to the driving sea. Helen said, "We must take the
    bedding first, it is ready."
The old mother: "You're very confident suddenly. You think you've made
    enough wretchedness to break my mind and make you
Commander here." Helen, vaguely, in her own thought snared: "What?
    No. Is a wind blowing, the trees on the cloud
Look hunched: and all my strength's gone: Oh mother,
Tell Reave to wait! Comfort him." "Reave?" She turned and went toward
    his room, then Helen remembered that suddenly
He seemed to dislike his mother: "Don't go in to Reave:
Oh, I was wrong," and followed her; and Luna followed
The two women. Helen said to Luna: "Take out the mattress and the
    covers: we'll have to go." The old mother
To Reave: "You called for that? Did you tell me you were going
    somewhere,
And I missed hearing?" His eyes avoided her, he answered:
"I'm going to the head of the rock to smell the rain.
Why not? I can't make Mark live
By smothering here." "The rock?" "Uh, what y' call the Landing.
I believe the air's free there." He closed his eyes
And fists, and smiled. Helen said sharply to Luna:
"The little package is mine: let it lie, I'll take it.
Bread and meat." Reave's mother looked back and saw
Her throat shuddering and swallowing as strained with sickness
At the thought of food. "Why: how long are you staying up there?"
"While our . . . the light lasts," she answered, and swallowed, and said,

"Olvidia's here if you need anything." The mother:

"Reave. This is not in your line, to run off from trouble.

She leads you I think." "Run?" He rolled his head on the thick neck. "*Run*,

To a man with no legs. And *she leads me*: you are very greedy to make
    humiliation perfect, ah?

I might have a grudge too . . . wi' that dog . . . ugh. Mother, mother:

You endure something and so do I: but bodily pain is ignoble and soils the
    mind. If ever

I should talk wildly . . . . no danger: I can bear much more than anything
    yet . . . . you'll not take it to heart,

Put it aside as just foam and nothing. I love you and respect you, and when
    you are bitter with me I know

How life has used you.

About the other thing: have you ever known me to turn back from
    something begun? I've grown touchy,

But not all changed." "In this raw air," she answered,

"In the likely rain to go up: you told me your trouble turned fiery after a
    rain." "I am ashamed,"

He said dully, "to leave you in sorrow. I can do nothing here, not even walk
    to Mark's room.

A man like me, crippled out of use, hurt out of patience and so forth

May's well go picnics. . . . D' y' see that star?" "What?" "The star."
    "There's no star, Reave." He drew his hand

Over his eyes and said, "No star? None? Oh, yes there is.

Thousands, but in the house we can't see them. Well, Helen.

Move me, ah? March."

                  That frame of redwood sticks

And canvas was laid on the bed against him, Reave shifted

The living part of his body onto it, the others

The lower part. Helen saw his jaws locked

Not to express pain, she heard the breath

Hiss through his nostrils, and thought that she must detach
Her nerves from feeling with his, or all her remnant
Of strength to help him would bleed away to no purpose: but a
    superstitious
Fear forbade any restraint of sympathy,
It looked too much like betrayal; and Reave might suffer
Some mystic loss. She took one of the whittled
Litter-handles, the old woman another, and Luna
The two at Reave's feet; so they conveyed him forth
And edged him onto the truck-floor. He felt his mother's
Eyes probe him, then to cover pain and the shame
Of helplessness: "You ought to rig up a mast
And tackle," he muttered with flat dry lips,
"To hoist your deck-load aboard." "Reave, for God's sake,"
Helen cried. "What?" he said. "Ships are bad luck I think."
"Fool." "Yes"; and she said panting, "Oh, you're quite right,
Call it a ship. I'll sit on the deck beside you.
Our lives are taken away from luck and given
Higher." The old woman looked at her lifted face
And began fiercely to speak, and looked at Reave's, and clutched
The broken board-ends of the floor of the truck
By his feet, where the steel binding was sprung. "I will stay with Mark,"
She said harshly. "It's been promoted," Helen said,
"From being the barge for calves to the butcher.
Now . . ." The mother: "I think, Reave, this woman
Is faithful now." "—A ship," Helen said, "exploring
The open ocean of pain to try if there's any
Shore." "You have not the courage," she answered.
"But as you deal with Reave I will deal with you,
And twice as much. I have nothing to hold me." She turned to the house
And the car moved; before she came to the door-step
She fell down in the path; but no one saw her,

For Helen looked at Reave, Reave at the sky,

And Luna drove. The old woman dragged her hands

Through the wet earth and stood up, lifting her yellow

Asturine face: as when a goshawk is caught in a steel trap at a pole's end,

That was feathered with a bird for bait, and the farmer comes with death in
   his hands and takes down the pole, she turns

In the steel teeth and outstares her captor with harder eyes.

                                            Pitching and

      slipping on stones

And greasy earth, the truck toiled up the farm-lane; Helen watched the
   lines in Reave's face, and risings

Of muscle in his cheek when he locked his jaws when a jolt racked him.
   Once, when the fore wheels and then the rear

Struck in succession and Reave's lips tightened, she laid her hand on his
   fist: "That was the cable," she said,

And wished that she had kept silence; and said, "It lies in the canyon mud
   like a killed snake: your enemy

Was under your wheels." But whether he heard her or not he made no sign.

                                                  At

      the turn to the county road

Mill Creek is bridged; the stream ran full, on the bridge was a whirlwind
   funnel of sticks and splinters, then Helen

Looked up the redwoods and saw the racing sky, and a ray of sun plunge
   like a sword, cut northward,

And be withdrawn. They climbed the cliff-cut zig-zag stair of the road;
   when they neared the crest

The blanket streamed up, stripped from Reave's feet, and Helen

With a sudden sea-gull cry caught it down again

And said "Oh, Reave!" as if waked from a dream

That drove toward some unbearable end. "We can't

Go out to the rock, but if you can bear it
We'll go on farther than that, we'll go on to town.
The doctor will have to do . . . at least something
To still your pain." "All the opium in India.
Brought low enough without that"; he muttered more,
But the streaming wind took it away, then Helen:
"Oh Reave be merciful: spare me once.
We couldn't tell that the storm was stripping the high places
When we planned this, down below, I can't bear it." The wind tilted the
     truck on the steep springs
When it gained the crest and turned quartering; Reave struck the floor with
     his hand, holding his body with the other to stay it
From rolling, and groaned, "I guess you can bear it." "You don't know," she
     said,
"What stands on the rock . . ." she stoppered her mouth with her knuckles
     against the teeth, and breathed through them, and said,
"You have no mercy: your choice is wise. Here is the gate."

XXII

                                                             At the
     cliff-line, in the lee of one of those heavily
Timbered platforms on the very brow, from which the lime-kegs used to be
     slung to the ship's hold,
They rested at length; but only the cripple's insane invincible stubbornness
     had brought them to it, by the gullied
Overgrown road. A broken shed on the staging, long ago unroofed by some
     former storm,
Still offered a brittle screen of standing planks, splintered, singing in the
     wind; Thurso's companions
Laid him in that shelter on the sea-brow platform. He gathered and
     governed pain in a long silence, and said,

"Did you see that riff-raff under the floor, in the joists and braces?"
"What?" Helen said dimly. "Sticks and grass: wood-rats' nests.
Kindling. When this spell of rain ends
We've only to drop a match and all the platform
Flies into ashes: while Luna pries the old engine-boiler
Down the cliff into the sea: we'll have our rock head
Clean as at first." She answered, "Oh: that?" and shivered
In the whirl of the broken wind, saying, "Reave: listen.
Do you think he minds?" "Hm?" "Your father. Because if he
Lives after his death, envying and doing evil,
Then death, that I have always been sick with fear
To think of, is not an end, and you and I
Might look down at our lives laughing
From a great height." "Dead as a dog," he said.
"I never thought anything else. Grieving for Mark
I may've talked foolishly. We'll erase his leavings
For pleasure and to clean the world." "You don't know.
I don't know. They won't tell," she said grievously.
"Another man, Reave, is dead also. They fall and fall
Like apples in a wind. Johnny Luna told me." She stood up
And called Luna from prying at the truck's mudguard,
Where it was bent to the tire by a stump of oak,
"Was it the Vasquez boys that told you?" she screamed
Down the loud wind. Luna climbed up the platform
And stood with his blank slate face bent from the storm,
Saying "What you want?" "I was so troubled this morning,
I hardly listened to you: didn't you tell me
Armstrong was killed?" He nodded gravely, and Helen:
"I'm glad. Are you glad, Reave?" "No. Rick Armstrong?"
He said groaning, turning himself on his shoulders,
"How did Rick Armstrong die?" "All in a minute,"
She answered, "how was it? In his car, Johnny?"

"He drive too fast at the bridge." "When was that?" Reave said.
"I don' know. Maybe las' week. Vidal Vasquez
He talking about." Reave said, "It's too bad.
He was a good fellow: but the single fault
I've never understood yet. Well. Time and chance." Helen, suddenly
   shaking like the erect boards
Behind her in the wind: "Is it nothing, nothing to you? It was something to
   me! Hush. I'll be still. I hoped
You'd feel an old debt paid, and be pleased, and I'd
Be dearer to you. He's dead, you understand? He's gone down. You live."
   Reave gazed up in slight wonder; Helen sighed
And turned to Luna: "That's all. Thank you for lying. It was no good."
   The Indian went carefully down,
And back to the car, clinging by the platform timbers in the current of
   wind.

        Helen crouched again
On the planks beside Reave's mattress, she kept jerking her hands together
   and drawing them apart; the screen
Of boards behind her whistled and clapped like something heard on a ship;
   the ragged skies and wreaths
Of mist rushed by, and crescent-moon-shaped flurries of foam on the
   streaked sea; the rock and the platform
Were driving up wind with dreadful increasing speed, the deck and the hull.
   She moistened her lips to whisper
Silently: "Mark's out of it. Oh happy, Oh happy! but the racing engines
Will burst with this. Is the time now?"

                 Reave never slept, he lay and
   looked up with broad light eyes
At the driven sky; the upper eye-lids cut the blue circles, the lower missed
   them; his face was motionless

Like worn hard wood, but all the while he felt pain. It was hateful of him
    to leave the duty to a woman;
Lie there fallen; wait to be saved; what had they come up for! And when
    she killed her lover to please him
He had not cared.

              She turned herself toward the clattering boards and
    undid the package,
And turned again, holding the things in her hands
Hidden in her lap. The engine in her side was quieter,
But the ship glided dreadfully faster, giddy with speed
She swayed upright and went around him to approach him
From the north side, so that her right hand
Was under his chin when she knelt down and kissed,
And babbling something of love drew his own sharp hunting-knife
Between the jaw and the jut of cartilage, with such
Hoarded unconscious violence that both the arteries,
And the tubes between them, and much of the muscle sheath
On the right of the throat were severed; his head jerked to the left,
The great wound gaped and sighed, all in a moment
Mattress and blanket, the planks, the whole world of sense,
Were painted with blood and foam. He heard her crying
She'd done it for love, he formed his lips to say "Bitch,"
But breath and the light failed; he felt the animal
Flurry of death waggle his arms and head,
No pain from the loins down. Then all was perfect
No-pain.

          Helen stood up from her deed
And said "I have the other thing in my fingers.
Oh Johnny Luna, go down and tell his mother
That the ship has found land." But when she looked,

Luna was still tinkering the truck. She ran
To the platform-end, and the wind threw her on the planks,
She lay on her breasts and thighs, crying "Tell the old woman
To come up here and see him like a king in Babylon
With his slave lying at his feet."

                                        Her face and the blood
Moved him to flee into the wind and down
The rock-path in the cliffside.

XXIII

                                        Reave's mother labored up the steep face,
    Luna behind her.
The wind had sagged toward the southwest and somewhat declined in
    violence, so that a wide-winged hawk
That had been hungry all day was able to hang in the birdless air of the
    rock head when they came up,
Probing with her eyes wild buckwheat bushes and sage and the polished
    leaves of the barren strawberry; she looked
Nailed to the firmament, her twitching wings like the spread hands of a
    crucified man fighting the nails;
But Helen imagined her a vulture and was screaming at her.

                                                        When
    Reave's mother came,
Helen made shift to sit up on the planks beside her slain man, and staring
    with enormous violet eyes
From a stained shrunk face, began to make words in a voice that was not
    her own: "I was afraid you'd not come.
I have to tell you. But now I've taken Reave's lifetime of pain upon me to
    spend in an hour or two,

And my throat's burnt, but I have to tell you
As clearly as I might be able, because you ought to understand that I am
    not vile to the very end,
And have done well. His death was rapid. But for mine, after I'd done it, if
    I'd taken any easy
Out, you'd have scorned me; and the watchful world might 'a' thought I'd
    done it unworthily, what I did out of pure love
And pity; or thought that I die to escape punishment. Don't come near me
    yet, for I've not finished. I read
In the Sunday paper, how they dug out the grave of a king in Babylon and
    found his women about him
With their skulls knocked in; I planned to honor
Reave in that way: he was like a king in some ways, and if he had found any
    great thing to do
He might have done greatly."

                        She fell, drawing up her knees, and the
    mother said: "What poison?" Helen made no answer,
But being asked a third time: "No," she answered faintly, "a woman's
    poison, a white one. The little tablets
I used for fear of having a baby, in our happy time." She fixed her eyes on
    the vacant air
Above the sea-edge: "Why there's that tiny tiny thing with the yellow mop
Come up to see us. Keep her off, please.
No, Hester. No. You may watch if you like but I alone
Am allowed to lie at his feet, my love is proved."

The old woman answered, "There's nobody." She crept on the platform for
    the wind threw her down, and crept past Helen
To Reave and said, "How did you do it? Did he let you do it?" Helen,
    coughing with laughter in the poison fever:

"Reave let me? Have you gone crazy? I knifed him while I kissed his
   mouth." She cried with pain
At the end of speaking, and the mother: "I knew he would never give in,
   why did I ask? You have done well,
You always were treacherous, you did it easily." She found the
   hunting-knife
And took it up from the blood against Reave's shoulder,
Then Helen cried, raising herself on her hands,
"You must not! You have no right. *I* alone saved him,
Alone to die with him." "When you die I will lay it down.
You are not to get well." Helen gasped, laughing
And retching, "Oh *that's* all? Old fool.
Those little white things, meant to fight the seed of our lovers,
Are seed themselves, I'm pregnant and swell fast,
Baby death, darling, darling."

                        She widened terrified
Eyes and said staring: "I can't
Be silent in pain like Reave: Oh, I did hope to.
I never dreamed, Oh, ooh; Oh, ooh." The old woman watched her
Attentively across Reave's body, and let the knife
Drop on the planks. Helen heard it, and after a long while
She said, stretching her throat, "Be merciful to me.
As I was merciful to Reave. I can't bear
The next hour. . . . Unless it would seem wrong?
Reave not be honored enough?" "I think your time
Is near," she answered.
"There is an end or I'd help you: it will be braver in us
Not to keep begging death out of the cloud
Before he is ready." But she crept under the wind
Around Reave's body and kissed Helen's hand, and remained with her
Tenderly until she died.

The platform is like a rough plank theatre-stage
Built on the brow of the promontory: as if our blood had labored all
    around the earth from Asia
To play its mystery before strict judges at last, the final ocean and sky, to
    prove our nature
More shining than that of the other animals. It is rather ignoble in its quiet
    times, mean in its pleasures,
Slavish in the mass; but at stricken moments it can shine terribly against
    the dark magnificence of things.

Luna came up the platform and stood shaking,
Leaned over against the wind; the old woman said:
"We can do nothing. She had a wasteful gallant spirit.
It is not poured out yet; go down for now."

Toward evening the seas
    thundered on the rock, and rain fell heavily
Like a curtain, with one red coal of sundown glowing in its dark. The old
    woman stood up
And fell, and stood up and called: "Now come, it is time.
. . . To bear . . . endure . . . are poor things, Johnny; to live
And bear what we can't strike back at: but we come to them
Unless we fall off before. . . . Has the car lights?
Help me: you'll have to carry all the weight. I am the last
And worst of four: and at last the unhappiest: but that's nothing."

III

Give Your Heart to the Hawks

1931-1933

CRUMBS OR THE LOAF

If one should tell them what's clearly seen
They'd not understand; if they understood they would not believe;
If they understood and believed they'd say,
"Hater of men, annihilating with a sterile enormous
Splendor our lives: where are our lives?"
A little chilled perhaps, but not hurt. But it's quite true
The invulnerable love is not bought for nothing.
It is better no doubt to give crumbs than the loaf; make fables again,
Tell people not to fear death, toughen
Their bones if possible with bitter fables not to fear life.
—And one's own, not to have pity too much;
For it seems compassion sticks longer than the other colors, in this
   bleaching cloth.

A LITTLE SCRAPING

True, the time, to one who does not love farce,
And if misery must be prefers it nobler, shows apparent vices;
At least it provides the cure for ambition.
One does not crave power in anthills, nor praise in a paper forest;
One must not even indulge the severe
Romance of separateness, as of Milton grown blind and old
In his broken temple against the drunkards:
The ants are good creatures, there is nothing to be heroic about.
But the time is not a strong prison either.
A little scraping the walls of dishonest contractor's-concrete
Through a shower of chips and sand makes freedom.
Shake the dust from your hair. This mountain sea-coast is real,
For it reaches out far into past and future;
It is part of the great and timeless excellence of things. A few
Lean cows drift high up the bronze hill;
The heavy-necked plow-team furrows the foreland, gulls tread the furrow;
Time ebbs and flows but the rock remains.
Two riders of tired horses canter on the cloudy ridge;
Topaz-eyed hawks have the white air;
Or a woman with jade-pale eyes, hiding a knife in her hand,
Goes through cold rain over gray grass.
God is here, too, secretly smiling, the beautiful power
That piles up cities for the poem of their fall
And gathers multitude like game to be hunted when the season comes.

INTELLECTUALS

Is it so hard for men to stand by themselves,
They must hang on Marx or Christ, or mere Progress?
Clearly it is hard. But these ought to be leaders . . .
Sheep leading sheep, "The fold, the fold.
Night comes, and the wolves of doubt." Clearly it is hard.

Yourself, if you had not encountered and loved
Our unkindly all but inhuman God,
Who is very beautiful and too secure to want worshippers,
And includes indeed the sheep with the wolves,
You too might have been looking about for a church.

He includes the flaming stars and pitiable flesh,
And what we call things and what we call nothing.
He is very beautiful. But when these lonely have travelled
Through long thoughts to redeeming despair,
They are tired and cover their eyes; they flock into fold.

AT THE FALL OF AN AGE

(The story of Achilles rising from the dead for love of Helen is well enough known. That of Polyxo's vengeance may be less familiar; it can be found in Pausanias' "Description of Greece," explaining the Rhodian worship of Helen as Dendritis, the tree-goddess.)

The scene is the fore-court of a noble dwelling on the island of Rhodes. Portico of the house, with steps of heavy stone and painted wooden columns, but all worn and old. Black pine forest on the hill behind. One great pine stands to the left of the steps, near the house-wall; it is old, with contorted boughs, one of which overhangs the steps. The time is nearly twenty years after the fall of Troy.

(Enter a shepherd and his little son, the shepherd leading a reluctant lamb by a noosed thong. They come from the right foreground, and go toward the left.)

THE SHEPHERD   The gods get hungry like you and me, so it has to die.

THE BOY   But you called her mine; you promised that I might rear her. Oh father.

THE SHEPHERD   I can't help that. You have a shepherd's eye and you chose the perfect one. *We* eat the runts and the lame, the Gods want perfection; the run of the season, that is neither poor nor perfect, is for wool and breeding. Choose again.

THE BOY   Only to lose again.

(A man comes in running, from the left.)

THE SHEPHERD   Hey. Fisherman?

THE FISHERMAN   *(breathless)*   You had better fetch in your flock, and tell Cowboy. Pirates I think.

THE SHEPHERD   What, what, what?

THE FISHERMAN   Ohey, the house! Who is at the door? A ship has landed.

THE PORTER   Who's there? A ship?

THE FISHERMAN   Armed men coming ashore from a black ship. I left
    Calcho watching.

> (*The porter turns in the doorway. Shouting is heard from within the house. The shepherd and boy scurry away out of sight, tugging the lamb.*)

THE PORTER   What kind of a ship?

THE FISHERMAN   (*breathless*)   Akh. Akh. The kind that people sail in.

> (*A few men with spears or pikes begin to come down between the columns; one is adjusting a leather helmet, another struggles clumsily with his shield.*
> *Calcho comes in from the left. He is a fisherman too, and carries the trident fish-spear of his trade.*)

THE FIRST FISHERMAN   Oh here is Calcho. Didn't they catch you?

THE PORTER   Where are they, Calcho? Raiding the pasture? Speak, man.

CALCHO   They are coming quietly up the path.

> (*The spearmen begin to form across the courtyard, at the foot of the steps. The first fisherman edges around behind them.*)

THE PORTER   What? Armed men?   (*turning*)   My lady . . .

> (*He moves to the side, to stand by one of the columns. Polyxo, the lady of the house, comes to the head of the steps, and speaks across the spearheads below her.*)

POLYXO   Tell me what you have seen, Calcho.

CALCHO

We dare not launch; the west is too full of wind; we drop our lines from
    the rock. I heard oars groaning;
That long black ship glided below us like a dream and came in and landed.
    These are some great lord's men;
I watched when they leaped the strake. They have fierce obedient faces;
    their life is outside them; they would do anything
Without winking. As for the woman with them . . .

POLYXO   A woman?

CALCHO   For

whom they laid the plank to the strand:
I watched and her beauty was like the thoughts of God, burning and calm.

POLYXO   We

    knew one like that:

Gold and fire and ivory: King Menelaus his adulterous wife: that Helen, for
    whose lawless luxury
Ten thousand died: the lord of my love and of this island among them . . .
    for a wanton. If this were that fountain
Of death! We've prayed for it: did the men speak like Spartans? I dream
    too much.

CALCHO   Not a word.

*(He looks behind him, and joins the defenders of the house, holding his trident as they hold their
pikes. The strangers come in, masked identically, moving like one machine. The woman with them
might be either their captive or their queen; a fold of her cloak is drawn over her face.)*

POLYXO

Who are you, strangers? It is peace I think?

*(The woman drops her cloak from her face and head; the hair is golden and the face ivory. An
exclamation like a sigh of wonder is heard among Polyxo's people.)*

HELEN   Peace and love, dear.

POLYXO   *(shuddering)*   Ah.

    Yes. Your face, Helen,
Has been much in my dreams. . . . My eyes are too old to see only the
    beauty among the tricks of the world.
What are these warriors?

HELEN   I'll tell you that in the house, when you are
    kind. Do you remember, Polyxo,
A day in spring, you and I were laughing together beside the flooded
    Eurotas? I garlanded
Your dear dark head with flowers before we bathed together, parting the
    green reeds of the bank.
Our skies were clear and no grief had come: you were my guest then.
Now I am yours.

*(The household spearmen have moved to right and left of the steps at the word "peace," so that the
space between the two women is cleared; Polyxo standing at the head of the steps and Helen in
front of her guard.)*

POLYXO　　　　　　　Grief has come; and that day is dead. . . . A man was
　　　here last year from Laconia
　　Passing to Egypt, who boasted that neither time nor grief nor weariness
　　　touched Helen's face. We judged him
　　A liar.
HELEN　　　You find me much changed, Polyxo.
POLYXO　　　　　　　　　　　　　　　Changed? A woman who
　　　has been a wild cause of misery and death
　　Will surely be pale with repentance; a woman famously unfaithful, surely
　　　purple with shame; a woman
　　Pursued by the ghosts of slaughtered men and a screaming city—could
　　　hardly escape marking I think:
　　The cheeks furrowed, and the eyes a haggard stare between the red eye-lids.
　　　. . . Nothing—nothing—nothing—
　　Not a line, not a mark. You have wandered through life uncaring,
　　　untouched, heartless, unmarked, and all your wickedness
　　Is like a song.
HELEN　　　　　　Must I not love you any more, once my dear friend?
POLYXO　　　　　　　　　　　　　　　　　　Whilst
　　I . . . Oh, your beauty is pure,
　　Young and burning and holy; you are not changed from the bride Menelaus
　　　unveiled or the young wife
　　The long soft eyes of Paris lustfully lingered on: whilst I—look at me.
　　　(She uncovers her head, throwing down the Tyrian head-dress; her thin gray-white hair, corded
　　　throat and wrinkled cheeks are seen.)　　　　　　　　　　　It
　　was no trick of mine
　　That drew ten thousand down to black death and burnt the chief towers of
　　　Asia. But you the Gods have made
　　To look pure forever. The Gods do strangely.
　　Perhaps . . . they leave justice to men.
HELEN　　　　　　　　　　　They are in their cloud; we know
　　　too little about them. We know

They love and surely reward the hospitable house. May I go into your
    house, Polyxo? I am homeless.
We have come far; weary are the waves.

POLYXO   Not yet. I am thinking what gift
    . . . Is Menelaus behind you
Baying on the trail? He will find it hard perhaps to raise the Greek princes
    a second time.

HELEN   My lord
    Grew old, and has left me, in the aging world. Carved stones contain him,
        with all the careful honors of death,
In high Therapnae.

POLYXO   Well—old. Some have died
    Young. You are all alone then? If any evil-disposed or remembering person
        should do you hurt,
No husband would come, nor no fierce lover, to find the quarrel and avenge
    you? It is bitter to be left alone.
I have learned that.

HELEN   Very bitter. Worse to be exiled. Old friends I see
    begin to regard you
Strangely and coldly; they let you stand at the door.

POLYXO   I have not only
    myself to think of, but all
This island people. You come questionably. Tell me who exiled you, for
    what new . . . we'll not say crime: the . . .
Adventures of one so immortally beautiful must not be called . . .

HELEN   Call
    them, Oh my lost friend, by any
Bleak shameful name that your heart can bear, but not me beautiful. That
    name is my hill of miseries. Many
Women are beautiful; and some have peace; and a few are happy. I am
    exiled indeed, but for no crime.

The sons of Menelaus by that other woman have always hated me. They
    inherit the kingdom, and I
  Am exiled.
POLYXO   Not without reason: they would give the people a reason.
HELEN   I
    am not here to be judged. A storm
  That struck Therapnae, and the living dead, perhaps had frightened them.
POLYXO   What
    is this? You shall tell me all the story
  Before you come in my door.
HELEN   (turning to her guardsmen)   Servants of Achilles: you see that
    friendship is a fading and fragile hope
  Among the living. With you in the high sepulchres
  It stands, if anything does. Oh soldiers, where will you take me, to what
    refuge, if I refuse
  To humble myself before this woman, but turn and shake off the eyes of
    Rhodes and enter the ship,
  Where will you sail to?
THE CAPTAIN OF THE GUARD
                            Queen: to the mound on the Asian foreland. You
    know our condition: that we have no home
  But the high, holy and quiet sepulchre. A ship is made to sail home: we
    shall hasten home.
HELEN   (shuddering)   Ah, Ah.
  I knew that!
THE CAPTAIN   The west wind still wildly blows.
HELEN   Oh soldiers: you know
    that Achilles your master loved me. Look north;
  You can see from here like a blue shadow on the raging sea
  Ancient Crete, and the snows of Cretan Mount Ida: take me there and
    leave me; leave me on the sand
  Like a beggar woman, and hasten home.

THE CAPTAIN   We must not beach the black

    prow again, we must hasten home.

HELEN

    To the burial-hill. To the wailing Trojan ghosts. To dust and ashes.

        (She turns toward the house.)   I will contrive to be humble.

    Polyxo: I am the woman

    Whom Theseus loved, and high-born Menelaus, and beautiful-throated

        Paris, and Deiphobus,

    And one greater than these more terribly, whom I shall name. I would

        rather have been a shepherd's daughter

    To run barefoot and milk the mountain ewes, and pat the curd into cheeses.

                                        Far

POLYXO

    better for you:

    Or else to be strangled at birth.

HELEN   Yet I remember the good gray elders of

    Troy, having seen their sons

    For my sake slain, and knowing me the poison in the city's heart, — yet

        when they passed me, walking like kings,

    They would look at my face with love, they never reproached me. I have

        memories of men doing nobly, to make me patient

    In the day of humiliation.

        (She stands in silence, struggling with her pride, while Polyxo bitterly watches. Helen continues:)

                      But Achilles,

    Violent and fierce, whom nothing could bind: for while he lived he dared

        affront Agamemnon the king,

    And had no reverence for beautiful human flesh, but pierced the shining

        feet of Hector slain

    And dragged him about and about the city at the chariot's tail, defiling the

        beautiful heroic body:

    But after he was dead he opposed

    The purpose of God. . . . He said my remembered face tormented him, he

        had no reverence but lusted for me,

In his life he had never known me, in his death he lusted. He wrestled with
    Death in the shut darkness; he broke
The mighty wrists and the mound of burial. He stood on the broken head
    of the mound and shouted to his men,
Whose graves pit the wide plain. They had never failed to obey him, they
    heard and rose. All the fierce Myrmidons,
Dark faces and fire in the hollow eye-sockets and earth-matted hair; staring
    they stood. These men here
Are of those that stood up.

> (*Movement of Polyxo's people. They retreat a little, but a line of the best draws across the foot of
> the steps again, so that Polyxo is seen again above spearheads. She herself shows fear, but says:*)

POLYXO   Go on. Tell it all. Whatever I resolve to do
    will not be shaken
By the lies of the poets you listen to in idle Sparta
Or lonely Therapnae in the long evenings.

HELEN   I would to God it were lies.
    Why do you hate me, Polyxo?

POLYXO
    Tell your tale.

HELEN   I cannot. I will not. Soldiers:
    Will you not speak?

THE MYRMIDONS   (*clashing their shields, and making a heavy pacing dance, as of bronze
puppets; but I think only the leader speaks.*)
                              We that broke the walls
And tore open the citadel of Asia,
And the holy city of Priam like a gored ship
Foundered in the roaring seas of our blood:
We have sacked the empire of Death also.
They planted strange seed in Asia who buried Achilles.
The earth had received us and we broke the earth;
The hands of God were upon us to hold us under;
We broke the fingers of God and Fate;

They planted wild seed in Asia who buried Achilles.
When we camped in the dead
Metropolis, we dead, there was nothing living but a wolf and a dog;
The very swallows were burnt
That used to twitter in the eaves of Troy.
Where Priam and the silken processions
Went delicately
By the great hewn stones: in the morning
We pissed on the stones and knew that we dead lived,
And went south from there
Fasting, until we came to a town and killed it.
Punic ships lay on the shore.
They planted strange seed in Asia who buried Achilles.
Oh high blue water
And whirling currents in the lee of islands,
Purple nights and blue days,
Were you not pierced, were you not trampled?
Bear witness how his great heart burned you,
Toward this woman he burned.

HELEN

Stand farther, soldiers. I cannot bear . . . Oh Polyxo, save me. Though
love is dead and friendship forgotten,
The living should guard the living, and a woman ought to have pity on a
woman . . .

THE MYRMIDONS

We beached at sundown
And struck in the night, in the gathered storm.
King Menelaus said "What are these?"
And the spear-point was at his beard.
"Dorian barbarians?"
Look under the torches, Oh King, that flare in the wind in the gates,
Look under the torches.

The Dorians have yellow hair; ours is earth-dark.
The Dorians have black iron helmets, ours are green bronze.
They planted strange seed in Asia who buried Achilles.
HELEN
Be silent, be silent! It is all true. There was only a little guard at
Therapnae. Our troops were north
On the borders, in the doors of the north. They took the high house and
held Therapnae. The storm raged, and the thunder
Shook the towers, while Achilles possessed me. It is true: he came and
possessed me. His body was not like death —
Only his eyes.
THE MYRMIDONS
We were the door-holders.
Our master went in and laid off his armor, and the queen of Laconia
Screamed once, and then sweetly smiled.
The wild male power of the world
Was mated with the perfect beauty.
While Menelaus outside the gate
Howled like a dog in the violet lightnings in the gaps of night
For spears, but all his were fleeing to the mountain.
And the Gods came down against us and we held the doors.
HELEN
You are not a rock but a woman: let me go in, let me go in!
From public shame, and this furnace of eyes.
POLYXO   Menelaus died?
HELEN   Not that
night. He did die,
Of old age, the next day. . . . I was compelled, undefended.
POLYXO   We are not
blind, we can see you are beautiful
Enough to have stung the body of a violent man in the very ashes. But I am
a woman, and not

A loving woman. Tell me, you dead and stationed soldiers, where is your
  master, this woman's lover?
I desire not to offend him by . . . any act toward this woman, if she is still
  claimed. We have no force
In our pastoral island to oppose the power
That humbled warlike Therapnae bristling with spears.
THE LEADER OF THE MYRMIDONS   You hide a knife
     in your mind, but not too darkly
For eyes that have looked through hollow death, and are whetted and
  disillusioned, nor too dreadful. We are charged
To keep this woman whom our lord has enjoyed intact of any less lover
  until she dies.
When she dies we may hasten home.
  HELEN   Will you plot against me before my
     face? And vainly. I can pity delusion
Even in dead men; whatever it is you would sell, she will not buy. My
  friend has grown cold, but not
Wicked; not monstrous: one can see that without looking through hollow
  death. . . . As to Achilles,
I will tell you, Polyxo. He went away from Therapnae in the stormy dawn,
  gathering his men,
Only detaching these few to guard me. He returned to the ships; and one
  had been burned, he took one of ours;
And sailed away to fetch west for the island Leuke, that white Atlantic
  splendor in the waves, to find there
The peace, he said, that even the most beautiful woman never can give. For
  there one is free of death's
Dreams as of life's. He will never return. I tell you because I trust you.
  POLYXO   That
     is true. Whatever you've done,
  Your blood is noble. The free-born
Trust gayly where a slave trembles. I have determined what I will do.

HELEN   Why
    are you trembling, Polyxo?
POLYXO
    We are not accustomed to seeing the dead land on this island. Come into
        the house. Come in. Let Helen
    Pass, but not those bronze corpses.
THE LEADER OF THE MYRMIDONS   We deliver her to you.
A VOICE AMONG POLYXO'S MEN   Oh
    beautiful woman trust her not!
POLYXO   Who spoke?
HELEN
    I will go in without fear, although I think that you hate me for some
        reason. I'd not seek shelter
    In a house of cold welcome, but choice has been taken from me. The ship I
        came from goes home to black
    And quiet death. One endures a cold welcome liefer than death; I will lay
        down all pride
    And like a suppliant go in. But why do you tremble, Polyxo?
POLYXO   Surely with
    eagerness. My house is honored.
        (Helen approaches the steps, and the spears part to let her pass. Calcho leans from among the spears
        and whispers as she passes in.)
CALCHO
    Beautiful woman turn back. Look: her pressed lips mean evil.
HELEN   Thank you,
    fisherman.
POLYXO   What did that man
    Whisper across the trident?
HELEN   Why, nothing, dear. He would bring me a
    speckled sea-trout or a great lamprey.
    He thinks I am used to kindness. Oh, why do you tremble so?

POLYXO   The chill

    at sundown. Time brings all things.

    (They go into the house.)

CALCHO   Evil is planned. Shall we let the most beautiful woman in the
    world fall into a trap, while we stand idle?

ONE OF THE MEN   Well, it's a pity . . .

ANOTHER   You think our lady lays traps because she had you whipped
    once: but well you deserved it.

THE MYRMIDONS

    Is there any stir in the house?

    Listen: or a cry?

    Farm-boys with spears, you sparrows

    Playing hawk, be silent.

    Splendid was life

    In the time of the heroes, the sun went helmeted, the moon was maiden,

    When glory gathered on Troy, the picketed horses

    Neighed in the morning, and long live ships

    Ran on the wave like eagle-shadows on the slopes of mountains.

    Then men were equal to things, the earth was beautiful, the crests of heroes

    Waved as tall as the trees.

    Now all is decayed, all corrupted, all gone down.

    Men move like mice under the shadows of trees,

    And the shadows of the tall dead.

    The brightness of fire is dulled,

    The heroes are gone.

    In naked shame Agamemnon

    Died of a woman.

    The sun is crusted and the moon tarnished,

    And Achilles has chosen peace.

    Tell me, you island spearmen, you plowboy warriors,

    Has anyone cried out in the dark door?

    Not yet. The earth darkens.

(Slate gray twilight has come; but later a high cloud catching light fills the scene with a confusing red radiance.)

At the fall of an age men must make sacrifice

To renew beauty, to restore strength.

We say that if the perfect beauty were sacrificed,

The very beauty that makes our death-cleansed eyes

Dazzle with tears, would be spread on the sky

And earth like a banner.

All men would begin to desire again, and value

Come back to the earth, and splendor walk there.

There is one perfection to be poured out, one lonely beauty

Left in the world, as lonely as the last eagle.

Has anyone groaned in the house? There it sounds.

A sharp clear broken-off cry like a snapped arrow.

CALCHO

Dead wolves, will her death feed you?

THE MYRMIDONS   Our trade was death.

And now we have known it, it is nothing evil.

CALCHO   Can we endure this?

(He and a few others are going up the steps, when Polyxo comes out and stands above.)

POLYXO   Clear the stones.

(Armed men are at her side; Calcho and his few followers return down.)

POLYXO   You need not press in, you shall see all. I have caught the
    panther.

O men of Rhodes, we sometimes exclaim against the great Gods, when the
    guilty seem to flourish, and the innocent

Fall unavenged. We are always rebuked at last. A murderer may flee to
    Caucasus but the broad eyes

Hardly turn and behold him constantly, and see the knife whetting or the
    noose hanging, in the very gorge

He runs to hide in, under the snow-shining walls and towers of the world.
    Do you remember my lord

Tlepolemus, the husband of my soul and my body? I have caught his
    murderer. Numberless thousands have died
By the war-making act of this one woman, the powers of Greece and the
    house of Priam: they are not perfectly
Important to us here enisled, but Righteousness counted them; and while I
    avenge Tlepolemus the Gods are here
Avenging all. I have two black men I bought from Egypt, whose minds are
    not made like ours, they feel
No shudder where a Greek would flinch; I bid them lead forth the
    murderess, so stripped and shamed as men who were stricken
On the plain by Troy . . . as Tlepolemus . . .
Ah Ah . . . was robbed
Of the hacked and dinted armor . . . all . . . that corselet I gave him: in
    the days when I was able to weep,
And prayed it keep safe his breast: the Greeks retreated from his body
    fallen in the dust, and grooms and foot-soldiers
Despoiled and stripped him, and left him naked under the glaring lion of
    heaven and the Trojan eyes,
White flower in the foul dust, the body I had held in my arms, the flesh
    that my mouth had clung to. . . . Shall I not
Shame this dead woman? . . . Come.

    (Helen is led by slaves from the door, her hands bound behind her back. The confusing red twilight
    somewhat veils her nakedness. Her head is held high, and the eyes clear, though she struggles against
    the bonds, breathing hard through parted lips. Her yellow hair is disordered, and hangs like a heavy
    fleece on one shoulder.)

HELEN   *(straining at the cords)*   Are you the stronger? Yet wretched
    to the end of time:
Contempt and a hissing: whilst I overcome by treachery am more than
    equal to all that may hurt me.
POLYXO   Here
    Is what made war. Look at it, because it will not be beautiful to-morrow.
    No warriors will quarrel for it.

No one will cut through death to come to it. Now, now, I say, the old
    aching hatred, the very bitterness
That fouled my wine with aloes and stained my meat with spilt gall,
    morning and evening all the empty years,
Is turned sweet; it is better to taste than honey; it smells more lovely than
    myrrh and frankincense
Hot from the south. You caught panther!
I am glad that you were a queen in haughty Therapnae; it will be harder to
    die; I am glad you are beautiful
Beyond fault, beyond nature: the ridiculous ugliness of death and
    corruption look the more dreadful to you;
I am glad you had many lovers, you will lie alone; I am glad time could not
    touch you nor age deflower you,
That your beauty is like the African crystal no point can scratch,
    unwoundable, uncontaminable:
For what comes now shall very suddenly unpolish it. Ah, Ah, Ah,
I am sick with delight. Call the black ravens, you beautiful woman.
Oh Helen, black crows and heavy-beaked ravens to be your lovers, to kiss
    your eyes. Call the mountains
Of Asia to look at you.
HELEN   Rhodians: your mistress you see has gone mad,
    you must prevent her — not for my sake,
For your own honor — from making this place forever abominable.
POLYXO   *(to a slave)*   Cast
    the rope over that branch.
I shall sleep sound at last, who have lain year after year tortured
    remembering. To-morrow coming
From the door at dawn, I shall see my enemy's face puffed purple and her
    breasts blackening, and the dragged neck
Not like a dove's, and those fine white feet
Perhaps all shrivelled, perhaps all swollen, who knows? God, who sent her
    here, knows. Why do you wait?

Fling the coil, slave, keep the noose in your hands. Hup! A good cast. I
    shall not sleep, but call
Torches, and feast all night.
HELEN   I see my dark shameful death. Hear me,
    Rhodians . . .
POLYXO   Let her speak, haltered.

(The slave makes to hang the noose on her neck, but when she looks at him he stands back in
    awe of her.)

VOICES AMONG THE PEOPLE
    We cannot suffer this. Oh Oh Oh.
    Spear the black men, hang up the old woman.
    Pikes and fire, ah? Like spitted pigs. We dare.

    (They move toward the steps.)

POLYXO
    I thought that you herd of dogs and peasants . . . Here, the guard.
        Peasants: here are the men
    Who fought at Troy, men to be trusted, my house garrison.

    (Fully armed soldiers, old men but dangerous, move mechanically in two files from the door, right
    and left of the group formed by Polyxo and Helen and the slaves, and make a fence of spears at the
    foot of the steps. They are masked with identical faces of old grim warriors; between them and the
    Myrmidons the island militia seethe like a rabble.)

POLYXO   Rabble, you
    know your boundary: the soldiers
    Of Tlepolemus. Few, but enough. These will not lust for a harlot. These
        are the men that saw
    The Gods fighting, when the rivers of the plain flowed fire and the earth
        roared like water. . . . Veterans of Troy:
    It is mine to avenge your labor and pain and your leader's death; it is yours
        to keep those plowboys in awe
    And herd those herdsmen.

THE MYRMIDONS

    Old men you ought to have died

    In your good years, not wearily

    Gone home to rust.

    If you had died and revived again

    Your hair would not be snowed under but brown as ours,

    And your eyes as fierce.

POLYXO   *(to the slave)*   I said, halter that woman.

    Between the dead and the living my hatred stands.

HELEN   Will you stand and let

    me be slain, you men of Rhodes?

POLYXO

    What, is life sweet? Cry out. Weep publicly. Show all your mind, make all

        your grief like your body naked.

    Surely it is all as beautiful as your body, and I shall be merciful.

THE MYRMIDONS

    It is beautiful to see men die by violence, but to watch a woman

    Killed, is the crown. Oh Queen, die boldly.

HELEN   I pray you on my knees,

    Polyxo.

    Life is too dear to be spent on pride. I am not afraid, but I love life.

POLYXO   I tell

    you, kneeling's

    Not half enough. You must act fear, if you feel none. Plead, scream.

    (Helen stands again, and wrenches at the cords, twisting her body.)

THE MYRMIDONS   *(coming nearer the house, pressing on the demoralized crowd)*

    Queen, life and death are no better than the two ears of a carrion-

    Battening dog; there is nothing to choose.

    We know them both, and their beauty is beyond them, their beauty is the

        value,

    As yours is your beauty. We also were sacrificed.

HELEN

    Dead wolves, fight for me. Save me. You could blow down this brittle
        stubble of Rhodian spears like summer

    Fire in the stubble. Flash your fangs, wolves. Fight, you bronze wolves. For
        I have the seed of Achilles in me.

    For your lord, for your leader's blood, not for me make war.

THE MYRMIDONS

    Beautiful blossoms of battle again and forever unfolding

    Star the earth, but we dropped petals of one

    Shall endure peace, not ever to behold them again nor to hear them,

    In the quiet places, in enormous neutrality.

    Oh perfectly beautiful, pain is brief, endure to be sacrificed.

    This great age falls like water and a new

    Age is at birth, but without your pain it could never be beautiful.

    The golden fleece of your hair, the straining

    Shoulders, the dove-throat, the breasts thrust forward by the strain of
        bonds,

    Shall yield their beauty to the earth and sky,

    The wonderful breasts their soul to all the flushed hills of earth,

    The long white thighs to the marble mountains.

    Mycenae is down in corruption but Athens will stand instead,

    The Dorians will make Laconia a land of helots.

HELEN

    Dogs, not wolves. Death-whipped dogs. Hear me, veterans

    Of Rhodes, old valiant warmen that fought in Asia—from the wall I
        watched you . . . No help, no help anywhere?

    I am brought to bay here between the bony mercy of unmanned old age
        and the eyeless pity of the dead.

    Do you see this ebony tool of murder hangs the halter on my throat, the
        strangling death?

POLYXO   Helen:

    Speak quickly, for your end hastens.

HELEN   I will speak. I have lived and seen the
     great beauty of things, and been loved and honored.
   If now I must die, it is come. Nothing on earth nor in ocean is hatefuller
     than death; at least I have not
   Wasted my life like this gray murderess, fouling with age, lying twenty
     years in the pit of time
   Grinding the rust on a knife.
POLYXO   Take for your portion agony and shame.
     Sweep room there below, guardsmen.
   Haul, slaves. May all that cause war, thus perish. . . . It is dark: torches,
     torches! People of Rhodes, we have caught
   And hanged a panther. Pelt the white body with pine-cones, pelt it with
     clods.
        (*While she is hanged, confused struggle in the brown twilight between the old guardsmen and the
        people. The Myrmidons chanting in their pacing dance take no part in it.*)
THE MYRMIDONS
   Wild swan, splendid-bodied,
   Silent at last, silent and proud, fly up the dark.
   Clash bronze, beat shields, beauty is new-born.
   It is not to be whispered in Argos that Helen died like a woman,
   Nor told in Laconia that sickness killed her.
   Strike swords, blade on blade, the daughter of God
   Hangs like a lamp, high in the dark, quivering and white.
   The breasts are thrust forward and the head bows, the fleece of gold
   Shakes on the straining shoulders, writhes to the long white thighs.
   When God looked down from heaven the mound in the Troad
   Swarmed like an anthill, what spears are those?
   Power that will pierce your people, God of the living,
   The warrior-ants of the anthill, the spears from the dark barrow . . .
        (*Torches are being brought from the house.*)
   Look under the torches, O King, that flare in the wind of night,
   Look under the torches.

No Dorians are we: they planted strange seed in Asia who buried Achilles,

Power to pierce death, helmeted heads cracking the grass-roots,

Power to be born again.

Come down and behold us O King of heaven and O hawks of Caucasus

Come down and behold us,

You African lions in the tawny wilderness roar in the storm,

For our master is joined with the beauty he remembered in death, with the
splendor of the earth,

While the King of Laconia howls like a starved dog

In the rain, in the violet lightnings, in the gaps of night, and we hold the
gates.

(*Polyxo comes between torch-bearers to exult.*)

POLYXO

High violent wind let the tree stand, leave me my vengeance. Slaves, hold
the flaring torches up high;

I can see a hanging whiteness in the wind and smoke. She ought to be
hideous now? How beautiful she is.

Hair veils the face. Where is my triumph? I am very happy. The high wind
swings her, slowly spinning

As if to show all her beauty. I did not wantonly, Oh beautiful woman; my
need compelled me. I have done

More than I dared; I have put my pain outside me; it is time to exult.
White mountains, ice-helmeted peaks

That wall the ends of the world, come here and behold my triumph. Where
is my triumph, has the wind snatched it?

There is no woman on earth so happy as I am, having slain my pain: yet it
seems that all present things

Slip away down hill, and I could weep for them.

CALCHO   (*coming behind her in the darkness and confusion*)   Old woman, revenge is a
slippery fish. This from Calcho.

(*He drives the trident into her side, and tries to escape. One of the guard strikes him down. Polyxo
has groaned and fallen on the steps.*)

THE MYRMIDONS   *(who have not ceased from their pacing dance)*
    Roar in the night, storm, like a lion, spare not the stars.
    They have planted wild seed in the air who lifted God's
    Daughter on high, wavering aloft, blessing the new
    Age at birth with the beauty of her body . . .

POLYXO   *(slowly, gasping)*
    Three spears? — that fish-spear — ah, ah, like a shark or tunny. Drag . . . the
        points, black man, the barbed points, out.
    Ah. Ah. Ah. No. Their claws catch in my entrails; her death was kinder.
        What whiteness
    Wavers up there over fires and anguish? Rhodes: I have no son . . .

THE MYRMIDONS   *(turning and going back by the way they came)*
    All is accomplished. Islanders gather the slain.
    Seed has been planted in Asia, seed in Therapnae,
    High in the dark, seed for the white eagles of dawn.
    For us the black ship on the shore, for us the black waters, the black
    Hollow of the mound. Heavily beat, bronze upon bronze.
    Clash, bronze; beat, shields; beauty is new-born.
    (The flame is blown from the torches by the violent wind.)

THE STONE AXE

Iron rusts, and bronze has its green sickness; while flint, the hard stones,
  flint and chalcedony,
Cut the soft stream of time as if they were made for immortal uses. So the
  two-thousand-year-old
Stone axe that Barney McKaye found in the little field his father was
  ditching kept the clear surfaces
Of having been formed quite lately. He wiped it clean on his sleeve, and
  saw, while he held it to show his father,
Between the knuckled fist on the spade-handle and the brown beard
  spattered with mud, the rounded hill
Toward the Dun River, the bay beyond, all empty of sails, and the cliffs of
  Scotland with yellow sun on them
Between two showers. His father looked at the stone. " 'Tis nothing: they
  do be callin' them thunder-stones,
I think the old people used them when short of iron." It was taken home to
  the cottage, however,
And there was lost at the foot of the mud-chinked wall, in the earth floor.

In
1815
The thatch took fire after a ten-day drought; the ruin was left abandoned;
  beautiful heather
Reclaimed the field. There was a Nora McKaye who married a McAuley,
Visited the site of her grandsire's cottage the week before they sailed for
  America. A digging rabbit
Had scratched the flint into view again, and Nora she picked it up from
  between the nettles and took it
To remember Ireland, because it felt fine in the hand and had a queer
  shape. In Michigan it was thrown out
With some cracked cups after she died.

There it was taken for a Huron tomahawk

By one clearing rubbish to make a garden, who gave it to his younger boy,
     who traded it for bantam eggs;
It wandered from hand to hand and George Townsend had it. He moved to
     California for his son's health
And died there. His son was a hardware merchant in Monterey, and
     displayed the stone axe beside the steel ones
In his window show, but after a time he gave it to the town museum. It lay
     dustily in harbor
Until the new museum was built, and there it lay on a shelf under bright
     glass, mislabelled
But sure of itself, intact and waiting, while storms of time
Shot by outside. The building stood up the hill by the Carmel road, and
     overlooking the city
Beheld strange growths and changes and ghastly fallings. At length the glass
Broke from its weary windows, then a wall fell. Young oak and pine grew
     up through the floors; an earthquake
Strewed the other walls. Earth drifted, pine-needles dropped and
     mouldered, the ruin was hidden, and all the city
Below it became a pinewood and sang in the wind.

White dawn grew over Mount Gabilan and Toro Mountain;

A tall young woman, naked except a deerskin and her sunburnt hair,
     stooped heavily, heavy with child,
To the coals of a hoarded fire in a dry stream-course. She awaked them,
     laying lichen and twigs to catch up the flame,
And crouching found that flint axe, which winter water had washed from
     the gullied bank; she found it with joy
And hastily went up the bank. Dawn like a fruit ripened for sunrise;

Monterey Bay was all red and yellow like the flaring sky. The woman called
  down the gully, "Oh, Wolf!
Wolf?" He came up between two pines, saying, "You have scared the
  rabbits." His beautiful naked body
Was as dark as an Indian's, but he had blue eyes. She answered, "I had to
  tell you: I found your axe
You lost yesterday morning; it was lying by the ashes." He took it and said,
  "That's a good thing.
I was greatly afraid I'd lost it, but here it is." She said, "How lovely the
  world beginning again.
Look, dear, there comes the sun. *My* baby be born as quietly as that."

TRIAD

Science, that makes wheels turn, cities grow,
Moribund people live on, playthings increase,
But has fallen from hope to confusion at her own business
Of understanding the nature of things; — new Russia,
That stood a moment at dreadful cost half free,
Beholding the open, all the glades of the world
On both sides of the trap, and resolutely
Walked into the trap that has Europe and America; —
The poet, who wishes not to play games with words,
His affair being to awake dangerous images
And call the hawks; — they all feed the future, they serve God,
Who is very beautiful, but hardly a friend of humanity.

STILL THE MIND SMILES

Still the mind smiles at its own rebellions,
Knowing all the while that civilization and the other evils
That make humanity ridiculous, remain
Beautiful in the whole fabric, excesses that balance each other
Like the paired wings of a flying bird.
Misery and riches, civilization and squalid savagery,
Mass war and the odor of unmanly peace:
Tragic flourishes above and below the normal of life.
In order to value this fretful time
It is necessary to remember our norm, the unaltered passions,
The same-colored wings of imagination,
That the crowd clips, in lonely places new-grown; the unchanged
Lives of herdsmen and mountain farms,
Where men are few, and few tools, a few weapons, and their dawns are
    beautiful.
From here for normal one sees both ways,
And listens to the splendor of God, the exact poet, the sonorous
Antistrophe of desolation to the strophe multitude.

GIVE YOUR HEART TO THE HAWKS

I

The apples hung until a wind at the equinox,
That heaped the beach with black weed, filled the dry grass
Under the old trees with rosy fruit.
In the morning Fayne Fraser gathered the sound ones into a basket,
The bruised ones into a pan. One place they lay so thickly
She knelt to reach them.

                    Her husband's brother passing
Along the broken fence of the stubble-field,
His quick brown eyes took in one moving glance
A little gopher-snake at his feet flowing through the stubble
To gain the fence, and Fayne crouched after apples
With her mop of red hair like a glowing coal
Against the shadow in the garden. The small shapely reptile
Flowed into a thicket of dead thistle-stalks
Around a fence-post, but its tail was not hidden.
The young man drew it all out, and as the coil
Whipped over his wrist, smiled at it; he stepped carefully
Across the sag of the wire. When Fayne looked up
His hand was hidden; she looked over her shoulder
And twitched her sunburnt lips from small white teeth
To answer the spark of malice in his eyes, but turned
To the apples, intent again. Michael looked down
At her white neck, rarely touched by the sun,
But now the cinnabar-colored hair fell off from it;
And her shoulders in the light-blue shirt, and long legs like a boy's
Bare-ankled in blue-jean trousers, the country wear;
He stooped quietly and slipped the small cool snake

Up the blue-denim leg. Fayne screamed and writhed,
Clutching her thigh. "Michael, you beast." She stood up
And stroked her leg, with little sharp cries, the slender invader
Fell down her ankle.

Fayne snatched for it and missed;
Michael stood by rejoicing, his rather small
Finely cut features in a dance of delight;
Fayne with one sweep flung at his face
All the bruised and half-spoiled apples in the pan,
A fragrant volley, and while he staggered under it,
The hat fallen from his head, she found one thoroughly
Soft-rotten, brown in the long white grass, and threw
For the crown of his dark head but perfectly missed,
Crying "Quits. We're even." They stood and warily smiled at each other
In the heavy-sweet apple air.

The garden was sunken lower than the little
  fields; it had many fragrances
And its own shadow, while the cows lay in the stream-bed, large sycamore
  leaves dropped on their flanks; the yellow
Heads of the hills quivered with sun and the straining sea-glare. Fayne said,
  "Where did it go, poor thing?"
Looking for the little serpent. Michael said gravely, "That's to remember
  me by. I wish I could do worse.
I'm going away." "What?" "From here again."
"Oh, no." "I am though." "No, Michael."
"Freckles," he answered, "didn't it ever occur to you
That it's fairly dull here? I'm going up to town again.
I've got to earn money and spend it and hear the motors."
She said dismally, "What about me? Who'll there be to talk to?"
"Lance of course." "I love him dearly: he's not fun exactly.

He wouldn't stick a rattlesnake up my leg."
"Gopher-snake," he shouted. They stood and laughed at each other,
And Michael: "I was over the ridge to Drunken Charlie's,
Fixing up a little party for Saturday.
There'll be a moon in the evening. I leave Monday."
Fayne said unhappily, "Help me pick up the apples
I poured on you."

II

Michael was taking Mary Abbey;
The Dolmans came, and Will Howard with two girls,
And Leo Ramirez with his sister Nell, so that the youth
Of the coast was all there. They met at Fraser's
And crossed the ridge; and were picketing the horses
Where they could ride no farther, on the airy brink
Above the great slides of the thousand-foot cliff.
They were very gay, colorful mites on the edge of the world. The men
    divided the pack to carry;
Lance Fraser, being strongest, took most.

Far down below, the broad
    ocean burned like a vast cat's eye
Pupilled by the track of sun; but eastward, beyond the white-grassed hump
    of the ridge, the day moon stood bleak
And badly shaped, face of stained clay, above the limestone fang of one of
    the Ventana mountains
Just its own color. Lance, looking back, saw his wife talking to Michael, her
    cinnabar-colored hair
Like a flag of life against the pale east. That moment he saw the horses
    plunging against the sky

And heard a noise like a sharp head of water from a narrow pipe; a girl
    cried out,
Lance dropped his pack and returned. Will Howard was looking for stones
But found none, but Lance found a burnt fence-post, relic of an ancient
    fire. The snake lay with raised head,
The rattle of its tail making that noise of sharp water running; a big rattler,
    but very small
At bay in the circle of the laughing men. Lance struck for its head, but the
    snake that moment struck at the rope's end
That Michael was flicking at it, so that Lance's blow failed, the fence-post
    broke to bits in his hands,
The snake not harmed; then Michael laughing with pleasure whipped the
    creature to death with the doubled rope
And set his heel on the head; Lance damned all rotten wood, his blond face
    flushing
Dark through the sunburn. Michael cut off the victim's
Tail with the ten rattles to give to Mary;
The other young men quieted the horses, and caught
One that had dragged away the bush it was tied to.
Lance would not wait, he picked up his pack and went
Alone down the zigzag path; but after a moment
His temper cleared.

                   Far down, short of the cat's eye ocean, they saw like a
    brown pebble
Drunken Charlie's hut in a gorge of the cliff, a feather of smoke, and his
    boat like a split berry
Of bladdery seaweed up the thin strand; and Lance stood waiting down the
    wild cliffside, his light brown hair
Golden with sun, his hat and the pack laid down. The warm wind up the
    mountain was wild with fragrance,
Chiefly the scent of the chiya bushes, that wear rosettes of seed

Strung on the stem. The girls squealed as they scrambled down, when the
  brittle traprock broke underfoot,
Small fragments ran over on the next below. When they came to the foot
  of the cliff Michael said, "Now," and offered
A bottle hot from his pocket. "It's time." Mary Abbey refused it but the
  others drank, from mouth to mouth,
Stinging fire from the slobbered bottle-neck.

                                              The sun was low
But had played all day on this southwestward
Cliff over the burning-glass water and the air
Still swirled with heat; the headland of Fraser's Point
Stopped off the trade-wind here. Fayne Fraser a little dizzily
Looked seaward, left of the blazing sun-track, and saw the track of the
  northwest gale and the running waves
Like an endless army of horse with banners going by off-shore; her eyes
  followed them, a ruled line southward
Of violent water, converging toward the bronze headland beyond headland
  of the mountain coast; and someone was saying,
"It's hot, we'll swim." "Before we eat," someone said.
The girls twittered together and clustered northward
To a little cove beyond a fair spit of rock;
The men remained on this side.

                              Fayne undressed beside Mary Abbey,
And was careful of words, because she'd sucked from the bottle more than
  she meant to, and had small experience of drinking.
She said carefully, "Where did those girls of Will Howard's come from?"
  "Nina told me," she answered: "waitresses
Down from the city on their vacation." "Honestly are they? I guessed it."
  "No," Mary said, "they're nice girls."

"That yellow-haired one, she's bad." "No," Mary said. Fayne said, "Did
     you see her face when she looked at Michael
Across that bottle?" "Oh, no," Mary answered. " . . . Well. Are you ready,
     Mary? Let's go."
They limped down to the waves, giggling and wincing.
Fayne had tied a broad handkerchief around her hair
To shed the spray; she swam out farther than others,
Mary remained along shore.

                         The other side of the rock-spit
The men had bathed, and had come up strand again
To dry by the driftwood fire; all except Michael,
Who loved to swim. Lance Fraser stood by the fire, his broad smooth chest,
     grooved between the square plates
Of heavy muscle, steamed and was ruddy in the glowing heat. He narrowed
     his eyes to look seaward
And saw Michael's left arm, over the speck of his head, lift, reach and dip,
Swimming side-stroke; two white arms flashing swanlike on either side of a
     handkerchief-hooded head
Emerged from the scales of light on the edge of the sun-dazzle. The
     swimmers approached each other,
And met this side the long brown stain of the breathing kelp-bed. Lance
     frowned,
But only thinking that they were too far out
And making a show of themselves.

                         On the pleasant water
Michael had called to Fayne, "I've something for you.
Come here a minute." She hardly dared, and thought
In the flashing joy of the sea, "Oh, the water covers us.
What have you got?" "Gin for girls.
We've got a fire on this side." They met laughing,

And reached the bottle from hand to hand and floated decorously
Separate again. Fayne looked toward shore, and saw the vast cliff in the flare
    of sundown soaring above
Like beaten gold, the imperfect moon-disk gold on its brow; the tiny
    distinct white shapes of men
Around their spot of fire in the flat blue sea-shadow. She breathed hard and
    said,
"My God how beautiful. Oh Michael, stay here at home."
He answered with a watery yell of pleasure, submerging his mouth
To roar as the sea-lions do.

                              Fayne trailed the bottle
And swam ashore. There was nothing to dry herself with;
The chill of the water had touched her blood, she sucked breath gustily
Through clicking teeth. She sipped from the salted bottle,
And dressed, but shivered still.

                                    She sunned herself by the fire,
Watching with fascinated speculation of pain
The antennae of lobsters like spikes of jointed grass
Above the heating water in a five-gallon tin
Writhe at the sky, lives unable to scream.

III

Under the vast calm vaulting glory of the afterglow, low smoky rose and
    delicately
Stratified amber, soaring purple; then rose again, luminous and virginal
    floating the moon,
High up a scoured hollow of the cliff
Cormorants were settling to roost on the jags and ledges.
They writhed long negro snake-throats and shot

Sharp heads at each other, shaking out sooty wings
And angry complaining cries.

                          Below, on the thread of beach,
The lonely fisherman who was called Drunken Charlie,
Fire glowing on his drugged eyes, wide beard and lank hair,
Turned meat on the grid over the barbecue-pit
And talked to himself all the time. Michael Fraser knelt
By a turned chest that served for table and poured
From a jug into cups, fierce new distillate
From Charlie's cliff-hidden kettle.

                         Fayne Fraser shook half-dried hair,
The color of the coals at the heart of the fire
But darkening as light decreased, and went to Lance
Who stood alone at the waves' edge, turning his back on the world, and the
    wet sand
Raised by his weight on either side of his foot-soles ran water and glistened
    in the still light. Fayne said
"Are you cross, dear?" She pushed up his rolled sleeve and clasped her
    fingers on the broad trunk of his arm
Above the elbow, "Dear, are you sad?" "I? No," he said, "what about?"
    "You haven't spoken to anyone
Since we were swimming." "Why should I? You were out too far, though."
    "Oh, I can swim.
And Michael was there to help me if I'd got tired." "By God no," Lance
    said, with a sharp vision in his mind
Of her bright nakedness, the shining whiteness and the red hair. She
    understood and said softly, "Well,
I didn't need help. But he's our brother." "Certainly; I didn't mind him," he
    answered. "But I did hate

To think that rabble of girls could look at you; it isn't decent." She said,
  "They didn't seem interested.
Come, drink and eat. Those waitress-women are passing the paper plates."
  He saw that vision once more,
The form and whiteness, the little gay-colored flower of the pubic hair, and
  groaned, as a thick bull
Alone in the field groans to himself, not knowing why the hot brow and the
  hooves itch for destruction.
Fayne to cure his unhappiness hasted and returned
Fetching two cups of the fire Michael was pouring.

                                        After they had eaten,
  twilight and moonlight came;
The fire burned smaller and brighter; they were twelve around it; and
  drinks were poured. The bearded fisherman seemed
Stiffly asleep, with open eyes like a drowned man's
Glazed by the yellow firelight. Tom Dolman and Leo Ramirez
Roughed at each other, and Nina Dolman
Sitting between them cried out; then Michael said,
"Get up and wrestle." All but the fisherman turned
To watch them circle clumsily on the damp sand
And suddenly lock, into one quadruped body reeling
Against the dark band of ocean and the low sky.
Ramirez had the low hold but Dolman was the heavier man;
They tugged and sobbed; Ramirez was lifted high
And writhed on the other's shoulder by the evening star,
But the strained column staggered and crumbled, the Spaniard
Fell uppermost and was the first to rise up.
Michael asked very gravely, "Who was the winner?
The winner may challenge Lance." Ramirez gasping and laughing
Said, "Drunk: not to that extent." "Then gather firewood.
The fire's got low."

The yellow-haired one of the two girls Will Howard
    had brought
Sat in the sand beside Lance Fraser; she leaned on his shoulder and held a
    cup to his mouth and said
"Please drink it for me: things are beginning to go round in circles." He
    drank; then Fayne on his other side
Grew suddenly cool and quite clear; she leaned across him and said, "That
    hair in the cup! Well, you drank it.
Her bleaches have made it brittle so it keeps falling." "Oh," the other
    gasped, "that's not true." "It's pretty," Fayne said,
"Only the black half inch at the roots. Is your name Lois? What's your
    name?" "Lois." "Lean the other way,
Lois." Then Lance said angrily, "Be quiet will you," and got up
To fetch more firewood.

                            A timber from one of the four ships
That have broken in half a century off Fraser's Point
Lay near and dry; Ramirez and Howard had brought it,
But the axe was lost in the sand. Lance up-ended it,
An ivory-white pillar under the moon,
Garnished with great iron bolts. He wedged his fingers
Into a crack and suddenly straining tore it in two;
The splitting made a great noise under the cliff,
The sea being quiet. Lance felt himself curiously
Numbed, as if the sharp effort had strained the whiskey
Out of his blood through the sheaves of his nerves;
His body obeyed as ever but felt a distance
Blocked off and alien. He took the halves of the timber
Under each arm and a bolt in his hand,
For two or three had fallen out of the wood,
This one straight, long and heavy. After he had laid
His logs on the fire he saw the fisherman's

Firelight-discolored eyes, and called "Hey! Charlie."
Still the man slept. Lance, wavering a little, reached
Over Will Howard's shoulder and took the cup from his hand,
Drank half, poured the other half on Charlie's long hair;
It dribbled into his beard; he coughed and awoke.
Lance said "D' you ever have rattlesnakes down here?
I snicked at one up the cliff with a rotten stick:
But this'd fix 'em." He gave him the iron bar;
Charlie posted it carefully up in the sand
Between his feet and answered, "Mm; but there's Injuns."
"What?" "All that was cleared out of the country.
Where did you think they got to? They ain't got ships.
Down here they are." The dark-haired girl that Will Howard had brought
Suddenly stood up from the fire, she went toward the sea and was heard
    vomiting. Charlie nodded and said,
"There's one o' them now. Most nights I see their fires away down the
    beach." Mary Abbey whispered to Michael,
"Don't take any more. Time to go home." "Ah no," he said, "dear, we just
    got here." Fayne came to Lance
And said, "Don't drink any more. Time to go home." He answered briskly,
    "Since when are you giving orders?"
"Since you're not fit to." She knew while the words made in her throat,
    "Now he'll be angry," a pale rush of anger
Ran to meet his; the memory of all his bad-tempered times, his heavy
    earnestness and lack of laughter,
Pierced like a mountain-peak the cloud in her mind, "Oh, I do hate you."
He stared, more astonished than angry, and saw her face
Lean, sharp, bled white, each freckle black as a mole
Against its moon-gleam pallor. "That's how you feel, ah?"
He turned his back. She thought, "He'll never forgive me:
Let him not," and saw the Dolmans, Nina and Tom,
Seeking the way up the cliff, Mary Abbey with them,

Fayne went and said, "Michael, I've lost my cup,
Aren't there any more cups?" "I'll hold the jug:
You hold your mouth." "Oo, I need water with it."
"No you don't." Half of the sip went strangling
Into her throat, half ran by her little chin
And trickled between her breasts. She looked at the fire,
Then at the moon, both blurred fantastically,
Red burrowed, white wavered high. Michael said, "My girl's gone."
Fayne said, "Oh, and yours?" He said "That's no sense. That's very."
She laughed and answered, "They don't."

                              The moon suspended in her
    great antelope-leap from the head of the cliff
Hung pouring whiteness along the narrow runway of sand and slide-rock
    under the continent's foot,
A watery glittering and secret place, walled from the world, closed by the
    cliff, ditched by the ocean.
Drunken Charlie dreamed by the dying fire;
Will Howard and Nell Ramirez were one slight point
Far down the white beach. Yellow-haired Lois
Spilled her drink and said, "Seeing is believing.
Come on, I'll show you." She smiled at Lance, "Come, dear.
Sadie's passed out; it's all right wi' Sadie,"
And to Leo Ramirez, "Come if you like, dark boy."
He swayed and stammered, "Responsible; sister Nell.
Keep an eye on young sister." "Ah, go and find her."
"Not till I see the picture on Sadie's stomach."
They wandered toward Drunken Charlie's little hollow skiff
And its black shadow, drawn up the moonlight sand.
Lance thought, "Here's a boat, let's break it," and thought with an ache of
    shame,

"I wouldn't think that, only being drunk." The center of his mind made
    savage war on rebellious out-liers
In breathless darkness behind the sweating forehead; while Leo Ramirez,
    seeing the bright fish-scales glued
With blood and slime to the boat-thwarts glitter like a night of stars, began
    to sing a stale song: "We'll always,
Be young and gay. We'll always, feel that way." Lois said "Shut up," and led
    them around the boat,
Her friend lay in the moonlight nestled against it. Lois knelt down and
    gently drew her by the shoulder;
She groaned in her sleep, resisting. Lois laughed, "The boys want to see it,
    Sadie," and tugged, and turned her
Onto her back, the stained pale face up to the moonlight; the teeth in the
    opened mouth glittered,
And sour breath crossed them, while Lois turned up the blouse, loosened
    the band and jerked up the linen shift
To show a three-masted sailing-ship tattooed with black and red inks on
    the soft white belly
Below the breasts. "My God," Ramirez said, "there it is."
Lois answered, "A fellow dared her," and looked for Lance,
Who trembled and said, "Cover her up, damn you."
Lois blinking drew down the blouse. Ramirez giggled,
"My God, a U.S. flag at the peak," and reached
Over Lois's shoulder to raise the cloth;
Lance struck and felled him, and stepping across him fallen
Leaned and strode toward the cliff and the red coals
That had been the fire.

        Drunken Charlie lay on the sand,
The iron bolt erect by his feet; Lance caught it up
And smashed the jug, and saw the remnant of whiskey
Glitter among the shards to sink into sand.

He ground his teeth; he saw in his mind in the stream of images
A second jug, and began to search for it.

                                        The tide had fallen, the steep
    ribbon of beach was but little wider,
But the sea was become so flattened that no waves flashed. Enormous peace
    of the sea, white quiet of the cliff,
And at their angle and focus a few faint specks of humanity happy in liquor
    or released in sleep,
But Lance alone. Then noises like the cries of a woman screaming, bird
    after bird of sharp-colored sound
Flew on the face of the cliff, tattered wild wings against jagged rock. On
    the cliffhead the patient horses
Turned their ears, grooving small wrinkles about the roots of the cartilage,
    but did not lift up their heads;
And the sea was not moved, nor the moonlight quivered. Will Howard was
    lying beside Nell Ramirez; they'd fallen asleep
Before he had his desire; they sighed and stirred in the sand. He murmured
    "Oh, somebody's got hysterics,"
And wriggled his fingers, which had grown painfully numb between her
    plump knees. But Lois, Leo Ramirez
And Drunken Charlie heard the sounds nearer; they went in a wind of fear
    to find out their fountain,
And Sadie awoke in the sand and followed heavily,
Falling but once, catching her clothes that slipped,
Whining at the hollow pain in her skull.

                                        Beyond a rock
Stood Lance, high white in the moonglaze, distorted, taller than human;
Lois said, "Dearie?" He babbled, "Oh Jesus Christ Oh Jesus Christ Oh
    Jesus Christ,"
Behind him in a great shadow of her hair darkened

By the rock-shadow Fayne turned her white wedge of face
With three holes in it. She was kneeling, bent S-shape,
And seemed to stare up from the very ground. She said "I think
It is finished. Water please. Water please.
He fell down from the cliff." Then Michael's feet were seen,
And thence the prone extended ridge of his body
Ending indefinitely under Fayne's face.
Lois cried, "He's hurt." But they dared not approach
For Lance standing between, high and twisted
Like a dead tree. Lance said "I . . ." Fayne cried,
"He fell down from the cliff." They all stood silent,
Lois's mouth opened and closed on silence
Three times, then asked, "Is he hurt?" Lance said, "Oh Christ.
I . . ." Fayne cried so that his words were hidden,
And stood up and said, "He has died. Michael.
He was climbing the cliff and fell, his foot caught in that bush;
He struck his head on that rock, on that edge of rock.
It is all—broken in. Oh, we loved him."
Ramirez said, "What for did he climb up there?"
"Have we drunk *water*?" Fayne said. But Lance began
To shake, like a tall dead mast of redwood that men are felling,
It is half cut through, each dip of the axe the sonorous timber quivers from
    the root up to the cloud,
He said "I caught them . . ." "He caught him," Fayne cried, "when he fell
    but he could not save him." "I killed . . ." "You are wild with sorrow.
He fell head down—whether you'd tried to catch him or not. You are not
    to blame." He said, "It is horrible
To hear the lies from her mouth like bees from a hot hive: I am the one,"
    but Fayne running to him
Made an animal moan in her throat in time to hide what he said. She came
    to Lance, and her face
Like a held spear, and said, "Drunkard.

Too drunk to be understood. Keep still until you can talk and be
     understood." He drew backward from her,
Shuddering like a horse from a snake, but when his back was against the
     rock he stammered, "I
Will find my time." "Yes," she answered, "be quiet now. To-morrow when
     you are better they'll understand you."
"Is he dead?" "Keep still. Will you shame his end
With drunkard babbling? For he was the dearest," she said, "in the world to
     all of us. Lovelier than morning light
On the mountain before the morning. There is not one of us would not
     have died for him: *I* would, *I* would, *I* would,"
She cried writhing, "but not lose Lance too. How can I plan to save him,
     I've got what I can't bear?
You are all our friends."
She set her hands in the masses of red-dark hair, dark in the moonlight,
     and tearing it, with her white face
To the white moon: "*That* eye's blind. Like Juan Arriba's old mare he used
     to beat on the face,
Her eyes froze white like that. He was larking on the cliff and fell." She
     seemed to be treading a tragic dance,
She was scuffling sand to cover the bolt of shipwreck that lay in shadow of
     the rock; she wrung her hands
And knelt moaning by Michael's head; she rose with blood on her hand and
     fibers of hair, and ran
To the rock under the cliff. "This rock killed him. He fell on this edge,"
     she drew her hand on the edge
And the rock was stained. Then Sadie was heard gasping from her poor
     stained face. One or two looked at her. "O-uh,"
She whispered hoarsely, "we was having fun!"

                                        Lance moved at length,
     like a dead man walking, toward his dead brother,

And stooped as one stoops to gather a sleeping child. Fayne ran and said,
    "No, the man. No, the man.
He has to come." Lance turned toward her his face like a paralyzed man's
Slack with peace, and said softly, "The man."
"He'd think wrong has been done. I can't think . . . coroner.
Don't take him up." "Home?" he said,
Seeming gently surprised; he gathered the body
Into his arms and walked along the foot of the cliff.
Fayne stayed behind a moment, the others following.
She cast quick looks over the rocks and sand;
One end of the rusty bolt was visible still;
She leaned toward it and fell on her face. She labored up
And went ten steps to the ebb and flung the iron
To the water edge.

       Lance walked along the foot of the cliff.
He turned, not where the path went up, and walked
Into the face of the cliff, and stood there walking
Like an ox in a tread-mill, until Ramirez
Showed him the path. Fayne went up behind him.

           Half way up
He awoke a moment out of his automatism
To feel failure and pain, his breathing like knives, and the failure
Of his eyes; it was impossible to see the path;
He checked a step and fell forward.

        Fayne came up to him
And stood; there was nothing that she could do. They lay
Very peacefully together, Lance's face
On his brother's breast. She looked across them;
Terribly far down the moonlight cliff crouched the dark sea.

Ramirez came up and stood. Fayne said they had not the strength to carry
    up either of the fallen, and so
They had to wait. They heard a faint breeze through the dry bushes; and
    the crying of sea-lions far down below,
Where eight or ten were lying in a circle by the softly heaving kelp-bed, as
    their custom is, and gazed
With great mild eyes at the sky and the night of water. Then they sing in
    their manner, lifting up sleek
Dark-shining muzzles to the white moon, making a watery noise of roaring
    and a lonely crying
For joy of life and the night.

                    At length Lance
Began to paw with his feet like a dreaming hound,
And some stones fell. He knelt and stood up
And took his burden and went up.

                    When they entered the sleeping
    farmstead,
Fayne led the horse; Lance held his brother and rode behind him.
It would be hard to tell which one was slain
If the moon shone on their faces. The horse stopped and sighed
By the garden-gate; Lance did not move to dismount,
But sat and held up his brother. Fayne came beside,
Reaching to help; Lance whispered "Ah, Ah, thank God."
"What?" "He may be saved, Fayne.
He is hot under the arms and I heard him breathe."
"You heard the horse breathe," she said. They lifted down
The unmanageable weight.

                  Oh ignorant penitents,
For surely the cause is too small for so much anguish.

To be drunk is a folly, to kill may call judgment down,
But these are not enormous evils,
And as for your brother, he has not been hurt.
For all the delights he has lost, pain has been saved him;
And the balance is strangely perfect,
And why are you pale with misery?
Because you have saved him from foolish labors and all the vain days?
From desires denied and desires staled with attaining,
And from fear of want, and from all diseases, and from fear of death?
Or because you have kept him from becoming old,
When the teeth drop and the eyes dim and the ears grow dull,
And the man is ashamed?
Surely it is nothing worse to be slain in the overflowing
Than to fall in the emptiness;
And though this moon blisters the night,
Darkness has not died, good darkness will come again;
Sometimes a fog will come in from sea,
Sometimes a cloud will crop all the stars.

IV

The moonlight from the west window was a square cloth
Laid on the floor, with one corner on the bed,
Lying over Michael's hand; they had taken him
To his own room. Fayne whispered: "Now we must tell them.
Your mother may die—her sick heart.
Don't let her die too bitterly. For this one night, dear,
Say nothing worse than 'Michael's gone.' Spare her something
Until she has cried. Four hours' mercy. By morning
That heart of hers will be seasoned." Fayne strained in the dark
To see his face. He answered in a short while,
"How many mornings I've come in here

And routed him out of bed. He always was a late sleeper.
Sound asleep mother." Fayne caught his arm. "Can't you hear me?"
"You," he said, "keep your hands off! . . . Until morning
I'll say he fell."

It was not morning, but the moon was down.
The old mother sat by the bed with her hand on Michael's, regularly her
  great fat-swollen body
Jerked with a sob, and tears were spurted from her closed eyes. Old Fraser
  sat with his fists evenly
Together on his knees, his bony face held erect, the brown eyes in their
  hollows red with lamplight.
Fayne heard the noise of a motor starting and left the room.

He was
  backing out the big truck,
The shed was full of the headlight glare, the ruby taillight glowed by the
  axle. Before she could come
It had crept out; its light swung up the driveway by the stooping sycamore
And picked from darkness the heavy timbers of the high corrals and the
  white bee-hives remote on the hill;
Fayne ran down the river of light to the gate and closed it, and stood in the
  gate for fear he might smash through;
But Lance came wearily to open; stooping, tall,
Black on the light. She said, "Oh, where?" "You know.
Tell dad to come to Salinas and get the truck;
There wasn't enough gas in the little one."
She answered, "Can the sheriff make us happy again?
Or the judge make Michael alive again?" "Open the gate."
"Yes, dear. *Listen* to me. When Arriba and his boys
Stole cows of ours, did you run to the courthouse?
We take care of ourselves down here. What we have done

Has to be borne. It's in ourselves and there's no escaping,
The state of California can't help you bear it.
That's only a herd of people, the state.
Oh give your heart to the hawks for a snack o' meat
But not to men." When she touched him with her hands
Pleading, he sighed and said, "If I'd been nearer
My decent mind, it would have been you, not Michael.
Did y' love him? Or was it only because you're female
And were drunk, female and drunk?" "Oh. Hush. I was begging him
Not to leave us, as I'm begging you. He promised me, dear.
He said he'd not go away. I kissed him for that: he was our brother:
And you came behind." Lance's blackness of his leaning bulk
Vibrated in the light-beam. "It'd be a pity for me then.
I can't see clear, in the dirty streaming memories . . .
Don't be afraid: your part will be secret.
I'll say I killed him for nothing, a flea-bite quarrel,
Being beastly drunk." "He was killed," she answered, "for nothing."
"It's a great pity for me then.
Open the gate." She clung to the timber bolt
To hold it home in the slot, and felt his mind
Tearing itself. "Lance. Lance? Sweetheart:
Believe . . . whatever you need to save you.
I won't give you up. You can't remember what happened;
I tell you he fell from the cliff. But if your dreadful
Dream were true, I know you are strong enough
To give your heart to the hawks without a cry
And bear it in lonely silence to the end of life.
What else do you want? Ah. Confession's a coward
Running to officers, begging help. Not you."

                                        She heard
The scrape of slow boots on gravel outside the light-stream,

Across the pulses of the idling motor, and suddenly cried,
"He fell from the cliff." An old man said in the dark,
"They ain't got consideration. Where was you going
This time o' night, after what's happened? Your dad wants you.
Your ma's took bad." Lance moaned and stood still.
Fayne said, "He was going to Lobos to telephone
The doct . . . the coroner. Dearest, you ought to go in.
She suffered great pain before, she was near death.
Old Davie will drive up the coast for you
When daylight comes." "Oh," he said stilly, and turned
His face to the fountains of light; it gleamed without meaning
In the stream of radiance like a stake in a stream,
Except that from exhaustion the pupils of the eyes
Failed to contract, so that their secret interiors
Of their chambers returned the light all sanguine.
At length he kneaded them with his fists and said,
"I can't see well. You'll have to help me find the way in.
It's not a trick of yours, uh?"

V

His mother lay on the floor,
For Michael's body lay on the bed. The sun of pain at her heart had rays like skewers of anguish
Along the left arm and up by the jugular arteries. She dared not move; her face stood wet-white and still,
With live blue eyes; but the clay-pale lips opened and closed. Old Fraser had swathed her in hasty blankets.
Fayne entered; Lance behind her stood swaying and stooping in the door and saw his father
Crouched beside the great cocoon of the blankets; and Michael in the bed above, and trinkets of Michael's

That hung on the wall, gleam in the lamplight. The violence of pain was
    brief; she whispered "better," and breathed
With greedy shallow passion; her eyes found Lance.

                                        Daylight grayed
    slowly into the room;
The lamp ran dry unnoticed. Lance and his father
Labored and carried the heavy old woman to bed.
Fayne brought them food, but Lance refused it. In the afternoon
He walked out-doors for a time, but nothing farther
Than the cattle-pens. Fayne must have been watching for him,
Because she went and walked by his side, and said,
When they were turned from the house, "Mary Abbey was here.
It seems she expected to marry Michael, though he never told us.
She cried a lot." Lance made no sign of hearing her.
Fayne said, looking up sidelong at his cheek and jaw,
Where the flesh hung thin on the bone: "Her grief's not
Like ours, forever; but sharp at present. If she ever
Imagined that you . . . how could we bear her looks? You are too strong,
    dear,
To lay on weaker persons a burden
That you alone ought to bear." He strode faster
And stopped, muttering, "He lies up there, like that.
And my mother, like that: and I have done it;
And you talk about Mary Abbey." Fayne said, "I have no time
To choose names, for a man is coming to-day
To question us. He's sent for. I have to tell you that you must choose
    whether to relieve
Your own weakness . . . conscience I mean . . . by easy confession,
Or bear the whole weight unhelped. The first way's easy: you'll be
    acquitted: you'll be left humbled and soiled,

But free; for confession is not enough; and you were too lost to remember
    anything clearly; and I
Am the one witness. I saw him climb on the cliff and fall. So your
    conscience will be well comforted,
And fairly cheap. Only your mother perhaps will die of it; your father and I
    will swallow our portion;
And the crowd at Salinas
Will have had a good time watching your face in court. It would be harder,
    if you've a snake in your heart,
To keep it shut there."

                    He was silent, and drew sharp breath and said, "A
    red-haired one. Ah.
A white one with a red brush. Did you do it with him
Or not?" "Leave that," she said stilly; "this choice is *now*."
He groaned and answered, "My mind's not quick like yours.
. . . I'll not lie to them." "Let me show your mind to you:
Be patient a moment still: if I seem cruel,
That's to save, all that's left. Look at yourself:
A man who believes his own sweet brother's blood
Lies on his hands: yet
Too scrupulous to tell a lie, for his mother's life.
Our minds are wonderful." He meditated, and answered
Heavily, "The sunlight seems dull but red.
What makes it red?" "Your eyes are sick of not sleeping;
Or there's a forest-fire in the south." "Our minds? Little bottles
That hold all hell. I seem too tired to feel it, though.
I'll think, I'll think."
"You have no time for thinking. He will come probably
Within this hour." "Who? Let him come. I'll tell him
God made them male and female but men have made

So-and-so. . . . I fall asleep while I talk . . . whiskey eh?
Lighted the sticky fire. It's not possible
I'd ever done it except that I stumbled on you
In the heart of guilt. I know that." "Believe it then,"
She answered shrilly, and stood twitching her lips
In the white freckled face, in the reddish light of her hair,
"If that will help." "Oh," he said.
". . . I wish you had picked from another tree."
She answered: "You are to say that you found him dying.
You heard me cry, and he was down by the rock.
Isn't that the truth exactly, because you remember
No previous thing? You heard me cry out; you came;
Michael was dying or had died. That's all. You carried him home.
. . . I wish he'd come."

                    But the man did not come
Until afternoon the next day. Dark weather, for a stagnant ocean of clouds
    was hung on the sky,
And what light shone came colored like the taste of metal through smoke
    of burning forests far to the south
That veiled the coast, so that it seemed brown twilight
In the house, in Michael's room. A lamp was lighted,
The death-wound viewed. "*Who* saw him fall?" "I alone.
My husband and others came when I cried." "Where is your husband?"
"With his mother," she answered faintly. "She had an attack,
Her heart, angina, and has to lie still. Shall I
Call him, sir?" her voice hardening, her eyes
Growing hard and narrow. "Pretty soon. Was this young man
In trouble about anything?" "No." "A girl?" "He was engaged
To Miss Abbey." "They had a quarrel, ah?" "No."
"Did he seem cheerful?" "Very." "They always do.

Yesterday I had to drive by Elkhorn Slough
Because a very cheerful old man opened his throat
With his nephew's pen-knife. I was two hours
Finding that place; the farmers around there they couldn't tell you
Whether Jesus Christ died on the cross
Or at the battle of Bull Run."

Old Fraser had stood
Nerveless and dreaming over the livid face
Since they uncovered it; abruptly he turned his head
Above his bowed shoulder, saying "It's enough.
Dog, blaspheme not. Go to your own place.
My son found death in recklessness, I fear in folly;
Write that and leave us alone; go hence and leave us
To mourn and hope." "Well, Mr. Fraser. You understand . . .'
"I am very patient," the old man said, thrusting
His hollowed face toward the other, the closely set
Inflamed brown eyes pushing like the burnt end of a stick
That has been used to stir fire; the man stepped backward.
"Did he say patient! . . . Well, is your husband here?"
Fayne's mouth jerked and froze hard, her hands quieted.
"I will call him. Come to the room down-stairs."
She said at the foot of the stair, "This way, sir. It's dark.
Will you have to go . . . to see the cliff, to see
The cliff?" "Hm, what's that?" "Where he fell."
"Can we drive there?" "No, ride and walk." "Look here,"
He said, "I've come sixty-five miles already.
You're sure it was accidental?" "Yes." "Well.
I always try to save the family feelings
When the case is not clear." He tried his pen,
Shook it, and wrote. Fayne watched, quiet and cold, thinking that Lance

Would not have to be questioned; he was saved now;
And saw the man to his car. When he had gone
She thought that now she could laugh or cry if she wanted to,
Now Lance was saved, but her nerves and her mind stood quiet. She looked
    at the dusty gate and the dark house-gable
In the stagnant air against the black cloud, and perceived that all events are
    exact and were shaped beforehand,
And spaced in a steel frame; when they come up we know them; there is
    nothing for excitement.

                    She went in,
And found Lance in the dark at the head of the stair, bent forward like a
    great bird. "Has he gone, Fayne?"
"Did you *know* he was here?" "I will live on," he answered, "seems to be
    best. I loved him well; he died instantly,
No anger nor pain. Davis has dug a place by the children's graves."

                                                        On
    account of the dull weather
And closing twilight the group on the hill-top was hardly visible in their
    vast scene. It was quite evident
That not only Pico Blanco against the north, and the gray Ventanas, but
    even every dry fold
And gully of the humbler hills was almost by an infinite measure of more
    importance
Than the few faint figures on the bare height,
The truck, and three saddled horses,
And some persons.
The old man swayed and shook, standing praying
At the head of a dug slot
Beside the pile of pale earth.

The heavy great brown-furred sky that covered all things made a red point
    in the west, lost it and darkened,
And the Point Sur lighthouse made a thin stabbing from the northwest.

Swaying on his heels and toes the old man prayed:
"O Lord our God, when thy churches fell off from thee
To go a-whoring after organ-music,
Singing-women and lecturers, then my people
Came out from among them; and when thy last church,
Thy little band, thy chosen, was turned at length
To lust for wealth and amusement and worldly vanities,
I cried against them and I came forth from among them.
I promised thee in that day that I and my house
Would remain faithful, thou must never despair;
I said, though all men forget thee thou hast a fort
Here in these hills, one candle burning in the infidel world,
And my house is thy people.

                    My children died,
And I laid them in this place and begot more children
To be thy servants, and I taught them thy ways, but they fell away from
    thee.
They found their pleasure among the ungodly, and I believe
They made themselves drunk with wine, and my dear son is fallen.
He died on the shore. One half of the curse of Eli has fallen upon me."
He covered his face with his knotted hands and stood gasping,
And said, "I loved him. Here he is, Lord.
Surely thou hast forgiven his sins as I have forgiven them,
And wilt lift him to thy glory on the last day."
The old man stood silent, lifting his face, and fixed his deep close-set eyes,
    like the eyes of an old ape,

Small, dark and melancholy under the bar of the brow, between the wide
    cheek-bones, fixed them far off
Across the darkening ridges and ocean upon that single red spot that waned
    in the western sky,
And said "The world darkens and the end is coming.
I cannot beget more children; I am old and empty,
And my wife is old. All men have turned their faces away from thee;
I alone am thy church. Lord God, I beseech thee not to despair,
But remember thine ancient power, and smite the ungodly on their mouths
And the faithless churches with utter destruction. For Jesus' sake, amen."
    While he prayed, Fayne watched Lance
With pity and fear; and Mary Abbey, who was there with her father,
Kept stealing glances at Lance through her wet eye-lashes.
She whispered to Fayne: "Oh Lance looks dreadfully.
I never knew he loved him so dreadfully."
Fayne answered, "Yes, he did"; and looked up at Lance
With pity and fear. "He looks as if he'd fall sick,"
Mary said. Fayne answered, "No, he is strong.
He hasn't eaten since Michael died; maybe
He hasn't slept." Mary said, wiping her eyes,
"His face is so sad and fine, like carved marble.
They say he carried him all the way home, up that cliff."
The old man ended his prayer, the redwood box
Was lowered with ropes; Lance had the weight at one end,
Old Fraser and Davis at the other. The ropes cut grooves
In the earth edges. While they were shovelling earth,
Mary Abbey, with a sudden abandoned gesture
Of the hand that had the handkerchief in it, ran up to Lance
On the scraped ground. "*Don't* grieve so." She reached and touched
His hand on the spade-handle. "It makes me afraid for you.
We all loved him: life has to go on." He jerked his hand,
And looked down at her face with startled eyes

So pale gray-blue that all the light that remained in the world
Under the low black sky seemed to live in them,
Stammering, "No. *No.* He fell from the cliff." She said, "I know, Lance.
We have to bear it. I loved him too." He gathered his dreaming nerves
Into the bundle again and said, "Oh. All right. Please keep out of the way
    for the time.
We have this to do." "Good-bye," she answered patiently. "Father's calling
    me."

          The pit was filled full and mounded;
Fayne came and said, "What was she saying to you?" "Nothing. Who?"
    "Mary Abbey." "I didn't see her."
"What, Lance? She came and spoke to you." "I'd rather be there with
    Michael," he answered. "Dear, you must rouse yourself.
Life has to go on." "Somebody was saying so, I think.
There's not a hawk in the sky." She answered from a hoarse throat, "After
    dark? What are you dreaming?
See, Davie's turned on the headlights." "I hate them," he said, "killers, dirty
    chicken-thieves."

          The farm-truck headlights
Shone on the mounded earth, and cast its enormously lengthened shadow
    and the shadows of a few moving
Persons across the world, with the beam of light, over mound beyond
    mound of bare autumn hills, and black
Ocean under the black-roofed evening.

VI

                  That night he returned again
To lie with Fayne in their bed, but like two strangers
Lying in one bed in a crowded inn, who avoid

Touching each other; but the fifth night
She laid her hand on the smooth strength of his breast,
He pretended to be asleep, she moved against him,
Plucking his throat with her lips. He answered, "After all?
You're right. If we're to live in this life
We'll keep its customs." He approached her confidently,
And had no power. The little irrational anger
At finding himself ridiculous brought to his mind
That worse rage, never before clearly remembered,
But now to the last moment; or imagined. He drew
His limbs from Fayne's without thinking of her, and lay still, with shut fists,
Sweating, staring up spirals of awful darkness, that spun away up and
    wound over his eyes
Around a hollow gray core with flecks in it. "I am damned unjustly. I did it
    in a moment."

          But Fayne knew nothing
Of the shut agony beside her; only she was troubled at heart, and
    wondering
Whether he had ceased to love her said tenderly, "Sleep,
Darling. I didn't mean. I didn't want.
Only I love you." He felt her instinctive hand
Move downward fondling along the flat of his belly.
He set it aside and spoke, so low that her ears
Lost every word between the hair and the pillow.
"What, dearest?" "I know it," he said, "they're dogs: that was exactly
Fit to tell dogs. I can be damned
At home as well." "Hush, dear." "I don't make a good murderer,"
He said, "I sweat." She was silent and heard him breathing,
And mourned, "Oh cover your mind with quietness to-night.
In the morning you'll face it down again. This will get well with time.
It was really only a dreadful accident." "Very damnable," he said,

"Very true." Fayne said, "We'll live, sweetheart, to feel it
Only a dreadful accident, and the sad death
Of one we loved." "That's your smooth skin.
The fires fester on mine. Will you do something
For me?" "Dearest, with all my heart." "An easy kindness:
Shut up your mouth."

           He got up after a time;
When he went out she followed, trembling. He turned on her
Outside the door. "I'm not going to Salinas,"
He whispered, "nor bump myself off either.
I'll not starve your hawks of their snatch o' meat.
Now let me alone for Christ's sake." She stood and saw him
Against the starlit window at the end steal down
The hallway, go past the stairhead, and enter the empty
Room of his brother. He slept there from that night on,
And seemed to regain calm strength.

VII

                      In the course of a month
Rain seemed at hand, the south wind whetting his knife on the long
    mountain and wild clouds flying;
Lance and his father set out to burn the hill to make pasture. They carried
    fire in forkfuls of straw
Along the base of the south wall of their valley; the horses they rode
    snorted against it, and smoke
Boiled, but the seaward end of the hill would only be burnt in patches.
    Inland, at the parched end,
A reach of high grass and sage might have led out the fire to the forest, and
    Lance rode up
To watch a flame down the wind to black out the danger.

He carried two barley-sacks and went to the Abbeys' trough
At the hill spring to dip them, to beat down the fire's
Creepings up wind. From that spur of the mountain
He saw the planted pine trees at Abbey's place,
And riding back with the dipped sacks, the vale
Of his own place, the smoke-mist, and Sycamore Creek
Wound like a long serpent down the small fields.
He set his fires and watched them rage with the wind,
Easily stifling their returns, riding herd
On the black line; then from the base of the hill
Red surf, and the dark spray rolled back by the wind,
Of the other fire came up roaring. The lines met
On the fall of the hill like waves at a river's mouth
That spout up and kill each other, and hang white spray
On cold clear wind.
A rabbit with blazing fur broke through the back-fire,
Bounding and falling, it passed by Lance and ran
Straight into the stem of a wild lilac bush,
He saw it was blind from the fire, and watching it struggle away
Up its dark pain, saw Mary Abbey coming down the black hill against the
    white sky,
Treading on embers. Lance turned and hardened in the saddle, and saw the
    vale below him a long trough of smoke
Spilled northward, then Mary came near and said, "I wanted to talk to you.
    I saw you ride by the water-trough."
He shuddered and said, "What? I'll watch the fire." "Fayne doesn't like me
    so well I think
Since Michael . . . . indeed I'm ashamed to be always around your house."
"I noticed you there," he said, carefully regarding
The dark braids of her hair, and the pale brown face
Seen from above. "I don't know," she said.
"My father says to go away for a time,

His sister lives on a place in Idaho.

But I wouldn't want to forget. But I told Fayne . . .

So I don't know. We could see that you grieved for him

More deeply than anyone else, and all these great hills are empty."

He said, "Is that all?" "Ah . . . ? Yes," she answered,

And turned away and looked back. Lance found that the bridle-leather

Had broken suddenly between his hands, and said "You won't get anything
    from Fayne; she's hard as iron.

Why do you follow us around? What do you think you'll find out?" She
    said, "Your grief is greater perhaps,

For you knew him longer. But you have Fayne and I have nobody: speak
    kindly to me. As I remember,

At first it came from seeing you and Fayne so happy in each other,

I wanted to be like that. I can't talk well, like Fayne,

But I read a great deal." He stared at her face and began to knot the bridle,
    his hands relaxing,

And said, "I must ride around by the oak-scrub and see that the fire has
    checked. I've got to be watchful always.

Will you stay here?" He went and returned and said, "Come down to our
    place whenever you are lonely, Mary.

My mother's quite well again. His death was . . . do people talk much
    about it?" She looked in wonder at his face,

And he with numbed lips: "What lies do they . . . can't you speak out?" "I
    never

Talked about it with anyone, since Nina Dolman

Told us that day. Truly there's nothing to be said by anyone

Except, he was bright with life and suddenly nothing, nothing, nothing,
    darkness."

Lance breathed and said sharply, "I wouldn't bet on it

If I were you. Mary, you are tender and merciful:

Don't come to the house; Fayne is like iron. You'd better

Run home and forget about us. Unless you should hear something

I ought to know." "What do you mean?" "Good-bye."
She saw his bridle-hand lift, she said "I've no pride,
I pray you not to leave me yet, Lance.
I loved him greatly, and now that bond hangs cut,
Bleeding on the empty world, it reaches after
You that were near him. Fayne and you. I was always
Without companions, and now I'd give anything
To be in your friendship a little." "Anything?" he said.
"You faithful women.
Fayne was five days. Mmhm, I have seen a vision.
My eyes are opened I believe."

He rode across the burnt hill,
Watching the wind swirl up the ashes and flatten
The spits of smoke. Past the singed oak-scrub he began to wonder,
If there was honey in the little tree, had . . . the dead
Tasted it before he died? "You'd better be off to Idaho.
. . . I shy from his name like a scared horse.
By God, I'd better get used to it; I've got to live with it."
He looked sharply all about the burnt solitude
To be sure of no hearers, and recited aloud:
"I killed Michael. My name is Lance Fraser.
I murdered my brother Michael. I was plastered,
But I caught 'em at it. I killed my brother Michael.
I'm not afraid to sleep in his room or even
Take over his girl if I choose. I am a dog,
But so are all."

The tall man riding the little bay horse
Along the burnt ridge, talking loudly to nothing but the ash-drifting wind;
  a shadow passed his right shoulder;

He turned on it with slitted eyes, and saw through the strained lashes
    against the gray wind a ghastly old woman
Pursuing him, bent double with age and fury, her brown cloak wild on the
    wind, but when she turned up the wind
It was only a redtail hawk that hunted
On the burnt borders, making her profit in the trouble of field-mice. Lance
    groaned in his throat "Go up you devil.
Ask your high places whether they can save you next time."

VIII

Leo Ramirez rode down on business
About redwood for fence-posts; he asked in vain
For Lance, and had to deal with old Fraser. When he went out
He saw red hair around the corner of the house
And found Fayne in the garden, and asked for Lance.
"I couldn't tell you. I saw him ride to the south.
He'll be home soon for supper." Ramirez stood
In troubled silence, looking at the earth, and said
"I wonder ought I to tell him . . ." Fayne's body quivered
Ever so slightly, her face grew carefully blank.
"What, Leo?" "Will Howard, for instance. Mouths that can't
Shut up for the love of God." "He drives the coast stage,"
Fayne answered carefully. Ramirez looked over the creek
At the branded flanks of the south hill, and no rain had come
To streak them with gray relentings. "He didn't see it,"
He said; "and those two janes on vacation
Went back to town the next day." He giggled, remembering
The sailing-ship stippled on the white skin,
And fixed his mind smooth again. Fayne said, "How dares he
Lie about us?" Ramirez's brown soft eyes
Regarded her with mournful wonder and slid away.

He said, "You was very quick-thinking." "What?" she said, "you were
    there.
And when I cried to him to be careful you looked
And saw him larking on the rock, and you saw him fall,
You could see very plainly in the awful moonlight.
These are things, Leo, that you could swear to." He nodded,
And slid his red tongue along his dry lips and answered,
"Yes'm." "So Howard's a liar," she said. "But don't tell Lance;
He'd break him in two. We'll all do very well,
All wicked stories will die, long long before
Our ache of loss." "Yes'm." She walked beside him
To his tethered horse, and charmed him with an impulsive hand-clasp
After he was in the saddle.

                        She stood with her face high, the great sponge
    of red hair
Lying like a helmet-plume on her shoulders, and thought she was sure of
    conquering security but she was tired;
She was not afraid of the enemy world, but Michael would never be here
    laughing again. On the hill,
In the hill he lay; it was stranger than that, and sharper. And his killer
Ought to be hated a little in the much love. The smells on the wind were
    of ocean, the reedy creek-mouth,
Cows, and wood-smoke, and chile con carne on the kitchen stove; it was
    harder to analyze thoughts in the mind.
She looked at the dear house and its gables
Darkening so low against the hill and wide sky and the evening color
    commencing; it was Lance's nest
Where he was born, and his great white body grew high and beautiful. Old
    Davie shuffled up from the calf-pens
Into the house; then far and high, like a tiny horn on the hill against the
    green-saffron heaven

Lance grew into sight, the man and the horse and the evening peace. He
    was well again; he was sometimes cheerful
Since the early plowing; his muscles needed strong labor. He was like this
    mountain coast,
All beautiful, with chances of brutal violence; precipitous, dark-natured,
    beautiful; without humor, without ever
A glimmer of gayety; blind gray headland and arid mountain, and trailing
    from his shoulders the infinite ocean.
So love, that hunts always outside the human for his choice of metaphors,
Pictured her man on her mind. He dropped from sight
In the hill thickets. She thought, "That's the direction
From the Abbeys' or farther south. Mary Abbey's
Quit haunting our house." The sky grew ever more luminous pale,
The hills more solid purple. At the valley sea-mouth pale rose layered over
    amber, and over the rose
Pale violet, high over the lifted hawk-wings of divided hills, to one fine
    twist of flamingo-feather
Cloud flying in the wind and arch of the world.

                                        A bat flitted up the still
    glimmer.
Fayne went up the drive and opened the gate
For Lance coming across the fields. He looked
As if he had fought, a victory; Fayne was silent;
He nodded, and said, "I've got it over with. You were right."
She saw a thin drift of blood on the bay's fore-leg;
A big brown bird hung from the saddle-thongs,
The half-spread sail of one wing clasped Lance's knee;
He had his rifle. "Another hawk, Lance?" "I've been there,"
He answered. "Oh, this? I pick 'em off when I see 'em.
I've been back to that place." "What place, dear?" "The . . .
Slaughter-house. Under the cliff. Ah: I looked around there.

And rubbed that . . . time into my eyes
Until it formed. Now I guess it won't mix
With every mouthful of air; I can call it to memory
Or shut it up." Fayne looked at his drawn face.
But she thought he seemed a degree restored
To natural goodness again, for he dismounted
And walked beside her. She smelled the prickly sweet fragrance
Of whiskey, and said: "That nasty old man was there.
Lance: you were careful with him?" "Care?" he said, "Hell.
We talked about fish. . . . I heard once about a fellow in jail
Kept banging his head on the wall until he died:
I'd liefer have done that than killed my brother.
I often . . . miss him." He stopped to tie up the hawk's feet
To the top wire of the fence; thence they went on
Without speaking.

                    At supper he said suddenly across the table, "Listen,
   dad.
Are not two sparrows sold for a farthing? When Mikey and I were little you
   used to have prayers in the evenings
And flogged us the times we snickered: why did you quit?" Old Fraser fixed
   his narrow-set apelike eyes
On Lance's face; they seemed to become one thrusting darkness, but he
   said nothing. After a time
Lance said, "But why did you quit?" "Because I grew old and powerless,"
   the old man answered. Lance: "What was that
You used to read about two sparrows for a farthing?" "The Book is there."
   He nodded toward the other room.
"Look it out for yourself." When they stood up from table Lance said, "I
   wish you would read it for us,
About the sparrows." "I will not," he said, "read for your mockery. I am
   utterly left alone on earth;

And God will not rise up in my time." But Lance: "Doesn't it say
No sparrow can fall down without God?" Fayne said, "Oh Lance: come
    on."
"No, no; I want him to read and pray.
What does that mean, fall to earth without God?
Does it mean that God fells it? Fayne and I
Know better than that: ah, Fayne? *We* know, ah?
But God connives.
Do read about the two sparrows." His roving glance
Came on his mother's blanched and full-moon face,
The pouched watery blue eyes, and the mouth always
Thirsting for breath. "No, no, I'll keep still, mother.
I didn't want to tease him, I was in earnest
To have prayers again."

                    But he remained in the room
Until his mother had gone up to bed, then instantly
Said, "Listen, dad. Be a good sport.
Are not two sparrows sold for a farthing?" Fayne had watched him
Sitting stone-still, only twitching his hands,
His face hollow in the lamp-shadow: she went quickly
And touched his shoulder; she smoothed her hand on his throat,
Saying, "Please, Lance, no more of that. Why will you do it?"
"Sh," he said, "I have him by a raw spot: keep out.
He spooned the gospel down my throat when I was a cub:
Why's he so tight wi' that farthing? Once, dad, you whipped Mikey
For spelling the name of God backward
Until the red crucifixion ran down his legs.
Do you remember the brave little brown legs
All smeared and welted?" The old man eyed him and said,
"You lie. He had a thorn-scratch that opened." "Booh," Lance answered,
"I won't quarrel with you. I want the truth:

Are not two sparrows sold for a farthing?" Old Fraser

Groaned, and the straight edge of the lamp-shade shadow

That crossed his broad face obliquely over the burning

Blackness of the eyes, but left the stiff mouth and jaw

In the yellow light, shook with his passion. He said, "My Master also

Was mocked cruelly by those he loved, desiring to save them. You have a
    strong body, and if I struck you

You'd take me by the wrists like a little child. I am in my house and I have
    no one to help me.

I am old and worn out; my strength is gone and white hair has come, but
    honor has not come. I say that God

Is not mocked; but a feeble ailing old man, who loved his boys too
    indulgently and has seen the blithe hands

Reach out for damnation, and the happy feet . . . Oh . . .

Is rightly mocked. Oh Lance, over Michael's death." Lance, pale and
    mumbling: "We all have troubles, old man;

Yours have come late. Well. Are not two sparrows . . ." Fayne cried,
    "Lance, Lance, for pity

Hush, whatever he did to you when you were little.

He earns peace now." "Mm," he said, "where's that? I've

Been trying to get him to call me about those sparrows:

The old man won't play; we've an ace in the hole too.

Here it is for nothing, old man:

I rode by the Abbeys' line-fence along the steep

Over Wreck Beach, and there's a young deer, a spike-buck

Hanging dead on the wire, made a bad jump

From the low side. The barbs caught him by the loins,

Across the belly at the spring of the haunches, the top wire.

So there he hangs with his head down, the fore-hooves

Reaching the ground: they dug two trenches in it

Under his suspended nose. That's when he dragged at the barbs

Caught in his belly, his hind legs hacking the air.

No doubt he lived for a week: nothing has touched him: a young
    spike-buck:
A week of torture. What was that for, ah?
D' you think God couldn't see him? The place is very naked and open, and
    the sea glittering below;
He hangs like a sign on the earth's forehead, y' could see him from China.
    . . . But keep the wind side.
For a loving God, a stinking monument." "Bosh," the old man answered,
And stood up, and puckering a miminy mouth: "Your little buck!
There is not one soul in hell but would take his place on the wire
Shouting for joy . . . . and few men past fifty." Lance also,
Made surly by the slow death of whiskey in his blood,
Stood up: "Your merciful God, that made you whip little boys. We're dogs,
But done licking those feet." He bulked in the old man's way to the door,
    towering in the shadow, and forced him
Toward the near corner. Fayne ran between them. "Tell me the truth,"
    Lance said, "do you believe in your God?"
Old Fraser, who had stood glaring like a bayed cat, suddenly dwindled; and
    felt outside the walled cube
Of lamplight under gray stars no Scottish nor Palestinian uplands but the
    godless hills of America
Like vacant-eyed bison lying toward the sea, waiting for rain. He moved his
    lips without breath, he struck
His throat and said feebly: "I am choked and dried up with the running
    sands.
I have prayed a great deal in vain, and seen the whole earth
Shed faith like leaves;
And the faces of sin round as the sun and morality
Sneered to death. I cannot
Live unless I believe. . . . I cannot live";
And stood all shrunken. Lance, awed: "My God, who'd ever 'a' thought
He could be plagued into honesty?" The old man

Cried fiercely: "I believe. Ah: tell your people to be careful
Of the God they have backed into a snarling corner,
And laugh off like a dirty story." "That's it," Lance answered.
"Dogs. We all are." He stood backward, the old man
Passed slowly, staring, saying "Make yourself ready if you can.
For I see you are changed."

                         Fayne shuddered and said,
"What does he mean?" "He? Nothing. He means *two* sparrows
For a farthing." She said "Lance. . . . Lance?"
He moved to leave her; she breathed and said, "Can you hear?
We were doing, what you thought. It seemed . . . . usual
That night: both drunk: he was going away. . . . So what you did, Lance,
Was justice." "Agh," he said, "nudge me wi' that, still?
I know it perfectly. What does it matter, what farthing
Sold them?" Fayne, sobbing: "Oh, then, we did not. It is not true.
I lied." "It would not be possible to tell you," he said,
"How little I care." She, with both hands at her white throat, but lifting
    her face:
"Yes. I can bear that. We've sailed I think away past the narrows of
    common faithfulness. Then care for this:
To be able to live, in spite of pain and that horror and the dear blood on
    your hands, and your father's God,
To be able to go on in pure silence
In your own power, not panting for people's judgment, nor the pitiful
    consolation of punishing yourself
Because an old man filled you with dreams of sin
When you were little: you are not one of the sparrows, you are not a
    flock-bird: but alone in your nature,
Separate as a gray hawk." "The very thing I was thinking," he answered.
"If you'd take your red hair and spindly face

Out of my lamplight I'd be alone: it's like a burst blood-vessel
In the eye of thought."

IX

Old Mrs. Fraser
Caught cold and remained in bed, the bronchial pain
Frightened her heart with memories of worse anguish.
Fayne went back and forth from the stove to the bed
Heating flannels, to lay them on the white upland
Between the blond mountains of falling flesh
That had fed Lance. Going by the curtainless window
She looked whether she could see him, across the fields
Or up the burnt hill. Not Lance, but a smaller figure
Was coming down the black hill under white clouds:
Mary Abbey: her father had horses enough,
Was she walking down here?

Lance's mother
Wished for that wintergreen oil again; Fayne rubbed it
On the white plain and the roots of great soft udders.
She could feel in her finger-tips the suck and rattle
Of phlegm in the breathing-tubes, the old woman coughing
And saying "I see there was four sheets in the wash again
From you and Lance; well dearie, don't fret.
He's just his father all over, crazy as hawks.
They get to thinking Antichrist and the Jews and the wicked Pope in
    Rome
And scunner at every arrangement for human comfort.
Then they come home like hungry sailors from sea.
You're all worn out in the morning; my feet are cold."
She coughed and panted; Fayne rubbed the oil. The old woman said,

"My feet are cold." Fayne answered sadly "I'll rub them."
"No, if you'd get me an iron; a fine hot flat-iron
Done up in cloth is a great comfort in bed.
Right often it's been a husband to me when my old man
Was prophesying around and a fresh cow
Cried all the night."

           Fayne went down-stairs for the iron
And heard a wonderful sound behind the house; she heard Lance laughing.
She looked from the door and saw old Davie by the lime-washed
   hen-house, leaning both hands on a long shovel,
Gaze at the ground; Lance crouched near by, with blood on his hands and
   something between his knees, red feathers,
That fiery old half-bred game-cock, that sent the dogs
Yelping for mercy. A little Cooper's-hawk was tethered in front of Lance to
   a driven peg,
One wing bloodily trailing; Lance pushed the game-cock toward it and the
   hawk fell, tripped by its wing,
But crutched itself on the other and came up again,
Erect and watchful, holding the earth with its yellow feet.
Lance pushed and freed the game-cock, that eagerly
Staring-hackled in his battle-passion
Leaped up and struck down; the hawk tripped by its wing
Fell quivering under the spurs, but a long-fingered
Lean yellow hand reaching up out of ruin
Plucked at the red king's breast: who charged again: one hawk-wing
Waved, and the talons mysteriously accomplished
Many quick bitter acts, whence the red king
Reeled out of hope. He crouched beyond tether's reach,
Propping himself on both wings, but the sinking head
Still stretched for fight; then dull-eyed, at strength's end,
Went staggering to it again. The yellow hands

Easily made him what would never any more
Chirp over bright corn to the hens or subdue a rival.

Lance came, and the little hawk ran quickly and fell
Onto its broken shoulder at the tether's end. Lance picked up the dying
    game-cock;
Red grains of wheat from the torn crop fell down with the blood. Fayne
    watched from the open door; she saw him
Turn at the click of a gate, and Mary Abbey came up from the creek-bed
    path. At sight of Lance
She stopped; her hands went up to her throat. He, frowning: "What do you
    want . . . Mary?" She lowered her hands
And stepping backward almost inaudibly said, "I . . .
Came the back way. I . . . came to see Fayne." She had hurried and was
    breathing hard. Lance stared at her,
And said "Go on in, confess your sins." He turned with his shoulder
    toward her; the bleeding bird in his hands
Stretched itself, thrusting back with the spurs as if it were killing its last
    rival, and suddenly died,
With a bright bubble of blood in the gaping beak. Old Davie laughed, but
    not Lance; the little hawk
Stood up and watched all with intent eyes. Mary stayed wringing her hands
    and Fayne came from the door,
Then Mary, half running toward her: "I hardly bear to see blood: let me go
    in." Fayne said to Lance:
"It won." "It will lose," he said in his throat, "when my heel is on it." She,
    gravely: "It fought well, Lance.
Have you hurt your hands?" "Ugh," he said, "nothing: the vermin." He
    moved toward the little captive, that looked up at him
With cold intentness; the blood had started again from its broken shoulder
    and striped the dead wing. Mary Abbey,

Shrilly, whipping the air with her hands: "Let me go!" Lance raised his
    foot to tread, but the victim's intent
Concentration of binocular eyes looked human; Mary cried shrilly: "They
    told me, my father said. . . . .
And Nina told me . . . Oh Fayne!" Lance, suddenly rigid: "What's that?"
    Fayne answered steadily and said, "Its life
Is little value to it with a broken wing. Come into the house." She
    answered "I am afraid."
But approached the door, whispering "What kind of a house, with blood
    sprinkled
Where you enter the door: what have you done?
His hands are red." Lance turned from the hawk and said with his teeth
    showing, "Tell your father
That I may soon be with this," he toed the dead cock, "our second-sighted
    old Scotchman has got a hunch.
But not with that, not caught alive." She fled from him
To the open door. Fayne, jerking her face but not
Her shoulders toward him said low: "You speak of things
Less real than nothing. It is not courage to make
Danger where there is none." She followed Mary Abbey
Into the door, saying: "Lance is not well. He loved his brother
Most deeply, and having heard of venomous talk
Makes the wound burn. Have you too been listening
To our enemies?" Mary, trembling in the house twilight:
"I know you couldn't speak calmly, if, if . . . Oh Fayne.
But every person . . . What have I done!" "Will you hush," Fayne said,
"Mrs. Gomez is probably not interested
In your girl dreams." Then Mary was silent, seeing
The dark ruler of the kitchen. Fayne took the iron,
And said on the stair, "I have to attend to Lance's mother:
You'd better stay with me. Then we'll walk." At the room door:
"Mary Abbey is here, mother."

Mary faltered

At the air of the room, the stove-heat and stale hangings in the air
Of wintergreen and eucalyptus. She stood close to the door,
And felt the weary mill turn in her mind,
Unable to think of any definite thing, painfully grinding, turning. Old Mrs.
    Fraser
Sniffed and said, "I can smell scorching cloth,
Did you try it with a wet finger? It ought to sizz
But if it whistles it will burn the sheets; Mary are you sick?
You look all blue by the mouth," she wagged her head in the pillow, "watch
    your heart." Fayne, kneeling
To slip the iron under the covers of the bed, tossed back her bright hair
    and said, "She's all right, mother.
Lance was having a kind of cock-fight in the back yard, that struck her pale:
    she's one of those delicate
Natures that die at seeing blood."

                The weary mill of the mind struck a
    hard kernel and seemed to fall
Down hollow waters: Mary leaned on the door-frame, clenching her fists
    not to go down with it, biting
Her white lip, the circle of sight contracted until only the blood-splatch of
    Fayne's hair was visible
At the hub of the whirlpool. She slid with her back to the steep door-frame
    and did not fall; Fayne helped her
To escape the room, the old woman far off proclaiming "It is her heart."

                                      Mary
    leaned on the newel
Of the stairhead to find her strength to go down, and said,
"I am so caught. And someone has daubed every
Beam of your house with it. All women have to bear blood

But mine has stopped. Please go first, Fayne,
For you don't hate me yet; now I can't bear
To meet . . . . anyone." Fayne slowly said, "It was Michael?"
"I am in terror," she answered, "of every living thing,
And him, and you." Fayne's triangular face,
The high cheek-bones and narrow jaw, thrust in the twilight
Opposite the other's white oval, as a small perching hawk
Thrusts with her head, forcing the shapes of things
To grow alive in the motion of the eyes
And yield up their hunted secrets: Fayne peered at her,
Trembling, and said, "Then follow."

                                        They went out the front way;
No one was seen; Fayne said: "It is horrible to be nearing New Year's
And still the dust and the sun, as if it could never rain. Would you like to
    be nurse to that old woman?
She's Lance's mother." Mary said faintly, stumbling on the plain path, "I
    have no mother: and the raging
Blue of your eyes hates me." "What you have heard," Fayne said, "is only
    the common lies of the shore.
It's natural for people to furnish a house with lies if it meets misfortune.
    When a man loses his property
He's called fool, or thief; when they see you crushed
By the sudden death of someone you love they begin to hint murder: it's
    human nature. If you're weak enough,
Believe them: it won't hurt us. But what are you here for?" She answered,
    leaning her hand on the post of the little gate
To steady her body: "I am not strong like you. I am in danger of killing
    myself, if . . .
Or if I believe them." "Better than you," Fayne said, "have died. Come on."
    A little way past the gate,

Mary said, "What is it? You too are trembling!" She answered, trembling,
   "Oh no: *my* life is easy. Dear,
We're friends, we mustn't make mysteries: tell me, won't you, what's all this
   web of trouble
You stare so white through? You can count on my loving friendship, and
   my
Forgiveness, if for any reason . . . My worst enemy
Will call me warm-hearted; and if I once had the name
Of being a jealous woman in my love for Lance:
Well," she said with a calm voice, her face twisting
Like a small white flame specked with flying ashes,
"That wears, it softens. And he . . . grows morose and strange,
Is not perfectly a splendor in my eyes any more.
I will confess that I cannot feel so warmly about him
As once I did. . . . Here above the bee-hives, Mary,
Nobody ever comes, and you could tell me
Everything safely; and if any advice of mine
Could help, though I am not wise."

                          They stood silently,
Turning their faces away from each other,
In a wind acrid with stale honey and the life of bees.
Mary Abbey shuddered and said, "I *came* here
To tell you. Oh, Oh. I used to seem to myself
Locked in, cold and unwishing; but . . . Michael's . . . love
Made April in me, and the sudden emptiness of death
Tore . . . I was much changed: you remember
How I clung to you in the desert of the days afterwards,
And tired you into dislike, until you turned
Hard eyes toward me. The first time I saw Lance alone
He was riding in fire and ashes; he was more unkind
Than you ever were." Fayne tasted

The crack in her bitten lip, and shut her eyes and said softly
"Go on, sweetheart"; but the dark-haired one
Only wept, and Fayne said "You've told me nothing,
Sweetheart." She answered "Are you still really my friend?
Don't look at me," and turned her face from Fayne,
Saying "I was so aching lonely. I only wanted
To be friends with someone: he really . . . he took me roughly
On the great lonely hill; it hurt, does it hurt at first
If you are loved?" Fayne had stopped trembling and stood
With bones and teeth showing through the skin of her face,
And trying to speak moaned slightly, and avoided
The little blind hand feeling for hers. "But still I
Strain and ache to be near him." Fayne took the hand,
And with her unfleshed mouth kissed Mary's hair,
And tried to speak, and with painful care: "Go . . . on . . .
Sweetheart?" "Then they told me that he killed Michael.
That was not true. Oh yes, I know, but I thought
If I loved where I ought to hate I would kill myself.
I have always been as regular as the new moon,
And this time, twelve days have passed. When I was troubling
About that, that was when they told me. I thought
About a coyote that was caught near our house
In two steel traps at once, so that it couldn't
Stand nor lie down." Fayne touched her teeth with her tongue
Until the stretched white lips came slowly to cover them,
And said, "Do you mean?" She answered, "I am so caught.
I know, I have a book about it. So I came here.
Your dooryard was full of blood." Fayne said, "Maybe you are.
He's travelled away past caring, and would let
Nature fly. I'd naturally. . . .
I have to control my starts, because Lance,
Who's worth ten thousand of *you*, hangs on the scale.

D' y' love him, *sweetheart?*" She turned her face toward her,

Saying, "Yes." Fayne mumbled and said, "I'd naturally . . .

It's babies like you . . . Listen to me.

I took Lance in my hand in that bad night

To fling at the world. We do not have to let the dogs judge for us. I told
him that we are our own people

And can live by ourselves: if we could endure the pain of being lonely. Do
you think *you* with Lance

Could strangle time? I am holding the made world by the throat

Until I can make it change, and open the knot that past time tied. To undo
past time, and mend

The finished world: while you were busy teething your young virginity. I
have to control myself.

Last year I'd 'a' let

Nature fly; changed your baby face wi' my hands,

Sweetheart: but I cannot risk: life has changed." "Oh Fayne! why did you
say . . ." "I'm not a tame animal,"

She answered, "the wild ones are not promiscuous. What would you do,"
her voice thinning to a wire, "if . . . Lance . . .

If it proved true, that you'd given your little dry heart and careful body

And anxious little savings of honor

For a prize to your lover's murderer: could you walk, eat, sleep,

While you knew that?" She said, "It is true then.

I had made up my mind: indeed I long for it.

Sleep: Oh, you'll see." Fayne drew in breath like one

Drinking in a desert passion, and said, "You've not

Enough courage." "Not for anything else," Mary answered;

"But that"; and began to go back down the dry hill.

Fayne followed, with eyes like the blue flame of sulphur

Under the fever of her hair, and lips reddening.

The moment of joy withered out of her face.

"I am fighting the whole people, do you think I'll risk:

For the pleasure of a small soft fool's removal,
Who'd weep it out to her father or leave a letter. . . . Oh, you: it's not
    true.
Lance is no murderer, you're innocent as far as that.
I saw with my eyes your unmourned lover
Clambering up the ledges in his happy drunkenness,
All alone, and the shale broke in his hands;
I saw him pitching down the white moonlight,
And heard the noise like a melon of his head on rock
In the clatter of the falling pebbles. Lance came up the sand
After I screamed." Mary Abbey stood swaying and said,
"If you knew my heart you'd pity me." Fayne, amazed: "Pity you
For having had Lance?" and said hoarsely, "When did you tell him
That you think you are pregnant?" "Oh, Oh," she stammered,
"Never. You hate me." "You're good at guessing," Fayne said.
"What do you want here, money to bribe a doctor?
We have no money here. Yet it seems I must help you,
Or worse will come. I know a woman in the city . . .
When you start east . . . But you must promise never to come back
Into the drawing net of our lives."

X

                    When Mary had gone,
Fayne went where Lance had been; but only the little hawk
Stood in the dust, hopeless and watchful, with its own misery
And a shadow of its own, between the privy and the hen-house and the
    back door. Fayne thought: would Lance
Be harmed if she should give it the gift? and fetched the axe from the
    wood-block, but forgot to be merciful
And went up-stairs. She washed herself, brushed her bright fleece, and came
    down.

GIVE YOUR HEART TO THE HAWKS   363

She found Lance at the fence-corner
Where the north pasture comes down to drink. He had looped his belt
    around the neck of a yearling colt
That had a head like a barrel; the little body and long knotted legs of
    nature, but the head enormous,
Like a barrel-headed beast in a dream. "Oh Lance, what ails it?" He stared
    at her
And answered, faintly smiling, "I guess a little
Message from someone." "What?" she said. "Nothing. We don't have
    rattlers
In the middle of winter." "Is it a rattlesnake bite?"
"They sleep in the rocks and holes, twisted in bunches,
They won't strike if you dig them up: but here
On his lip are the pricks." He unhaltered
The shuddering colt. "Stumble away poor thing.
That was a mean trick, to sting the innocent."
Fayne said, "Was it a rattlesnake bite?" "Mm: but
What sent it up?" "This weather," she said, "the vicious sun."
"Fine hawk's-weather, ah? Did Mary what's-her-name
Tell you her young sins?" Fayne quivered, closing her eyes,
And answered at length, "She's sick." "So are we all."
"*I* am not. . . . Lance, you are generous: if you found a stranger
Starving, and gave her . . . *him* milk and bread, and came
Home and you found someone of yours starving;
Your father, whom you don't love, but you have to owe him
A kind of duty . . ." "Why didn't you say brother?"
She fixed her eyes on his face and sighed and said, "I am speaking
Of the living.
. . . And he begged you for the mouthed cup, and what was left
Of the broken loaf?" He made a sound of impatience
And turned, but Fayne took his hand, still marked by pressure
Of the strap that had held the struggling colt: "Would you let him starve?"

"No. What about it?" "That . . . stranger . . . you fed seems to be sorry
    about it. I suppose she was starving.
I have some angry rinsings of pride in me
Make begging bitter." "*That's* it," he said. "I could 'a' laughed at you
In the days before I was damned. I'm learning. The mares have their
    seasons but women always." "I will bear anything,"
She answered sighing, her narrow white face opaque with tolerance. "I was
    not always perfectly patient.
If you were safe I'd have twisted a knife in her fluty throat. My knife is
    patience." "I know the very
Place," he said. "Come on, I'll answer his note. The very place."

                                                      They
    went up by the dry
Gully through the starved and naked pasture; the autumn hunger of horses
    and the patient hooves had left
Hardly roots of the grass, and the yellow dust was reddened with sundown.
    They saw lean horses drift off
Along the ridges on the darkening sky, and far on the last knoll
Three slabs of redwood standing like erect stones, quite black against the
    red streak and slate-color cloud,
Lonely and strange. Fayne, breathless with labor up the long slopes, cried
    hoarsely, "Where are you going? Oh Lance,
Not there?" "There," he said. "No. I won't. No.
What agony in you . . . not here." "On his earth," he answered. "It would
    make us despise ourselves. Oh, do not hate him.
He did no wrong, he was happy and laughing-natured, and dear to us all."
    "Come on," he said, "or go home.
Choose." She went slowly away down the hill, and returned and said, "I
    love you and I want . . . not what you think,
But near enough. And the dead know nothing." "I wouldn't bet on it," he
    said; "the drunk did." "You are wildly wrong,"

She answered, "Oh horribly," and embracing him strained up to his throat
Her whitened lips.

                She felt the bare crumbled earth,
The dark home of the dead and serpents,
Under her back, and gave herself eagerly,
Desiring that gift that Mary meant to destroy,
And herself had never wanted before, but now
To accept what her rival dared not keep,
Take and be faithful where the other fled, had some bitter value;
And faith and the world were shaken; Lance might be lost,
The past might prove unconquerable: no, she could save him: but yet
She'd bind the future.

                This time Lance did not fail.
She feared his caution and schemed against it, quite needlessly,
For he had wandered beyond prudent thoughts;
But when they were going away in the twilight, "Ah vile.
Vile," he said, "your hawks have worse poison in their hook beaks
Than any ground-nest of rattlers." She answered, "I am not to tell you
What my hope is." "On top of his bones, dogs in a boneyard."
She answered languidly and bitterly, "I ought to have let you
Go to Salinas. I did not know that your mind . . .
I would have waited for you all the long years.
I did not know that your mind needed men's judgment
And the helpless appraisals of the world to help you. You stood so strong,
Separate, clear, free in my eyes: and I did violence to you
When I kept you." She felt a trembling about him
And saw that he did not hear but was watching shadows
Fleet in the air: "Sea-gulls. They are gulls, Lance. Look how beautiful
The long sharp silent wings in the fading light
On the bare hill." "He took it very quietly," he answered;

"We are all dogs, every one." "Oh," she said, "the world's full
Of evil and foolishness but it is terribly beautiful.
If you could see that, Lance." "What? By God they won't, not alive.
But then comes hell." "I pray you, I pray you, dear,
Not to begin to think strangely: that's for your father, who often
Walks his road all staring between hedges
Of Christs and Satans: but you will rub your mind quiet
Like the face of a crystal; there is enough to see
In the dark lovely shoulders of hills, the cows and horses, the old gray rocks
    and the folk around us,
Without tapping strange dreams. . . . Oh, we'll live well."

XI

The rain held off; for two hundred and forty days there had been no rain
But one sun-drunken shower. The creek was dry rock and weary gray roots;
    the skin of the mountain crumbled
Under starved feet; the five carcasses of hawks that Lance had hung on the
    fence-wire dried without odor
In the north wind and rages of the sun.

                                        Old Fraser walked under the
    moon along the farm-drive beside them,
Saying "Lord if thou art minded to burn the whole earth
And spat off the dust from thy hands, it is well done,
The glory and the vengeance: but if anywhere
Rain falls on hills, remember I beseech thee thy servant's place,
Or the beasts die in the field." While he was praying
The moon was dimmed; he felt a flutelike exultance
Flow up from the V of his ribs to his wrinkled throat:
He was not abandoned: and looked aloft and saw
A little many-colored man's-palm-size cloud

Coasting the moon from the southeast, the storm-side.

The old man exalted himself; he had power upon God; and anxiously

Repressing his joy for fear it waste the event

Beforehand, compelled his heart to remember bitterness,

His two sons lost, one dead, the other in rebellion,

And poverty and scorn and the starved cattle. "Oh Lord God,

As in old time thou didst choose one little people for thine out of all the
    earth,

So now thou hast chosen one man, one old man, foolish and poor: but if
    thy will was made up

To punish the earth, then heed not my voice but arise and punish. It is rank
    with defilement and infidelity

And the music of the evil churches." He saw a shining white form at the
    garden-gate, and for a high moment

Believed that some angel, as unto Abraham . . . It was Lance,

Perfectly naked, and Fayne his wife behind him

Walking in her white night-dress, who spoke pleadingly,

But Lance went on. He came with stiff hesitance,

And seemed not to look down at the latch but opened the gate.

The old man watched and waited in the tool-house shadow.

Lance passed the gate and stood in the open dust

Like a blind marble pillar-stone, the icy moonlight

Washing his body, pouring great shadows

Of the heavily moulded muscles on the hairless breast,

And the ripple of strength on the smooth belly; he stood

And babbled and called: "Mikey. Oh Mikey. Come home.

I'll be *it* to-morrow again. It's getting too dark to play,

Don't hide any more, buddy, for the owls are out.

If you'll come in I'll let you have my cornelian,

And the heron's eggs that I found." Fayne took his hand,

"Lance, Lance, wake up," and stroked the smooth power of his arm,

Her face caressing his shoulder. He said, "Hurry, they're blaming me.

They think you're lost." Fayne said, "I can't bear it, Lance.
Mikey's in the house. He's come in already." The old man
Came forward out of the shadow; Fayne heard and stared at him.
Lance said, "Damned liar. Ma's not . . . mare.
People ain't made like . . . dirty . . ." and babbled words
That could not be understood. Fayne said, "Sleep-walking.
Did he ever before . . . what can I do?" Lance moaned,
She reached her arm around him and stroked his face
With the other hand; the old man saw her hair
Against the wide white breast like a burst of blood
Deep in the moonlight, then Lance flung her aside
As white foam flies from the oar, saying still in the dream-drunken
Sing-song, "Oh no you don't: this is not dogs' meat.
Or you'll have to kill it before you paw it.
The angels wi' the hooky beaks. . . . What in hell," he said
Sharply, "who's there?" "I, Lance. Oh come to bed, dear.
You wandered out in your sleep." "No: that spying devil,"
He said, "hm?" "Your father, your father, Lance.
He was here when you came." "Oh. . . . Did I talk?"
"Hardly a word. Nothing, dear." "I sleep better
Alone," he said, "now."

    The old man looked up at cloud-flecks
Like algae breeding on clear deep well-water around the moon,
And looked at Lance, and returned up the drive. Lance said, "Do you wear
    white? Hitch it up on your breast,
The teat is bare. Why did he turn away without speaking?" "He saw you'd
    wakened." "Black will look fine,"
He answered, "wi' the fiery hair. I want you to marry again, you'll have
    chances."

                    The sky in the morning
Was layered with cloud, and it drove from the southeast; the old man kept
    working his mouth in silent thanksgiving
For answered prayer; and the wind came down from heaven and smoked in
    the fields. The sky cleared for a time,
But that was natural; the wind increased. It ran quartering the little valley;
    ashes from the hill
And mountain dust entered all cracks of the house. It raged on the salt pool
    at the creek sea-mouth
By the caverned crag that storms have worn spongelike; it reaped the heads
    of the waves on the wide sea, and lay
Like a quivering steel blade on the necks of the herbless mountains.

                                                            Far

    away northward in San Francisco
It blew the filth of the street into the faces
That walked there; one was Mary Abbey's little pale oval
Lost among thousands. She moved unevenly, fast and lagging,
And looked with terrified eyes at the gilt street-number
Scribed on a window; beyond a mean plush-curtained restaurant
The number stood over a door. She stood choking,
And read on a brass plate in the doorway: "Dr. Eisendraht,
Eye, ear, nose, throat"; a wind-scoop of sudden dust
Blurred the letters and filled her eyes. She went on
With faint small steps, and at the street-corner
Tried to stand still, and was jostled. Not wearing gloves
She spurred blood from the back of her left hand
With the nails of her right: the pain helped her go back
And enter the door and find the stairway. She had to sit long,
Waiting her turn; she was served impersonally

And dismissed, fainting or able, to the desert wind
And dust and multitude down the mean street.

At Sycamore Creek

Lance's mother was wiping the table oil-cloth
For the noon meal, the film of the wind's dust, and suddenly
Fell into a chair; Mrs. Gomez came in with knives and forks on the plates
    and found her, and Fayne
Came at the cry; they couldn't take her up-stairs until Lance came in. They
    helped her slip to the floor,
And brought a pillow, then Lance came in. Fayne said, "She is weak but
    better, the pain is passing." The old woman
Mountainous laid on the floor wished to lie still for a time. Lance knelt by
    her side. "All right, mother.
As long as you like. Fayne," he said gravely,
"Will you come to the door a minute?" Fayne went, and outside the door
    said, "What do you want, Lance? You scare her
Wi' that secret look." "I was not afraid to go in after him, I want you to see
    him. The question is
Whether my eyes have begun to sing lies to me.
He came from the orchard walk and went in the shed.
I know you have courage. A frightful branding. Oh," he sighed,
"That's the point." She looked at his face and followed him,
And reeled in the dry fierce wind in front of the house;
But he leaning his back on the stiff wind
So that his shirt moulded the groove between
The great bands of lean power from the shoulders: "Well. Do you see him?
In the shed door." "No." "It was closed, he opened it.
You can see that it's open? Now I'll catch him.
Come." He ran suddenly and leaped the garden-gate.
But Fayne must stop to unlatch it, and when she came
Lance had gone into the shed and around the motor-truck

That stood within. Fayne said, "Wind broke the peg
That held the clasp of the door: see, here's one piece.
That's why it's open." She heard the roof straining
Over the imprisoned storm. Lance said "Did he pass you?
Ah?" She answered, "We must go away from this place.
For you, it's haunted. Your mother, whom I think you love, is just now
Lying low between life and death, and you leave her
To chase the wind, and the foxes of your eyes. Do you love him so?
Or hate him?" He answered, "The fire's burnt through his cheek,
His back-teeth grinned at me through the horrible scar.
I'll be there soon." "What fire? . . . Are you dreaming punishment?
Oh, that's the vainest craziest falsehood of all.
Leave that to your poor old father." "We go down
Into blackness," he stiffly answered,
"And neither you nor I nor the old man
Knows what happens there. This was Michael: if I should dream him
I'd dream the skull knocked in, hm? What I saw's
The cheek burnt through." "I will not let go and lose you," she answered.
    "Probably," Lance said, "he'd have lied
If I could have caught him."

                    In the afternoon
Fayne saw from the window above the kitchen a small gray object
Making a singular dance in the flying dust.
The little hawk which Lance had shot but not killed
Was dying; they had dropped it a strip of beef that dried in the sun,
And given it a dish of water, and not again
Remembered it, though it stood up grimly and watched
Whoever passed to the privy. The water was blown
Out of the dish; no matter, it had never drunk.
Now it was flapping against the wind,
Fluttering the natural wing and trailing the broken one,

Grotesque in action as the blackcock at dawn
Making his dance of love; but this was of death.

In the night Fayne said: "That little hawk died. Oh be quiet now;
You've shot them out of the sky. . . . Dear, I am to blame
Like you, and yet I'd be as happy at heart
As a fed bird that glides through the high air
If you were not tearing yourself." He made no answer,
She heard the wind tear at the roof, and said,
"I love this place. But time has changed, let old Davie
And your dad farm it now, it is full of memories
And very fit for old men. You and I
Will take three horses for all our share of it,
And travel into the south by that deer-track
Where the planted foot is on the face of the mountain and the lifted foot
High over the gray face of the sea: four or five days
Only the eagles will see us, and the coasting ships
Our fires at evening, and so on southward. But when we get to Los Angeles,
    dear,
You'll put your great white shoulders to work
For passage-money, we'll sell the horses and ride
In a ship south, Mexico's not far enough,
The Andes are over the ocean like our hills here,
But high as heaven." "Fancy-work," he mumbled. "Ah. Low as hell."
Fayne said, "No. Listen: how the air rushes along the keel of the roof, and
    the timbers whining.
That's beautiful; and the hills around here in the cloud-race moon-glimmer,
    round rocks mossed in their cracks with trees:
Can't you see them? I can, as if I stood on them,
And all the coast mountain; and the water-face of the earth, from here to
    Australia, on which thousand-mile storms

Are only like skimming swallows; and the earth, the great meteor-ball of
    live stone, flying
Through storms of sunlight as if forever, and the sun that rushes away we
    don't know where, and all
The fire-maned stars like stallions in a black pasture, each one with his stud
    of plunging
Planets for mares that he sprays with power; and universe after universe
    beyond them, all shining, all alive:
Do you think all *that* needs us? Or any evil we have done
Makes any difference? We are a part of it,
And good is better than evil, but I say it like a prayer
That if you killed him, the world is all shining. It does not matter
If you killed him; the world's out of our power, the goodness and splendor
Are things we cannot pervert, although we are part of them,
And love them well." He heavily answered: "Have you finished?
Don't speak of . . . him . . . again." She began to answer,
Thought, and was silent.

XII

                         She fetched a pair of rawhide panniers
From the harness wall in the barn, remembering that Michael
Less than two years ago had whittled the frame, and Lance
Shaped the hairy leather and stitched it with sinew thongs.
That was the time they three in delight and love
Rode south by the sea-eagle trails to Point Vicente and Gamboa's
For seven days' hunting, when Fayne shivered with happiness,
Riding between the most beautiful and strongest man
For husband, and the gayest in the world for brother, on perfectly
Wild hills and by rushing streams.

She packed the panniers,
And balanced the weight, mixing her things with Lance's.
The wind had ceased and no rain had fallen, but the air grown colder
Whipped up her courage to believe Lance would go,
And find life, in new places. His mother was well again;
And on the farm all things had come to a pause; he was not needed.
The hay-loft was emptying fast: but Lance could not make it rain by
    staying!

         While she packed the panniers
A little agony was acting under the open window, between the parched lips
    of the creek.
One of those white-crowned sparrows that make sweet voices in the spring
    evenings in the orchard
Was caught by a shrike and enduring death, not the bright surgical mercy
    of hawks, but slow and strangling.
Its little screams quivered among the gray stones and flew in the window;
    Fayne sighed without noticing them,
And packed the panniers.

             When Lance came up at evening she showed
    him what she had done: "We'll go to-morrow."
He said he'd not leave the place in trouble, "Even dogs are faithful. After
    the first good rain I'll go."
The reasons she made only angered him.

             Late in January
Fell rain mingled with hail, and snow in the nights. Three or four calves
    died in a night, then Lance
Had occupation with what survived; and the north slopes of hills were
    sleeted with magic splendor
That did not melt.

GIVE YOUR HEART TO THE HAWKS   375

Fayne was drying dishes while Mrs. Gomez washed
them; she dropped a cup
With the dazzle of the white hill in her eyes when the sun came out;
Then Lance's mother filled up the door and said,
"That Mary Abbey is here." Fayne answered clearly,
"I broke a cup. She is in Idaho I think."
The old woman: "She's thinner. Oh Fayne, there were only seven
Left of the dozen": she gasped, remembering Michael: six were enough.
"She's got something to tell you." Fayne said, "Being out of our net
Has she flown back? Where's Lance?" and passed the old woman
As one moves a door to pass through a doorway,
But found no one; neither in the front rooms
Nor on the garden path when she opened the house-door.
Then she returned to Lance's mother and asked,
"Where has she gone? Where was she?" but found no light in the answers,
Only that Mary looked waxy as a little candle,
Her heart must be terribly weak, she looked all blue by the mouth,
And must have come a wet way.

Fayne felt the jealous
Devil fingering her throat again, tightening her breath,
And hasted and found Lance; but he was alone;
In the lower creek-bed, lopping all the twigs from the willows, making a
    load, to be chopped fine
And mixed with little portions of hay. She saw him reaching up the dwarf
    stems, as tall as the trees,
The sky-cold knife, the purple twigs at his feet, and said, "Have you seen
    Mary Abbey?" "What?" "Mary Abbey."
"You said she'd gone." "Well, she did go: she was up at the house just
    now"; and knowing her own bitter absurdity
Fayne trembled, saying, "Was she here?" He looked into the hollow
    creek-bed behind him; what was Fayne seeing

To make her tremble? "No," he said. Fayne, trembling with anger: "I'll tell
  you what she went east for: she was pregnant.
She stopped in San Francisco to be fixed up." "That's bad," he said; "poor
  child";
He slashed the twigs. Fayne tortured her hands together until the pain in
  the knuckles made her able
To smell the wounds of the willows and say steadily, "What will you do
Now she's come back?" "Oh," he answered. She stood waiting; he slashed
  the twigs and dropped them, saying, "Let her stay there.
I've been thinking, Fayne. I've been able to think, now the heat's broken.
  We have no outlet for our bad feelings.
There was a war but I was too young: they used to have little wars all the
  time and that saved them,
In our time we have to keep it locked up inside and are full of spite: and
  misery: or blindly in a flash:
Oh," he said stilly; "rage
Like a beast and kill the one you love best. Because our blood grows fierce
  in the dark and there's no course for it.
I dream of killing all the mouths on the coast, I dream and dream." She
  said, "Will you go to-morrow?"
"No. When the grass grows up. I'm bound to save what I can for the old
  people, but knives and axes
Are a temptation. Two inches of grass." She stood gazing; he saw the blue
  of her defenceless eyes
Glance at his knife-hand. "Don't be a fool," he said, "I can be quiet forever.
  Have you seen the old man
When he looks at me? I think he knows." "That is impossible," Fayne
  answered. "Why?" "For his mind is like
A hanging rock; he'd go mad when you crossed his eyes. But if he learned it
  after you'd gone away
He could absorb it, like the other dreadful dreams that he eats." He
  answered, "Davis has known for weeks.

I can tell that." "We have friends," she said; "faithful ones." "Did you say
    that poor child
Was . . . what did you say?" Fayne hardened and answered, "Your mother
    saw her."
"I mean . . . no matter," he said.

                              In the night she lay
Unable to sleep; she heard the coyotes howl
And shriek on the white hill, and the dogs reply.
Omens and wraiths waked in her night-weakened nerves,
Reminders of the vague time when wolves were terrible
To one's ancestors; and through all the staring-gaps of the night
She kept thinking or dreaming of Mary Abbey,
Who had come to the house and then lacked courage to stay, and must no
    doubt
Be suffering something.
But Lance to-night slept quietly; he'd enjoyed the good fortune
Of useful and active labor out-doors, in the cold
Beautiful weather. He was so concentrated
On the one spot of anguish
That nothing else in the world was real to him. The Abbey girl
Was never real to him; not even while . . . Fayne heard her own teeth
Chipping each other in the angry darkness . . .
Nor whether she'd been in trouble.

                              The little wolves on the hill
Lifted their tumult into a tower of wailing; Fayne saw clearly in her mind
    the little muzzles
Lifted straight up, against the star-lit gray shoal of snow, and the
    yellow-gray clamor shot up the night
Like a church-spire; it faded and floated away, the crackling stars remained.
    "They smell," Fayne thought,

"The dead calves, and no doubt have found them. They've feasted,
And now they sing. . . . Nothing is real to Lance but his wound;
But when we get away from this luckless place,
Which yet I love,
Then gradually the glory of the outer world
Will become real; when he begins to perceive the rushing and shining
   storm and fragrance of things,
Then he'll be well."

              A drift of thin rain fell in the morning;
The white vanished from the hill. The third day,
Fayne, going to spy for fear Mary might come
Where Lance was working, found old Davis in the driveway
Talking to a tall thin man on a red horse;
A Spanish man whom Fayne had not seen before,
But felt that she'd seen the horse. She eyed them and said,
"What does he want?" Davis, turning his back on the stranger,
Covertly touched his forehead and drooped an eye-lid.
"He works at Abbey's. This is the famous Onorio Vasquez,
The cowboy that sees the visions. He wants to tell you: you can send him
   off if you want to. Have you heard
About Abbey's girl?" "What?" Fayne asked, her eyes narrowed, lips thinned.
   "He says she put herself out.
The young they ain't got consideration for nobody." "What do you mean?"
   "Jumped off a pier I believe.
A telegram came in their mail yesterday. Her dad's gone up to San
   Francisco to view the body.
—So his hired man can roam." Fayne's mouth jerked, her eyes widened. "I
   cannot understand what you mean,
Davie," she said; but gazed at the Spanish-Indian, the hollow brown eyes
With a bluish glaze across them, in the shadow of his hat, in his bony face.
   "Jumped off a pier,"

Davis answered with patient enjoyment; "it seems she kept her address in
  her hand-bag on account of traveling,
So they telegraphed." "Did you say that she died!" He nodded, "Mmhm:
  wa'n't made for a fish, didn't have gills.
The young ain't got consideration for things like that." "Mary!" Fayne said,
  her hand at her throat.
She drew deep breath, and sharply lifting her face toward the silent
  horseman: "What are you waiting for,
Your news is told?" He, in better English than one expected,
In the soft voice of his race: "You are very sorry:
Excuse me please. I only saw her a little and she went away
After I came to work: she was beautiful with patient eyes but I think it is
  often good to die young.
I often wish." "She came to this house," Fayne said, "two days ago: how
  could she . . . in the city? She was here
The day before yesterday." "No, that was the day," he answered, "she died."
  Fayne stared at him
Without speaking; he was half dazzled by the wide blue of her eyes below
  the fire-cloud of hair,
He looked at the brown earth. "What time did she . . .
What time?" Fayne asked. "Don't know." She said slowly,
"I think it is . . . strange." She hardened. "Nothing. Have you come
To tell us any other thing?" "Yes," he said proudly,
"I ride on the hill and see a vision over this house. You have heard of
  Onorio
Vasquez? That is my name." Old Davis made a derisive noise in his throat;
  Fayne, thinking "Visions?
Apparently we too . . ." said quietly, "I never heard of you." He, saddened:
  "It does not matter." But Davis, the grizzled
Thatch of his lip moving to make a smile:
"Now that's too bad: for the man's famous. He's got six brothers
And every one of them knows him, every Vasquez on the coast.

If they can't steal meat nor borrow a string of peppers they listen to brother
   Onorio
Telling his dreams all through a winter night;
They don't need nothing." She answered, "If you have nothing to do here,
Go and help Lance." And to Vasquez: "Tell me what it is
You have to say." "You know a place in the south call' Laurel Spring? No?"
   he said. "Near Point Vicente.
I never been: my brother Vidal has been. He told me a rock and an old
   laurel tree
Is cut by the wind into the shape of the rock, and the spring runs down.
   He made a beautiful place
The way he told; we are much Indian, we love such places."
Fayne answered, "I am busy just now." He: "Excuse me please.
I ride on the hill and every day
Watch the old war in the sky over this house;
I hurt my heart with my eyes. Sometimes a naked man
Fighting an eagle, but a rattlesnake bitten him;
Sometimes a lion fighting a tide of dogs;
But sometimes terrible armies out of the east and west, and the hacking
   swords." Fayne gazed at him
And said, "Is that all?
I have just heard that my best friend has died:
I cannot think of these things." He said "The two armies
Destroyed each other, except one man alone
Walking among the bodies of horses and men
That blocked the sky; then I heard someone say,
'Let him lie down with the others.' Someone say, 'No.
At Laurel Spring he will wash off the blood,
And be cured of his wound.' I cannot live
Until I tell you." "Is it on the way
Into the south?" Fayne said. "Yes: on the trail.
My brother Vidal . . ." "I believe many lies

Are told about us," she said. "Have you heard talk
About this house?" He picked at the hair rope of the halter
On the horn of the saddle. She said, "I can guess
What you have heard. . . . May I call you Onorio?
Because it was kind of you to come down: and thank you
For telling me about your vision." She went nearer to him,
To reach his eyes under the eaves of his hat.
"Do you know Leo Ramirez?" "Him? Yes." "Have you talked to him?
He could tell you about it. He and I alone
Saw my husband's brother climb on the cliff and fall.
Ask him and he will tell you the truth. The others lie:
To amuse idleness I guess. If they had your great power
And saw the spirits of the air, they'd never do so.
But would you think the spirits of the dead?" Her face
Flashed at him, soft and hard at once, like a wet stone.
"Nothing," she said. "This present world is enough
For all our little strength. Good-bye Onorio. If you hear anything
Come down and tell me . . . at Abbey's or anywhere . . .
For nobody comes down to see us any more,
On account of those wicked . . . lies . . ." While she spoke
A sob broke through and she hid her face. He from above
Looked down at her bent head and the wild color
And foam of her hair; he reached and touched her hair
As if it were a holy thing. Fayne, in a moment
Quelling her tears: "I'll remember
About the way south, that fountain. I am very unhappy
For my lost friend." She turned hastily away
And left him, and found Lance.

                              She sobbed, "Mary Abbey
Will never come back. I . . . I liked her well enough

If she had not . . . Oh Lance." He was flaying the leather from a white and
    red calf, kneeling to work.
He rested his red-stained hands on the carcass and looked up with vague
    eyes. Fayne remembered, "At Laurel Spring
He'll wash the blood . . ." "Hm?" he said, "what?" "Mary . . . What am I
    doing," Fayne thought, "I oughtn't to tell him
While his mind is like this"; and clearing her face if she could, making a
    smile, said carefully, "What
Do you want the skin for?" "I've nothing to do," he said, "for the time.
    Rawhide has uses. I ground my knife
After all the willows were cut. Occupation." "A sort of bloody one," Fayne
    said carefully. "Well," he said,
And tugged at the skin with his left hand, making small cuts with the knife
    against the cling of the flesh.
She stood and watched, and furtively wiped her eyes. He looked up again:
    "No fat to scrape off." He dipped
The knife in the shrunken flesh between ribs. "Amazing," he said, "how the
    beasts resemble us, bone for bone,
And guts and heart. What did you say about Mary Abbey?" "No," she
    answered, "nothing. I was too unkind.
I think how lonely she was." "Oh. You mean Mary Abbey. I wish to
    God . . ."
He stopped speaking and tugged the skin, making small cuts
At the tearing-place. Fayne said, "Did you ever hear
Of Laurel Spring, down the coast?" She saw his wide shoulders
Suddenly stiffen, a shadow shot over in the air
And Lance's white-blue eyes rolled after the bird,
A big black one, with bent-up wing-tips, a flesh-color head
That hung and peered. He sighed and pulled at the skin, slicing the fiber.
Fayne said, "A vulture. They're living high now." "Mm," he said, "*they
    know*: they're always stooping over my head.

I thought it was something else." "You've shot them out of the sky," she
    answered, "there are no hawks." "Aren't there!"
He said, and hushed.

                              After a time Fayne left him, and looked back
When she came to the ridge of the hill. She saw the brown breast of earth
    without any grass, and the lean brown buck-eye
Thicket that had no leaves but an agony of stems, and Lance
Furiously stabbing the flayed death with his knife, again and again, and
    heard his fist hammer
On the basket-work of the ribs in the plunges of the hiltless blade. She
    returned; when he saw her he was suddenly still.
She said, "Whom were you thinking of?" He gazed in silence as if he
    thought that he ought to remember her
But could not. "Who was being stabbed . . . in your mind, Lance?"
    "Nobody. We are all dogs. Let me amuse myself."
"Me?" she said steadily. "No." She sighed and said, "I was going to tell you
    . . . I will. Mary Abbey's dead."
She watched his blood-flecked face and his eyes, but they stood still. "Oh,"
    he said coldly. "What did she die of?"
"Unhappiness. She drowned herself." "Too bad." He said no more, and
    Fayne stared and said: "When your mother saw her
That day, she was not real but a pleading spirit; she was dying in the north.
    We never pitied her."
"Is she frightened?" he said. "Who? Your mother? I have not told her."
    "Don't then."

XIII

                    He stood up slowly,
And wiped the knife on the hair side of the skin;
He looked up the darkening wind and said, "It is going to rain."

Fayne said, "Then will you go?" seeing his fixed face
Against the lit cloud, so that the sanguine flecks
And smear under the cheek-bone were not apparent,
Only the ridge of the face, the unrounded chin
Higher than her eyes. He turned in silence and passed
Heavily over the grassless earth, but soon
Fayne had to run to keep up. Near the house
They came to Davis pouring water into the hand-pump
Of the old well to prime it; who said, "The water's
Quit in the pipes; the crick's not dry up yonder,
I guess a rat in the intake . . ." Lance answered hoarsely,
"Fish it out then. Where's the old man?" Fayne said
"What do you want, Lance?" "The old man." Old Davis gaped
At his changed face; Fayne saw the water clamber
Up the sides of the can in the shaking hand
In little tongues that broke and ran over, "Hey, hey,"
Davie stammered, "y' got to consider," but Lance touched him
With only the finger-tips, then the man raised
One arm and pointed northwestward, slant up the hill.
Lance turned and ran; Fayne followed him, but could not now
Keep up, old Davis hobbled panting behind them;
At lengthening intervals the little ridiculous chase
Crossed over the creek-bed under sycamore trees,
Past buck-eye clumps, and slant up the bare hill
Below the broad moving sky.

                         Tall spikes of a tough weed
With leather leaves grew at a place on the hill;
A few staring-flanked cows tongued the gray leaves
But would not crop them, and broke the stalks. Old Fraser stood
Against a fence-post and watched; he saw the herd

A red and white stippling far down the slope, and the serpent-winding
   creek-bed, the salt pool of its end
Behind the sand-bar, and the sandstone fang in the mouth of the valley,
   from which the shore hills over sky and water
Went up each way like the wings of a sombre archangel. Lance came from
   behind
And said, "I have run my course. I cannot go on forever." The old man,
   broken out of his revery,
Looked blindly at the wide chest, red hands and stained face, as if a pillar
   of mist had come up and stood
Threatening above him. "You," he said harshly, "what do you want?"
   "Judgment. I cannot go on alone,"
And in a boy's voice, "Oh judgment. I have done . . .
I need, I need." The old man's brown apelike eyes got him clear at length,
   and became after their manner
A force of thrusting, like a scorched bar of fire-hardened wood. "Go
   home," he said, "drunkard.
If there is no work in the field for your . . . hands . . . what blood is that?"
   "My brother's," Lance said. Fayne came too late,
And sobbed for breath, in her throat a whining, and said, "He was skinning
   a calf down there, he was . . ." Lance passed
Between them and leaned on the fence-wire with his hands together and
   dragged the palms of his hands to the right and left
So that the barbs of the wire clicked on the bones of his hands through the
   torn flesh. "And mine," he said.
Fayne heard the tough noise of tearing, and felt in her own entrails through
   the groin upward an answering anguish.
Lance turned, hissing with pain, and babbled: "For no reason on earth.
I was angry without a cause and struck him with iron and killed him. The
   beast in me
That wants destruction. I mean Michael you know, Michael I mean." Old
   Fraser staggered, saying quietly,

"Has he had drink?" Fayne said "He . . ." she looked up at Lance's
    beautiful head and stained gray face,
But the lower zone of her vision could not avoid his hands, and thick blood
    falling from the shut knuckles:
Where was that readiness of mind, her thoughts were wailing away on the
    wind like killdeer, which flitter singly
Crying all through the white lofts of the moonlight sky, and you never see
    them. "Am I going to tip over
For blood, like Mary?" She stammered: "He . . .
Ah God. I'll tell you. . . ." Lance said, "This is mine. I have come. Keep
    that woman away from me until I speak.
She fooled me into concealment, time and again, Oh cunningly. I have
    fallen through flight after flight of evil
And harmed many." Fayne gathered her mind and said, "This is it. This is
    the thing. He made love
With a girl and she has just died: now he hates me and he hopes
To take all the sins of the world onto his shoulders, to punish himself. It is
    all like a mad saint.
You trained him to it. But I saw Michael . . ." Lance said, "I remember an
    iron bolt for my shipwreck
Stood in my hand": he opened the ripped palm and the red streamed: "I
    struck." "Climb," Fayne said,
"Up the awful white moon on the cliff and fall, I saw him. It is Mary
    Abbey
Has killed herself." Lance said, "How your power's faded. You'll never
Fool me or the world again. I would not die
Until I had told."

            Davis came up, and saw
Lance head and shoulders against the sky like a dead tree
On which no bird will nest; the others at his base

On the brown hill, Fayne saying "Oh weak as water,
How will this help you bear it?" Davis, choked
With haste on the hill: "Ah. Ah. What's he been doing?" Lance held
His two hands toward his father, suppliant, but clenched
To save the blood. "What shall I do?" The old man
Stepped backward without an answer. Fayne said, "Because
The Abbey girl drowned herself, Lance thinks his finger
Helped push her down: but she was sick in her dreams
And might 'a' done it for anyone: the rest's invention
To punish himself. I am the one to hate him
Meddling with that sick child, but I love him
And will not lose." Davis, eyeing certain flakes
And scraps on the red thorns of the wire, sighed "Ah
That was a ghastly thing," and stood swaying,
Yellow and withered. Old Fraser's burnt wandering eyes
Fixed on him, the old man said: "Which is the liar?
Did Lance do it?" Lance opened his palms toward him
As if they would take and hold, saying "Tell the truth.
I will not bear to live in the dark any more."
Davis groaned "Ay. It's true I guess." Fayne: "Ah Ah coward.
Because he held his hands at you." She said to old Fraser:
"People hate you and your enemies made this story
Because you still had a son after Michael died.
This is what they have whispered so long, and Lance has heard it
And uses it to stab himself." Lance said, "It is horrible
To hear the lies from her mouth like bees from a hive
Hot in the sun. I was Michael's death;
And I cannot bear it in silence. Only I pray you all to keep it
Hidden from my mother: you can do that
With a little care, with a little care, she cannot live long.
Make a story to save her." Old Fraser, suddenly

Covering his face: "*Me* . . . has anyone cared a little to save
Lest I live to the bitterness?" He passed among them
With tottering steps, tasting the way with his hands,
And down the hill toward home. Lance stood and muttered,
"What did he say, did he answer me?
He's honest, I bank on that."

                              A short way down
The old man stumbled and nearly falling stood still a moment;
Then turned his course up the hill and seemed to make haste
With short weak steps. Lance watched him and followed soon,
But turned fiercely on old Davie: "Back to work. Off.
That rat in the intake." And to Fayne: "How death
Makes even a rat powerful, they swell like clouds.
Leave me, will you." She answered, "I will never leave you.
But you, Davie, go home." "Hm?" Lance said, "never? You take your time.
Tie up my hands then; I think the seepage dulls me
More than the hurt helps. Here's a handkerchief:
Your dress is old." She tore it, and while she bandaged him
They stood, the old man trotted on. Lance dully wondered:
"Why did I come to him; because he believes in God?
What the hell good is that? Hm? Oh, to put it
Out of its misery." "I know you have been in torture," Fayne said.
"And now you have done unwisely but yet we'll live: not here, but certainly,
    fully
And freely again. You might have spared that old man.
Our joined lives are not weak enough to have gone down
In one bad night. . . . Oh Lance," she prayed suddenly, "have mercy on
    me. While you tear and destroy yourself
It is me that you tear."

He went on, she followed. On the high knoll
ahead
Stood the bleak name-posts of those three burials, one new and two old,
   erect against the sinking gray sky,
And seemed to rise higher as the clouds behind went down. The old man
   was struggling across a gully this side.
Fayne breathlessly said, "Lance, Lance, can you hear me? He is going up to
   Michael's grave, where his wild mind, that you've
Not spared, is to find some kind of fall, some kind of decision. Do you
   remember, dear, that you took me
To Michael's grave a while back? You were so angry.
But that was the break of our bitter frost.
And maybe there, or maybe afterwards at home in bed: sometime you put
   new life in my body.
Do you remember that I begged you for it? I could not bear
That that sick child and not I . . .
Through me you go on, the other threw you away. Remember, whatever
   destroying answer
Is to gore us now,
A spark of your life is safe and warm in my body and will find the future.
   There is some duty in the parcel
With being a father; I think some joys too. But not to destroy yourself,
Not now I think." "Sing to yourself," Lance answered.
"I am sorry if she died sadly, I've worse to think of."

Fayne saw old Fraser, crooked and black against the light cloud,
Totter up the hill-top and drop himself down
By the new name-post, but he stood up again
Before Lance and Fayne came. He screamed, "Keep off,"
And picked up clods of the herbless earth and threw them,
But Lance went up without noticing. "What must I do?"
He prayed, "I cannot live as I am." Old Fraser

Suddenly kneeling covered his face and wept,
And said "What has God done? I had two sons and loved them too much,
And He is jealous. Oh Lance, was there no silence in the streaming world
To cover your mouth with, forever against me?
I am not. Not hangman. Tell your story
Where it belongs. Give yourself up.
Must I take you?" "That's what I thought of at the very first,
But have been deluded awhile," Lance answered quietly,
And turned to go down. Fayne cried, "What good is this? Oh but how
    often,
Father, you have spoken of the godless world: is that what Lance is to go to
    for help and punishment?
When they came to put a serum into your cows, what did you say? You
    would not trust an old cow to them,
Will you trust Lance? If he were as red as Cain . . . when hunters come
    and break down your fences here
Do we run to the law? Must we run to it
For a dearer cause? What justice or what help or what understanding? I told
    him to give his heart
To the wild hawks to eat rather than to men." Lance gripped her elbow
    with the tips of his fingers,
And pointing at the empty air past the old man: "See, he looks pleased wi'
    me,
And happy again." She looked first at Lance, then at the vacant air. "How
    could he help but forgive you,"
She answered, "he knows it was not hatred but madness.
Why must you punish yourself, you loved each other": and to the old man:
    "Is God's hand lamed? Tell Lance
To lean on your God; what can man do for him? I cannot remember," she
    said trembling, "how Cain ended.
There were no prisons I am sure?" Lance said, "He looks well.
No scar at all and his eyes laughing. Ah, Ah, look!

He waved his hand at his grave and laughed. I'll tell you, though,
He's not real. Don't mistake him. It makes me glad,
But it's bright nothing. Now it's gone: see?" The old man, suddenly
Erect and shaking against the gray cloud: "I will have no part in this
    matter.
It is written that sevenfold vengeance on the slayer of Cain. Go. Go. To be
    a fugitive and be a vagabond,
And tramp the earth hard that has opened her mouth for thy brother's
    blood. No wonder the sweet rain could not fall.
I say flee quickly, before the dogs . . . . should I give
My son to be judged by dogs?" Fayne said, "Do you hear him, Lance, he
    has answered you. We must go away south,
As I've been praying." Lance said, "It has all been useless and blind. I am
    back in hell." He sighed and went down
The way Fayne led, old Fraser behind them crying:
"If you had listened in the days before: now it is night,
And who shall hear? but the sharp feet of pursuers: yet look how Christ's
    blood
Flows like a fiery comet through heaven and would rain sweetness
The fields refuse."

                    Fayne said, "I am going to tell your mother
That you've got work as foreman on a farm in the south,
A dairy I'll say, near Paso Robles. You've got to go and earn wages
Because we're to have a baby. But next summer
She'll see us again: we'll come visiting: do you understand?
You must not let her think that you're going for good;
She couldn't bear that perhaps; but cheerfully say good-bye,
You'll save the sorrow, that's your wish, perhaps even
The ticking of her tired heart. Can you do it, Lance?
No," she said sadly when she looked at his face.
"I'll say that you've gone ahead. You had to go suddenly

To get the job." "By God," he said, "I can do my own lying,
And smooth a face of my own, come on and watch me.
It is *my* mother." "Your hands, Lance." He moaned impatiently.
"How will you say they were hurt?" He moaned, "Hobbled, hobbled.
Never an inch. That's the first rule in hell,
Never to step one inch until it is planned.
. . . In the feed-cutter." Fayne said "I daren't. Yes, at the end.
I'll find clean cloth to bandage them. You must wash.
Get Davie to help you ready the horses.
The pack is ready, only we must put food in it."
He answered, "I am sick of life. I have beaten at the last door
And found a fool."

XIV

Beyond Abbey's place
The trail began to wind up to the streaming cloud.
Fayne looked back: Abbey's was hidden, the awful-memoried cliff
Crouched indistinguishable. Lance said fiercely,
"What do you see?" "Nothing." Fayne led the packhorse
To save torture of his hands; Lance rode behind.
He stopped on the rounding of a high fold of the hillside
And turned himself in the saddle, with his finger-tips
On the withers and on the croup. Fayne stopped. "Did you see," Lance
    said,
"The look of the man that watched us by Abbey's fence?"
"What, Lance? I am quite sure you are wrong: there has been no one
Since we left home." "Then I was mistaken.
. . . I see nobody following. If they come after me
I'll kill them; I am not going to be interfered with now.
My trouble's my own affair. I'd cut my heart out

To make him live: that's out of the question. I have beaten like a blind bird
    at every window of the world.
No rational exit. No cure. Nothing. Go on. No," he said, "wait.
You know it's our last chance to see home. There are our hills but the
    valley's hidden. There's Fraser's Point,
Do you see? The small jag: like a beak, ah? And," he said slowly, "the curve
On this side, glimmering along . . . that cliff you know.
Looks like flat shore." "Dear," she said faintly, "it would be better not to
    look back. We're going far. Come."
"Worn flat I suppose by my thoughts, walking around, up and down,
    walking around. Don't talk about it.
I can even pick out the hill where we stood this morning, that posted hill.
    I'm a little run down in health,
Perhaps these haggles in my hands will poison. Go on: I've seen enough."
Around the corner of the hill, where wet earth hushed
The stony hooves, "Did you tell me," Lance said,
"That my mother saw Mary . . . what did you tell me?
When she died?" Fayne felt a tired hope of joy:
He was thinking of someone else than Michael at least.
"Your mother saw her the day she died; probably the hour
And very moment. She thought that she asked for me,
But when I came, the presence had disappeared."
"What about it?" he said, "there's no sense in it." "No.
That's the manner of . . . spirits. She had a clear sweet nature,
Candid and loving." Lance answered, "I am much troubled
About leaving my mother. The skin looked bluish again
Around her nostrils: we ought not to have left her." Fayne heard
An angry repeated crying high up in the air;
She was careful not to look up, but stealthily
Looked back at Lance; and said, "She was happy, dear,
When I told her about the baby; she was full of plans.
And we'll write often." He was glaring up at the sky,

His face menacing and pale. Fayne said, "Lance?"
And when he did not answer, herself looked up and watched a great soaring
    bird,
White-tailed, white-headed, a bald eagle, wide over the mountain and shore
    scribing his arc of flight,
Tormented by a red-tail hawk that sailed above. The hawk dived,
    screaming, and seemed to strike,
The eagle dipped a wing with reluctant dignity
And sailed his course. "Oh, you can't kill them all,"
Fayne said, "from here to Mexico." "I don't want to.
They win, damn them."

                              They climbed at length to the cloudy ridges
Where the high trail went south; they rode through the clouds and in
    windy clearings
Would see enormous declivities tilting from the hooves of the horses down
    wells of vapor to the sudden shore's
Thin white surf on a rock like a grain of sand. Two or three times
Fayne heard Lance stop; she sat in the cloud and waited until he came.
    When the ridge and the trail widened
They rode abreast; then she saw that he'd stripped
The bandage from his right hand, but one thin layer
The wound gaped through. "Oh Lance, it is all exposed: was it too tight?"
    "Too stiff." "I must fix it.
Have you thrown the linen away?" He said with a shamed face, "Let's be
    friends, Fayne. I feel somebody
Behind us; and I can tell you I won't be caught. I have my gun: I can't
    manage the trigger
Wi' that muff on my hand." "You are right," she answered with a flash of
    joyful fear; "but it is certain
That no one's following. Your wrist looks swollen." "No," he said; "but it
    is strange and pleasant to have left the place

Along with you. Your hair is like a fire in the cloud." She answered, "We
    have changed worlds." "Wait for me,"
He said, and turned and went back. Hearing him speak, but not able to see
    him through the blind vapor,
She struggled in a kind of nightmare to turn the packhorse
To go back to him; she dropped the hair rope and struck
Her mount with fists and heels. As it leaped, Lance
Grew out of the fog, towering on his little horse.
"What was it? What did you see?" "Ah, nobody.
I could 'a' sworn."

            He was always listening as they went on,
And looking back, if the steam of the world cleared
Over the draft from a gorge. Fayne suddenly stopped
In the blind coil and drizzle of the cloud. "Are you there, Lance?
Are you all right?" "Hm? Yes," he answered, "I know it.
But I never can see him." Fayne said quietly, "Perhaps he is.
As when your mother saw Mary Abbey. But they're not real,
As you and I are, and the hard mountains and the horses and the wet cloud.
    He is not an enemy: we never
A moment hated him, but always loved and were sorry. But he is only an
    echo of our own troubled
And loving thoughts." Lance laughed like the sudden bark of a dog:
    "Eavesdroppers
Have got to take what they get. But *what's* real, ah? How do you know?" "I
    never thought of it," she answered,
"But I can tell you. What eyes, ears, fingers, can feel; and come again the
    next day
And feel again: that's real. You may see visions but you cannot touch them;
    but if you could touch them too,
Yet they don't last. . . . Did you ever hear of a place called Laurel Spring?"
    "No. Any water would do.

It's growing toward night." "I was thinking about a man named Vasquez,"
    she answered,
"That sees visions."

        The trail had come lower,
They rode in dropping skeins of the cloud, a slight cattle-track
On a steeple-roof slope so sheer and high
That every stone the hooves kicked out rolled down
Into deep water; but had dwindled from sight down the pitch of distance
The first quarter of its fall. The sea-west heaven
Opened an eye, whence the last of the sun
Flamed, like a fire fallen into a well
Flashing before it is drowned, that makes the black disk of water
As bright as blood; and the wild angry light streams from the bottom up
    the stained wall
And washes with color every cold stone: so from the floor of the world a
    fountain and flood of roses
Flew up to the height, those two riders might have seen
Their own blue shadows on the red cloud above them;
Then the eye of the west closed. Color was there
But no radiance, here the gray evening gathered.
Lance's mount suddenly stumbled; Fayne cried out;
And they rode on. Lance said, "Now he's ahead of us;
The horse shied when he passed; I couldn't see him.
It's trembling still." Fayne said, "No wonder. If it had fallen
It would roll from here to the sea; Oh keep your feet
Light in the stirrups. Your bay's getting too old, Lance.
To-morrow it must take the pack; you'll ride the pinto."
"*To-morrow!*" he said. Fayne turned and looked and said nothing, feeling
    intolerable sadness
Grow over her mind like the gray darkness covering the world; for a
    moment it seemed they were not escaping

But only dragging the trap; and the twilight darkened. There was no
    stopping here;
They rode like flies upon the face of a wall;
The tired horses must stick if they could, and go in darkness
Until some flat place found. Fayne was tired too,
And shook in the cold. "Lance, Lance, ride carefully.
If you should fall I'll follow. I will not live
Without you." He laughed "Ha!" like the bark of a dog.
"No danger here, we are going in the perfect owl's eye.
Michael has gone ahead to make ready for us.
You know: a camp." "What?" she said. "*You* know: a camp.
We'll come to it." "Oh Lance, ride carefully." A kind of shoulder on the
    wall
Showed in the dark, and a little noise
That Fayne thought was the sea. Lance called behind her,
"Hello. Are you there?" She said, "Here, Lance." "Uhk-hm.
The other fellow; not you." She thought "I can't bear it,"
And said quietly, "It's water my horse has found.
It must be a little creek; I can hear it falling."
They stopped and drank under the whispering bushes,
And found no place to lie down. There were no stars,
But three ship's lights crept on the cavernous depth
And made a constellation in the under-world;
Lance said "Damn you, go on." Fayne understood
By the useless curse how his mind stared. The horses
Paced on with heads down, and around the fold of the hill
Stopped of themselves. Here in a shallow gully
There seemed to be room to camp, between the sharp slope
And a comb of bushes.

                    Fayne saw a glimmer move in the dark
And sobbed to restrain a cry; it was Lance's hand

From which he had slipped the bandage; the wound and its wet exudate
Shone phosphorescent: the right hand: the hand that had done it. Or can
    pain shine? In a moment Fayne thought more quietly:
"Is it infected, could infection shine in the dark like decaying wood?" He
    was feeling the earth for sticks
To start a fire; she dipped in the pannier and found the matches. In the red
    firelight she examined his hand:
Feverish, a little; but less than his lips and eyes: Oh when would the strain
    end? "Let's make a big fire,
This our first night of freedom, and keep ghosts away." She took the
    short-handled axe from the pannier side
And broke dead wood with it. "We'll make a bright eye up here for the
    night, in the high blackness, for the hollow night,
For the ships to wonder what star. . . . I'll tell you what star,
You streaming ships: the camp-fire of Lance and Fayne is the star; we are
    not beaten, we are going to live.
We have come out of the world and are free, more hawk than human, we've
    given our hearts to the hawks to keep
In the high air." Lance laughed "Ha! Owls you mean. Welcome." He kept
    his hands
From the fire-heat, and would take no food.

XV

                                        The famished horses
Moved in the dark; Lance ground his teeth in sick sleep;
Wind whispered; the ocean moaned; that tinkling water
Fell down the rock. Fayne lay and was cold; she wondered
Whether it was Laurel Spring perhaps; then perfectly knowing
That all the leaves were oak, she was compelled
To creep away in the darkness and crush leaves
To smell their nature. "I was not like this

A year ago," she thought wistfully, "to lie wakeful
And stare at the words of a fool; in the high sweetness
Of mountain night." Her solitary mind
Made itself a strange thought: that Lance would be saved and well,
But she herself would die at the baby's birth,
After some happy months: it seemed to lead hope
Into the line of nature again; for nobody ever
Comes off scot free.

           She slept a little; Lance woke
And felt his hands aching, and thought, "It cannot be true
That I killed. Oh yes, it is. At every waking.
And there is no way to change it." Night was grown pale
In the way to dawn, and many dark cold forms
Of bush and rock stood quietly. But moving creatures
Troubled the stillness, Lance heard the steps of pursuit
Along the trail from the north, more than one rider;
Then his long-frustrate and troublesome life
Flaming like joy for the meeting, shook its bewildered elements
To one sharp edge. He was up, and moved quietly,
Willing to let Fayne sleep, in the sunset cloud
And pillow of her hair. His puffed hot fingers buckled
In a moment without fumbling the holstered belt
That had the gun; he caught the short-handled axe
That magnetlike drew his hand; and the world was suddenly
Most cool and spacious.

           Four lean steers
Led by a barren cow were along the path.
They had come to drink in the dawn twilight, and now
Remembered a grass-plot southward. Where Lance met them
The trail was but a hair of passage stepped in the face

Of a leaning clay cliff; the leader stopped,
Was pushed from behind, and trying in her fear to turn,
Splayed with both fore-feet over the slippery edge,
Felt the axe bite her neck; so leaping out blindly
Slid down the pit. They were horsemen to Lance, his enemies,
Albeit a part of his mind was awake and faintly
Knew what they were; the master part willed them to be
Men pursuing a murderer; they were both cattle and men
At the one moment. For being men, hated; for being cattle,
The hand was more free to strike, the fiery delight
More pure of guilt. The steer came on, not angrily,
Dull and unable to turn, dipping his new-moon horns,
Lance whining with joy and reckless of his own body
With both hands on the axe-helve drove the sharp steel
Into the shoulder; it broke right through the shoulder-blade
And nicked the broad ribs below. At the same moment
The curve and base of a horn found Lance's thigh
And pushed; but he with his weight flung forward
In the fury of the axe-blow went over the head
Onto the shoulder, and a moment clung there, as when an old
    mountain-lion
Has hunted under the spite of fortune for many days, until his bright hide
    is ruffled, and the ribs
Lift up the hair; he comes by a secret way and crouches in the alder-leaves
    an hour before dawn
Over a pool where the deer drink; but not a deer but a cow-elk comes to
    the pool,
And stands in the glimmer and the trembling twilight, and stoops her head:
    the puma watches, his lustful mind
Can even taste the hot flesh through the rough hide, and smell the soft
    heavy fountain of blood; he springs,

And sticks on the shoulder, blunting his teeth against the great bones of the
    neck; but the elk does not fall,
But runs, and beats her death against the low branches, and scrapes him off:
So Lance fell off from the steer's shoulder, and was ground
Between the flank and the cliff, as the numbed fore-leg
Failed and recovered. The weight lifting, he stood
With his back to the steep wall and violently
Pushed the great hairy quarters with all his power
Of both his arms; the hind hooves fell over the edge,
And the fore-legs, one crippled, scraped the stiff clay
In vain for foot-hold, the great hurt bulk went down
Standing, but fell in a moment and slid in the chasm.
The others had turned and fled.

                  Fayne saw her lover
Come swaying and shining against the gray sky
Over the abyss of darkness, and she had seen the steer fall.
Lance held the axe. "Ah, Ah," Fayne cried, "strike then. Strike. Finish it.
    We have not lived pleasantly,
And I have failed." He threatened her, laughing with pleasure. "I have not
    had such pleasure in the days of my life.
Did the dogs think they were hunting rabbit? Surprised them, ah, ah?" She
    said, "Your hands have opened again
And dripping fast." "More?" he said, hearing the horses that stamped and
    snorted beyond. "Oh, good. If they get me,
Remember it's a grand end." He ran and struck
The nearest; it was holding its head ready for the axe, backing and straining
On the taut halter, and went down on its knees; the second stroke
Chopped horribly along the neck, the third ended the pain. Lance crouched
    and looked at the head, and wearily

Rose, and said slackly, "There was no way out, here, either. My own horse
    you see.
I must 'a' been . . . I have been troubled.
Beating my face on every glass gap and porthole . . .
And get a beaten face.
Were those more horses?" Fayne had stood rigid; she said,
"Steers." "Why didn't they shoot? . . . Oh . . . Steers. *That's* it.
Yet I hate blood.
See how it springs from the ground: struck oil at last, ah?
I felt like this, that time. So we've tried a long time
And never found
My exit: I think there's none: the world's closed.
A brave fellow, a tethered horse.
A natural butcher."

                    One of the fallen fore-legs
Paddled its hoof on the earth and Lance said faintly, "I've come to the
    point
I cannot even put him out of his pain."
He dropped the red axe; Fayne saw his own blood spring from his palm
When he let go. "I think," he said, "have I got the gun on me?
Will *you* finish him off?" "He is dead," she answered.
"Listen, Lance." Her throat was twisting and beating upward with hot
    nausea; she swallowed and said,
"Dearest. This is only a stumble on the way. We are going on. You will be
    well after this.
You are dreadful with blood but you are too beautiful
And strong to fail. Look, dear,
How the clear quivering waters and white of dawn fill the whole world; they
    seem to wash the whole mountain

All gently and white, and over the sea, purifying everything. If I were less tired

I could be full of joy." She pressed her hands to her throat and swallowed and said, "Where you and I

Have come to, is a dizzy and lonely place on a height: we have to peel off

Some humanness here or it will be hard to live. If you could think that all human feelings, repentance

And blood-thirst too, are not very important in so vast a world; nor anyone's life;

Nor love either, the unlucky angel

That has led me so far: we'll go on, we'll not fail. All over the mountain

The eagles and little falcons and all the bright cold hawks—you've made friends with them now—are widening

Their wings to wash them in the cool clearness, and over the precipices launching their bodies like ships

On the high waves of dawn. For us too

Dawn brings us wandering; and any ghost or memory that wants to follow us will be sore in the feet

Before the day's end. We're going until the world changes, you and I like the young hawks

Going hunting; we'll take the world by the throat and make him give us

What we desire."

          He stood bent over, smiling sidewise, watching the drip from his hands, and said,

"You do it quite bravely. No doubt you are right, and I must take your guidance without a word

From this time on. What next? I'll go wash. Faugh.

What a hell of red to be stuck in; you're out o' luck,

Loving a butcher." She answered with her hands at her mouth, struggling against her sickness, "I'll come in a moment

And help you to clean your hands and bandage them again." He went back
   by the trail, but she
Vomited with grievous labor a little water and followed him.

                                              Now all the
   world was quite clear
And full of dawn, so that Fayne saw from the trail
The jutting shoulder of the hill, guessed at in darkness,
Was a great rock, lengthened by thick hard foliage
Of mountain laurel, which grew above it, and the wind had carved
Into the very nature and form of the rock
That gave it shelter, but green for gray. She remembered
With a wild lift of the heart, "He'd wash the blood
In Laurel Spring, and be healed of his wounds,"
But Lance had not gone to the stony basin, but stood
Out on the ledge of the rock, and was looking down
The straight vast depth, toward the beauty of the ocean
Like a gray dove's breast under the dawn-light. She could not call to him
Before he leaped and went down. He was falling erect
With his feet under him for a long time,
But toward the bottom he began turning in the air.
One of the roots of the mountain concealed his end
On the shore rocks. Fayne lay down in the trail
And thought that when she was able she would go down to him,
One way or another. " . . . That would be happiest.
But then he'd be extinguished forever, his last young spark
That lies warm in my body, bought too dear
For gulls to eat . . . . and I never could help you at all,
And now has come the wild end.
I could not keep you, but your child in my body
Will change the world."

She climbed slowly down,
Rock to rock, bush to bush. At length she could see him
Lying softly, and there was somebody bending above him,
Who was gone in a moment. It was not so dreadful
As she had feared; she kissed the stained mouth,
And brought smooth stones from the shore until she had covered
Her love against the vultures and salty gulls;
Then climbed up, rock to rock, bush to bush.

IV

Solstice

1933-1935

RETURN

A little too abstract, a little too wise,
It is time for us to kiss the earth again,
It is time to let the leaves rain from the skies,
Let the rich life run to the roots again.
I will go down to the lovely Sur Rivers
And dip my arms in them up to the shoulders.
I will find my accounting where the alder leaf quivers
In the ocean wind over the river boulders.
I will touch things and things and no more thoughts,
That breed like mouthless May-flies darkening the sky,
The insect clouds that blind our passionate hawks
So that they cannot strike, hardly can fly.
Things are the hawk's food and noble is the mountain, Oh noble
Pico Blanco, steep sea-wave of marble.

LOVE THE WILD SWAN

"I hate my verses, every line, every word.
Oh pale and brittle pencils ever to try
One grass-blade's curve, or the throat of one bird
That clings to twig, ruffled against white sky.
Oh cracked and twilight mirrors ever to catch
One color, one glinting flash, of the splendor of things.
Unlucky hunter, Oh bullets of wax,
The lion beauty, the wild-swan wings, the storm of the wings."
— This wild swan of a world is no hunter's game.
Better bullets than yours would miss the white breast,
Better mirrors than yours would crack in the flame.
Does it matter whether you hate your . . . self? At least
Love your eyes that can see, your mind that can
Hear the music, the thunder of the wings. Love the wild swan.

WHERE I?

This woman cannot live more than one year.
Her growing death is hidden in a hopeless place,
Her death is like a child growing in her,
And she knows it, you see it shine in her face.
She looks at her own hands and thinks "In a year
These will be burnt like rags in the crematory.
I shall not feel it. Where I? Where I? Not anywhere."
It is strange, it gives to her face a kind of glory.
Her mind used to be lazy and heavy her face,
Now she talks all in haste, looks young and lean
And eager, her eyes glitter with eagerness,
As if she were newly born and had never seen
The beauty of things, the terror, pain, joy, the song.
— Or is it better to live at ease, dully and long?

THE CRUEL FALCON

Contemplation would make a good life, keep it strict, only
The eyes of a desert skull drinking the sun,
Too intense for flesh, lonely
Exultations of white bone;
Pure action would make a good life, let it be sharp-
Set between the throat and the knife.
A man who knows death by heart
Is the man for that life.
In pleasant peace and security
How suddenly the soul in a man begins to die.
He shall look up above the stalled oxen
Envying the cruel falcon,
And dig under the straw for a stone
To bruise himself on.

DISTANT RAINFALL

Like mourning women veiled to the feet
Tall slender rainstorms walk slowly against gray cloud along the far verge.
The ocean is green where the river empties,
Dull gray between the points of the headlands, purple where the women
    walk.
What do they want? Whom are they mourning?
What hero's dust in the urn between the two hands hidden in the veil?
Titaness after Titaness proudly
Bearing her tender magnificent sorrow at her heart, the lost battle's beauty.

NORTHERN HEATHER

Dark ancestral fields,
Dark wet deserts of heather like a weedy shore
That waves, their voices
And flashing have fled far away from, the sea-floor stillness
Alone is left;
The ebb is established, the tide never returns;
The sun is not ever
Noisy, nor life blowing bugles: in the ebb of the mind
Between two poems,
When imagination is clearly a trap and all words
A noise about nothing,
You, treacherous north-Ireland beauty, beautiful as death,
Whisper in my mind:
"Oh cease, come home. Resume darkness. Nothing
Is lovelier than silence.
Why will you climb up the turrets of another folly?"

LIFE FROM THE LIFELESS

Spirits and illusions have died,
The naked mind lives
In the beauty of inanimate things.

Flowers wither, grass fades, trees wilt,
The forest is burnt;
The rock is not burnt.

The deer starve, the winter birds
Die on their twigs and lie
In the blue dawns in the snow.

Men suffer want and become
Curiously ignoble; as prosperity
Made them curiously vile.

But look how noble the world is,
The lonely-flowing waters, the secret-
Keeping stones, the flowing sky.

PRAISE LIFE

This country least, but every inhabited country
Is clotted with human anguish.
Remember that at your feasts.

And this is no new thing but from time out of mind,
No transient thing, but exactly
Conterminous with human life.

Praise life, it deserves praise, but the praise of life
That forgets the pain is a pebble
Rattled in a dry gourd.

THE TRAP

I am not well civilized, really alien here: trust me not.
I can understand the guns and the air-planes,
The other conveniences leave me cold.

"We must adjust our economics to the new abundance . . ."
Of what? Toys: motors, music-boxes,
Paper, fine clothes, leisure, diversion.

I honestly believe (but really an alien here: trust me not)
Blind war, compared to this kind of life,
Has nobility, famine has dignity.

Be happy, adjust your economics to the new abundance;
One is neither saint nor devil, to wish
The intolerable nobler alternative.

ROCK AND HAWK

Here is a symbol in which
Many high tragic thoughts
Watch their own eyes.

This gray rock, standing tall
On the headland, where the sea-wind
Lets no tree grow,

Earthquake-proved, and signatured
By ages of storms: on its peak
A falcon has perched.

I think, here is your emblem
To hang in the future sky;
Not the cross, not the hive,

But this; bright power, dark peace;
Fierce consciousness joined with final
Disinterestedness;

Life with calm death; the falcon's
Realist eyes and act
Married to the massive

Mysticism of stone,
Which failure cannot cast down
Nor success make proud.

SHINE, REPUBLIC

The quality of these trees, green height; of the sky, shining; of water, a
clear flow; of the rock, hardness
And reticence: each is noble in its quality. The love of freedom has been
the quality of western man.

There is a stubborn torch that flames from Marathon to Concord, its
dangerous beauty binding three ages
Into one time; the waves of barbarism and civilization have eclipsed but
have never quenched it.

For the Greeks the love of beauty, for Rome of ruling; for the present age
the passionate love of discovery;
But in one noble passion we are one; and Washington, Luther, Tacitus,
Eschylus, one kind of man.

And you, America, that passion made you. You were not born to
prosperity, you were born to love freedom.
You did not say "en masse," you said "independence." But we cannot have
all the luxuries and freedom also.

Freedom is poor and laborious; that torch is not safe but hungry, and often
requires blood for its fuel.
You will tame it against it burn too clearly, you will hood it like a kept
hawk, you will perch it on the wrist of Caesar.

But keep the tradition, conserve the forms, the observances, keep the spot
sore. Be great, carve deep your heel-marks.
The states of the next age will no doubt remember you, and edge their love
of freedom with contempt of luxury.

SIGN-POST

Civilized, crying how to be human again: this will tell you how.
Turn outward, love things, not men, turn right away from humanity,
Let that doll lie. Consider if you like how the lilies grow,
Lean on the silent rock until you feel its divinity
Make your veins cold, look at the silent stars, let your eyes
Climb the great ladder out of the pit of yourself and man.
Things are so beautiful, your love will follow your eyes;
Things are the God, you will love God, and not in vain,
For what we love, we grow to it, we share its nature. At length
You will look back along the stars' rays and see that even
The poor doll humanity has a place under heaven.
Its qualities repair their mosaic around you, the chips of strength
And sickness; but now you are free, even to become human,
But born of the rock and the air, not of a woman.

WHAT ARE CITIES FOR?

The earth has covered Sicilian Syracuse, there asphodel grows,
As golden-rod will over New York.
What tragic labors, passions, oppressions, cruelties and courage
Reared the great city. Nothing remains
But stones and a memory haunting the fields of returning asphodel.
You have seen through the trick to the beauty;
If we all saw through it, the trick would hardly entice us and the earth
Be the poorer by many beautiful agonies.

FLIGHT OF SWANS

One who sees giant Orion, the torches of winter midnight,
Enormously walking above the ocean in the west of heaven;
And watches the track of this age of time at its peak of flight
Waver like a spent rocket, wavering toward new discoveries,
Mortal examinations of darkness, soundings of depth;
And watches the long coast mountain vibrate from bronze to green,
Bronze to green, year after year, and all the streams
Dry and flooded, dry and flooded, in the racing seasons;
And knows that exactly this and not another is the world,
The ideal is phantoms for bait, the spirit is a flicker on a grave; —
May serve, with a certain detachment, the fugitive human race,
Or his own people, or his own household; but hardly himself;
And will not wind himself into hopes nor sicken with despairs.
He has found the peace and adored the God; he handles in autumn
The germs of far-future spring.

                         Sad sons of the stormy fall,
No escape, you have to inflict and endure: surely it is time for you
To learn to touch the diamond within to the diamond outside,
Thinning your humanity a little between the invulnerable diamonds,
Knowing that your angry choices and hopes and terrors are in vain,
But life and death not in vain; and the world is like a flight of swans.

AT THE BIRTH OF AN AGE

(The story is derived from the closing chapters of the Volsung Saga, the action of which refers itself to a date fairly correspondent with the end of the Greco-Roman age and the beginning of this one.

The theme of self-contradiction and self-frustration, in Gudrun's nature, intends to express a characteristic quality of this culture-age, which I think should be called the Christian age, for it is conditioned by Christianity, and — except a few centuries' lag — concurrent with it. Its civilization is the greatest, but also the most bewildered and self-contradictory, the least integrated, in some phases the most ignoble, that has ever existed. All these qualities, together with the characteristic restlessness of the age, its energy, its extremes of hope and fear, its passion for discovery, I think are bred from the tension between its two poles, of western blood and superimposed Oriental religion. This is the tension that drew taut the frail arches of Gothic cathedrals, as now it spins the frail cosmogonies of recent science and the brittle utopias of economic theory. This tension is really the soul of the age, which will begin to die when it ceases.

In modern times the direction of the tension has shifted a little; the Christian faith is becoming extinct as an influence, compensatorily the Christian ethic becomes more powerful and conscious, manifesting itself as generalized philanthropy, liberalism, socialism, communism, and so forth. But the tension is relaxed, the age prepares for its long decline. The racial pole is weakened by the physical and especially the spiritual hybridization that civilized life always brings with it; the Christian pole is undergoing constant attrition, steadily losing a little more than it gains.

I believe that we live about the summit of the wave of this age, and hence can see it more objectively, looking down toward the troughs on both sides, than our ancestors could or our more remote descendants will. . . . . Is it necessary to add that I am not speaking as one of the prophets? These are only ideas that came to me while I was writing what follows, when I wondered "Why does Gudrun act this way?" Thence they added themselves to the thought of the poem, and are noted here to explain one tendency of its thought. The others seem clear enough.)

I

When the north and the east crawled with armed tribes toward mindless wars,
Barbarians like a shieldful of knives flung random, clashing together, stabbing, gashing or missing
Through the north darkness, Goth, Hun and Vandal, Saxon and Frank, and down the hopeless frontiers of Rome:
Three men leading three hundred came to the edge of the forest to a murdered farm. Hoegni said laughing,
"Hey for the owner!" And Gunnar: "Ay. He hangs there." For a haltered man
Hung in the oak above the fire-crumbled walls. "This is the place she named to us: the dead man's farm,
A hill over a plain, a hanged man, a choked well, a stream at the hill-foot. Let them drop the gear."
But Hoegni: "I say go on," jutting his chin to the south, the sharp yellow beard,
"We'll meet the sooner. Aah, camp here waiting
While they loot Gaul?" "Wolf-eagerness is a treasure in warriors, caution in kings," answered Gunnar,
Called king for being the head of a little clan between the Saxons and Franks; his eyes were royal
Over the thick brown beard, deep and ice-blue, dark-browed, "If Gudrun comes, and gives bonds and promises,
Yet I shall probably turn you back and lead home. I am not in love with letting my naked face

Into the bear's mouth." His brother Hoegni groaned and laughed but not
    spoke. Then Carling his youngest brother,
A boy still, beardless, brave face, wide eyes, bright hair: "*I* shall not turn.
    Look, brother, how it is clouded
With herds of horses like a summer heaven, clouds beyond clouds, I never
    saw anything nor heard a poem
So beautiful as this plain.
Yonder must be the Horde's encampment: like a hundred cities: and the
    horses, the horses, the many-colored,
At pasture around it like a vast wheel. There, there, and there, are the
    towers of smoke from the burnt towns.
Yonder a band of war-men far off goes galloping on some great raid. Sigurd
    had a horse;
He called him Grayfell." Gunnar said: "Listen, boy. You shall have horses
    to ride if we go down there.
But Sigurd is not to be named. Sigurd is not to be named. Remember we
    are making peace with Gudrun,
Who is our sister, and has grown powerful too." Hoegni laughed, Carling
    said, "I know. It is a pity.
Oh Gunnar it seems to me that my spirit,
After the close fields and forest at home, flies towering up to the sun like a
    noon eagle
Above this plain, the space the distance, the immense green freedom
    glimmering to blue: as if I could almost
See Rome from here." Hoegni said, "Live and we'll see it: if those Goths
    have left anything. Meanwhile we'll feed.
They'll have to hack firewood from the owner's oak, it's all that's left him.
    He will not care." "Oh Hoegni!" Carling
Answered, "Oh Gunnar! When Gudrun comes and we've dearly greeted
    her, then let us
Not seek the Hun's camp nor friendship with him, but suddenly help
    ourselves to keen horses and alone together

Go and see Italy.

Oh Gunnar! *that* would be the high path for heroes, no talk, no alliances. I
know Sigurd would do it

If he were living. Ride southward like a pointed storm of wild swans, like a
flying lance-head, an axe-head,

Carve our own valley through the Huns and Romans." "What a pity,"
Hoegni said,

"To be a fool at sixteen. I warned you Gunnar,

Leave Fool at home." "A flight of horsemen," the youth said gladly, "this
way. Oh look, Oh the lovely fellowship,

Like a long arrow burning with dust for smoke." "You have young eyes. Ay.

That will be Gudrun. How many?" He answered, "They ride by fours, less
or more. Some ten ranks: forty perhaps."

"Hardskin and Swayn," Gunnar said. "Ay," they answered. "Patrol the
wood-path until I call you.

You east and he west.

Not to be embraced from behind as well. She left us in white anger, I will
not trust her yet."

II

Gudrun dismounted and came to her brothers; tall, blonde and pale, clad in
a wine-dark gold-threaded

Wide cloak, snatch of some Byzantine altar, sweetly smiling came Gudrun;
a black-haired slave-woman,

A face like white wax, walked at her side; on the other a swarthy
sword-wearing Hun, who scowled and spoke.

Two more behind him watched hard under slant brows. Then Gudrun:
"*Dear* brothers! Gunnar: will you bid your men

Go ten steps back? Timor here . . . this dark-browed battle-rememberer

Is Timor, he is lofty in my lord's attendance. My three brothers, Timor.
He is full of safeguards, being as he says

Accountable for the priceless treasure of my person.

GUNNAR   *(waving his men back)*   Well, sister. Twenty.

GUDRUN   My

    Timor is very faithful,

And fears . . . never death . . . torture. Can that be Carling? Oh my dear,

    Carling, how beautiful you have grown!

I always loved you.

GUNNAR   We were most happy, Gudrun,

    In your dear message. Jealousies die but love is immortal. We have come at

    great pains through the wet woods

Only to see your face. I say *only,*

Because it is certain that we are wealthy enough

Without Hunnish alliances. Our thought in coming is toward you only; to

    see the loved face, salute

The dear lips, and return.

HOEGNI   And ask you how it feels to be married to a

    toad, for every man told us

Huns look like toads: and by God it's true. Pop eyes, no noses, toad

    color . . .

GUDRUN   Hoegni!

    Be wary of your words a little.

HOEGNI   Not *I.*

GUNNAR   As to the precious gatherings of

    Gaul and Italy: what's gold?

We came for love's sake.

GUDRUN   *(to Hoegni)*   He understands it well enough,

    Though for scorn he won't speak it.

HOEGNI   Tim—Timy you mean? For scorn

    you say? I am telling you . . .

GUDRUN   *Understand me,*

    Hoegni. My lord and his race are not mocked. The emperor of northern

    and middle Europe, all from the Caspian

To the North Sea.

HOEGNI   Not a toad? Nose-holes
  Where a nose ought to be . . .

GUDRUN   And soon I believe to conquer and rule
      the whole nation-written
  War-weary tablet, all the king-scarred earth.

HOEGNI   Not *me*. . . . That is a
      marvelous piece of a victory
  Worn on your shoulders, Gudrun. Well, you look young still.

GUDRUN   And for
      gold: look at these
  Bracelets that bruise my arms; and this neck-chain.

HOEGNI   Oh, he loads you.
      Save up, save up,
  Lest winter come.

GUDRUN   The chain's for King Gunnar. No: I pray you, brother,
      take it with my love. Though I was bitter,
  That was quite long ago. And now I live among foreigners . . .

GUNNAR   How your
      lips writhe! Don't cry, my dear,
  I'll not refuse it nor the love either, but joyfully . . . Let me kiss you
      Gudrun, why do you cover your face?
  I'll kiss the tears.

GUDRUN   It was caught in my hair. There. You've a tress with it.
      Ah, Gunnar,
  Little you know!

GUNNAR   Dear sister. I am far more glad that our love is born
      again
  Than for all these great links of gold.

GUDRUN   And for my . . . brother Hoegni,
      these . . .

HOEGNI   Don't do it

If it hurts you so. You're white as death,

Snow-girl.

GUDRUN   I remember you used to call me that. We were near the
    same age.

HOEGNI   But now those blue eyes of yours

Have wolves in 'em.

GUDRUN   The better to see you with, dear! Well, I've been
    through . . . and seen stark battles: but if

These eyes grow hard: not toward my brothers, Hoegni. By-gones are
    by-gones, that wound's hid . . . healed I mean.

You never knew me to lie I believe? So take the bracelets. I guess them
    nearly the weight in gold

Of Gunnar's chain.

HOEGNI   Thank you, Gudrun. I wish to do you sometime a
    worthy service. Why, men

Have fought to death for less than a hundredth fraction

Of this heavy glitter.

GUDRUN   It's nothing: we swim in it. Carling dear: I've
    something . . . I find myself

Wet-eyed to look at you.

Because you were much younger than me and Hoegni. . . . I'm not false,
    I'll hide no thought, if you'd been tall

At that time, I believe you'd have helped me. Who knows? Hush, dear, let
    me dream. This is very vain talk

About an old woe. The snows of that year are melted and so is my heart,
    and I am Attila's wife.

You look like ghosts, ah? All but Carling. Oh, it's wiped out.

I thought you, Carling, too noble-minded . . . young I should say . . . to
    care about gold, and so have chosen you

A steel jewel, only a sword, yet a rare one. Give it to me, Jukka.   (*She takes it
    from one of the dark warriors behind her.*)   It is said there were great
    enamel-workers
And godlike smiths in Gaul before the back-and-forth grovellings and wash
    of war
Wiped out all.

CARLING   Oh Gudrun! What are these gems? Why, the hawk-head
    hilt
Is like a firebrand.

GUDRUN   The blade, the blade. The hilt's nothing, a gem-crust.
    Nor the scabbard either. See
How cunningly they let the delicate-colored threads of enamel
Into the fierce blank steel.

CARLING   Oh Gudrun.

GUDRUN   Hawk or eagle the pretty
    tracery, who cares? It's pretty, ah?
I begged it of my lord when he was merry.

CARLING   I cannot tell you . . . Oh
    Gudrun.

GUNNAR   By God, what a smith. I think
You've the best, brother.   (*to Hoegni, quietly, nodding toward the oak*)
            I don't like those two, the ravens.

HOEGNI   Mm?
    Those?
Children of nature, attracted by meat like you and me. They take the
    eyes first.

GUNNAR   Caw caw, damn them!
Though they're God's birds. Is she true?

HOEGNI   It's true gold.

CARLING   (*admiring the sword*)   Oh Gudrun, the
    beauty, the power, the balance! And as for the edge:
Look at my thumb: I barely touched it to feel it.

GUDRUN   Oh, Oh, my gift!
                                                        But
CARLING
    I love the slight cut.
    I think it's magical: see, I streak my own blood on the silky blade, that
        makes it mine for my life-days
    Faithfully. Oh sister, I'll do such deeds with it . . . some deed for the poets
        to remember in all the fire-lit music-filled
    Evenings of time. Sigurd's great beautiful bone-biter, the sword
    That he called Anger, never did such a deed . . . Oh! . . . I didn't mean, I
        didn't want . . .
    I adore his memory.
HOEGNI   Fool.
GUDRUN   I know, dear. Hush, Hoegni, let him alone.
    We may love Sigurd and yet
    Not hate his . . . killers. He was too great to need any memory but
        thoughts of love . . . to need any
    Reprisal. His fame's not slain. . . . What'll you call the sword, Carling?
                                                                          I
CARLING
    thought of calling him
    Sea-eagle. Ah Sea-eagle you'll fly in Rome,
    You'll dazzle the south.
ONE OF GUNNAR'S MEN   (shouting from a distance)   Troop of horse, a long
    one.
ANOTHER   From the west by the wood's edge.
HARDSKIN   (farther off)   A thousand horse.
    (Gunnar and Hoegni draw sword, so do the Huns.)
HOEGNI
    Bitten, by God.
GUNNAR   I will never believe, Gudrun, no never . . . Timor: we
        are here
    As friends, probable allies . . .

HOEGNI   Baited and trapped, with a yellow glitter
And milky talk.   (shouting)   Stand to it. Ham-string 'em, that stops 'em.
    (to Timor)   . . . Well?
Toad? Let's begin.

GUDRUN   (cuffing her slave-woman, who was about to scream)
                        You are too excitable, you shame me red, brothers,
    before
These quiet dark lords of the East. Those are the horses to mount you.
    Each man of that troop leads a spare horse.
And thus you trust me! I could not allow you to *walk*, you and your people,
To the Emperor's camp.

GUNNAR   Ay? Why do they come from behind and cut us
    off from the wood?

GUDRUN   They come from the pasture.

GUNNAR
    So it takes five hundred men
    To bring us mounts?

GUDRUN   For your escort also. There's rough work
    On the plain.

GUNNAR   There'd be rougher
    If my poor woodsmen forked themselves over horses.
    No, Gudrun.

GUDRUN   The Huns despise you if you come walking.

GUNNAR
    Are we your prisoners?

GUDRUN   Why, brother!

GUNNAR   No? Then farewell, Gudrun.
    We carry back to the great fir-woods, the lonely tarns
    And little clearings, magnificent memories
    Of wealth and kingly splendor and kindness, and a sister's great
    Forgiving heart.

HOEGNI   And toads. . . . Come home with us,
    We'll make you queen of the North.
CARLING   Oh. I want to ride with her.
GUDRUN
    But since I . . . love you, my brothers: how could I let you go? I'd even
        keep you
    By force. You see: by force . . .
    Of loving persuasion. I could hardly persuade my Huns
    To let such warriors as you . . . not join the Horde.
    Gunnar: he will conquer the whole world, there's not a doubt:
    All the wealth, all rings of gold, all tribes of men, all the meat and drink:
    It rolls to his feet like a ball. . . . Hoegni:
    Do you love battles?
HOEGNI   In moderation, in moderation.
GUDRUN   This would be out
    of scale for you, then.
    Now the great crowning battle of the world is making, to dazzle all war
    Before and after, will be fought on this plain within three days. For Rome
        has bandaged all her sick legions
    Into one sword, ransacked her waning moon for man-power, and bought
        peace with the West-Goths
    (Whose king Theodoric is eight feet tall) to try odds against us. They have
        joined the two armies like axe and helve
    For one huge stroke. Their last one.
HOEGNI   Is Caesar a tall man too?
GUDRUN   Which
    Caesar? None fights. They've an active general,
    What's his name? I can't think. They are hundreds of thousands together,
        and ours are three hundred thousand, with the East-Goths,
    Vandals, Gepidae, Franks . . .
HOEGNI   Boo, said the goose
    Counting duckweed.

GUDRUN   What?

HOEGNI   Tell it to the Swedes, not to us.

GUNNAR   No, no,
        we don't doubt
    Your good faith, sister: yet there's a dreamy quality
    About these numberings of multitude. How could such hordes be fed?

GUDRUN   Ours,
        are experienced.
    They tap their horses' neck-veins and suck the blood, then stop the wound
        and ride on. Or a man's at a pinch,
    Ah, Timor? The Goths and Romans I imagine starve. . . . Oh, this
    Meeting will exceed all measure, enormous, a sword-mountain: you'll stay
        and see it? And, Carling, after we force them—
    For the sun will fall out of heaven before Attila
    Fails of a victory—the whole fragrant south will lie open, unlocked and
        helpless, all the sun, all the honey,
    Rich gardens, rare fruits, all kinds of artist-work. We'll ride on the golden
        strands of blue seas and drink nothing
    But purple wine, hear nothing but little Greek slaves
    That sing like nightingales.

GUNNAR   Will you swear by the holiest,
    By Woden hanged on tree; and by all the Gods of the Huns too, and all
        other Gods,
    That you mean well by us?

GUDRUN   I cannot imagine why you mistrust me.

GUNNAR   Will
        you swear?

GUDRUN   Why should I? You have no choice.
    And you mistrust me vilely. And what are the Gods, who sees them? My
        Huns have traveled the whole world and now
    Laugh at the Gods. Yes, I will swear.

GUNNAR   By Woden hanged on the tree?

GUDRUN   Oh,

    clearly. And by all the Huns' Gods,

And the Roman Christ.

GUNNAR   You will be sick and die

    If you break oath. Well, Hoegni?

HOEGNI   I want to see old Hardskin straddling a

    horse, that's what I want.

CARLING

    They'll go. Oh Gudrun how beautiful you look. One to stand shining

    And sworded for the Decider of Battles in the eagle sky

    In the poem that I've been making.

GUDRUN   Do you make poems, Carling?

CARLING

    Things are so beautiful. Your face, like a white sword

    Lifting against the blue. I'll make better ones.

GUDRUN   Sing me a poem

    While we ride down. I need it. Life narrows on me,

    All its events are vicious, whichever I choose.

III

(In front of the curtains.
    Sentinels post themselves in the midst. Men enter and stand conversing at the extreme right.
    Gudrun and her brothers, her slave Chrysothemis, and the Hun Jukka, come in from the left.)

GUNNAR   . . . The pastures are wide and rich, yet all the grass is bitten to
the roots. What was that river we forded?

GUDRUN   I told you. The Marne. We have to wait here until the
trumpet is blown; no one may enter before Attila.

HOEGNI   I wish him joy of it.

GUNNAR   Marne; the Marne. What a language. Hoegni: did you notice
the herd of thick-flanked brood-mares? I believe there were at least two
thousand. These things are out of our scale of thought.

HOEGNI   Bah!

GUDRUN   This building is an old broken place, curtained for the feast. The broken country-house of some dead Roman. The curtains look richly purple in the evening sun, don't they, Carling? If blood would keep its color, what a dye. And cheap.

CARLING   Does he not come to bring you in? As I remember Sig . . . I remember Sigurd used to?

GUDRUN   No.

GUNNAR   Tell me, sister: what do they do when their mares foal on the march?

GUDRUN   (impatient)   Ah! Another time. Ask Jukka.

GUNNAR   I have asked him a number of questions, he only gabbles. It is essential for a ruler to understand . . .

GUDRUN   Will you . . . I am trying to make a quietness in my mind.

HOEGNI
    Yes. I have watched you, Gudrun. You are mad with pride.
    You think you have married the mountain of the world. Sigurd was not
        enough . . .

GUNNAR   By the honor of God, brother!
    Keep the peace, will you?

HOEGNI   Aahh . . .

GUDRUN   I'll tell you plainly then. I am ill
        in my mind.
    Pride? No: hardly. I was proud while Sigurd lived, before you killed him,
        but as things are
    I've won back a little . . . power . . . not pride. Perhaps you will be able to
        tell me, being wise, Gunnar,
    Why it is that I. For it seems that I still love you, for all your. I am not
        able. We're the one blood,
    And were gay when we were little together,
    Yet, when the warmth wins, I remember that yours was the cold
        contemptible mind that planned his death

Because your woman wound you up to be envious. And the cynical hand
Was my brother Hoegni's. And how cowardly it was done.

HOEGNI *(handling his sword-hilt)* I guessed you. Bring on your niggers.

GUNNAR You are bound by the highest and most dangerous of oaths,
Gudrun.

GUDRUN *(impassively)*   . . . So that
my heart is in heavy trouble between love and hatred,
Two snakes in one coil. Which can neither endure nor destroy each other,
but each is swollen to bursting with venom
From the other's jaws, it spurts on my heart. Ah? Well? . . . Well, that's
how it is wi' me.
I was saying, to do you a harm would never make Sigurd live, nor be any
comfort to myself, so breathe easily. Carling's a poet: do you think killed
men want justice, Carling? Don't answer. I think they're nothing, they're
lucky. I believe nothing.
After you've traveled and seen ten thousand corpses
You'll keep your poems in the way of nature.

GUNNAR Indeed, sister, these questions about death are mysteries to all
of us; it is wisest perhaps . . .

GUDRUN The men with the red straps wound to the knees are
East-Goth nobles. That tall man, who is talking to the Hun, is Alberic the
Frank. Yonder are two lords of the Gepidae. I love to see kings cooling
their heels at my husband's pleasure.

GUNNAR And those to the left, Gudrun?

GUDRUN Huns. Don't question me! I am not patient.

*(A trumpeter appears between the parting curtains. He sounds the trumpet, and announces in
Hunnish and in Gothic:)*

The Lord of Lords has taken his seat. The Masters of War have taken their
seats.

HOEGNI The Toads have squatted.

(The curtains draw aside, and they enter.)

434   SOLSTICE

IV

(It is the atrium of a ruined Roman country-house. The walls at this end are broken down; the wall seen slant on the left is arcaded with freestone columns, the near ones broken, the farther entire. Strange guests have stopped here since the owner fled.

The wall at the back has no colonnade but is adorned with wall-paintings; the panels to left and right indistinguishable, the great central painting scarred but clear. It represents Prometheus bound on Mt. Elboros, the snow-veined rocks, the wound and the vultures.

Planks on trestles range parallel to the walls, making an L-shaped table. On the far limb of the (inverted) L, below the colossal Prometheus, Attila is seated among his generals. He is swarthy, thick, gray-haired, with a flat Mongolian face, and robed in barbarous magnificence. He is already feeding and drinking.

Gudrun will take a place near the angle of the L, keeping Carling on her right, allowing Gunnar to sit on her left, toward Attila and beside Timor. Gudrun's slave stands behind her. Hoegni sits between Carling and Jukka. The other guests, Huns, Ostrogoths and so forth, are coming in and finding places, and servants are busy.)

GUDRUN   *(standing at her place)*   My lord. . . . My lord.

ATTILA   *(at length turning his face toward her)*   All right?

GUDRUN   This is King Gunnar, my brother, of whom I spoke. And my other brothers.

ATTILA   Mm. Welcome.   *(turning back to one of the Huns)*   I say if Arval fails taking Troyes as he slacked at Orleans, that is the end for him.

GUNNAR

Noble Attila:

Our sister having by message invited us

We come with clear good will and kingly confidence

To behold her face, and yours, and the glory of the Horde.

She has flown high, she was nourished in a high nest.

We have strong places northward and power of warriors,

Though fewer . . . horses, I believe . . .

And not as a guest from wandering, but as the king

Your brother-in-law, retinued with quiet swords . . .

ATTILA   *(turning and staring)*   Hm?

GUNNAR

We acknowledge your hospitality.

ATTILA   Well, well.

Sit down. I remember she spoke of you.

HOEGNI   *(aloud)*   Toad of toads.

GUNNAR   But as for

alliance,

And to ride with your host . . .

ATTILA   Jukka! Converse with him for me.

(turning to Blada, who sits next him)   So you'll sweep the banners around their

loose end, curl it up and cut for the center: the plain is wide.

BLADA   Ay, Master. They'll have reserve, I must have more weight than

can be delayed . . .

JUKKA   *(to Gunnar)*   He say he ver' glad you here.

GUNNAR   He seems a laconic man. Between kings, courtesy should be

religion.

HOEGNI   Whisper, Gudrun. How does it feel? They say the Black Forest

women have to do wi' wolves, but a toad, my God! Have you got warts?

GUDRUN

Do not tempt me . . .

JUKKA   *(to Gunnar)*   He make plan 'bout . . . big fighting. Soon he drink

more, then make speech to you maybe.

GUDRUN   . . . toward a black duty. I have what I sought in

marriage, that's power. I am not hardened yet

To its uses. . . . Oh Oh, Carling, I wish I had died with him.

There were blue campions around him beside the spring,

All changed in color, his blood had filled all their cups.

I wish the wet red earth sweet with young flowers

Had swallowed my life with Sigurd's, for I am not strong enough to be his

avenger. (Nothing, Jukka,

Oh nothing: an old feud of our tribe.) Gunnar:

Look down the table, you see the three boys beyond Blada and Bela-Nor?

They are sons of Attila. He has no other male relatives, for he killed his
brothers, it is their custom. These fresh boys will cut each other's throats
when the time comes. You'll leave early to-morrow, I shall arrange it.
Tell Hoegni . . . tell Hoegni his hand . . . was crueller than mine. Carling:
Stay with me?

CARLING   I long to. You are good and beautiful, and here is the main
    door of the world. . . . I am Gunnar's man.

GUDRUN

Because I am lonely and hate myself. And though this camp-life is always
    dangerous, and has no root

In nature, nothing but wars, rapine and wandering; this people would need
    ennobling to pass for wolves:

But Gunnar too and Hoegni are murderers. If you should ever do anything
    glorious they'd knife you for it.

In the back.

GUNNAR   I am glad you are not an oath-breaker. You cannot have him.

GUDRUN   Can
    I not?

GUNNAR   You'll go home with us, Carling.

GUDRUN

You make him unhappy and nothing is decided. Drink, brother.
    (*The trumpeter comes in, on the serving-side of the table, drops on one knee before Attila, and
    whispers to Blada.*)

BLADA   The bishop of Troyes, Master. One of those Roman holy-men.
    He came through the lines at Troyes saying he had gifts for you, so they
    brought him here. What was his name? What?

THE TRUMPETER   Lupus, my lord. Bishop Lupus.

ATTILA   We lack entertainment since the juggler was brained. Ah? Bring
    him in.

HOEGNI   (*to Gudrun*)   Are you done raging? What's a juggler?

GUDRUN   (*to Carling*)   The poor man was doing tricks for them. At first
    they threw pennies, but when they were drunk they threw bones.

(*Bishop Lupus and his followers are led in, and set to stand facing Attila. The bishop is a tired white-bearded old man, noble in distress. His robe is torn and soiled; he carries a crozier.*)

ATTILA
Well, old beard? Talk.

BISHOP LUPUS   I come to plead for a Roman town
Your troops are troubling; that your majesty may deign to spare it for a fit
    ransom. I am the unhappy shepherd
That has to kneel to the wolf.

ATTILA   Your name?

LUPUS   I thought they had told you.
    I am the unhappy bishop of Troyes,
    Which lies like an egg in your hand to spare or crush.
                                                Spy! Do you hide

ATTILA   (*like a play-actor, pretending vast anger*)
    your name?

LUPUS   Lupus, my lord.

ATTILA
    Lupus. I thought so. Unmasked, ah? This seeming-reverend benign old
        man, that styles himself
    A shepherd: what kind of shepherd? A stealthy ravening and murderous
        wolf. I'll pluck that mock-saintly beard,
    See the great fangs grin in the jaws.
                                        It is only my name, my lord, I cannot

LUPUS
    help it. Your majesty
    Delights in mockery.

GUNNAR   (*to Gudrun*)   What is this ah-ah-ah talk, so smooth and soft?
    Do you understand it?

GUDRUN   (*who has drawn a straight bright dagger from a hidden sheath, and plays with it on the
    table before her, regarding it gravely, as if she were reading it like a sad poem, in silence but with moving
    lips.*)   Roman. No.

GUNNAR   I wish I could understand it.   (*seeing the dagger*)   That is a nice
    brave thing, do you cut your meat with it?

GUDRUN   I keep it clean.   *(turning to her slave-woman)*   Chrysothemis: what
   are they saying?

   (Chrysothemis interprets in her ear from time to time, Gudrun does not listen, but reads her knife.)

ATTILA   *(continuing, to the bishop)*

                Well, then: what ransom?

LUPUS   All that we have in the
   city, except a few loaves of mercy
   Against starvation. For if you destroy the hive you'll have the honey, my
      lord, but burnt and damaged.
   Much rather take the honey and let the hive live, and season after season
      returning take
   New tribute.

ATTILA   You have a great store of wealth then.

LUPUS   Oh, little, my lord.
   The Goths have stripped us yearly, and the Alans
   Before them: we can only give all that we have.

ATTILA   All, hm? That's to say, *all*.
   Including your virgins,
   Young wives, all other livestock.

LUPUS   My lord, I have stood humbly before
   you bearing your mockeries.

ATTILA   Very well.
   Open your gates to-morrow in the morning, my officers will examine your
      houses.

LUPUS   You are right, Attila,
   To judge me both fool and coward, that I have prayed mercy
   Where no mercy is.

ATTILA   You guess badly again. I am as full of mercy as the comb is of
   honey. But unfortunately I have not enough wine for all my people, nor
   beer either. We must drink the rivers.

LUPUS   I doubt your meaning, my lord. We will roll out all we have,
   every keg, every jug.

ATTILA   It is not enough. Your misfortune is that your city is on the
    Seine and pollutes the water. My horses bloated when we passed there. And
    now that we move west again: you understand? For sanitation, for
    sanitation. Man, woman, and child: every soul that drops excrement.

LUPUS
    You are great and cruel, and are pleased to mock at us.
    I have borne it humbly. I have been deceiving you, Attila: you are not the
        mighty one here. You range the dark world
    From the Danube to the western sea; no man resists you, no power confines
        you; your numbers like the shore sands,
    And deadlier and crueller than the sea waves; so that the tall white ignorant
        heathen that humble Rome
    Horde upon horde fall helpless before you.
    They fall and scream at your feet; you ride them like horses or you drive
        them like deer. . . . Yet I say to you
    That the King whom I serve sometimes weeps in his sleep, pitying Attila.
                                                                        Ho!
ATTILA
        In the pillow?
    Patternoster, ah? Patternoster. We know you. . . . What is that hook?
                                                                        For
LUPUS
        though you are great on earth,
    And seem to prosper invincibly: alas, there is only one little step for a man
        between life and death,
    Vast pride and bloody destruction.
ATTILA   I step, but not down. What is that
    hook in your hand? Answer.
LUPUS   My crozier.
    The shepherd staff, the sign of my office.
ATTILA   Hm? . . . Dog!
    (*Attila glares at him in silence, with a stagey look of black ferocity. Lupus begins to tremble, but
    returns the stare with courage.*)
GUNNAR   (*to Gudrun*)   What now, what now? What did he say?

GUDRUN   He is trying to scare the old man.

HOEGNI   Eh: Gudrun. What d' y' keep reading your knife for? Has it
    runes in it?

GUDRUN   This? . . . I will tell you.
    It is clean and straight. It speaks to me. It says: "Justice.
    Faithfulness. Honor. Courage. Duty." . . . But I am not able.
    I am not just, but a woman with kindred.
    Not honorable, not faithful to the eagle I loved.
    But passive, corrupt, merciful.

HOEGNI   Do you say so! Sheathe it then.

ATTILA   Hear me, companions. I have wound this babbler in the net of
    his own words, and he has confessed. He is the spy of a great king (that
    soaks pillows), and he is sent to hook me down with that hook: do you see
    that hook? See it jiggle in his hand. Judge.

HUNS AND GOTHS   (some in earnest, others shouting with laughter)   Death. Flaying.
    The blood-eagle. By his beard hang him.

LUPUS
    Lord Christ, I entrust my spirit to thy wounded hands
    Very cheerfully. Speak to thy Father, Lord,
    For the poor people of my city; and that he have mercy
    Even on Attila.

ATTILA   You tremble, however. Wait! . . . Reprieved, old man. I never
    offend a God on the eve of battle. My secretary Gratiano will arrange a fair
    ransom with you before you go home: he is a Christian too. Now . . . . . .
    What's this picture on the wall behind me? Is it your God? Gratiano thinks
    so.

    (The sun is setting, its level rays burn on the painting. Attila's imposing shadow, at the feet of the
    Prometheus, moves as he turns.)

LUPUS   No.   (He wavers, as if to fall.)
    I have tasted death. I wish to remember that it holds no bitterness;
    But lined with eternal life, solemn with joy.
    As for that picture . . . The picture, my lord?

ATTILA   Come, come.

LUPUS   (*wearily, passing his hand over his forehead*)   A fable of the pagans; we read it in school. A wise giant that loved mankind: the God of the pagans crucified . . . I mean hanged him for it.

ATTILA   Bah. I took the ransom because I thought your God was here. Drink, friends, it's a sick world! . . . Why was *yours* hanged?

LUPUS   What did you say, my lord?

ATTILA   Yours too was hanged for loving mankind.

LUPUS   Yes . . . yes. I am terribly tired. He gave himself willingly.

ATTILA   It is all the same thing. Keep your feet, old man! If you fall your city falls.   (*The bishop sways and faints, but is held up from falling by the priests with him.*) Ricimer: why was yours hanged?

RICIMER, A GOTH   Who? Me, master?

ATTILA   When you swear by your hanged God, when you promise me faithfulness. Was he hanged for loving mankind?

RICIMER   Ho! We love our friends, not mankind.

GUNNAR   (*to Gudrun reading her dagger*)   *You* have sworn, Gudrun.

RICIMER   We say that he hanged himself up as a sacrifice to himself. They hang up heroes and white horses to him but that's not enough; he wanted the greatest sacrifice. There is nothing greater than himself, so he hanged himself up. Or another story . . .

GUDRUN   (*suddenly standing*)   I, my lord! I, my lord!

ATTILA   Eh? Go on.

GUDRUN   I was brought up in it. We think there's a great wisdom in pain that's hidden from the happy.
Woden's our God of Gods and no power could hurt him: then he must hurt himself to learn it: how else,
Wisdom's higher half? It's false, though; I learn nothing. I . . . Oh tell me, my lord, do the dead care
What the living . . . what we do?

ATTILA   Take care of your words; we are feasting, not prophesying.

GUDRUN   Or even a punishment

Is death? Quick pain and eternal quietness: that's a reward. Or do they lie
     groaning? Ignorant, my lord?

But I can't act without knowing! Ask your companions, Attila, ask your
     lords of war, Attila!

What: have you sent so many thousands to death, and not know what death
     is?

Never frown at me, my lord, I am not drunk,

Or only on the bitterness. Because my spirit's been rushing back and forth
     all day and dashing itself

On both sides of decision like a fish in a doubled net. I can neither do it
     nor not do it . . .

I'll speak quietly.

ATTILA   *(scowling)*   Do what?

GUDRUN   I will tell you. . . . I pray you to let the old
     man lie down, my lord. We are cruel

In needs and nature, but not to use it for amusement. That old sick
     innocence.

HOEGNI   *(to Carling)*   Boy: slip away before it explodes. Gunnar and I are
     hanging on a widow's hair: never fear, we'll take some with us: but you
     . . . . survive, survive. Do as if you were drunk and must find a place to
     relieve yourself.

CARLING   You mistake her terribly.

ATTILA   Gudrun: we never allow women to drink with us: I honored you
     because you seemed white and still and well-bred. I was wrong to make an
     exception. You do for the bed but not the board.

Keep standing, old man; on your feet! or all's lost.

When it grows dark I'll set a torch-bearer by you

To light you all night: if you fall we sack Troyes. I am not to be moved by
     women. You old white weariness,

Can you not watch with me for one night?

I too am aging, the snows of time in my hair like winter on the black
   pinewoods that wind that Grecian
Fire-mountain Aetna: the frightful heart never cools, and when the fire
   bursts forth where is the snow?
But still I am aging, and carry the enormous burden of the world. Night
   after hollow night my friends here
Eat flesh, drink and wax merry, my armies that cover all the plain feed by
   straw fires and sleep, my companions
Rest in their tents; but for me no slumber, no rest, no relief. My herds of
   horses
Lie down under the stars before dawn, the herders forget to herd them, all
   the mounted sentinels
Nod lower, their heads droop over to the horses' manes. The last drunkard
   sleeps in his song; the inveterate
Gamblers dicing for bits of conquest, by a candle hooded with double
   leather, let fall their yellow
Eyelids, their fingers relax. Even the little flowers of the fields have closed
   their faces and sleep . . .
Who watches then? Who takes care? Who upholds
The troublesome and groaning earth, revolving it like a vast iron ball in the
   torrent of his mind, devising
Its better courses? Which one of your Caesars? Or does a Goth
Uphold the whole earth, night and day, never sleeping? Is it Attila? And yet
   your thankless Romans and brutal
West-Goths conspire. Whom I shall crush with one mangling battle, in
   streams of blood exterminate rebellion
And settle the world; no man again to make war, no man to be masterless,
   but laboring in orderly peace
Under my lordship, the peace and happiness of the whole earth. . . . Hold
   up your face, man.
If you fall, or fail to attend me, remember: every roof burnt, every man
   slain, each woman and child

For a sport to the horse-herders. Eh, old man? . . . Tell me:

I, watching all the nights through, toiling all day, sustaining the earth: am I
    not like your God

That gave himself up to torture to save humanity, because he loved them?
    . . . Take off your hands from him!

Let him stand alone. . . . Eh? Answer.

LUPUS   Have mercy . . .

ATTILA   And who,

except my own people stuffed with incessant spoils,

Has any gratitude? You in Troyes, shutting your gates? The Romans, that
    opened their mouths to swallow the earth

And have choked on it? Or Theodoric the Goth, bought with Rome's gold?
    I shall not leave one alive.

HOEGNI   *(to Carling, as Gudrun rises again)*   Make off, will you. Warn our folk
if you can.

CARLING   She is good. You are dreaming.

GUDRUN

My lord, you are great and men are ungrateful. You have told your
    sufferings, our pity is moved. May I mention mine?

I shall make no disturbance; I have found decision and can speak quietly.
    My prayer is for simple justice,

And you only in the world have power. I have stood in your favor.

ATTILA   Promotion for your brothers, I suppose. Let them earn it in the
near battle, it will taste the sweeter.

GUDRUN   *(sighing sharply)*

Ah. A kind of promotion. Yes, my lord.

My youngest brother is perfectly without guilt in the matter: he must be
    saved. And my brother's men

Are guiltless: I pray you let them go home.

ATTILA   Hm? Stop there.

Twilight's a bad counsellor. Bring in the torches.

HOEGNI   (gently)   Snow-girl:

    Snow-girl: do you expect to outlive us?

    We are not disarmed.

GUNNAR   (out of the corner of his mouth, to Hoegni)

                    Hold your hand, brother. That would finish it.

    Patience and cunning may find the ford yet. . . . Gudrun . . . sister . . .

        (Torch-bearers have come in. Some take their places behind the top of the table, so that the
        Prometheus is illuminated, but Attila a thick overbearing bulk against the light; others, at Attila's
        gesture, stand opposite Gudrun and her brothers, and one by Lupus; much of the company is in
        shadow, but these brightly lighted.)

GUDRUN   Carling

            dear, can't you quiet them

    Until I have finished speaking? . . . You remember, my lord, how curiously
        I inquired (and never an answer!)

    On the subject of death? But now I think that if it is good I will do them
        good, for I love them.

    If evil, evil: for I hate them too. The thing they did to Sigurd I will do to
        them. (And quite ready

    To tempt it myself, Hoegni. Jukka: watch him. He threatens my life.)

    Ah but this is a miserable story, my lord, of spites and jealousies

    In a back-woods corner between the swamp and the trees. In winter we have
        no sun and bleach white, in the spring

    We kill each other; blue campions blossom. You can hardly imagine our
        heavy narrowness, one thought a year

    And there it sticks. You plains-riders pass over and look at new things.

    I knew an eagle in my youth, but the warrior-woman

    Brynhild had enjoyed him when he was a boy.

    She married my brother Gunnar here, still loving Sigurd,

    Who was mine. . . . Wave the torch-man, my lord, nearer my face

    While I speak of him, because I must praise him

    For Brynhild's reasons. Myself being wedded to the Hun-king, the captain
        of the earth,

Would hardly . . . care . . . to remember

How beautiful (to that bison-boned woman I mean) Sigurd appeared. Oh,
he was tall, and rather

Pale than ruddy, with golden blown hair and eyes like the . . .

He was like a lonely eagle in the van of attack and like an iron tower
(Brynhild

Believed) in the closed battle when it bled at his base. Yet gayer at the feast
and gentler than any girl . . .

At least of such as we breed northward . . . She preferred him to Gunnar
and wooed him secretly and he disdained her.

I too was a little scornful, because the woman was built too big and
masculine to go about sighing

With eyes like a sick wood-pigeon's,

Then Brynhild in a cold and patient fury wrought on her husband, my
brother here, saying daily

That Sigurd outbraved him, Sigurd was the better man, Sigurd plotted to
wrench his kingdom away,

And so forth, and we in ignorance. The more noble are the more helpless
in these whispering wars. So they killed Sigurd.

Gunnar my brother and my brother Hoegni knifed him from behind, while
he was kneeling to drink

At a spring in the forest and you observe, my lord,

That my face has not twitched nor my tongue faltered; the wrong I suffered
led me up to the sun

Of your countenance and burns to a benefit.

ATTILA   Gives you that icicle look:
  Hm?

GUDRUN   The whole world is injured
  If wickedness flowers unpunished.

ATTILA   What do you want?

GUDRUN   The woman, my lord, killed herself. Here are the men. I told
the story to amuse you.

ATTILA   You have a crooked mind. If you know what you want I will do
   it.

GUDRUN   That my brother Carling be spared, because he had no part in
   the matter, he was then a young child.

CARLING   Oh . . . *Gudrun?*

GUNNAR   *(standing)*
   My lord she has not shown you the half of this business.
   We are here as your guests and hers . . .

HOEGNI   *(laying his sword on the table in front of Jukka)*   Take it, toad.   *(rising while
   Jukka reaches for it)*   I have its little twin.

   *(He leans across Carling, striking at Gudrun with his dagger; but Carling, his right arm engaged
   under Hoegni's weight, catches the blade of the dagger in his left hand.
   Chrysothemis screams. Jukka and others overpower Hoegni from behind. Gunnar, leaping back
   and half drawing his sword, is overpowered by Timor and others.)*

ATTILA   *(roaring with angry laughter)*   Ho! . . . Are you hurt?

GUDRUN   *(to Carling)*   Your hand, your hand!

CARLING   *(his hand raining blood on the table)*   What have you done, Gudrun!

ATTILA   *(angrily shouting)*   I say are you hurt?

GUDRUN   My . . . No, my lord. My little brother . . . Oh,
   Chrysothemis, tear your linen and tie it up. Here, here.   *(Gudrun gives her the
   dagger that she had been playing with)*   Cut strips. . . . Not hurt, my master. My
   brother took in his hand the blade . . .

ATTILA
   What kind of death will you choose for them? . . . Drink, friends, it's no
   harm.

GUDRUN   I . . .   *(moaning over Carling's hand)*   Does it hurt? Oo, Ooh . . .
   am so awakened
   From such a dream . . . *I* was not the one
   That wanted them, that wanted . . . Oh no, my lord; and I do pray
   you . . .

ATTILA   *By God,* again?

GUDRUN As in a nightmare

We do what day would damn us for, I have been wanting . . . What have I done!

My brothers, my lord: I grew up wi' them. . . . As if I had walked in the narrow cave of a dream and could never turn,

But now have wakened. No, no, no. If he struck at me,

He knew that I was mad and trying for his life. . . . Oh, truly my lord

It was only a play of mine to amuse you. I have sisterly grudges, I sought to frighten them.

ATTILA Ay? We've drunk too much

For you to jest with.

GUDRUN It went too far. Yes, my lord.

ATTILA Well, Timor? Ah?

Whatever she wants,

They have brawled at our table. Take them out, do what my law requires. Leave the pale boy.

HOEGNI *Damn* you, Carling, that saved the toad's slut! But there, boy. Take heart. Live merrily.

JUKKA (*to Hoegni*) Come on, you. Your last walk.

TIMOR (*to Gunnar*) Come.

GUDRUN (*who has been standing death-white and passive, with eyes staring at no mark*) I am in such a hell . . .

GUNNAR

Nobles of the Goths: is this justly done?

You princely East-Goths and Franks . . .

It was sworn to me by Woden hanged on the tree, by the agony of God . . .

(*A hand is clapped on his mouth.*)

ATTILA (*sharply, to Lupus*) *Keep on your feet*, Bishop the beard.

GUDRUN (*to Chrysothemis*) Give me that! (*She takes the dagger and sets the point against her breast*) Attila, my master! If anyone comes near me before I speak

. . . or if they are taken off before you have heard me . . . I know not that you care, but I'll do this.

ATTILA   Fool.

GUDRUN   Perfectly, my lord. That is my name. One who swore
        vengeance by the great self-tortured God
    I then believed in; and consecrated my helpless life to it, went spying
        through the world for power to accomplish it . . .

        (Her eyes rove continually, watching against interference.)

    Tell your servants to stand away from me, my lord,
    Or in goes the needle-point. . . . I heard that the power in the world was
        Attila: I knew not then that I was to love you,
    But solely playing my life to kill Sigurd's murderers . . . That was my
        constant passion, whether we rode
    In Greece or pleasured in Persia, or on the mirage-
    Glimmering Hungarian plain. At length we campaign in Gaul; I laid the
        trap when we crossed the Rhine,
    And sprung it by the Marne, and I cannot bear it.
    I seem contemptible to Sigurd but let him lie. Let them go!
    Oh, Oh, quietly. I promise.
    For two reasons, my lord: for if I have accomplished my brothers'
    destruction it will seem to all men that I love Sigurd dead more than you
    living. And also I shall kill myself.

ATTILA   These are dreams from the wine-cup bottoms. You have drunk
        yourself mad.

GUDRUN   Forgive me, Carling. . . . Hands off!

RICIMER THE GOTH   Master. . . . For undoubtedly they are guests; and
        it seems a crooked occasion. Might it be well to wait judgment until the
        morning?

        (Two messengers have come in. They are dressed for the field, capped with iron and stained with
        riding. The gaudily dressed trumpeter is with them, trying to prevent them.)

THE TRUMPETER   No, no, no, let me announce you.

ONE OF THE MESSENGERS   It is haste.

GUDRUN   Oh noble Ricimer! Pray to my master!

(*The messengers stand beside Bishop Lupus and his companions.*)

ATTILA   What. You're well splashed. You, Haiga?

HAIGA   Master. They have made forced marches and have forded the
Seine at five miles from Troyes. Your servants there are vigilant.

ATTILA   It is time.

HAIGA   I have ordered raids, we shall have a few captives for questioning.
The horses are being brought in.

ATTILA

This is not courage. These wretches rush on their fate like trembling
culprits

That pray the executioner to hurry the stroke. Dear hearts! it's ready. I
shall so hug you, Theodoric,

And you. Roman Aetius . . .   (*to Haiga*)   You will tell me the rest after we
clear the hall. . . . Out, you unneeded. For the forest-men: take them and
tie them up and set a guard: your business, Jukka. Except that pale boy:
treat him with honor. Set a strong watch on their people. . . . For this old
white-muzzled sheep-dog . . . go pray, totter-knees. Give him a tent. Out
with you.   (*As they go out*)   Close the curtains, we take counsel.

V

GUDRUN   (*standing this side of the closing curtains; with Chrysothemis. Carling has left her, going
with his captive brothers*)

Do you see him forget me, that pale bright thankless boy? Yet his blood's
What washed my courage away and made me a merciful . . . piece for
contempt. We are all four

That bright foul blood. That foul bright . . .

Am I insane or what? Look how Attila lights for action like a joy-fire, how
Hoegni flamed up for it . . .   (*tearing at herself*)   Oh! Wet punk. You were
born a Roman.

CHRYSOTHEMIS   I? Yes my lady, a Greek.

GUDRUN   Men stole you from your parents when you were ten years old.

CHRYSOTHEMIS   Yes.

GUDRUN   You were beaten without mercy, raped and starved and sold to a trader, and so began your pilgrimage. If your robbers were laid at your feet, what would you do?

CHRYSOTHEMIS   Alas, my lady. Nothing.

GUDRUN   How, nothing?

CHRYSOTHEMIS   I would let them go. We were taught to forgive evil and love our enemies. But also I have known too much suffering ever to wish to inflict it, even on the wickedest . . .

GUDRUN   (striking her)   Coward. Slave. A slave by nature.

(They go out.)

VI

(*The scene is empty and darkened. Again and again horses are heard galloping from a sudden start: Attila's messengers to the four quarters of the field. The curtains are darkened out of sight, so that the person who comes in seems to walk abstract and alone, on a great plain at night. He sweeps the plain with a broom.*)

THE SWEEPER

I am sweeping the Catalaunian plain,
Seine to Marne, Marne to Seine.
Back and forth, south and north,
For another battle this old earth.
North and south,
Blood of your sons will fill your mouth.
West and east,
Warrior's fall is worm's feast.
East and west,
Who can say but death's best?
Here a track for the Hun stallions,

Here a stand for Goth battalions,
I must make all smooth and plain
Along the Catalaunian plain.
Here the legions, here for a king . . .
To fall . . . here for a king . . .
I forget the rhyme, I cannot help it. At every new era we have to learn a
new set of verses, but damn this tinkle-tankle.
God curse all rhymes
I have to learn because of changing times.
Fair, ah? I made it out of my head. Times change and we have to tag along,
Learn a new song.
I am the wind, I am the rain
Over Chalons and along the plain,
The tortured grass to grow again . . .
Wi' poppies in it too. The stars shine weakly. . . . Stop. What are *you*?
(*Two heroic shadows pass in the air.*)

ONE OF THE SHADOWS
Weep for the living, Brynhild, not for us dead.
We cannot be betrayed nor betray ourselves;
We have power, though unwilled; and only shadows of pain.
(*They fade and pass.*)

THE SWEEPER   (*shivering*)   Booh!
I am the wind, I am the rain,
Sweep the Catalaunian plain,
The dead they flit, the living remain,
Lives like grass and blood like water,
The women will breed and it's no matter.
(*He goes out, sweeping.*)

VII

(Starlight. A few distant red campfires.)

CARLING   *(entering alone)*   What was that? . . . Nothing. But their guards
never sleep. Gunnar and Hoegni are held in a pit under a wall, bound hand
and foot, and I am not allowed to come near them. I will glide through the
army and rouse our people. We'll show these brown men whether the
western axe has an edge, whether Gunnar is a king or a servile Goth.
We are few, but the many sleep. What does it say in the poem? Let only a
   few but resolute arise,
The tyrannies of darkness are not invincible. The soul of man is greater
   than the winter giants. Ah sweet sword,
Sea-eagle how you vibrate against my thigh. We never guessed that so soon
   . . . Ah? We are going to act
A nobler poem than any sung one: if I shake it's with eagerness. That red
   torch Antares
Stands high in the south of summer midnight and we shall hew out of here
   before dawn. Now. Quietly.

(He goes out.)

VIII

*(Interior of a tent, lighted by a small lamp. Darkness outside. Chrysothemis lies asleep in a corner
of the tent.)*

GUDRUN   A slave's dream, but a sweet one,
   That love is her law and God. She has slept on it, with a little breath of a
     Roman prayer, her hand
Under her cheek.
                "Snow-girl," he called me, the pet-name, even in his
   hissing anger. And poor Gunnar's
Pitiful bewildered kingliness. . . . Yes? Was not Sigurd

Pitiable too? No, never, in his life or death. Betrayed, then? Betrayed and
    stabbed, cowardly and shamefully.
I have given my life and lived with a loathed husband, made myself the
    Hun's flattering harlot, to avenge it.
Lived in the filth of the camp, lain in the sweat of his bed, my cold white
    body accepting entrances
It ought to have died not to endure. No wonder my mind's divided in two:
    how can I tell
Which half's the real one? . . . It's because I've lost religion; travel and the
    Christians corrupt me. I see the armies
Like worms crawling, and the Gods a cloudy growth of deception, and laws
    and justice only habitual
Fear and imposed violence.
                                I'll kill the half of my mind and not change
    again: how they'll laugh at me
When safe at home. But Oh, the futile proceedings of life henceforward, its
    purpose gone, disgraced
And beggared, sold for nothing, empty and vile. Empty and vile. Yes, but
Lordly Sigurd is nothing either; Sigurd is ashes. What value in ashes? that
    desire nothing,
And are not desired; no courage in ashes, no joy, no loveliness, no eyes, no
    song. Am I to have killed
My brothers for the sake of a cup of ashes? . . . Yes, but if Sigurd and the
    wish to serve him die out of me,
Then Sigurd is dead indeed. Oh . . .   (staring)   I am in such a hell of
    emptiness . . .
I will not change. I have forgiven them. Wake up, will you.   (shaking
    Chrysothemis by the shoulder)   Up!

CHRYSOTHEMIS   Ah, no, my lady, I am sure
    It can't be lost. I laid it in the cinnamon-wood casket
    With the other silver.

GUDRUN   You must get up.

CHRYSOTHEMIS   Yes, my lady.

GUDRUN   They took my

brothers to that cellar-hole

Under the broken wall by the linden tree, near Blada's encampment. You'll
bear them a message for me.

Tell them I pledge my life for theirs and will see them safe. Tell them that,
as you say so grandly,

"Love has conquered." I have the will and the power. . . . But after that.
After that, woe to me harborless,

Without direction or virtue. Well. Go.   How long I have prayed to die.

CHRYSOTHEMIS

    Oh not at night my lady

Through the fierce camp!

GUDRUN   Poor doll, what do you fear, you were deflowered twenty years
ago. No one will touch you, you are known for mine. And you are old, you
are old.

CHRYSOTHEMIS   *(kneeling)*   I dare not. I cannot, though you kill me.
They are horrible.

GUDRUN   You are not wise, my dear. There is a worse wolf here than in
the hundred thousand. I have tied up his jaws as well as I can, but speak
softly.

    (Chrysothemis goes, but stops outside the tent, in the light from the tent-flap, wringing her hands.)

GUDRUN   Assure them they're safe, and will soon be free. . . .

Little Christ-God of hers: apparently you are the last of the Gods for
Gudrun, who has sloughed them all. You'll never go far in the world: I wish
you could. A few women, a few slaves; but the nature of things is a wolf
and your throat in his.

A woman and the Roman slaves. I was a little more than a woman, and not
a slave, though put to it

To do craftily, when I made the plan and brought it perfect. I have played
the slave's part until it fits;

Ah? Slaved myself to the Hun and sold away my body's and spirit's nobility
for an exact

Payment of nothing, what a bargain.

I have been bewildered. This is the curse of having been childless; the
unspent milk swims in my blood,

Honor, action, fierce faithfulness cannot live in me; but female, female
mercy, female compunctions,

And be inferior forever. You! Chryso!

CHRYSOTHEMIS   *(wringing her hands)*   I stand between death and death.

GUDRUN   She's
gone: I forgot. No matter.

This other message is mine to carry, on my knife's point.

(She goes through the tent-flap and comes on Chrysothemis, who drops to her knees.)

GUDRUN   *(coldly)*

Baby. Get up and follow.   *(Noise of horses galloping)*   Wait while the horsemen
pass: Attila's message-birds

That fly all night when killing's in the air. He is filthy to touch or smell but
a man of war. I

Could respect him. Come. . . . Ah? *That's* something.

(Distant shoutings and anger in the darkness. Clash of arms, as of an enemy raid driven into the
encampment)   Have they pulled
open the iron flower of battle

Untimely under weak stars? Listen it's pretty. Shine, killers.   *(A stampede of*
horses is heard. Men calling from all directions. The central anger seems moving distantly, from left to
right.)   What! Will
your Christians

Fight? It makes Tyr and Woden itch in my blood, all the unbelieved
absurdities like thirsty fleas.

Wonderful, to feel one's mind for a moment unfixed from misery.

Baby, come. I want to see it.   *(drawing Chrysothemis by the wrist)*   Come I say.

(*Gudrun's tent-sentinel has been standing motionless in the darkness. He comes into the light that shines from the tent-door.*)

THE SENTINEL   Regret, my lady, it is not fitting that our lord's lady . . .

GUDRUN   Quiet, you. Guard my gear.   (*shuddering*)   What was *that?*

SENTINEL   . . . wander through the night camp . . . My lady?

GUDRUN

Blind I have been. I never thought of it, mixed in my misery. My own folk's death-shout. My own blood spilling

Made me merry just now. I drove 'em to it: Carling has called their troop and I am the fool.

SENTINEL   My lady . . .

GUDRUN   Follow down then.

(*They go into the darkness.*

Men are heard roundabout, moving in the darkness, calling to each other.)

Which way? — I said the bridle. — Is it you, Katta?

A VOICE   (*farther back*)   Nothing: some riotous captives. They are being dealt with.

A VOICE   Go back to your places and lie down.

A VOICE   Help me turn the horses if you are mounted, Katta. This is no storm.

IX

(*A length of broken wall. There are many dead at the wall-foot. A campfire flickers to one side; toward the center, warriors of the Huns, and men with torches. Others are investigating the fallen. Blada enters.*)

A HUNNISH CAPTAIN   My lord Blada! They brought it on themselves, we only quelled them. . . . The Chief will understand.

BLADA   I hope so. You are responsible. You must understand that this was the clan of the Lady Gudrun.

THE CAPTAIN   They started up suddenly and attacked.

BLADA   Have you questioned your prisoners? And there are live men in the heap, I can hear them gasping.

THE CAPTAIN   I have sent for a Frankish man who can gather their language. Here he comes I think. — Merovech? Come here.

A HUN SOLDIER   (*lifting up Carling from among the slain*)   Here is one living, an arrow right through him. And still grips a broken sword-hilt.

ANOTHER SOLDIER   Oh! That youth was their leader.

BLADA   Question him, Frank. What were they attempting?

MEROVECH   Were you their leader, young man? What is your name?

CARLING   (*painfully*)   A free . . . fool. Whoever you are, you had better be lying here . . . than serve the Hun.

MEROVECH   Come, come, your name.

CARLING   Nobler than yours.

MEROVECH   (*to Blada*)   I cannot do well with him: his mind wanders.

ANOTHER SOLDIER   (*turning over a wounded man*)   Ho! Here is one of the two that were bound in the cellar-pit, whom they set free.

BLADA   (*to Merovech*)   Try that one. Quick: he is going out.

MEROVECH   (*kneeling over the wounded*)   Were you a chief of theirs? Your name, your name.

HOEGNI   (*whispering*)   Go to hell.

MEROVECH   I wish to be your friend. You have death in your belly.

HOEGNI   (*whispering*)   I will tell my name . . . to your master the Hun but not to you.

MEROVECH   (*to Blada*)   He says he will tell you his name, but not to me.

   (*Blada stoops close to hear him. Hoegni strikes a dagger into his skull and shouts:*)
Hoegni! Do you like it?

MEROVECH   God!

THE CAPTAIN   Ah . . . rat . . .   (*driving the lance he carries through Hoegni's body*)

MEROVECH   You need not have troubled: both dead already, both dead.

THE CAPTAIN   Oh noble Blada. He can't have died thus: help me!

MEROVECH   He can't have lived very well, the long blade in his brain and the hilt his horn. My God, a one-horn, a unicorn.

THE CAPTAIN

    Oh tent-pole of battles we shall miss you to-morrow.

    Oh star of the horses. . . . God, God, it's not possible.   *(To a soldier)*

    Report this to Lord Timor . . . no, no, to Jukka first. Oh dreadful

    accident! Straighten his body, draw out the dagger.

A SOLDIER   How the dead forest-man grins in his yellow axe of a beard.

    (Gudrun comes, with her tent-sentinel and Chrysothemis.)

GUDRUN   I know what has happened. Are any living?

THE CAPTAIN   The noble Blada! Murdered, murdered.

MEROVECH   My lady!

GUDRUN   *(quietly)*   I see.

    I have come to ask about my brothers: have you killed them all? I bear the

        blame: but for pity . . .

    I am slack and patient you know, I can bear anything and smile at it, so

        answer me. Two of them were

    Captive, one a brave boy.   *(She sees Hoegni's body.)*   Oh. . . . It was cruel. . . .

        Is anyone alive?

THE CAPTAIN   My lady: a dreadful accident.

    The noble Blada . . .

GUDRUN   I see. Where's Ca . . . King Gunnar? Were any

    taken

    Alive?

MEROVECH

          I have come just now. There's a fair boy still breathing . . . If you

    look carefully

    You'll see twin flecks of light in the heap: he's down but his head's lifted:

        his eyes in the torchlight . . . strange, eh? . . .

    Fixed on us.

CARLING   Gudrun: come here. But do not touch me for the pain . . .

    I never guessed: nobody speaks

    About the pain . . .

GUDRUN   (*moaning above him*)

Oh, Oh.

CARLING   I roused our men, hoping to save my
    brothers. You and I between us
    Ha' done it, we've done it. . . . I dreamed of being a poet and a warrior
    and am a piece of skewered meat. The sword
    You gave me snapped, it was rotten with enamellings. I hate you, but not
    for that. Look along by the wall-foot,
    Gunnar like a dead lion.

GUDRUN   Oh his mouth bleeds and fills: beasts! help
    me will you . . .

CARLING   (*painfully*)   Drown yourself, Gudrun.
    Save pain.

GUDRUN   Die, dear . . . dear . . . dear . . . Quietly; like sleeping. Poor
    wet forehead. Oh, never? Oh how you shudder.
    Again? . . . Again? . . . The last.   (*rising*)   Now
    Blood-men be quiet. One beautiful and innocent, worth all your Horde
    And smoky victories has died.   (*seeming to weep*)   Oh. Oh. . . . I am false to
    the bones: I feel nothing: only weariness
    And sticky fingers.

MEROVECH   My God! the Chief!

    (*A stir among the soldiers. Attila enters, with Jukka and others.*)

ATTILA   Where?   (*seeing Blada's body and Gudrun standing near it*)   To your tent.
    A *man* has died.

GUDRUN   Many have, my lord: from time to time.

ATTILA   (*to the captain*)   Are you of Blada's men?

THE CAPTAIN   Oh, master. Timor's.

ATTILA   (*to a soldier*)   You?

THE SOLDIER   Truly.

ATTILA   Can you follow Bela-Nor as boldly? Your master would have led
    the encircling charge to-morrow, the hook that brings home the battle: he
    was my right hand and is cut off: Bela-Nor must lead it. You and your

comrades will know that he is in Blada's place, it is Blada's soul in him. You will know. Your leader is not dead, his soul has gone into Bela-Nor. Do you hear, Blada's men?

SOLDIERS   Ay! Master. Bela-Nor!

ATTILA   For these rioters: if any lives, kill.   *(to Gudrun)*   And you. . . .
T' your tent!

GUDRUN
Well, I bear the whole blame. I have managed neither justice nor mercy; slacked and let happen.
I am one of those cowards that let go the bridle and brutal chance rule all. I ought to be whipped to death.
But who's to do it, Attila? You?

ATTILA   Are you mad?

GUDRUN   No. Slacking again.
Look, I pray you: this one's
The best corpse of them all, his hand still bandaged from saving my precious life, his brave sword snapped.
A lovely boy but not formed for war. He had beautiful music in his breast, and if he had lived might possibly . . .
Ha' charmed cockroaches.
And take care of my poor little slave-woman: be kind, be kind. I've lived wi' masterly killers,
Taking instruction.   *(Her knife-blade winks in the torchlight.)*

ATTILA   Catch her hand!

GUDRUN   Do this to the Romans
to-morrow.
(She has carefully placed the point on her breast, and drives it in convulsively with both hands, a gesture of straining embrace, and falls. The by-standers cry out. Chrysothemis kneels by her.)

CHRYSOTHEMIS   Oh. Dearest . . .

JUKKA   *(stooping by the body)*   Master.

ATTILA   It is deep?

JUKKA   To the bottom. It is finished.

ATTILA   (*furiously*)   Stand away from her then! . . . . Ah the white beast.
What ailed her in God's name? She wanted her brothers killed . . . wanted,
   not wanted, gets what she wanted,
And drinks a knife. It makes me mad, Jukka: I liked her well.

CHRYSOTHEMIS   Dear
   Savior, care for her spirit.
She was bewildered, and she was kind. She might have come to thee.

ATTILA   All
   these long white women have devils.
Pah — the eve of battle — the same spiteful hour —
My right-hand friend and my favorite too. A cursed omen.

> (*He stands, blackly brooding.*
> *Meanwhile a thin, fractional, insubstantial Gudrun disengages herself from the body of Gudrun*
> *and stands beside it, among the living but neither seen by them nor seeing them, and stares with*
> *wide empty eyes.*)

ATTILA   (*to Gudrun's tent-sentinel*)   Why did you not catch her hand? Whose
   man are you?

THE SOLDIER   (*in terror*)   My lord my lord. I was not near enough.
   Timor's.

ATTILA   He can spare you.   (*to the Captain*)   Have him bound: and bind
   the slave-woman. Bury them living in the Lady Gudrun's grave, not to lack
   attendance.

CHRYSOTHEMIS   (*moaning*)   Oh. Oh.   (*But neither she nor the soldier offers*
resistance.)

ATTILA   For high-born Blada whom I loved: bury him not until after the
   battle. There will be thousands of Goths for him, thousands of Romans.

GUDRUN'S SHADOW   (*with vague monotonous voice, delirious after the shock of death*)
I know not moon nor stars,
How low you lie lynx.
You must 'a' bled in the wars.
Edgyth to whom he drinks,
Or Fredegond:

Me to womb he thinks . . .

JUKKA   *(to Attila)*   May I speak? . . . Shall we convey the bodies to their tents, master?

ATTILA   Do it. Their tents? Yes, do it.

JUKKA   I'll have beds brought to carry them.   *(To a soldier)*   You, Elvi. And you. You. From Blada's quarters: hide stretched on spears, or what you can find, but hastily.

GUDRUN'S SHADOW

Tall sit the wolves around

The lynx in the snow,

Hanging their tongues beyond

Their tails I know.   *(calling)*   Chrysothemis!   *(quietly)*   No, no. I know.

In a row around the red pool

In the snow.   *(calling)*   Sigurd?   *(quietly)*   Snow, no.

ATTILA   *(over Gudrun's body)*   She looks less than tall now.

Lying wantonly with what a craving mouth. I ought to have . . . what she asked for . . . whipped to death . . .

GUDRUN'S SHADOW   *(which has already moved to some distance from the body)*

Oh when my (mother's) maiden lynx

Bled on the spear in the snow.   *(calling)*   Father?   *(quietly)*   No: snow.

Folded close will my petals open

When the tenth moon has broken

Silence?   *(calling)*   Mother?   *(quietly)*   No snow either.

I am in the whom alone.

ATTILA   *(touching with his fingers the face and throat of the body)*

I ought to 'a' killed you when you came riding that first time. You were damned from the first. Farewell,

Harlot-gold hair.

(He withdraws from the body and turns his back on it, while men come in with stretchers.)

GUDRUN'S SHADOW   My darkness begins to crawl. . . . Lynx are you there? . . . I begin to remember a loathsome thing

That the living call life.   *(She stands staring.)*

ATTILA   *(to Jukka)*   D' y' think it'll dawn clear?

JUKKA   Master? Oh, ay, I think so. There were low clouds but the moon outsoars them. I think we shall have perfect weather, my lord.

ATTILA   We had better.   *(fiercely)*   Attend to that business: see it done with dignity.

GUDRUN'S SHADOW   Am I to go down the darkness eternally
    Chewing such a filthy cud of memories between my eye-lids? Poor
        youth-broken Carling whimpering
    In the dead men's hay-cock . . . and Hoegni the poison-white sidelong
        slayer . . . the plain careful fool
    Gunnar making a speech. Or a horrible beater of drums like Attila. Or
        myself, whored and treacherous
    Plotter too weak to see it through.   *(tearing at herself)*   Shadow cannot hurt
        shadow,
    No knife can save me.

        (The bodies are being borne away, accompanied by torch-bearers: and with Gudrun's,
            Chrysothemis and the tent-sentinel are led. Chrysothemis screams suddenly, and Attila turns.)

JUKKA   Stop that. Strike her mouth.

        (She is silenced; the bodies are taken out. Attila shudders and draws his cloak to his face.)

THE CAPTAIN   *(to Jukka, quietly)*   The Chief . . . look.

JUKKA   Oh master. If I dare: what is it . . .

ATTILA   *(making a noise like anger)*   There was none like Gudr . . .   . . . Blada.
    Things are not right here, do you feel that? There is no tension in the air.
    Always before a battle we've lain
    Twitching in the stored womb of thunder, where the hair starts from the
        skin, men ha' snapped at each other
    Like famished hounds, horses neighed all night. Now: by God, listen. Not
        a fierce note in the camp.

GUDRUN'S SHADOW   Ah, but
    My eagle. Conquering Sigurd, for whose dead sake . . . I suppose there is
        no meeting among the dead;

But each in his lonely darkness, after the drunken insanity and sweat of life,
  remembers disgust.

ATTILA

Nothing. Murmurs. Sleepy patience, walking horses, stinking omens.

JUKKA   Master, we have Attila.

ATTILA   Oh, ay, we'll cook them and eat them. Come. . . . Aetius and
  his Romans: Theodoric his West-Goths and so forth: when I gather them
  in my mind, then they are under my hand. I am still Attila.

(Attila and Jukka go out with their following.)

GUDRUN'S SHADOW   *(while soldiers heap the fire, and hold torches to strip the*
better-furnished of the slain)

For my killed eagle. Love, the base instinct, the leader of captivities. How
  low you lie, lynx, I've sweated pleasure

Under Attila's brown bag of a body when I thought of his power. Love?
  . . . I think my deformity

Was only ambition: to fly at the highest.

Therefore I valued Sigurd, famous for killing, but horrible Attila's ten
  thousand to him. Oh, vile

Vile heroic flesh. Brynhild have him

If any residue's to find, I know he hankered. Worthy of each other, both
  heroes, dog-wolf and bitch-wolf.

But I will give myself to the earth-hating wind, in hope to be washed clean
  of the stains and scalding

And that crime of being born and praying to find the black honey of
  annihilation in some comb of darkness

Back of the stars. At worst I shall find no deeper defilements nor no worse
  captivities. Fling me far, wind.

(She goes out.)

X

(The Sweeper, as in VI, passes along the closed curtain, carrying his broom. He seems inhumanly remote and tall, in spite of the bonhomie of his mask.)

THE SWEEPER   A fair field, as they say, well swept.
I've labored all night and seen the yellow lions of day
Creep on the Argonne hills peering for prey.
Plenty: they're breaking each other's bones already. Go it, Goth. Sick 'em,
Hun. Now I can take a few hours off and back to work in the afternoon,
for—
Hun brag and hound bay,
This broom decides the day.
Roman hold and Hun ride,
My broom will decide.
Strictly according to orders: I'll recite them for you. First: to blow
Attila back to the Danube. Second: to clear the air of the chittering
ghosts of the slain. Third: to pat down the battle-corpses and gloss over
everything.
So much anger, so much toil,
All to make soil.
So much fury to feed grass
Comes to pass.
All the horror, all the pain . . .
What's horror and pain? If I could understand the words I might remember
the rhyme.   *(scratching his head)*   . . . Well, but
Some day cabbages and vineyards
Will spring out of the warriors' inwards.

(He goes out, absent-mindedly sweeping.)

XI

(Gudrun, at first alone. The factors of the scene do not become visible until she perceives them.)

GUDRUN

    Thin storm, no farther? The air hisses and fails, dying like a sick snake. Far
        down below me the meteors
    Spin green fire-threads; almost infinitely far down, the glaciers make faint
        light at the mountain-foot.
    The peak is hidden in that cloud of stars. . . . Ah, it's not here,
    What I was hoping. My knife was a fool and could only thread the meat of
        the breast, missed this unlucky
    Point it was sent to find . . . spirit, soul . . . *me* apparently . . . the dead
        body's lost dog,
    Howls in the silence. Will it starve at last? Or is it perhaps . . .
    Immortal? . . . that would be a sick thing.
                          I thought this height had no
    human stain: but someone . . . The star-vapor
    Drifts off and clears him. Another of death's white lies I suppose.
        (*A figure becomes visible, standing on a rock a little higher than Gudrun.*)   Red
    stars in his hands and feet, a blood-comet
    Cut in his side. He is berserk-naked, young and gray-haired, one of the
        shieldless that burn young.
    He seems to be praying to the peak, as our childish priests used to pray to
        oaktrees . . . and other handless Gods . . .
    (*addressing the young man*)
    And get the same answer. What are you praying for, annihilation? If you
        find it, tell me.

THE YOUNG MAN   Did you believe in me once, that you rub salt in my
    wound?

GUDRUN   What? No. If you are the Roman God that my slave described
    to me: how bleak your heaven is.

THE YOUNG MAN

    I was deceived; and love is a fire; I cannot end until my banked longing
        burns itself out.

SINGERS   (*coming up from below, and going about the rock the young man stands on*)

> . . . No angel flew
> To unwind us when the flesh died,
> No light no song for a guide,
> I cannot guess how we knew
> The way up to you.
> I died in childbirth crying to you.
> I died of old age in your faith.
> I of a crueller death.
> All my life was my flying to you.
> We on the spear and sword,
> Fighting for Christian Rome.
> The running pestilence, Lord.
> Open the enchanted home,
> Open the glory of God.
> Savior, I on the road
> Running to your wars.
> Open the joy, break back the stars.
> Because my faith
> Haughtily trampled on death.
> The wings, the victory, the shrill
> Song on the height.
> The violent blossoming, the life the light
> After the mortal strife.
> He will tell us the gate is open: be still.
> The star-gates. Endless life.

THE YOUNG MAN

> When I could not bear it . . . Betrayed children, I was deceived before I
>   deceived you. I have stood here long
> And seen my betrayed come to my feet, and bitterly seen the soul more
>   mortal than flesh, and found

No blood to weep for it. When the earlier dead came crying to me, my first
   martyrs, from jails and gibbets,
Who had endured all evil for my sake, led by my words to misery, my
   promises to death by torture:
And even my own dear friends whom I had touched with my hands . . . when
   I could not bear it,
I lied and said "Life is here. Wait but a little, my Father is preparing your
   places behind the stars."
They waited in hope, soon they were nothing. They faded and wasted and
   were gone away, but not into joy.
I will not lie to you. You are dead; your lives are finished; there is nothing
   more. The spirit is a distant echo
From the other mountain, dying in a moment. Or a blown fading smoke of
   burnt grass. My dream was a fool.
My promises were a love-drunken madness. Alas that you are too weary
   shadows to cry out and curse me
And drown my long self-torment in your seas of bitterness. If Judas for a
   single betrayal hanged himself,
What for me, that betrayed the world?

SINGERS
   Our Savior says
   Wait, for the star-gates move;
   While I gaze on his face,
   While I faint on his love.

THE YOUNG MAN
   You have not understood me. I would not deceive any soul
   Again forever. While I lived I saw my people beaten and deprived, therefore
      I imagined a world
   Beyond life, out of time, righteousness triumphing. I saw it so clearly,
      towers of light, domes of music,
   God's love the wings and the flame. But sometimes I thought my vision was
      only a symbol of much greater realities.

Thus passionately I raised myself up to be mocked and pitied. . . . There
　　is nothing good after death.
As to God: I know not whether he is good. I know not whether he exists. I
　　have stood and gazed at the star-
Swarming cloud. . . . Out of huge delusion
My truth is born. It has nothing to do with the dead; I loved the living and
　　taught them to love each other.
Even now on earth my love makes war upon death and misery, not like a
　　sword, like a young seed,
And not men's souls, but far down the terrible fertile future their children,
　　changed and saved by love,
May build the beauty of an earthly heaven on all our dead anguishes, and
　　living inherit it.

SINGERS

Do you hear? He says that we inherit
Heaven on the instant and the roofs are tiled
With the flame-wings, the high-singing angels, the rose-color wings, the
　　wild
Fire-color wings, the violet-fire feathers and spirit over spirit
For tile over tile overlapping from the ridges downward . . .

OTHER SINGERS　　　(hoarse voices; a heavier tune)

The arrow is like air but the held spear enters.
The pike is a pearl, pushes its path.
Ha! says the sword, ham-strings the horses.
The hooking halberd, the Hun from the saddle-ridge,
Ha! says the halberd . . .
　　　　　　　(more quietly)　　the fear, the pain.
The knees that sag while the blood runs out, the dizzy sickness,
The choking struggle, the horror of death . . .

GUDRUN

Another variety of dreamers. They pass like pulses from a cut artery. I saw
　　Hoegni in the press

Furiously stabbing imaginary princes; and Blada leading his lonely fancy of
   ten thousand horse,
   His private death-dream.
OTHER SINGERS
   Claw, green cat,
   Roll it home to Roua.
   Cat of the standard!
   You have felt the claws, Goth?
   The teeth excel them.
   (quietly)   Oh, the terror.
   The darkness of wounds, the fallen riders, the red agonies.
OTHER SINGERS
   Wolves for your hunger horse-meat and Hun-meat.
   Weary not, West-wolves, worry to the bone.
   Crush bone and kill, Christ is the conqueror.
   (quietly)   The horror, the hidden cowardice,
   The stifling agonies.
GUDRUN   What a wretched fisherman is death,
   That lets his catch lie kicking in the nets of delusion like living men. . . .
   A sudden silence has covered them.
THE YOUNG MAN
   The cloud that veiled it: Oh breaking, breaking. The stars like dust flee
   apart, perhaps for the face of God . . .
   (The height clears. It is the great cliff under the mountain-peak, precipitous, with a shallow
   concavity and over-balance, like the face of a breaking wave. A vast form, in appearance youthful
   and human, beautiful and powerful, is bound against the rock, hanging on heavy chains from the
   wrists, and bleeding from wounds. The figure resembles the Prometheus painted on the wall of the
   ruined house where Attila feasted; but this is more beautiful, and not a painting.)
THE YOUNG MAN
   I hoped. I am finally betrayed and perfectly fooled to the end. It is only my
   dream of my own death
   Hanged on the sky. Blind stars, return.

SINGERS

Oh stars return, Oh mind

Remember the earth or be suddenly blind.

I see the pride of an eagle nailed up alive.

A leopard pierced with spears that transfix the stone.

Enormous helpless shoulder-storms of an eagle nailed there: yet strive,
  wings, strive.

Sharp strength come down, be free. Oh lonely virtue, Oh alone

Beauty and power. Bright snake nailed on the stone.

GUDRUN

Leopard, serpent, eagle? Wounded power? Oh, but lovelier. The hanged
  God that my childish blood loves.

This is my barbarous blood from the north, from the sick swamps and the
  heavy forest, white fogs and frosts,

My vicious blood . . . was it spilt? . . . my vicious love flies to him like
  sighing fire like the tides of the sea.

I know not moon nor stars, how low you lie lynx, I have come to my love, I
  have found him. Here is the dignity

We adored in rocks and waters, the reticent self-contained self-watchful
  passion of the gray rock,

The greatness of high rivers going west; here is the comeliness I knew in
  heroes, the high beauty of the helmets,

The praise of Sigurd; here is the pain in myself and all. Here is reality,

All that my living eyes ever saw was phantom

Shadows of this. Myself too: I was nothing but only a sigh toward him. For
  this I killed my brothers,

For this I let Sigurd be killed: I never knew myself

Before this moment: I know that I consented in Sigurd's death. Layer after
  layer I am stripped

Of falsehood under falsehood and fear under fear, and know my naked
  center in the flame of reality,

The sun of this beauty, the song of burning. To this I am willingly
sacrificed, I have come to my love, I have found him,
I have aped him and shared his life, like the white horses the Swedes hang
up to Odin, from the porch lintels
Of pillared Upsala.

THE YOUNG MAN   He is not a phantom. The stubborn violent rays and
strain of reality
Glow from those tortured limbs, I know them, I have found what I was all
my life seeking, and all my death,
The power my life-delusion called Father, and never feared him and never
. . . hated him . . . before this time.
I wish the waters of Palestine had been white fire, devouring the flesh with
the spirit before I sought to him.
I wish my mother had been slain with a sword before she conceived me, or
shame had killed her when the unknown seed
Knocked at the womb. He is terribly beautiful.
He is like a great flower of fire on a mountain in the night of victory, he is
like a great star that fills all the night,
He is like the music and harmony of all the stars if all their shining were
harp-music. He has no righteousness,
No mercy, no love.

SINGERS
Peace, and the vast
Expanse of the soaring storms, the peace of the eagle
Forever circling
Perfectly forever alone, no prey and no mate,
What peace but pain?
His eyes are put out, he has fountains of blood for eyes,
He endures the anguish.
But if he had eyes there is nothing for him to see
But his own blood falling,
He is all that exists . . .

GUDRUN   It is bitter in me

    That I fled out of life, while I see the beauty of power overcoming pain,
        and the earnest eyes.

    I think that Gunnar was born a fool, and now I know Carling. Hoegni had
        a glimmer of the beauty, he burned

    A little pure, if pure killer. And Brynhild beautifully did evil and died.
        Sigurd . . . a noise

    Flung up by fortune. I have come to my love, if only in a partial vision: his
        greater part

    No poet can know.

THE YOUNG MAN   The fire on the mountain

    Lights all my depth: I see the ridiculous delusion that gave me power and
        the ways that led up to Golgotha,

    The delusion dies, the power survives it. I am not conquered. I set myself
        up against you, Oh merciless

    God not my father. On earth an old wave of time is fallen and a new one
        draws

    From the trough to tower higher: my spirit is the light in it, I am
        remembered, this age is mine.

    I have bought it with the stubborn faith of my people, and my own

    Insane idealism, the wine of my wounds, the tension of intolerable hope.
        Let me remembered

    Be a new spirit of mercy in the new age, a new equality between men, that
        each

    Unblinded behold the beauty of all others: thence happiness and peace . . .
        my longing chokes me . . . When men are happy

    Let them cut the crosses out of the churches, no man remember me.

GUDRUN   He

    is beautiful, this easterner, but like a child

    Desiring what men despise. Happiness? For all the living? How
        shamefacedly we should have to kill it

As if it were evil. Hoegni'd run white and stabbing through the world, and
  well stabbed, Hoegni. I can't think why.
SINGERS   (*Scattered multitude, seen moving among the rocks at the Hanged God's feet, or like*
meteors across the sky at his knees.)
If once I could see the poplars again that ring the cistern
Whiten their leaves
I could bear to have died.
They are fed with sun and the flashing water, from the high thunder-cloud
Falls a stray wind
To the mountain foot.
  —What enemy has maimed you and nothing perfect?
The cloud on the mountain is black, on the plain a small golden dust-cloud
Where men race horses;
The cool round cistern's
Blue eye glitters, the pale poplars for eyelashes; dark
Rises the mountain
To the roaring cloud.
  —Oh wounds of God, storm of stars, broken wings.
At Cartagena on the broken sea-wall spikes of white grass
Used to be shuddering,
You saw blue water
Through the spikes of dry grass, Oh why must I weep for those
Pale rays wavering
In sea-clear wind?
  —I would the enemy that wounded him had killed him.
The Christmas fir-trees crack with burdens of snow, how low
Low you lie lynx,
The torn throat's flow
Is red but the wolves glitter with frost and snow, their spears
Red in a row
Around the red pool.
  —He is beautiful, I fear his wounds are not mortal.

Ah Sigurd that I was mourning Adonis the mistletoe lance,
Hoegni nail hard
The hero's hands
To the eagle wings, make him more than a man, die for me Christ,
Thammuz to death,
Dermot go down.
What boar's tusk opened God's flank, what enemy has bound his wrists,
Nailed him on the eagle
Wave of the mountain?
Die, dear . . . dear . . . quietly like sleeping, Carling, drink sleep.
Oh how you shudder.
Again? Again?
The cool black water Oh red lips of fever, burning harsh lips,
Dear, die. Oh dreadful
Agony of God can you never die?
The mountain storm-cloud of stars, mounded and towering, multitude,
    thunder-cloud
Dark with the blinding arrogance of light: what a black
Lightning from that!
—I say have you learned from the Roman Christ to be meek and hang
    there,
For love of humanity perhaps!
Hanged like a beast's hide?
Bound captive who looks like power, like the eagle of battles, when you
    shudder in the agony huge bands of strength
Move in the arms to the groove of the breast as if you might conquer many
    but an enemy has conquered you. By craft then?
Or like the young Jew
For you loved your enemy perhaps!
—Why do you call him impure, there is no impurity in fire there's pain,
Me Attila and Christ defiled in vain.
The grave slow sunset bleeding at the end of enormous lands,

Always to bleed,
Never go down,
I would I had worn my life with a little valor while I lived
And the earnest beauty of things
Was always reproaching me.
—O sola beatitudo,
Lonely bleeding star
So high, so high
Over the multitudes.
I believe because it is unbelievable, there is my victory.
—What is that rushing in the air,
That moaning on earth?
—Witches and Maries at the foot of the gallows
And over the post and the peak and the superscription in the furiously
    pouring
Rage of the stars
Riding Valkyries.
—Come up Grimalkin my long-nosed sister. —Is it you, Birdalow?
—Naked and greased
Swim in the storm.
—I am old and have flapping breasts. —Bind a birth-strangled man-child's
February bud
In the hollow between them.
—Oh hell's the horror. —*Hush!* —Hell's the horror. —Shut your mouth,
    woman!
Lord Satan wishes
That hell hushes.
—Blood fire in the mouths of eternal furnaces, Oh Oh no hope no help no
    end, save me Christ.
—No. You must be sacrificed.
—I'll hang with my lord then, my beautiful honey-love Satan. —Snow no.
    It's God.

Satan was burnt. —Ai! —But to nothing.
Gone, destroyed, nothing.
—Loathing? —Snow, nothing.
—Oh lucky prince.
—Do you hear the storm of the wind rattling the gibbet
Chains? The lynx has got out of chains, what reins
Will now bridle him? —The wind's idle hymn,
The girls on black horses, the chaste Valkyries.
—And who is to lead us in that day?
The gnomes of the chaste machines? —Not they.
—What, the scared rich?
—Snow: the sword.
—Into the ditch.
—Man has no nobler lord.
—Now the age points to the pit, all our vocation
Is to teach babes to jump. —Oh sterile
Process of Caesars, all the barren Caesars.
—Look at us, God, we are part of you: not defiled? Not imbecile
Children sold for the seventh
Share in a toy, a motor or a music-box, push-button comforts, a paper
    world?
I would the enemy that wounded you had killed you.
I would the shores and the valleys were sheeted with fire and the mountain
    volcano's
Vomit on the plains, when the feet were burnt off we should fall on our
    hands and fire
Lap at the wrists and cut them and the faces fall in it. We are many, and
    strangely
Powerful, knowing metals, knowing drugs, we have counted the stars, we
    have conquered the mastery of wings, and there's not one of us
Worthy to live, pure enough, proud enough. —So they say.
What, they think life is great?

I have had my day:
Life is too little to love, too little to hate.
Temperately share the house
With beetle and louse. —At the head of the beautiful glen
The mountain is crowned with dawn and his purple shoulders . . .
There are fox-gloves here, at the foot
How the sea flames.
  —The sun will come through it in a moment,
Saying "I desire to die, let me die.
I hate myself, I writhe from myself in fountains of fire
And fall back frustrate, something escapes, wastes into light, waste is my
    want,
I pour my body on the eyeless night
And a few planets the rain
Of golden pain,
But knowing that annihilation's no promise, but on and on
New flesh catches old bone . . ."
INHUMAN VOICES
  I am the whale's way. What, for *their* woes? I am the old
Dragon of blue water.
  — Rock and the snow, Aconcagua, Gosainthan, Kinchinjunga, all
High-builded cloud-knives,
Heads of the earth, here is our sky-head.
  — Blazing I gaze, I am the sun, never to find
Purpose nor worth: why do I shine? Why shall I die? I am the sun.
  — Fire-swarm of wheeling vultures of light, torch-multitude
Turning in the emptiness,
Hungry for darkness, I am the galaxy. — Darkness for all-heal?
I am an old
Out-lier, a cloud of
Coal-black vultures, universe of slag, caught in the fork. I have eaten
    darkness. — I am the shoreless

Ocean of stars, crazy to shed

My desire from me. — I am power,

Pushing so close against the fountain that I can hardly

Distinguish myself from him; I am the doer, pale with desire, never to
know

What is my want, where is the end; stone-eyed and lightning-

Handed and sleepless.

VOICES

What horse will you ride, Katta? — The crazy black.

I was broken yesterday.

Life was an idiot dreaming, death's his kept ape.

— Sir, we guessed that last August in Macedonia,

The night we turned atheist by a dry-weed campfire

Drinking bitterness and spitting vinegar. — Hush it thunders.

THE HANGED GOD

Pain and their endless cries. How they cry to me: but they are I: let them
ask themselves.

I am they, and there is nothing beside. I am alone and time passes, time
also is in me, the long

Beat of this unquiet heart, the quick drip of this blood, the whirl and
returning waves of these stars,

The course of this thought.

My particles have companions and happy fulfilments, each star has stars to
answer him and hungry night

To take his shining, and turn it again and make it a star; each beast has
food to find and his mating,

And the hostile and helpful world; each atom has related atoms, and hungry
emptiness around him to take

His little shining cry and cry it back; but I am all, the emptiness and all,
the shining and the night.

All alone, I alone.

If I were quiet and emptied myself of pain, breaking
these bonds,
Healing these wounds: without strain there is nothing. Without pressure,
without conditions, without pain,
Is peace; that's nothing, not-being; the pure night, the perfect freedom, the
black crystal. I have chosen
Being; therefore wounds, bonds, limits and pain; the crowded mind and the
anguished nerves, experience and ecstasy.

Whatever electron or atom or flesh or star or universe cries to me,
Or endures in shut silence: it is my cry, my silence; I am the nerve, I am
the agony,
I am the endurance. I torture myself
To discover myself; trying with a little or extreme experiment each nerve
and fibril, all forms
Of being, of life, of cold substance; all motions and netted complications of
event,
All poisons of desire, love, hatred, joy, partial peace, partial vision.
Discovery is deep and endless,
Each moment of being is new: therefore I still refrain my burning thirst
from the crystal-black
Water of an end.
My lips crack with their longing for it,
My wounds are fires, the white bones glitter in my iron-eaten wrists, blood
slowly falls, blinding white bands
Of fire flow through the strained shoulder-blades, so that I groan for an
enemy to kill: there is none: I alone.
Stars are condensed from cloud and flame as it were immortally, and faint
and have ceased, and their slag finds
After enormous ages the mother cloud; self-regenerating universes all but
eternally

Shine, tire, and die; new stars fling out new planets, strange growths appear
   on them, new-formed little lamps of flickering
Flesh for the same flame.
                                    . . . On earth rise and fall the ages of man,
   going higher for a time; this age will give them
Wings, their old dream, and unexampled extensions of mind; and slowly
   break itself bloodily; one later
Will give them to visit their neighbor planets and colonize the evening star;
   their colonies die there; the waves
Of human dominion dwindle down their long twilight; another nature of
   life will dominate the earth,
Feathered birds, drawing in their turn the planetary
Consciousness up to bright painful points, and accuse me of inflicting what
   I endure. These also pass,
And new things are; and the shining pain. . . .
                                    Every discovery is a
   broken shield, a new knife of consciousness
Whetted for its own hurt; pain rises like a red river: but also the heroic
   beauty of being,
That all experience builds higher, the stones are the warring torches, towers
   on the flood. I have not chosen
To endure eternally; I know not that I shall choose to cease; I have long
   strength and can bear much.

I have also my peace; it is in this mountain. I am this mountain that I am
   hanged on, and I am the flesh
That suffers on it, I am tortured against the summit of my own peace and
   hanged on the face of quietness.
I am also the outer nothing and the wandering infinite night. These are my
   mercy and my goodness, these

My peace. Without the pain, no knowledge of peace, nothing. Without the peace,

No value in the pain. I have long strength.

SINGERS

The long river

Dreams in the sunset fire

Shuddering and shining.

— All the drops of his blood are torches.

I am one with him, I will share his being.

— Alas to me the deep wells of peace are a dearer water.

GUDRUN

I will enter the cloud of stars, I will eat the whole serpent again.

SINGERS

His beauty redeems his acts, it is good for God

Not to be quiet, but for men not to live long.

— Forever if I could: his intelligencer

Spying the wild loveliness.

— But after I have rested as it were a moment

Against the deep wells, and then

I am willing to eat the whole serpent again . . .

The river down the long darkness

Shining writhes like a fire,

The stars return.

GRAY WEATHER

It is true that, older than man and ages to outlast him, the Pacific surf
Still cheerfully pounds the worn granite drum;
But there's no storm; and the birds are still, no song; no kind of excess;
Nothing that shines, nothing is dark;
There is neither joy nor grief nor a person, the sun's tooth sheathed in
    cloud,
And life has no more desires than a stone.
The stormy conditions of time and change are all abrogated, the essential
Violences of survival, pleasure,
Love, wrath and pain, and the curious desire of knowing, all perfectly
    suspended.
In the cloudy light, in the timeless quietness,
One explores deeper than the nerves or heart of nature, the womb or soul,
To the bone, the careless white bone, the excellence.

RED MOUNTAIN

Beyond the Sierras, and sage-brush Nevada ranges, and vast
Vulture-utopias of Utah desert,
That mountain we admired last year on our summer journey, the same
Rose-red pyramid glows over Silverton.
Whoever takes the rock pass from Ouray sees foaming waterfalls
And trees like green flames, like the rocks flaming
Green; and above, up the wild gorge, up the wild sky,
Incredibly blood-color around the snow-spot
The violent peak. We thought it was too theatrical to last;
But if we ship to Cape Horn, or were buying
Camels in Urga, Red Mountain would not turn pale for our absence.
We like dark skies and lead-color heights,
But the excellence of things is really unscrupulous, it will dare anything.

AVE CAESAR

No bitterness: our ancestors did it.
They were only ignorant and hopeful, they wanted freedom but wealth too.
Their children will learn to hope for a Caesar.
Or rather—for we are not aquiline Romans but soft mixed colonists—
Some kindly Sicilian tyrant who'll keep
Poverty and Carthage off until the Romans arrive.
We are easy to manage, a gregarious people,
Full of sentiment, clever at mechanics, and we love our luxuries.

SOLSTICE

Under this rain-wind the sombre magnificence of the coast
Remembers virtues older than Christ; I see the blood-brown wound of the
    river in the black bay,
The shark-tooth waves, the white gulls beaten on the black cloud, the
    streaming black rocks. Ah be strong, storm.
Pride and ferocity are virtues as well as love. I call to mind the dark
    mountains along the south,
The rock-heads in the cloud and the roaring cliffs, the redwoods cracking
    under the weight of wind,
These things wash clean the mind.
We even can face our lives, to bear them or change them. I call to mind
Against our meanness, the bitter crawling meanness of human lives — not to
    damn all — Madrone
Bothwell's white eyes and straight black hair; as once I saw her on Mal Paso
    bridge with one of her children
Above green waves; and once taming that watch-eyed horse they kept in
    Aguilar
Canyon-mouth, crushing his bare shoulders between her great knees. She
    had power; she was free and proud. She was not
Bred of this country, but the coast is the poorer now she is gone.

                                                         This
    was the manner of her going away:
She lived in the old house at Caliente Creek and had sent her cowboy
Vidal Vasquez north to the Big Sur post-office, to fetch the side of bacon
    and the drum of oil
She had ordered left there by the coast stage. He returned with two letters
    also, he was afraid to deliver them

And Mary Oliveras took them in. She held the hand of Madrone's little
　　daughter Gloria in her left hand
And the letters in her right. Vidal stood staring in the door behind her.

　　　　　　　　　　　　　　　　　　　　　　　　　　Madrone
　　Bothwell
Tore open, read, and let fall. Then she stood up against the cloudy sea-light
　　that filled the window,
Dark on the gray, so tall that her head was above the glass, and said in her
　　low voice: "Let him come.
He has the power, let him try." She stooped and lifted the letter like a
　　noxious insect between two finger-tips
And dropped it on the stone hearth, and the other with it unopened.
　　"Vidal have you a match? Light that
Before it crawls." While he leaned, stooping against the smoke-blackened
　　limestone, Madrone took
Her little daughter by the wrist, so fiercely the child was afraid and drew
　　away toward Mary. Madrone said "No
Dear I won't hurt you. The court has given him the children,
It seems I am a woman of a bad reputation, unworthy to be a mother. If I
　　walk very
Softly I may see them once in a month,
And a slight pension until I'm able to get work. Do you hear me? To me.
　　On good conduct."
She moved in the room like a lioness and said: "He will not have the
　　children. But I must warn you we are homeless,
He has sold the place." She passed between them and turned in the door,
　　saying "Ah Vidal. Is the wind south?
It will soon storm." He answered "It's raining ma'am." She turned her oval
　　face, cold and composed

Under the black mane, and went out; but when they saw her passing the
    window her head was bent
And her hands at her mouth.

                              The silvery rain-light
Tarnished and reddened; suddenly night
Poured from the ridge of mountains over the sea and put out the sunset.
    Madrone walked on the round
Wave of the hill above the house-roof as if she were
Herself the rain-wind; the cold fingers trickled through her thick hair and
    flowed on the great arch
Of her breast-bone, down the high plain between the far-parted hills that
    had fed children. When her soaked clothing
Clung like bondage to her throat she tore it.

                              In the house Mary Oliveras
Lighted two lamps and cooked eggs and meat; she fed Ronnie and Gloria
    and ate food with Vidal,
Rolled cigarettes and smoked them; then she and Vidal went out searching
    the night,
Through thin rain calling. A spear of storm glanced up from the Rat Creek
    ridge cracked the deep cloud, the invisible
Moon poured whiteness through a high fleece above, and something on
    earth responded, some spot of white
In a black gully. Mary Oliveras regarded it and saw it move, but when she
    stood on the brink
Thorns caught her, the sharp clay mouth bearded with cactus, and
    bayonet-stands
Of brazen yucca. She stood back crying "Is it you? Oh, Oh," straining her
    senses into the darkness,
The chuckle of waste water: the flag of the wide white breast and arms, the
    oval white face

Moved in the pit and dawned; saying "Ah. I will come up I am satisfied."
  "Oh Christ Oh crown of thorns,"
Mary cried, "did you fall in? Ai Vidal! come." "Stop screaming. I *came* in,"
  she answered. "These gentle things
Are not like shame." She cried "Vidal! Por aqui vente corriendo. Ai, ai,
  querida,
Can you come up?" She climbed up, slipping on the wet slope, stroking the
  earth with her finger-ends,
The black mane loose on her great white shoulders and the torn garments.
  "These friendly burrs my
Comforters: I am afraid I have hurt them a little, I have rolled in them."
  "Oh why do you torture yourself,
Not the first time?" She stood by Mary Oliveras, her head and shoulders
  above her like a white peak
From the forest of the mired and broken clothing, she said "Ah? I?
For my sins. Because I gave my virginity to a dog. Because I never
  cuckolded him
Publicly enough. Because I am human, that's the dirt of the world Mary,
  and hate and lacerate . . .
Can *you* bear it without loathing?" "Woman?" She looked up and said,
  "Oh how you're bleeding! Amiga are we worse
Than men?" "Do you think so?" she answered tenderly. "If I were a man
I'd find a knife for it."

                    The hot spring that names Caliente Creek
Breaks from the headland cliff, and overflowing their improvised rock and
  cement basin cascades
Into the creek-mouth: Madrone used to come down here at dawn to bathe,
  and later Mary or she
Would bathe the children. There are three smoking springs in the
  mountain: here and at Big Creek and at Tassajara,

Within ten miles, besides the great guarded fountains of the south at Paso
    Robles: the earth is still young,
Hot-blooded, hot with desire, shuddering from time to time like a mare in
    heat: the mountains roar then,
There is thunder underground.

                           And the sky is young, in winter: there
    had been such bursts of rain in the night
That no one slept under the voice of the roof, or to dream of shipwreck.
    When the revolution of dawn
Shook the wet air, before there was any light in the world, one of the
    children screamed in a dream
And the rain stinted. Madrone went down from the house between the
    night and the half-light and saw the gray breath
Of the hot spring drift north, against the stone-hard darkness and body of
    the sea. She washed her lacerated
Body and all the heavy cordage of her nightfall hair, and stood up steaming
    in the cold twilight,
Long-legged, deep-ribbed, great-shouldered, nothing soft, not even the
    dark-eyed breasts; but like a great engine
Built for hard passions and violent labor, and in the bone girdle of the hips
    to breed warriors. The channelled mountain
Stood against dawn; the sea was the color and roughness of a shark's flank,
    wounded by the flooding creek
As if they had torn its side with the gaff when they hauled it in. Tilted
    from sea to rock-head the rain-sky's
Enormous carvings of flat blue slate on silver rushed north.

                                 She rode all
    morning
In the mountain in the blowing rain, as if compelled to revisit many known
    places she would have to leave now;

The whirlwind-shaped laurel where the buck bled; the madrone tree where
   she met and enjoyed that tall white Lance
Fraser in his youth but in wrath they parted; the flood-spoiled trout-pool;
   the rock where she had cursed God and lived
Rose suddenly between two rain-veils; the gap where the wild pigeons cross
   in their thousands . . . When the horse fell
On a clay slide, she tethered him there and climbed on foot Marble Peak,
   through the cheval-de-frise
Of limestone fragments like fossil bones, trying to tire herself into
   prudence against the future,
Oh patience, Oh prudence, to be wise once, dreading the cold
Fury that comes in a moment and tears
Before it knows. She remembered how it comes, like the entrance of a devil
   from the red stars
Crying to be black and cease.

                                    She stood on the peak leaning against a
      dark wind
With hail-stones in it and saw through the guardian lashes of her slitted
   eyes the grizzly-bear
Backs of the mountains and the towers of rain; from Black Cone in the
   north to Twin Peak and that orchestral
Tumult of nameless mountains over Devil's Canyon; the black gorges and
   ocean, the distant snow-ridges,
Unnatural white patches on the storm-purple east. She thought "I am sorry
   to leave you beautiful mountains,
God keep you wild," and went down.

                                    She tired the horse, not herself, and
      returned home
Walked in the house like a caged lioness, having no occupation now the
   place was not hers,

Let the fences fall and the hay rot and the herd perish. Mary Oliveras came timidly

Saying "Nelson." Madrone said "What?" She answered "I shut the door in his face. It's a fine storm." Madrone

Went out and saw him settling dejectedly in the wet saddle in the solid rain.

"Well?" she said. He answered, "Oh Oh. Mrs. Bothwell, I came to tell you I'm sorry . . ." "That's not my name,"

She answered, "I have washed since." "I couldn't help it," he said, "they subpoenaed me." "So you confessed

All?" she said smiling. "You poor scoundrel. But cheer up, man, they'd plenty of evidence without you. You weren't

My only sin." "No ma'am I lied until I got scared. They'd Mrs. Temple and that blab Will Howard,

And Rambler the detective that sat on the hill wi' field-glasses. 'N' the gopher-face

Lawyer chopping at me got me confused." His blond face twitched with remorse, his horse hunched its back

And shuddered in the stinging sleet. Madrone said "Oh well. Come in and drip. It's dog's weather, ah?" "Oh," he said

Gratefully, "I thought you'd curse me." "No. We're *all* lice." She called Mary Oliveras to make a fire for him,

And left him by it.

A car was heard in the farm-drive,

And men came to the door. Mary Oliveras was screaming through the locked door, Madrone came down

And said, "Is it the dog? Go up and be with the children: *I* will speak to him," but said to Nelson

And Vasquez: "Stay." She opened the door and saw four whitish faces against the dark purple ocean.

Bothwell's was one; he was tallest, his chest and belly bulged his big
  overcoat; but lean-faced, strong blue eyes
And a stiff mouth. "Is it you, Andrew? What, have you brought an army?"
  He regarded her with calculating
Eyes pinched against the wind-squall and said, "You had my letter?" "I am
  hoping for better terms; not down
Level with those yet. What's the army wi' banners? Witnesses?
Bodyguard?" "Mr. Stevens," he said: a man with a coarse face and overshot
  jaw: Madrone
Turned sharply in the door and said, "Nelson:
Gopher-face is it?" But Nelson hesitated by the fire, Bothwell said, "My
  attorney. And Mr. Rambler . . ."
"Oh," she said, "the man wi' field-glasses." "My friend
Mr. Black," Bothwell said heavily, "who's bought the place." "Ah," she
  answered, blazing on the man
With steady eyes, so that he stepped a little backward instinctively,
  "comical to be kept waiting
On your own door-step
That you have bought.
I think you are not a cattle-man?" "We plan to develop the place as a
  resort, Mrs. Bothwell.
I've had the spring-water analyzed: we hope to build a hotel on the
  sea-cliff." She blazed with her white eyes
Between the black lashes and said, "A stew-pot for nature-
Lovers and sick drunkards." She stepped back from the door and the men
  entered.

        Nelson and Vasquez
Withdrew themselves to a far corner. Madrone said, "Are there chairs? The
  place is a little out of gear,
I am rather sitting among the ashes you know.

And there seems to be such an army of you." "No, we go back at once,"
    Bothwell answered,
"Not to keep the children on the road too late. The children." He looked
    sharply at her,
But she looked down and was trembling. She stood and trembled, and
    breathed and said, "I have not been a bad mother.
No doubt you have the law in your pocket and Mr. . . . your lawyer here
    whose name I can't think of . . .
Loaded to instruct me that I am helpless. Because loathing came over me, I
    let go everything, ate lies
And was tricked easily. Yet
You'll have to show better cause than a court order. What do you plan to
    do for them?" "Certainly," he said.
"They'll live at home with me. They'll have pleasures and advantages you
    cannot possibly: radio, motion-pictures, books,
The school, the church. And when they're old enough to go up to
    college . . ." "Wait," she said, "that's far.
You will have to tell me what kind of a woman Constance is. I can hardly
    imagine that any . . . woman
Debased or deceived enough to marry you
Will not be a beast or a fool toward my children. Describe her." The
    lawyer intervened, "Now, Mrs. Bothwell,
Easy! I can assure you . . ." "She is not under discussion," Bothwell said,
    speaking awkwardly
Through lips like flints, "Where are they? Up-stairs?" "I will not let myself
    go again," Madrone answered,
"I will try not to insult anyone. They are mine and not hers, so that I have
    some interest
In knowing: but I can guess. Do you love them so much? Why do you want
    them?"

They heard the old clapboard walls

Scream on their nails in a sudden storm-gust and Bothwell said: "If you
care for them as you pretend

You'll not delay us, and keep them half the night on the road in the storm.
It will take four hours

From here to town." "I do not love them

Extremely," she answered. "But still they are carved-out pieces of me: how
could I help being curious about

Their pitiful futures? It is a horror

What the time does. You, that were once no worse than a drunken cowboy,
a trick rider at dude-ranches."

"Talk," he said,

"So that I'll know it's you; but the power's mine. Bring them down." She
trembled violently and breathed and said,

"Is it talk?" She looked at Nelson and dark Vasquez, they stood like mice
in a corner while the other men

Watched from the fireside. "I am rather unhelped,

But I believe," she answered, her eyes like white unnatural snowlines under
the storm-cloud hair,

"I am still the stronger. . . . Vidal: you and Nelson had better go away
from this house," she said tenderly,

"Why should you taste our damnation? Ride and find a roof somewhere,
it's evil weather." And to Bothwell:

"Your power? It is not your power but the world's. I am quite alone, how
can I fight the law that you have

Made for you, the blue knife between mother and children? I never
understood that the world cares,

Or could come between." "Apparently," he said. "Will you bring them
down?" "Ronnie and Glory have been so sweet to me,"

She answered. "Be glad of that," he said, "when your demon

Drives you again. I'll go up and fetch them." She stood against him in the
doorway and said,

"There never has been a time when you were not weaker
And less than I. How can I be humble or submit? Do you know what
    mountains
In me hate you? There are no mountains on the earth like them,
Neither Everest nor the white mountains I saw
When I was born. Do you think you can overcome me? You? Go up to
    them." She stood out of the doorway
And let him run up the stair and find them.

                                While she
With a high ice-cold face over the northern hell of ice and emptiness that
    filled her mind
Went from the stair door toward the outer door. Stevens the lawyer
    attempting to speak to her, she looked down at him
And he was stilled; she passed him and stumbled against the door as if she
    had no eyes, and went out,
A caught whirlpool of wind struggled in the house behind her. The door
    blew
Shut. Then Rambler remembered his calling, and followed into the evening
    cloud-light and the horizontal
Whips of quick rain. She stood in the storm as if they had carved and set
    up an image of human despair
In the shape of a western woman
On the end of the world toward the last ocean and all mankind long extinct
    it stood there; but she heard the door,
She turned the eyes of a whelp-robbed lioness and said, "What do you
    want? Oh, you're the field-glasses.
Come here. It's a stinking trade, but we're all
In the same slime-brook." He said, "Nothing, ma'am," and saw that she was
    walking random. He was glad to return in-doors
Out of the storm-whipping.

Madrone approaching him had struck her shoe
On a brown metal bar in the mud path; the poor spy instantly slid out of
her thoughts.
It was one of those abalone irons, valueless things, used and let fall,
A chisel-shape blade from the broken springs of an old wagon or motor:
they use it to pry the giant
Shellfish from the tide rocks; she thought it might do to kill with. She went
around the house-corner and saw
Bothwell's long car stand in the drive, and knew in a moment with a cold
clear and intent mind
How she could kill it. She opened the hood of the engine and pried and
broke a bomb-shape thing from its bearings
And flung it to the trees below. The gas-line dripped stinking blood and
the car died. Madrone, not raging,
Not in a torrent, with a cold crystal and intent mind: "I think you won't
take them to-night,"
And closed the hood. She stood and saw the gray white-scaled ocean darken
toward evening,
And heard the oak-branches roar, and watched the long black-roofed car
shudder in the wind as if it were alive,
But it was dead.

Bothwell came out with Ronnie dressed warm for
traveling; behind him Mary Oliveras
Weeping brought little Gloria. The children's eyes were not much
frightened but wide with wonder. Madrone
Cried desolately, "It would be better for them to die. Will you take them
from me?" He said "Are you there?
Listen to me." He set Ronnie in the car and said: "Mr. Black wants
possession by New Year's,

And that's ten days. So you'll have to come up to town before long, then
   you can see them. Come Christmas day
And see them shine." Her face writhed, and for a moment the pupils in her
   white eyes made them turn black;
She breathed and said humbly, "May I? For I have promised them one or
   two little things, pitiful keep-sakes
They'll hardly notice in their new affluence, but let me give them." "Why
   certainly. Madrone," he said
Hesitantly, "I bear no grudges." She clenched her hands and breathed and
   said, "Why should you? For it seems
You have the victory. What now can save them
From lives much worse than death, decaying to an average, growing to be
   like
All the other insects that fill the cities and defile the country? That listen to
   imbecile songs and love
To breathe each other, and eat and drink and make love in common,
   swarming for pleasure; and from time to time
A war or a revolution rakes them up like dry straws in a stack and burns
   them, they hurrah with joy.
Better the babies died than such lives for them. Do you want them to be
   like *me*? Do you want them
To be like *you*?" "My God," he laughed, "say quieter good-byes. . . .
   We've got to live. Listen, Madrone,
You'll have some things to send up: Do you need money?" "I am going to
   my father's place in the Rockies." "That's fine!"
He answered gladly. "Except that my father is dead you know and the place
Sold long ago. There is such a mania
For dying and selling." He answered, "We'll settle these things when you
   come to town. I know," he said, "it's a wrench.
I'm sorry for you." Her eyes startled him.

                                He pressed on the steel button;
the starter whirled, but the engine

Would not answer one word. After he had whirled and whirled it in vain
    many times Madrone said humbly

That she was sorry, she'd been wild with pain at losing her babies. She'd
    pay the damage

Out of her little pitiful . . . allowance

That had been promised. "*By God* you will. Get out and look into the
    engine, Rambler." "You needn't look,"

She answered, "I did it thoroughly. . . . Who has the victory?" "I," he said.
    "Rambler:

Look under the hood. If it can't be fixed, there's a car here. There in the
    shed." "That's mine," she answered.

He said, "I was going to let you have it. But now if the thing will hang
    together till we get to town:

We can squeeze in."

                      The increasing wind

Pressed Rambler against the mudguard while he stared at the engine, as if
    he were pasted against the mudguard.

Madrone leaned on the wind like a falling tower her strong body, saying
    stilly, "That worn-out car

Is mine and mine. I took it from my father who wisely hated this man, I
    stole it to escape in.

I robbed my father for love of this man: whom now I am horribly

Changed from *loving*.

There is no honor left." Rambler looked up at Bothwell and shouted
    through the wind: "Nothing doing.

God what a wreck." Madrone went toward the shed leaning on the wind;
    Bothwell reefed his big overcoat

And followed hastily: "I'll watch you by God or you'll smash that one too.
    Come on, Stevens."

When she opened the shed-doors
The fierce wind from the south took them like sparrow's wings and broke
    them backward and tore the hinges,
One of the wings tore free and flew in the air, fell on gray grass; the heavy
    roof-timbers
Writhed on their bolts. Madrone laughed whitely at the crashes and
    answered, "It is not enough." She took the old car's
Ignition key from its slot, she offered it to Bothwell and seemed to have
    given it to him, she said "I was getting
The key to give you." He said, "Give it then." She passed him by, laughing
    and saying "What, have you dropped it?"
He followed her and she stood on the steep of the mountain beside the
    shed
And flung the key. Caught by the wind it made a strange far flight,
    compounded of two impredicable
Curves and three forces. She said, "Who has the victory?" and the men
    running down the steep face
In hope to find it, she laughed in the wind and mocked them: "Look sharp,
    for the night is coming. Not there: look farther.
There in the briars for I saw it fall: put your hands in
And snuffle for it. Fetch Fido, fetch Towser."

                            That moment the
    magnificence and fire of the sun at setting
Found the one single flaw in the planetary cloud, for which it had been
    sounding with golden plummets
All day in vain. A fountain of intense light
Poured on the ocean and sprayed and scattered; but now too late for gold,
    redder than blood, great waves
Of blood-color light, that stained the sea they came from, and
    treacherously

From below stabbed the cloud, dyeing its unguarded belly with fiery blood, and beat the sea-wall

Mountain so that it rang like a gong

Resounding with sanguine light. Every rock, leaf and stone, each grain of earth, each blade of dead grass,

Each pool and course of water, each horn of the herd, bird in the air, deer on the hill; each eye,

Each hair,

Caught light and lived in it, distinct and particular and perfect, and fiery red. The ignition key, that toothed slip

Of tarnished metal down the mountain sea-face,

Shined like a star, a red one, among the spikes of black grass beside the wild buckwheat bush: nobody

Not blind could fail.

Madrone watched them find it

And wrung her hands, feeling, not thinking: "Who steers the light like a red ship? Who is able to open

The clouds and close them?" Her face white and dead; in the fading red glare her face for a moment was the only white

Thing in the world; and the twisted mouth exposing white teeth of one dead by violence. She covered her face,

And said to Bothwell "He has given it to you." Then stooping and shrunken against the wind

Went toward the house; but turned a little and went toward the broken car where her children were. Mary

Oliveras was there alone with them; the men by the shed, Bothwell starting the car. Madrone said coldly:

"I love them so. Let me alone with them.

I am not fighting rats any more, but in the pit

With a great enemy. I have to say good-bye to my babies." Mary got out of the car; Madrone

Turned while she entered it and said: "Go into the house: bring me my
    purse
From the drawer in my room." Mary stood still and said, "Purse?" "Fool,
    bring it quickly," she answered, blazing
With her white eyes.

                    Then little Gloria, who spoke always clearly, rang
    like a silver bell:
"Good-bye mama." "You?" she answered. "So you're glad to go?" The
    child, seeing her face when she turned, suddenly
Began to weep by itself, but Ronnie who was older answered: "No, mama.
    Father says that it's better.
He'll give us things. And he says that it's wrong to hide here, we have to
    learn
How to help people." "*I* had some things to give you for Christmas." "Yes
    mama." "This was not one of them," she answered,
Her face like a white star, "but it's the best." It hung by a cord, hidden
    around her neck
Under her clothing, an amulet she wore according to her nature, a sharp
    sheathed thing, that had skinned game
And gelded calves; she lifted her arm and drew it from the high plain
    between the hills that had fed them,
Then Gloria shook her curls and said "No"; but Ronnie, "Oh thank you
    mama." She answered, "Do you know God
Wants you to take a journey?" "Father does," Ronnie answered, "what's
    God?" "My enemy," she answered;
"Aren't you too hot?" The wind made thunder in the top of the car,
    Madrone unbuttoned the child's
Coat at his chin and said from her cold and intent mind: "Sister's too hot."
    She unbuttoned Gloria's,

And said, "Don't look." He looked and saw the hand on the chin, and his mother's face
Stiffen while she slashed and dragged.

                                              His scream was drowned
In the noise of Bothwell starting the car, and the solstice wind. Madrone said, "I am sick, Ronnie,
I am so afraid of you." He choked and drew into himself, and said with a face like an old man's: "Will you . . . *me?*
Why, mother?" "I hate him so. I need, I need. It is better for you." "I always knew
Since I could speak," he said, "look at her blood. I thought how beautiful it is but I always knew.
Oh poor Glory. Does it hurt?" He screamed, "Help! Oh! Let me live!" Madrone answered, "I have seen
What kind of life. I am willing to help you."

                                      The car came out of the shed and stood at some distance,
Prow toward stern with this car. Mary Oliveras returned from the house. Madrone said, "I've had lovers,
But never a friend before you alone. Now help me carry the children to the other car. Take Glory.
I will take Ronnie." Mary made a harsh rattling noise in her throat, such as the dying
Make in their throats. Madrone said "Hush, don't wake them, I wish to surprise
Bothwell. Oh lift her tenderly for she was precious." Mary turned away and stood out of the car,
Gray-faced, her mouth ridiculously gaped open its widest and stuffed with silence, as if the jaw
Were dislocated, she looked toward the south and fell

Beside the wheels. Bothwell came and said "What!" Madrone answered:

"She cannot bear to part from the children, she is not strong. Tell your
    friends, Andrew,

To carry her into the house.

You cannot leave her here in the storm on the wet soil." Stevens attempted
    to lift her up,

Then Rambler helped him; they took her in. Madrone said, "Andrew: must
    you surely take my children from me?

You see how vicious it is, when even this poor woman who is not their
    mother." He said "I must,"

And then coming near saw her face clearly. He stumbled backward and said,
    "What have you done what have you

Done." "If you'll take your son," she said, "I will take your daughter

To the other car. Or is your mind changed?" He scrabbled with his hands
    like epilepsy in the car doorway

Reaching for the boy's loose little body; when he plucked at it

The head slipped over, the great wound in the slender neck opened its lips.
    Madrone took Gloria

Into her arms and left the car by the opposite side. Black was approaching
    from the other car;

Madrone passed him and said "She's asleep,"

And propped up the small body on the rear seat of her own car, but the
    running motor's vibration

Made it fall sidewise. Madrone returned to Bothwell's and looked in to see
    him

Kneel on the blood-lake floor, praying, "God, give him life. God, make
    him live." "God cannot," she answered,

"I did it." "Dear God. For the sake of *your* son. Make him alive." Black,
    standing sick with amazement

By the car step: "My God what has happened? Is the child dead?" "This
    hell's not yours,"

She answered. "What," he said, "is the child dead?" "Yours will come

In its time," she answered, and said to Bothwell: "God cannot.
Whose victory?" He looked up at her with blind unknowing and
    question-tortured eyes, like the questioning eyes
Of a hurt dog, and said "Are you a devil? Oh I have dreamed of you." She
    answered, "You too look changed."
"Dear God," he said like an incantation, "for *your* son's sake." "God
    cannot," she answered.

                    The raging wind
Raved in the oak-branches and darkness began. Madrone said "I have to
    take him into my car.
Get out of my way." Bothwell's mind returned to him and said, "He is
    dead." "I did it," she answered.
He turned the headlight switch, in hope to make what seemed unreal really
    unreal. The light
Stared into horizontal rain and the end of the world. She said, "This car is
    dead, we have to
Take him to mine. Don't you remember?" "I remember you.
Stevens!" he shouted. "Mr. Stevens and Mr. Rambler," she answered, "are
    in the house. And Mr.
Black has run into the house."

                        She pushed by him, reaching for the
    child's body, but when she touched it
Bothwell's hands found her throat and joyfully
Felt the fierce bands of flesh harden, then submit, and the cartilage
Ply in his fingers. She reeling blindly along the seat of the car reached her
    bare knife and nicked
Both his wrists with it, and breathed, and said hoarsely, "You are hurting
    him.
I will kill you if you hurt Ronnie." "God, make him live." "God cannot,"
    she answered.

                    The house door opened,
The red light of a smoking lamp scarred the black wind. Madrone said
    hoarsely, "Quick now, they're coming.
Let me have him to save him, I'll save his life." "What?" he said, "Oh!"
She answered, "*This* car is dead.
But in the other. Let me get by you." She gathered the small body tenderly
    into her arms
And carried it across the darkness, leaning on the wind, and set it by its
    sister's. Bothwell followed submissively
And stood beside it. Madrone returned to Bothwell's car, the three men
    were there;
Their eyes not yet adjusted to the change and darkness
They had come to the car's light from the house light. She answered
    hoarsely, "I've saved the children, they are not here,"
And reaching down the black wind sought for her purse
In the mud by the wheels, where Mary
Falling had dropped it. Stevens shouted "Where are they?" "Saved," she
    answered. He said, "What are you looking for?" "Like you:
Money. In the mud." Rambler, in the car,
Set his hand on the sticky seat-cushion and suddenly cried, "Ah Ah, my
    God," and reaching forward
Across the seat-back found the push-button switch and lighted the car's
    interior. Madrone picked up
Her purse from the lighted mud by the step and said
"I am equal with you." She stood with red hands, but the men were staring
    into the dreadful stains
Inside the car. She returned to the other.

                            Bothwell was standing praying
    "God, make them live. *Dear* God . . ."
"God cannot," she answered. He extended groping hands like a blind man
    toward her to ward her off, and suddenly

Screamed "Take her. She is here." "Drunkard," she said and entered the car
    from the other side and let in the gear.
Bothwell running clung to the seat where his children were. The other men
Came blind, dodging the headlights, Madrone said as she passed them,
    "Andrew went mad and has hurt the babies.
I am taking them to a doctor." The car gathered speed, Bothwell fell off
    from it.

Madrone with the murdered flowers
That her womb formed slid down the driveway through the cut night,
    slipping from side to side in the mud,
She reached the road and ran north. Sick pain came over the rage, but she
    thought of nothing, the play was done.
At Aguilar Canyon she stopped at the bridgehead and washed herself
In the cold stream under the comets of light from the car's eyes. She looked
    and found a torn cloth
That had been used to wipe down the windshield, she dipped it and washed
    the dead children's faces; and there was a rug
In the car; she set them up on the seat and spread it up to their chins.

Slides

from cut banks,
Rocks and root-slipped redwoods and lakes of water lay over the road, but
    she wove around them. The time
Was eternal hell or only two or three hours and she came to the lighted
    gas-pump at Carmel Highlands.
No one was there; when she cursed them with the car's horn, then a man
    came. He filled the tank and told
The price of gasoline and said "My God are they sick?" "They are asleep,"
    Madrone answered. "My God," he said,
"Their eyes half open." "This is not your hell,"

She answered, "Yours comes. I am taking them to a doctor." "My God!"
    he said. "Will you look at the oil-measure,"
She said, "a quart?" He poured the oil in and said "My God they're dead."
    "So will you be."

                She turned
By the Carmel bridge and drove up the Carmel river-valley, thinking that
    Bothwell might have been able
To telephone to Monterey. That forest-service wire from Big Sur: she
    ought to have ham-strung the horses.
She drove up the quiet winding valley and thought of blood
On the hocks of horses. In the oakwood near the steep road that branches
    off to Cachagua a double lantern
Stood in the road to stop her; she roared the engine and drove straight at it
    to run through it: it was only the eyes
Of a tall mountain-lion, that bounded up the cut bank. There was snow by
    a bush
Where it leaped up.

                   The great final sky-ridge was all heavy with snow,
    pines waved in the wind, glittering
In the car's eye-light, needles of frost. Here the car slipped and stalled in
    snow-sheeted clay
Close to the summit. One of the rear wheels dug a grave for itself; when
    Madrone stopped the engine
She heard the wind crying in the pines, and the moon came out. She broke
    branches and strewed them, the wheel
Churned them down and went deeper. She said to the dead children,
    "Darlings,
You don't need to wake up: I think there's a kind of a little spade with the
    other tools

Under the seat." She put her right hand under Ronnie's thighs, his head in
    the hollow of her left shoulder,
She lifted him and set him on the front seat. Gloria fell over sidewise and
    she lifted her
All random, and turned her face to hers; hot-lipped kissed the cold mouth
    and suddenly terribly cried
"Oh . . Oh . . Oh . . Oh . . Oh," her voice
Like a she-wolf's howling on the white hill, "What have I done?" She
    stopped, and set Gloria upright
Beside Ronnie. She moved the seat and taking the shovel dug the wheel
    clear, and paved the incline
With stones and branches. She tucked the lap-robe closer around her
    children, saying coldly, "I could have saved you
Some other way. I was too senseless-confident
Until the degradation had you in its hands, I did what a senseless
Caged beast killing her cubs . . . Oh . . Oh . . Oh . . I beast
I did it." She moved away from the car, tall and alone, terrible on the white
    mountain, tearing
At her own throat and her long black hair; and returned and said
"Now we must go." She thought that Ronnie answered, "Leave us here,
    mother."

                    She heard him without amazement,
And said, "Not here." She thought that he answered, "We have never seen
    snow before. So white so white. Leave us
Here, mother?" She said, "Sweetheart, where we are going to the snow lies
    deep, the mountains wear it all summer.
They stand like great pinto horses spotted with snow, grazing, with their
    heads down; little lakes
As round as cups and as blue as your eyes
Are at their feet." He answered, "We'll never see them, mother. We look so
    strangely our small dead faces,

The people would surely stop you and take us from you." She said, "They? Dogs." "We'd rather stay here, mother,

In the mountains where we were born. Can you see the ocean from here?" She turned and stared and said "No . . . yes."

The child answered, "You know he could never find us up here. . . . Your face looks terrible. . . . *Please* leave us here.

. . . For we are terribly afraid to be with you, your eyes are terrible.

. . . Mother, you can have *new* babies.

. . . *Please* don't look at me mother your eyes are terrible . . ." Madrone

Left him and went away up the bank to an open place; she dug the pit in the black earth,

When she returned Ronnie said, "We are just as happy, mother, as if we'd lived." She made no answer.

She wrapped the children in the lap-robe over head and eyes and laid them to bed in the wet earth

And said, "Sleep. Sleep. Poor pawns forever. Sleep Gloria. Good-bye Gloria. Oh you were lovely

Ronnie and Gloria."

It snowed again and the bodies were never found. Gopher and ground-squirrel

And the rooting boar break up the sod in so many places on the high hills. If the children

Could see from where they lie hidden they'd see

What a great surf of mountains beats from the distant ocean up to their dwelling-place, wave over wave,

Waves of live stone; and low storm-clouds fly through the gorges like hunting eagles. Or if it were summer,

They'd see the quail and the mountain woodpecker walk above them, hawks flying, and the great white clouds; they'd see

The sea-fog drawn over the farthest ridges taut as a drum, the dry white stream-beds, the strained

Crystal of the air. It is likely the children are never able to see the wild
    beauty of things.
You almost think you hear them crying in the earth because the thirsty
    roots have drunk their blue eyes.
But no, there is not a sound.

                          Their mother drove east through thickening
phantoms
And is thought to have died of thirst in the desert or have killed herself,
    because she was hunted like the last wolf
And never found. Her car was found overturned in a desert gully off an
    abandoned road;
That was perhaps the place where the phantoms caught her; the wolf-hunt
    failed.

I cannot tell; I think she had too much energy to die. I think that a fierce
    unsubdued core
Lives in the high rock in the heart of the continent, affronting the bounties
    of civilization and Christ,
Troublesome, contemptuous, archaic, with thunder-storm hair and snowline
    eyes, *waiting*,
Where the tall Rockies pasture with their heads down, white-spotted and
    streaked like piebald horses, sharp withers
And thunder-scarred shoulders against the sky, standing with their heads
    down, the snow-manes blow in the wind;
But they will lift their heads and whinny when the riders come, they will
    stamp with their hooves and shake down the glaciers.

V

Such Counsels
You Gave to Me

1935-1938

REARMAMENT

These grand and fatal movements toward death: the grandeur of the mass
Makes pity a fool, the tearing pity
For the atoms of the mass, the persons, the victims, makes it seem
  monstrous
To admire the tragic beauty they build.
It is beautiful as a river flowing or a slowly gathering
Glacier on a high mountain rock-face,
Bound to plow down a forest, or as frost in November,
The gold and flaming death-dance for leaves,
Or a girl in the night of her spent maidenhood, bleeding and kissing.
I would burn my right hand in a slow fire
To change the future . . . I should do foolishly. The beauty of modern
Man is not in the persons but in the
Disastrous rhythm, the heavy and mobile masses, the dance of the
Dream-led masses down the dark mountain.

AIR-RAID REHEARSALS

Unhappy time why have you built up your house
So high that it cannot stand? I see that it has to fall:
When I look closer I can see nothing clearly, my eyes are blinded with rain.

I see far fires and dim degradation
Under the war-planes and neither Christ nor Lenin will save you.
I see the March rain walk on the mountain, sombre and lovely on the green
  mountain.

I wish you could find the secure value,
The all-heal I found when a former time hurt me to the heart,
The splendor of inhuman things: you would not be looking at each others'
  throats with your knives.

THE PURSE-SEINE

Our sardine fishermen work at night in the dark of the moon; daylight
or moonlight
They could not tell where to spread the net, unable to see the
phosphorescence of the shoals of fish.
They work northward from Monterey, coasting Santa Cruz; off New Year's
Point or off Pigeon Point
The look-out man will see some lakes of milk-color light on the sea's
night-purple; he points, and the helmsman
Turns the dark prow, the motor-boat circles the gleaming shoal and drifts
out her seine-net. They close the circle
And purse the bottom of the net, then with great labor haul it in.

                                                        I cannot
    tell you
How beautiful the scene is, and a little terrible, then, when the crowded
    fish
Know they are caught, and wildly beat from one wall to the other of their
    closing destiny the phosphorescent
Water to a pool of flame, each beautiful slender body sheeted with flame,
    like a live rocket
A comet's-tail wake of clear yellow flame; while outside the narrowing
Floats and cordage of the net great sea-lions come up to watch, sighing in
    the dark; the vast walls of night
Stand erect to the stars.

                        Lately I was looking from a night mountain-top
On a wide city, the colored splendor, galaxies of light: how could I help
    but recall the seine-net
Gathering the luminous fish? I cannot tell you how beautiful the city
    appeared, and a little terrible.

I thought, We have geared the machines and locked all together into
    interdependence; we have built the great cities; now
There is no escape. We have gathered vast populations incapable of free
    survival, insulated
From the strong earth, each person in himself helpless, on all dependent.
    The circle is closed, and the net
Is being hauled in. They hardly feel the cords drawing, yet they shine
    already. The inevitable mass-disasters
Will not come in our time nor in our children's, but we and our children
Must watch the net draw narrower, government take all powers, — or
    revolution, and the new government
Take more than all, add to kept bodies kept souls, — or anarchy, the
    mass-disasters.

                    These things are Progress;
Do you marvel our verse is troubled or frowning, while it keeps its reason?
    Or it lets go, lets the mood flow
In the manner of the recent young men into mere hysteria, splintered
    gleams, crackled laughter. But they are quite wrong.
There is no reason for amazement: surely one always knew that cultures
    decay, and life's end is death.

BLIND HORSES

The proletariat for your Messiah, the poor and many are to seize power
and make the world new.

They cannot even conduct a strike without cunning leaders: if they make a
revolution their leaders

Must take the power. The first duty of men in power: to defend their
power. What men defend

To-day they will love to-morrow; it becomes theirs, their property. Lenin
has served the revolution,

Stalin presently begins to betray it. Why? For the sake of power, the Party's
power, the state's

Power, armed power, Stalin's power, Caesarean power.

This is not quite a
new world.

The old shepherd has been known before; great and progressive empires
have flourished before; powerful bureaucracies

Apportioned food and labor and amusement; men have been massed and
moulded, spies have gone here and there,

The old shepherd Caesar his vicious collies, watching the flock. Inevitable?
Perhaps, but not new.

The ages like blind horses turning a mill tread their own hoof-marks.
Whose corn's ground in that mill?

THE WIND-STRUCK MUSIC

Ed Stiles and old Tom Birnam went up to their cattle on the bare hills
Above Mal Paso; they'd ridden under the stars' white death, when they
    reached the ridge the huge tiger-lily
Of a certain cloud-lapped astonishing autumn sunrise opened all its petals.
    Ed Stiles pulled in his horse,
That flashy palamino he rode — cream-color, heavy white mane, white tail,
    his pride — and said
"Look, Tom. My God. Ain't that a beautiful sunrise?" Birnam drew down
    his mouth, set the hard old chin,
And whined: "Now, Ed: listen here: I haven't an ounce of poetry in all my
    body. It's cows we're after."
Ed laughed and followed; they began to sort the heifers out of the herd.
    One red little deer-legged creature
Rolled her wild eyes and ran away down the hill, the old man hard after
    her. She ran through a deep-cut gully,
And Birnam's piebald would have made a clean jump but the clay lip
Crumbled under his take-off, he slipped and
Spilled in the pit, flailed with four hooves and came out scrambling. Stiles
    saw them vanish,
Then the pawing horse and the flapping stirrups. He rode and looked down
    and saw the old man in the gully-bottom
Flat on his back, most grimly gazing up at the sky. He saw the earth banks,
    the sparse white grass,
The strong dark sea a thousand feet down below, red with reflections of
    clouds. He said "My God
Tom are you hurt?" Who answered slowly, "No, Ed.
I'm only lying here thinking o' my four sons" — biting the words
Carefully between his lips — "big handsome men, at present lolling in bed
    in their . . . silk . . . pyjamas . . .

And why the devil I keep on working?" He stood up slowly and wiped the dirt from his cheek, groaned, spat,
And climbed up the clay bank. Stiles laughed: "Tom, I can't tell you: I guess you like to. By God I guess
You like the sunrises." The old man growled in his throat and said
"Catch me my horse."

                    This old man died last winter, having lived eighty-one years under open sky,
Concerned with cattle, horses and hunting, no thought nor emotion that all his ancestors since the ice-age
Could not have comprehended. I call that a good life; narrow, but vastly better than most
Men's lives, and beyond comparison more beautiful; the wind-struck music man's bones were moulded to be the harp for.

THE COAST-ROAD

A horseman high-alone as an eagle on the spur of the mountain over
    Mirmas Canyon draws rein, looks down
At the bridge-builders, men, trucks, the power-shovels, the teeming end of
    the new coast-road at the mountain's base.
He sees the loops of the road go northward, headland beyond headland,
    into gray mist over Fraser's Point,
He shakes his fist and makes the gesture of wringing a chicken's neck,
    scowls and rides higher.

               I too
Believe that the life of men who ride horses, herders of cattle on the
    mountain pasture, plowers of remote
Rock-narrowed farms in poverty and freedom, is a good life. At the far end
    of those loops of road
Is what will come and destroy it, a rich and vulgar and bewildered
    civilization dying at the core,
A world that is feverishly preparing new wars, peculiarly vicious ones, and
    heavier tyrannies, a strangely
Missionary world, road-builder, wind-rider, educator, printer and
    picture-maker and broad-caster
So eager, like an old drunken whore, pathetically eager to impose the
    seduction of her fled charms
On all that through ignorance or isolation might have escaped them. I hope
    the weathered horseman up yonder
Will die before he knows what this eager world will do to his children.
    More tough-minded men
Can repulse an old whore, or cynically accept her drunken kindnesses for
    what they are worth,
But the innocent and credulous are soon corrupted.

                                                  Where is our
    consolation? Beautiful beyond belief
The heights glimmer in the sliding cloud, the great bronze gorge-cut sides
    of the mountain tower up invincibly,
Not the least hurt by this ribbon of road carved on their sea-foot.

MEMOIR

I saw the laboratory animals: throat-bandaged dogs cowering in cages, still
    obsessed with the pitiful
Love that dogs feel, longing to lick the hand of their devil; and the sick
    monkeys, dying rats, all sacrificed
To human inquisitiveness, pedantry and vanity, or at best the hope
Of helping hopeless invalids live long and hopelessly.

                                          I left that great
    light room where pain was the air
And found my friends dehorning cattle in the field above Rio Piedras
    Canyon. (The buyers require it now,
So many horned beasts have injured each other in the gorged trucks
And crowded cattle-cars up to Calvary.) I watched the two Vasquez boys,
    great riders, drive the scared steers
Into the frame that clamps them and holds them helpless. Bill Flodden with
    a long-handled tool like pruning-shears
Crushed off the horns and the blood spouted; Ed Stiles, our knower of
    bawdy stories, the good-natured man,
Stands by to cake the blood-fountains with burning alum. These fellows are
    fit for life, sane men, well-buttoned
In their own skins; rarely feel pain outside their own skins: whilst I like a
    dowser go here and there
With skinless pity for the dipping hazel-fork.

                                    Blank rises the limestone
Mountain Pico Blanco, blue runs the sea. No life here but some gray
    bushes, lupine and sage,
No creditor of pity, sage and satisfied plants, for it rained this morning.
    Here in the sanctuary
I need not think beyond the west water, that a million persons

Are presently dying of hunger in the provinces of China. I need not think
    of the Russian labor-camps, the German
Prison-camps, nor any of those other centers
That make the earth shine like a star with cruelty for light. I need not think
    of the tyrannies, that make the tyrants
Ignoble and their victims contemptible. I need not think of the probable
    wars, tyranny and pain
Made world-wide; I need not . . . know that this is our world, where only
    fool or drunkard makes happy songs.

HELLENISTICS

I

I look at the Greek-derived design that nourished my infancy—this
  Wedgwood copy of the Portland vase:
Someone had given it to my father—my eyes at five years old used to
  devour it by the hour.

I look at a Greek coin, four-drachma piece struck by Lysimachus: young
  Alexander's head
With the horns of Ammon and brave brow-ridges, the bright pride and
  immortal youth and wild sensitiveness.

I think of Achilles, Sappho, the Nike. I think of those mercenaries who
  marched in the heart of Asia
And lived to salute the sea: the lean faces like lance-heads, the grace of
  panthers. The dull welter of Asia.

I am past childhood, I look at this ocean and the fishing birds, the
  streaming skerries, the shining water,
The foam-heads, the exultant dawn-light going west, the pelicans, their
  huge wings half folded, plunging like stones.

Whatever it is catches my heart in its hands, whatever it is makes me
  shudder with love
And painful joy and the tears prickle . . . the Greeks were not its inventors.
  The Greeks were not the inventors

Of shining clarity and jewel-sharp form and the beauty of God. He was
  free with men before the Greeks came:

He is here naked on the shining water. Every eye that has a man's nerves
behind it has known him.

II

I think of the dull welter of Asia. I think of squalid savages along the
Congo: the natural
Condition of man, that makes one say of all beasts "They are not
contemptible. Man is contemptible." I see

The squalor of our own frost-bitten forefathers. I will praise the Greeks for
having pared down the shame of three vices
Natural to man and no other animal, cruelty and filth and superstition,
grained in man's making.

III

The age darkens, Europe mixes her cups of death, all the little Caesars
fidget on their thrones,
The old wound opens its clotted mouth to ask for new wounds. Men will
fight through; men have tough hearts.

Men will fight through to the autumn flowering and ordered prosperity.
They will lift their heads in the great cities
Of the empire and say: "Freedom? Freedom was a fire. We are well quit of
freedom, we have found prosperity."

They will say, "Where now are the evil prophets?" Thus for a time in the
age's after-glow, the sterile time;
But the wounds drain, and freedom has died, slowly the machines break
down, slowly the wilderness returns.

IV

Oh distant future children going down to the foot of the mountain, the
    new barbarism, the night of time,
Mourn your own dead if you remember them, but not for civilization, not
    for our scuttled futilities.

You are saved from being little entrails feeding large brains, you are saved
    from being little empty bundles of enjoyment,
You are not to be fractional supported people but complete men; you will
    guard your own heads, you will have proud eyes.

You will stand among the spears when you meet; life will be lovely and
    terrible again, great and in earnest;
You will know hardship, hunger and violence: these are not the evils: what
    power can save you from the real evils

Of barbarism? What poet will be born to tell you to hate cruelty and filth?
    What prophet will warn you
When the witch-doctors begin dancing, or if any man says "I am a priest,"
    to kill them with spears?

NEW YEAR'S EVE

Staggering homeward between the stream and the trees the unhappy drunkard
Babbles a woeful song and babbles
The end of the world, the moon's like fired Troy in a flying cloud, the storm
Rises again, the stream's in flood.
The moon's like the sack of Carthage, the Bastille's broken, pedlars and empires
Still deal in luxury, men sleep in prison.
Old Saturn thinks it was better in his grandsire's time but that's from the brittle
Arteries, it neither betters nor worsens.
(Nobody knows my love the falcon.)
It has always bristled with phantoms, always factitious, mildly absurd;
The organism, with no precipitous
Degeneration, slight imperceptible discounts of sense and faculty,
Adapts itself to the culture-medium.
(Nobody crawls to the test-tube rim,
Nobody knows my love the falcon.)
The star's on the mountain, the stream snoring in flood; the brain-lit drunkard
Crosses midnight and stammers to bed.
The inhuman nobility of things, the ecstatic beauty, the inveterate steadfastness
Uphold the four posts of the bed.
(Nobody knows my love the falcon.)

NOVA

That Nova was a moderate star like our good sun; it stored no doubt a
  little more than it spent
Of heat and energy until the increasing tension came to the trigger-point
Of a new chemistry; then what was already flaming found a new manner of
  flaming ten-thousandfold
More brightly for a brief time; what was a pin-point fleck on a sensitive
  plate at the great telescope's
Eye-piece now shouts down the steep night to the naked eye, a nine-day
  super-star.

                    It is likely our moderate
Father the sun will sometime put off his nature for a similar glory. The
  earth would share it; these tall
Green trees would become a moment's torches and vanish, the oceans
  would explode into invisible steam,
The ships and the great whales fall through them like flaming meteors into
  the emptied abysm, the six-mile
Hollows of the Pacific sea-bed might smoke for a moment. Then the earth
  would be like the pale proud moon,
Nothing but vitrified sand and rock would be left on earth. This is a
  probable death-passion
For the sun's planets; we have no knowledge to assure us it may not happen
  at any moment of time.

Meanwhile the sun shines wisely and warm, trees flutter green in the wind,
  girls take their clothes off
To bathe in the cold ocean or to hunt love; they stand laughing in the
  white foam, they have beautiful
Shoulders and thighs, they are beautiful animals, all life is beautiful. We
  cannot be sure of life for one moment;

We can, by force and self-discipline, by many refusals and a few assertions,
    in the teeth of fortune assure ourselves
Freedom and integrity in life or integrity in death. And we know that the
    enormous invulnerable beauty of things
Is the face of God, to live gladly in its presence, and die without grief or
    fear knowing it survives us.

GIVE YOUR WISH LIGHT

By day and night dream about happy death,
Poor dog give your heart room, drag at the chain,
Breathe deep at dawn, wish it were the last breath,
Imagine the leaden ball planted in the brain,
The seed of that superb flower, dream the brave noose
That loves the neck so dearly it lets the life loose,
Dream the fierce joys of war where men like drunken
Jesuses fling the supreme gift at each other,
"Take blessedness, take it deep in your breast, brother . . ."
Dream on, dream all these joys, life might look shrunken
In lack of dreams. Give your wish light, give it room.
You know you will never untimely attempt the tomb.
— Go in to your bride by daylight before the crowd
As if sweet death were a whore? You are too proud.

THEBAID

How many turn back toward dreams and magic, how many children
Run home to Mother Church, Father State,
To find in their arms the delicious warmth and folding of souls.
The age weakens and settles home toward old ways.
An age of renascent faith: Christ said, Marx wrote, Hitler says,
And though it seems absurd we believe.
Sad children, yes. It is lonely to be adult, you need a father.
With a little practise you'll believe anything.

Faith returns, beautiful, terrible, ridiculous,
And men are willing to die and kill for their faith.
Soon come the wars of religion; centuries have passed
Since the air so trembled with intense faith and hatred.
Soon, perhaps, whoever wants to live harmlessly
Must find a cave in the mountain or build a cell
Of the red desert rock under dry junipers,
And avoid men, live with more kindly wolves
And luckier ravens, waiting for the end of the age.

Hermit from stone cell
Gazing with great stunned eyes,
What extravagant miracle
Has amazed them with light,
What visions, what crazy glory, what wings?
— I see the sun set and rise
And the beautiful desert sand
And the stars at night,
The incredible magnificence of things.

I the last living man
That sees the real earth and skies,
Actual life and real death.
The others are all prophets and believers
Delirious with fevers of faith.

THE GREAT SUNSET

A flight of six heavy-motored bombing-planes
Went over the beautiful inhuman ridges a straight course northward; the
    incident stuck itself in my memory
More than a flight of band-tail pigeons might have done
Because those wings of man and potential war seemed really intrusive above
    the remote canyon.
They changed it; I cannot say they profaned it, but the memory
All day remained like a false note in familiar music, and suggested no doubt
The counter-fantasy that came to my eyes in the evening, on the ocean
    cliff.

        I came from the canyon twilight
Exactly at sunset to the open shore, and felt like a sudden extension of
    consciousness the wild free light
And biting north wind. The cloud-sky had lifted from the western horizon
    and left a long yellow panel
Between the slate-edge ocean and the eye-lid cloud; the smoky ball of the
    sun rolled on the sea-line
And formless bits of vapor flew across, but when the sun was down
The panel of clear sky brightened, the rags of moving cloud took
    memorable shapes, dark on the light,
Whether I was dreaming or not, they became spears and war-axes, horses
    and sabres, gaunt battle-elephants
With towered backs; they became catapults and siege-guns, high-tilted
    howitzers, long tractors, armored and turreted;
They became battle-ships and destroyers, and great fleets of war-planes . . . .
    all the proud instruments
Of man imposing his will upon weaker men: they were like a Roman
    triumph, but themselves the captives,
A triumph in reverse: all the tools of victory

Whiffed away on the north wind into a cloud like a conflagration, swept
    from the earth, no man
From this time on to exploit nor subdue any other man. I thought, "What
    a pity our kindest dreams
Are complete liars," and turned from the glowing west toward the cold
    twilight. "To be truth-bound, the neutral
Detested by all the dreaming factions, is my errand here."

THE ANSWER

Then what is the answer? — Not to be deluded by dreams.

To know that great civilizations have broken down into violence, and their tyrants come, many times before.

When open violence appears, to avoid it with honor or choose the least ugly faction; these evils are essential.

To keep one's own integrity, be merciful and uncorrupted and not wish for evil; and not be duped

By dreams of universal justice or happiness. These dreams will not be fulfilled.

To know this, and know that however ugly the parts appear the whole remains beautiful. A severed hand

Is an ugly thing, and man dissevered from the earth and stars and his history . . . for contemplation or in fact . . .

Often appears atrociously ugly. Integrity is wholeness, the greatest beauty is

Organic wholeness, the wholeness of life and things, the divine beauty of the universe. Love that, not man

Apart from that, or else you will share man's pitiful confusions, or drown in despair when his days darken.

THE BEAKS OF EAGLES

An eagle's nest on the head of an old redwood on one of the precipice-footed ridges

Above Ventana Creek, that jagged country which nothing but a falling meteor will ever plow; no horseman

Will ever ride there, no hunter cross this ridge but the winged ones, no one will steal the eggs from this fortress.

The she-eagle is old, her mate was shot long ago, she is now mated with a son of hers.

When lightning blasted her nest she built it again on the same tree, in the splinters of the thunder-bolt.

The she-eagle is older than I; she was here when the fires of 'eighty-five raged on these ridges,

She was lately fledged and dared not hunt ahead of them but ate scorched meat. The world has changed in her time;

Humanity has multiplied, but not here; men's hopes and thoughts and customs have changed, their powers are enlarged,

Their powers and their follies have become fantastic,

The unstable animal never has been changed so rapidly. The motor and the plane and the great war have gone over him,

And Lenin has lived and Jehovah died: while the mother-eagle

Hunts her same hills, crying the same beautiful and lonely cry and is never tired; dreams the same dreams,

And hears at night the rock-slides rattle and thunder in the throats of these living mountains.

It is good for man
To try all changes, progress and corruption, powers, peace and anguish, not to go down the dinosaur's way
Until all his capacities have been explored: and it is good for him
To know that his needs and nature are no more changed in fact in ten thousand years than the beaks of eagles.

ALL THE LITTLE HOOF-PRINTS

Farther up the gorge the sea's voice fainted and ceased.
We heard a new noise far away ahead of us, vague and metallic, it might
    have been some unpleasant bird's voice
Bedded in a matrix of long silences. At length we came to a little cabin lost
    in the redwoods,
An old man sat on a bench before the doorway filing a cross-cut saw;
    sometimes he slept,
Sometimes he filed. Two or three horses in the corral by the streamside
    lifted their heads
To watch us pass, but the old man did not.

                                            In the afternoon we returned
    the same way,
And had the picture in our minds of magnificent regions of space and
    mountain not seen before. (This was
The first time that we visited Pigeon Gap, whence you look down behind
    the great shouldering pyramid-
Edges of Pico Blanco through eagle-gulfs of air to a forest basin
Where two-hundred-foot redwoods look like the pile on a Turkish carpet.)
    With such extensions of the idol-
Worshipping mind we came down the streamside. The old man was still at
    his post by the cabin doorway, but now
Stood up and stared, said angrily "Where are you camping?" I said "We're
    not camping, we're going home." He said
From his flushed heavy face, "That's the way fires get started. Did you
    come at night?" "We passed you this morning.
You were half asleep, filing a saw." "I'll kill anybody that starts a fire
    here . . ." his voice quavered
Into bewilderment . . . "I didn't see you. Kind of feeble I guess.

My temperature's a hundred and two every afternoon." "Why, what's the
   matter?" He removed his hat
And rather proudly showed us a deep healed trench in the bald skull. "My
   horse fell at the ford,
I must 'a' cracked my head on a rock. Well sir I can't remember anything
   till next morning.
I woke in bed the pillow was soaked with blood, the horse was in the corral
   and had had his hay," —
Singing the words as if he had told the story a hundred times. To whom?
   To himself, probably, —
"The saddle was on the rack and the bridle on the right nail. What do you
   think of *that* now?" He passed
His hand on his bewildered forehead and said, "Unless an angel or
   something came down and did it.
A basin of blood and water by the crick, I must 'a' washed myself." My wife
   said sharply, "Have you been to a doctor?"
"Oh yes," he said, "my boy happened down." She said "You oughtn't to be
   alone here: are you all alone here?"
"No," he answered, "horses. I've been all over the world: right here is the
   most beautiful place in the world.
I played the piccolo in ships' orchestras." We looked at the immense
   redwoods and dark
Fern-taken slip of land by the creek where the horses were, and the yuccaed
   hillsides high in the sun
Flaring like torches: I said "Darkness comes early here." He answered with
   pride and joy, "Two hundred and eighty-
Five days in the year the sun never gets in here.
Like living under the sea, green all summer, beautiful." My wife said,
   "How do you know your temperature's
A hundred and two?" "Eh? The doctor. He said the bone
Presses my brain, he's got to cut out a piece. I said All right you've got to
   wait till it rains,

I've got to guard my place through the fire-season. By God," he said joyously,
"The quail on my roof wake me up every morning, then I look out the window and a dozen deer
Drift up the canyon with the mist on their shoulders. Look in the dust at your feet, all the little hoof-prints."

GOING TO HORSE FLATS

Amazingly active a toothless old man
Hobbled beside me up the canyon, going to Horse Flats, he said,
To see to some hives of bees. It was clear that he lived alone and craved
   companionship, yet he talked little
Until we came to a place where the gorge widened, and deer-hunters had
   camped on a slip of sand
Beside the stream. They had left the usual rectangle of fired stones and
   ashes, also some crumpled
Sheets of a recent newspaper with loud head-lines. The old man rushed at
   them
And spread them flat, held them his arm's length, squinting through
   narrowed eye-lids—poor trick old eyes learn, to make
Lids act for lens. He read "Spain Battle. Rebels kill captives. City bombed
   Reds kill hostages. Prepare
For war Stalin warns troops." He trembled and said, "Please read me the
   little printing, I hardly ever
Get to hear news." He wrung his withered hands while I read; it was
   strange in that nearly inhuman wilderness
To see an old hollow-cheeked hermit dancing to the world's echoes. After I
   had read he said "That's enough.
They were proud and oppressed the poor and are punished for it; but those
   that punish them are full of envy and hatred
And are punished for it; and again the others; and again the others. It is so
   forever, there is no way out.
Only the crimes and cruelties grow worse perhaps." I said, "You are too
   hopeless. There are ways out."
He licked his empty gums with his tongue, wiped his mouth and said
"What ways?" I said "The Christian way: forgiveness, to forgive your
   enemies,

Give good for evil." The old man threw down the paper and said "How
    long ago did Christ live? Ah?
Have the people in Spain never heard about him? Or have the Russians,
Or Germans? Do you think I'm a fool?" "Well," I said to try him, "there's
    another way: extermination.
If the winning side will totally destroy its enemies, lives and thoughts,
    liquidate them, firing-squads
For the people and fire for the books and records: the feud will then be
Finished forever." He said justly, "*You're* the fool," picked up his bundle
    and hurried through the shadow-dapple
Of noon in the narrow canyon, his ragged coat-tails flapping like mad over
    the coonskin patch
In the seat of his trousers. I waited awhile, thinking he wished to be quit of
    company.

             Sweet was the clear
Chatter of the stream now that our talk was hushed; the flitting water-ouzel
    returned to her stone;
A lovely snake, two delicate scarlet lines down the dark back, swam through
    the pool. The flood-battered
Trees by the stream are more noble than cathedral-columns.

                        Why do we
    invite the world's rancors and agonies
Into our minds though walking in a wilderness? Why did he want the news
    of the world? He could do nothing
To help nor hinder. Nor you nor I can . . . for the world. It is certain the
    world cannot be stopped nor saved.
It has changes to accomplish and must creep through agonies toward new
    discovery. It must, and it ought: the awful necessity

Is also the sacrificial duty. Man's world is a tragic music and is not played
    for man's happiness,
Its discords are not resolved but by other discords.

                                                   But for each man
There is real solution, let him turn from himself and man to love God. He
    is out of the trap then. He will remain
Part of the music, but will hear it as the player hears it.
He will be superior to death and fortune, unmoved by success or failure.
    Pity can make him weep still,
Or pain convulse him, but not to the center, and he can conquer them. . . .
    But how could I impart this knowledge
To that old man?

                      Or indeed to anyone? I know that all men instinctively
    rebel against it. But yet
They will come to it at last.
Then man will have come of age; he will still suffer and still die, but like a
    God, not a tortured animal.

CONTEMPLATION OF THE SWORD
(April, 1938)

Reason will not decide at last; the sword will decide.
The sword: an obsolete instrument of bronze or steel, formerly used to kill men, but here
In the sense of a symbol. The sword: that is: the storms and counter-storms of general destruction; killing of men,
Destruction of all goods and materials; massacre, more or less intentional, of children and women;
Destruction poured down from wings, the air made accomplice, the innocent air
Perverted into assassin and poisoner.

The sword: that is: treachery and cowardice, incredible baseness, incredible courage, loyalties, insanities.
The sword: weeping and despair, mass-enslavement, mass-torture, frustration of all the hopes
That starred man's forehead. Tyranny for freedom, horror for happiness, famine for bread, carrion for children.

Reason will not decide at last, the sword will decide.

Dear God, who are the whole splendor of things and the sacred stars, but also the cruelty and greed, the treacheries
And vileness, insanities and filth and anguish: now that this thing comes near us again I am finding it hard
To praise you with a whole heart.

I know what pain is, but pain can shine. I know what death is, I have sometimes

Longed for it. But cruelty and slavery and degradation, pestilence, filth, the
   pitifulness
Of men like little hurt birds and animals . . . if you were only
Waves beating rock, the wind and the iron-cored earth, the flaming insolent
   wildness of sun and stars,
With what a heart I could praise your beauty.

                                          You will not repent, nor
   cancel life, nor free man from anguish
For many ages to come. You are the one that tortures himself to discover
   himself: I am
One that watches you and discovers you, and praises you in little parables,
   idyl or tragedy, beautiful
Intolerable God.

                    The sword: that is:
I have two sons whom I love. They are twins, they were born in nineteen
   sixteen, which seemed to us a dark year
Of a great war, and they are now of the age
That war prefers. The first-born is like his mother, he is so beautiful
That persons I hardly know have stopped me on the street to speak of the
   grave beauty of the boy's face.
The second-born has strength for his beauty; when he strips for swimming
   the hero shoulders and wrestler loins
Make him seem clothed. The sword: that is: loathsome disfigurements,
   blindness, mutilation, locked lips of boys
Too proud to scream.

                    Reason will not decide at last: the sword will decide.

OH LOVELY ROCK

We stayed the night in the pathless gorge of Ventana Creek, up the east
    fork.
The rock walls and the mountain ridges hung forest on forest above our
    heads, maple and redwood,
Laurel, oak, madrone, up to the high and slender Santa Lucian firs that
    stare up the cataracts
Of slide-rock to the star-color precipices.

                             We lay on gravel and kept a
    little camp-fire for warmth.
Past midnight only two or three coals glowed red in the cooling darkness; I
    laid a clutch of dead bay-leaves
On the ember ends and felted dry sticks across them and lay down again.
    The revived flame
Lighted my sleeping son's face and his companion's, and the vertical face of
    the great gorge-wall
Across the stream. Light leaves overhead danced in the fire's breath,
    tree-trunks were seen: it was the rock wall
That fascinated my eyes and mind. Nothing strange: light-gray diorite with
    two or three slanting seams in it,
Smooth-polished by the endless attrition of slides and floods; no fern nor
    lichen, pure naked rock . . . as if I were
Seeing rock for the first time. As if I were seeing through the flame-lit
    surface into the real and bodily
And living rock. Nothing strange . . . I cannot
Tell you how strange: the silent passion, the deep nobility and childlike
    loveliness: this fate going on
Outside our fates. It is here in the mountain like a grave smiling child. I
    shall die, and my boys

Will live and die, our world will go on through its rapid agonies of change and discovery; this age will die

And wolves have howled in the snow around a new Bethlehem: this rock will be here, grave, earnest, not passive: the energies

That are its atoms will still be bearing the whole mountain above: and I many packed centuries ago

Felt its intense reality with love and wonder, this lonely rock.

SINVERGUENZA

They snarl over Spain like cur-dogs over a bone, then look at each other and shamelessly
Lie out of the sides of their mouths.
Brag, threat and lie, these are diplomacy; wolf-fierce, cobra-deadly and monkey-shameless,
These are the masters of powerful nations.
I wonder is it any satisfaction to Spaniards to see that their blood is only
The first drops of a forming rain-storm.

OCTOBER WEEK-END

It is autumn still, but at three in the morning
All the magnificent wonders of midwinter midnight, blue dog-star,
Orion, red Aldebaran, the ermine-fur Pleiades,
Parading above the gable of the house. Their music is their shining,
And the house beats like a heart with dance-music
Because our boys have grown to the age when girls are their music.
There is wind in the trees, and the gray ocean's
Music on the rock. I am warming my blood with starlight, not with girls' eyes,
But really the night is quite mad with music.

STEELHEAD, WILD PIG, THE FUNGUS

I

The sky was cold December blue with great tumbling clouds, and the little river
Ran full but clear. A bare-legged girl in a red jersey was wading in it, holding a five-tined
Hay-fork at her head's height; suddenly she dartled it down like a heron's beak and panting hard
Leaned on the shaft, looking down passionately, her gipsy-lean face, then stooped and dipping
One arm to the little breast she drew up her catch, great hammered-silver steelhead with the tines through it
And the fingers of her left hand hooked in its gills, her slender body
Rocked with its writhing. She took it to the near bank
And was dropping it behind a log when someone said
Quietly "I guess I've got you, Vina." Who gasped and looked up
At a young horseman half-hidden in the willow-bushes,
She'd been too intent to notice him, and said "My God
I thought it was the game-warden." "Worse," he said smiling. "This river's ours.
You can't get near it without crossing our fences.
Besides that you mustn't spear 'em, and . . . three, four, you little bitch
That's the fifth fish." She answered with her gipsy face, "Take half o' them, honey. I loved the fun."
He looked up and down her taper legs, red with cold, and said fiercely, "Your fun.
To kill them and leave them rotting." "Honey, let me have one o' them," she answered,
"You take the rest." He shook his blond head. "You'll have to pay a terrible fine." She answered laughing,

"Don't worry: you wouldn't tell on me." He dismounted and tied the
    bridle to a bough, saying "Nobody would.
I know a lovely place deep in the willows, full of warm grass, safe as a
    house,
Where you can pay it." Her body seemed to grow narrower suddenly, both
    hands at her throat, and the cold thighs
Pressed close together while she stared at his face, it was beautiful, long
    heavy-lidded eyes like a girl's,
"I can't do that, honey . . . I," she said shivering, "your wife would kill
    me." He hardened his eyes and said
"Let that alone." "Oh," she answered; the little red hands came down from
    her breast and faintly
Reached toward him, her head lifting, he saw the artery on the lit side of
    her throat flutter like a bird
And said "You'll be sick with cold, Vina," flung off his coat
And folded her in it with his warmth in it and carried her
To that island in the willows.

                                    He warmed her bruised feet in his hands;
She paid her fine for spearing fish, and another
For taking more than the legal limit, and would willingly
Have paid a third for trespassing; he sighed and said
"You'll owe me that. I'm afraid somebody might come looking for me,
Or my colt break his bridle." She moaned like a dove, "Oh Oh Oh Oh,
You are beautiful, Hugh." They returned to the stream-bank. There,
While Vina put on her shoes—they were like a small boy's, all stubbed and
    shapeless—young Flodden strung the five fish
On a willow rod through the red gills and slung them
To his saddle-horn. He led the horse and walked with Vina, going part way
    home with her.

Toward the canyon sea-mouth
The water spread wide and shoal, fingering through many channels down a
broad flood-bed, and a mob of sea-gulls
Screamed at each other. Vina said, "That's a horrible thing." "What?"
"What the birds do. They're worse than I am."
When Flodden returned alone he rode down and watched them. He saw
that one of the thousand steelhead
Which irresistible nature herded up-stream to the spawning-gravel in the
mountain, the river headwaters,
Had wandered into a shallow finger of the current and was forced over on
his flank, sculling uneasily
In three inches of water: instantly a gaunt herring-gull hovered and
dropped, to gouge the exposed
Eye with her beak; the great fish writhing, flopping over in his anguish,
another gull's beak
Took the other eye. Their prey was then at their mercy, writhing blind,
soon stranded, and the screaming mob
Covered him.

Young Flodden rode into them and drove them up; he
found the torn steelhead
Still slowly and ceremoniously striking the sand with his tail and a bloody
eye-socket, under the
Pavilion of wings. They cast a cold shadow on the air, a fleeting sense of
fortune's iniquities: why should
Hugh Flodden be young and happy, mounted on a good horse,
And have had another girl besides his dear wife, while others have to
endure blindness and death,
Pain and disease, misery, old age, God knows what worse?

II

Perhaps their wildness will never die from these mountains.
The eagle still dawns over the ridges like a dark sun, the deer breed, the
    puma hunts them, the rattler
Has his fangs, fleet hawks have the air. The timber-wolves were all killed,
    some rancher's German shepherd-dogs
Ran with coyotes and bred a new kind of wolves, strong and more cunning,
    fierce killers. And the grizzlies
Extinct, a wealthy amateur up the Carmel Valley brought in wild pigs
From the Urals to stock his hunting-park: they overswarmed it and broke
    his borders and roam the coast-range, beautiful
Monsters, full of fecundity, bristled like a hedge at midnight; and the boars
    with long naked
Knives in their jaws. They lair all day in impenetrable manzanita-thickets
    of the farther mountain
And whet their knives at night on the farmer's apple-trees.

                               A gang of
    them returning toward the gray of dawn
Through Flodden's plowland, old Bill Flodden and his boy Harry ran out
When the dogs yelled, but Hugh stayed warm in bed beside his young wife;
    only when he heard rifle-shots
Yawned, stretched himself and went out. It was raining softly, things were
    dim gray and black and the trembling sky,
The dogs making a noise far away, the old man calling them. They had
    bayed something
In the steep chaparral at the base of the mountain. Hugh went up and said
    "Pig?" The old man said "I
Pinked him in the butt, he's too mad to run." The dogs raved in the thicket
    and as light increased, oozing
Down the black mountain-sides like water from a sponge

To spread on the gray floor of the valley, you saw the chaparral surface
    waving in ship's keel wakes
Where the boar charged the dogs, little quick rushes, one of them jagged
    up into a piercing death-scream,
A dog was caught, but nothing to be seen except the greasewood-
Tops waving. The old man: "I'm going in there and kill the bastard." Hugh
    said "Like hell you are." The old man said
"He got a dog." Hugh said "He'd get you too. You can't see past your face
    in that swither." Old Flodden,
His voice cracking falsetto with passion: "I've got a knife." Hugh said "Old
    fool: it's a boar in there?
You might as well stand on the railroad tracks at Monterey
And fight a freight-engine with a knife." Flodden answered, "When y' get
    old: you'll be old some day.
Look at me for God's sake." He was half dressed, naked from the waist up,
    wide sagging shoulders
Oily with rain-water, and pearls of rain on the pale hair in the groove
Between his big sagging breast-muscles; his belly sagged on the belt that
    had the sheath-knife. "Hm? Love of women?"
He said plaintively, "I get so damn' tired hearing your bed-springs creak in
    the evenings." Hugh said, "Where's Harry?"
"Up the hill on the other side, watching if he comes out." "Let me get the
    gun from him, I'll
Go in with you, father." He answered, "Got to have some fun," and rather
    delicately for one so thick-bodied
Slipped into the bushes, parting them with the barrel of his rifle, and
    disappeared. The dogs were silent.
Hugh called to Harry for the other rifle.

                          However, it was not required.
  The old man searched and searched

Vainly all through the thicket; he found the two living dogs, meek and
    subdued, and the dead one
Trampled in a jelly of its own entrails, but the tall boar had vanished, like a
    piece of sea-fog
That blows up-canyon into warmer air and instantly vanishes.

                                                 It was now

   broad daylight, and old Flodden
Returned out of the thicket, jeering at the cowardly dogs: that moment a
    heavy
Noise like distant cannon-fire roared at the mountain-top, the horses
    pasturing in the valley below
Raced up the opposite slope; then some great stones and a storm of
    fragments came bounding
Down the rock-face, felled an oak-tree or two, and cut several straight
    paths through the brush and chaparral.
The winter had been very rainy, a high blade of rock
Had settled and split away and rolled down; but it seemed as if the
    mountain had said something, some big word
That meant something, but no one could understand what it meant. Or the
    other mountains did.

III

June Flodden and Florrie Crawford were gathering mushrooms
In the green field, and Florrie found a thick-stemmed toad-stool with a
    close purplish cap,
She plucked it and giggled at it, showing it to June, who couldn't think
    what she meant; then Florrie formed
An oval doorway between the finger and thumb of her left hand, she forced
    the odd-looking fungus

Into the slot and made it play back and forth. When its head broke off

She screamed with pleasure, threw it on the ground and trampled it, her
little white teeth grinning maliciously, "I'd love to

Do that to all of them." She looked at June

And June had laid down the sack of mushrooms and hid her face in her
hands and wept. Florrie said "Oh

June! What's the matter?" "Nothing . . ." "Did a spider bite you?" June
shook her head.

She had two-colored hair cut at her shoulders, the outer locks were harvest
yellow and the mass under them

Pale shadowy brown. Her hands covered her face and Florrie saw a bright
tear trickle on the fingers.

She patted her twitching shoulder. "There, there. Hush dear. Are you
going to have a baby, that's not so terrible."

June wept aloud and said "No. Now I never will." "Why, what's the
matter?" "Hugh," she answered, and gasped "He's

Untrue to me." Florrie answered, "Good Lord. I thought

Something terrible had happened." June lowered her hands to look at her
friend's face and saw the black hair

Through tear-filled eyes in the clear sunlight haloed with rainbows, and said
solemnly, "Nothing

Worse could happen. If I knew who it was I'd shoot her." Florrie, eagerly:
"Oh tell me dear,"

Laying her arm around her shoulder and her cheek

To the wet cheek; they made a beautiful picture on the green field starred
with white stones and mushrooms

In rath sunlight of March, the dark head against the blond one, the soft
young bodies touching each other;

Those long grave slopes and limestone precipices of Pico Blanco lifting
beyond.

Florrie said,
"My Tom: you know how homely he is; you wouldn't think that a sick
　　heifer would look at him. Well:
A dozen times. I always know what to do." June sobbed "Oh, Oh,
What do you do?" "No, I won't tell,
Until you tell me your story: how do you know Hugh's cheating you?
　　Come up to the rock behind the oak-tree
And tell me everything; I'll teach you how to be happy, Tom and I are
　　happy."

　　　　The rock was a great lichen-grown
Fragment that must have fallen from the mountain centuries ago; chance
　　and the weather had carved a rough
Bench in its base, where Florrie made June sit close to her and stilled her
　　tears; from time to time a hard sob
Interrupted the story. June said that Hugh
Would sometimes ride away all the afternoon and into the evening. When
　　he returned he always
Said he'd been looking for a strayed steer and she had believed him. But
　　then she noticed . . . "I can't tell that.
Florrie I can't." "Darling you must tell all or how can I help you?" She
　　looked away from her friend
And whispered in a ragged voice, "I noticed after those times when he'd
　　been away, he never wanted to . . .
Oh . . . what we did every night when we went to bed. He turned away
　　from me." Florrie compressed her lips
For fear of smiling, and said "That's bad." June said "At first I thought he
　　was tired, riding so far.
But when I feared that he was unfaithful to me I prayed to die. I went down
　　to the river
And dreamed of drowning myself; it was too cold, no hole was deep
　　enough. Then Hugh rode by.

I scooched behind a bush and he didn't see me and I followed down
Clear to the sea." Florrie said "No, darling.
Don't tell me you kept up with the horse." She answered "You know that
    empty cabin at the river-mouth
With cypress trees around it: his horse was tied to
One of those trees." "Oh, Oh! What did you find?" "I didn't dare to go
    near. I went and sat
On the sand far away, and heard the wretched noise of the waves and
    watched his horse." Florrie said
"Did they come out?" June said "There was a bird on the beach, a great
    ugly pelican,
Starving to death, his feathers tarred with oil from a ship so he couldn't fly.
    He leaned on his wings
And they were like two crooked black fishing-poles. I guess that bird and I
    were the very wretchedest
Lives in the world. And the gray sea glittered, the river ran through the
    sand; after while they came out.
She seemed to be a little thing but I couldn't look. What shall I do?"
    Florrie said "Ha? Every time
That he does it, you do it. That's what I do wi' my Tom: that's the great
    secret." June said "I can't
Tell what you mean." She answered, "Take any pleasant young man, they
    are all willing. You'll find revenge
Is sweeter than love or honey." June said "I'd rather drown myself. I'd
    rather be like that wretched bird,
Ugly and alone and hopeless, waiting to die by the glittering sea." "Ah, Ah,
    never say die,"
Florrie answered quickly, "it's wicked for a married woman to talk like that,
    we must not be abject. Look, darling:
There's the first yellow violet, yellow outside and brown underneath, just
    like your hair."

NIGHT WITHOUT SLEEP

The world's as the world is; the nations rearm and prepare to change; the
    age of tyrants returns;
The greatest civilization that has ever existed builds itself higher towers on
    breaking foundations.
Recurrent episodes; they were determined when the ape's children first ran
    in packs, chipped flint to an edge.

I lie and hear dark rain beat the roof, and the blind wind.

                                        In the morning
    perhaps I shall find strength again
To value the immense beauty of this time of the world, the flowers of decay
    their pitiful loveliness, the fever-dream
Tapestries that back the drama and are called the future. This ebb of
    vitality feels the ignoble and cruel
Incidents, not the vast abstract order.

                              I lie and hear dark rain beat the
    roof, and the night-blind wind.

In the Ventana country darkness and rain and the roar of waters fill the
    deep mountain-throats.
The creekside shelf of sand where we lay last August under a slip of stars
And firelight played on the leaning gorge-walls, is drowned and lost. The
    deer of the country huddle on a ridge
In a close herd under madrone-trees; they tremble when a rock-slide goes
    down, they open great darkness-
Drinking eyes and press closer.

Cataracts of rock
Rain down the mountain from cliff to cliff and torment the stream-bed.
    The stream deals with them. The laurels are wounded,
Redwoods go down with their earth and lie thwart the gorge. I hear the
    torrent boulders battering each other,
I feel the flesh of the mountain move on its bones in the wet darkness.

                                                        Is this
    more beautiful
Than man's disasters? These wounds will heal in their time; so will
    humanity's. This is more beautiful . . . at night . . .

HOPE IS NOT FOR THE WISE

Hope is not for the wise, fear is for fools;
Change and the world, we think, are racing to a fall,
Open-eyed and helpless, in every news-cast that is the news:
The time's events would seem mere chaos but all
Drift the one deadly direction. But this is only
The August thunder of the age, not the November.
Wise men hope nothing, the wise are naturally lonely
And think November as good as April, the wise remember
That Caesar and even final Augustulus had heirs,
And men lived on; rich unplanned life on earth
After the foreign wars and the civil wars, the border wars
And the barbarians: music and religion, honor and mirth
Renewed life's lost enchantments. But if life even
Had perished utterly, Oh perfect loveliness of earth and heaven.

SELF-CRITICISM IN FEBRUARY

The bay is not blue but sombre yellow
With wrack from the battered valley, it is speckled with violent foam-heads
And tiger-striped with long lovely storm-shadows.
You love this better than the other mask; better eyes than yours
Would feel the equal beauty in the blue.
It is certain you have loved the beauty of storm disproportionately.
But the present time is not pastoral, but founded
On violence, pointed for more massive violence: perhaps it is not
Perversity but need that perceives the storm-beauty.
Well, bite on this: your poems are too full of ghosts and demons,
And people like phantoms — how often life's are —
And passion so strained that the clay mouths go praying for destruction —
Alas it is not unusual in life;
To every soul at some time. *But why insist on it? And now*
For the worst fault: you have never mistaken
Demon nor passion nor idealism for the real God.
Then what is most disliked in those verses
Remains most true. *Unfortunately. If only you could sing*
That God is love, or perhaps that social
Justice will soon prevail. I can tell lies in prose.

SUCH COUNSELS YOU GAVE TO ME

I

A young man carrying a battered straw suit-case
Climbed slowly the wavering cattle-track from an off-set
Gorge of Mal Paso Canyon, and across the hill
Toward Howren's place. He staggered from time to time
With illness or extreme fatigue. Behind him in the magnificent after-glow
    of November sundown
The two brightest of planets hung close together, like brilliant
    condensations of the amber light
Above the crimson; the sky overhead was still blue and pale. The young
    man was perfectly alone
On the white-grassed hills under the sky, he was like a hardly noticed
    thought of unhappiness passing
Through a great serene mind. But when he approached
The fall of the hill toward Howren's he saw apparently
A person on the verge, outlined against the darkening
Commissure of the farther hills, intently gazing
Into the valley. The young man's tired and dulled mind,
Bred in these hills, taught in the city, reverted easily
Toward his dead childhood; he thought it might be one of the watchers,
Who are often seen in this length of coast-range, forms that look human
To human eyes, but certainly are not human.
They come from behind ridges and watch. But when he approached it
He recognized the shabby clothes and pale hair
And even the averted forehead and concave line
From the eye to the jaw, so that he was not surprised
When the figure turning toward him in the quiet twilight
Showed his own face. Then it melted and merged
Into the shadows beyond it; the young man thought heavily

That in his state of mind and body hallucination
Was not surprising. He went and stood for a time
Just where the figure had stood, in the same attitude,
Staring down at the farmhouse roof. He thought
That twenty years ago, but no doubt a little
Later at night, his mother then a young girl
Of sixteen or seventeen, slender and wistful
Of body, and the strong coarse man his father had lain
In a bed under that roof welding their naked
Bodies together, "and I that stand here, with all my
Inflamed hopes, work, wretchedness, final disaster,
Am the result. Go to it, dear parents." He watched undazzled
As if the farmhouse roof and the twenty years
Had become glass. "I have something here in my pocket
To undo all your bed-work." He imagined the terrible
Life-race of the myriad half-cells of one
Ejaculation, racing up the wet uterine
Darkness to find one bride. One finds her and enjoys her
And has a future, poor fool; the others die frustrate.
Like competition in the world outside: for one that wins,
Thousands of others wither in the wet darkness.
Like competition in the world. But if the poor passionate tadpole
With all his genes in him could have foreseen *what* prize
He was winning . . . . he'd 'a' sculled the dark stream less eagerly.

                                                                 The

    boy went down
Through the pale twilight; they had lighted lamps in the house.
He stood and looked in a window, hoping to escape
Meeting his father to-night, or any man,
In this dejection. He saw Grace Gomez pass
Silhouetted against the lamplight with a pile of plates

To set the table; she propped them on her big belly; her hands
Held them, her belly carried them. He heard noises
From the hill behind, and stumbled away from the house
To stand behind an oak-bush and watch them pass,
Horse, man and dogs, and the pig's carcass. His father had shot
One of the great wild pigs, and was sledding it
Home from the hill, driving to the heavy-timbered
Farm-gate, built like a gallows, where he used to hang them
For flaying and quartering; but first he went to the house
To fetch a helper and a lantern. When he returned,
And the two far dark figures in their aura of reddish
Lanternlight at the gallows-foot: the boy took up
The suit-case and went in-doors.

                                  His mother stared at him
As if she were seeing a spirit. "Oh Howard, what's happened?"
"Nothing. I'm sick. Well, I've cracked up, I can't go on
Unless he'll help." The pupils of her eyes dilated,
"He," she said with no change of countenance but the momentary
Waxing and waning of the pupils, which the boy saw
Because her face was toward the lamp and his eyes
New from the twilight; she said "How did you come?" "Begged rides.
I know he won't: I'm prepared." His sister came in,
Hearing their voices. "Howard!" "Hello, France." The mother said
"What do you mean, prepared?" "Oh . . . prepared. Prepared for it.
I can't talk to him to-night, mother, I am half dead.
Let me lie down."

                              She brought him supper to his bedside
And he was very hungry but the odor of food
Turned his face white. He said he had failed a mid-term
Examination; he knew the subject all right,

His mind went blank and splinters like a broken mirror.

He worked at night in a restaurant—"why food nauseates me—

And janitor-work in the biology lab.

Studies are stiffer this year. Well: Cracked up.

You know, mother, I've got to be first or nothing. There's a young Jew,

I just nosed by him last year, but the class-idiot

Can beat me now. I can't . . . you know . . . concentrate?"

If his father would lend him thirty dollars a month

He could go on. Mostly nerves, losing sleep. They'd given him

Tuberculin test at the infirmary, positive reaction,

That was nothing important. Only he could not

Go on unhelped.

            She sat by the bed kissing his hand

And said "Mine was like that." He said "It would take more money

Through medical . . . what, mother, your hand?" "Mind," she answered.

"That time after France was born. What you said: bright splinters

Around a blank." "Oh," he answered quietly, "to encourage me. Don't
   worry, I'm quite sane.

Only drained, drained." "I want you to rest this year,"

She answered, "start fresh next year." "I might be raving by then

And shipped off to the booby-hatch for a real rest,

Like you." She said "You were three years old. When I came home

You were five years old." "If you hadn't come home

I'd have grown up like *him*, exactly the I.Q.

Of a wild hog. Whatever happens, mother, mother,

I'm grateful to you." He sighed and turned

From her face and the lamp. She extinguished it

And turned in the darkness, bending over the bed

To kiss his cheek, he said "Mother. If you

Still sleep with him be very careful, you are still young.

It would be cruel to breed another like me" . . .

He spoke clearly but without inflection: he was perhaps
Already asleep, but she stood back from the bed
Without kissing him. She listened to the breathing of his exhaustion, the
    gentle moan
At the start of each expiration; whispered again
"Good-night, dearest," and tip-toed out.

                                    Sleep deepened over him
Like heavy ocean, more like coma than sleep; his mind made no appreciable
    dreams,
But crawling blindly about his body like a numbed spider on its web of
    nerves, here it shook a filament,
There a dark ganglion faintly glowed for a moment and returned to
    darkness, a pin-point nexus of brain-cells
Grew phosphorescent and faded and faintly glowed again; little superfluities
    of meaningless chemistry;
Besides the tidal glowing and paling, and traffic-light rhythms
Of nerves that govern breathing and heart-beat, arteries and viscera.

                                                  While
    outside the boy's body and the house
Orion swam slowly from the hills the southeastern sky. Procyon came up.
    Dry east-wind began to move
Across the hills, it creaked in the house and made strange flappings in the
    old roof. Sirius came up
To crackle in heaven like a blue diamond, little spurts of color. About that
    time a small constellation
Of nerve-cells began to glow in the sleeper's brain, and his mind dreamed
An image, a vaporous distortion rather, as if he saw a small cloud like a
    frog, and it had frog-skin
At the lighted spot. This faded quickly, the exhausted elements of life
    fought against consciousness, even

The fractional consciousness that makes a dream. Some gland poured
    opium into the blood.

                    Sirius flamed higher,
The Pleiads went over westward, the nerve-cells recharged their exhausted
    batteries; a whisper went through gray starlight
That the earth was turning over toward morning. Then strands and galaxies
    of nerve-cells flickered in the brain,
And thin swords through the cord and body, and the boy dreamed
That he and others in the laboratory were nailing a dog to wings, driving
    sharp horse-shoe nails
Between the pads of the fore-paws into the shafts of the wing-frames. The
    dog vanished from the dream, the dreamer
Himself flying wide over the city, crucified to wings; one of the spikes tore
    out through his palm
And he pitched down, falling along the facade of a public building.

                                            He
    saw the rainbow-
Haloed flame of a candle through sleep-wet eyelashes,
His mother in her night-dress standing holding it. "What?" "Oh screaming
    so,"
She answered. He saw the candle tremble in her hand,
Why was she terrified? They stared at each other through the jigging
    candlelight,
Both faces haggard from the deeps of sleep, their intimate
Resemblance appeared more clearly, the narrowed oval
Outline, the droop of the mouth-corners, the high-bridged
Bone of the nose, the blond pallor and the hollow cheeks,
They were two coins of one minting. "Howard . . . dearest
Are you all right?" He said "Will you let me alone

At night at least." "You were crying the way a dog." "One of those falling
    dreams,"
He answered, "wings over Spain or something. Go back to bed."
She looked all about the room. "What did you mean
When you said *prepared*?" "I haven't the faintest idea
What you're talking about, mother. Prepared?" She said "I'd kill myself
If anything should happen to you." "What? Nothing will happen.
I am not well and had a nightmare, that's all.
Your teeth are clacking with cold: go back and warm yourself
Beside your . . . husband," he said and looked curiously
At her eyes—would the pupils widen?—but could see neither
Blue iris nor black center in the shaking candlelight,
Only long obscure shadows. She said "You don't need
To be cruel to me, my life's not joyful." "Our minds are pits, mother,
Depth under depth and level under level. What color
Are France's eyes?" "What, dear?" "They are brown, aren't they?"
She said, "What do you mean?" He: "Nothing whatever.
It occurred to me." He noticed that her shivering stopped,
The candle-flame burned steady in the quiet air.
He had never so much admired her. "Brown, like my father's,"
She said. "What of it?" "Nothing." He smiled in himself
Thinking about the scrap of Mendelian theory
Picked up in high-school: blue eyes recessive, brown dominant:
Therefore blue-eyed parents cannot produce
A dark-eyed child, the dark-eyed-producing element
Is lacking in them. If it were present in either,
That one would be dark-eyed, for dark eyes are dominant. At first it had
    frightened him.
And he refused to believe it. After he accepted it
He avoided his mother for a time, and from this time forward
Found feverish interest in all the sciences of life: to know, to know,
To understand, to discover . . . the springs of life . . .

There his hungry mind found its bent and direction
And so continued. These waves of passion had gone over him
In wild secrecy and loneliness, forming his life;
But now that he grew adjusted to knowledge, that secret
Connivance in his mother's fortuitous or passionate adultery made her
More real and dear, not merely a mother, a living woman,
With her own loves and lawlessness. He said "Good-night,
Mother. I'll promise not to dream any more,
At least out loud." "Good-night, dearest . . ."

                                       After she was gone
He got up and went stealthily about the darkness
To find his coat on the chair-back. He folded it
And laid it under his pillow; he had a precious
Thing in the pocket. In the morning he was still tired and ill,
But having the KCN snitched from the laboratory,
The open-sesame of sudden death in his pocket,
One could run through the rigmarole.

II

                                  They had hooked the tendons
Of the wild pig's hind legs over the ends of a single-tree
And hung it by a rope through the ring, high in the gate-frame.
They'd gutted it the night before and were now flaying it,
They had got down to the shoulders. Howren, bent double,
Peeled the left fore-leg, Jim Gomez knelt in the dust,
Working on the right shoulder, snicking away with the knife
Through fat and fascia, tugging at the heavy hide
With the other hand. Above them the massive red-and-white-marbled
   column of the body

Hung naked against the background of yellow hills; to Howard it was so
    repulsive
That he could hardly come near, for feeling the carcass a monstrous
    crucified phallus, or a horrible fat man
From a hot bath, the dressing-gown falling off.
He ground his teeth and came near, said faintly and angrily
"Good-morning." Jim Gomez, Grace's boy, a boy his own age,
Looked up and grinned; Howard's father stood erect and said
"Hello. Heard you were back," wiped his right hand
On the bristle side of the hide, held it out. Howard touched it, the
    jaw-muscles
Lumping in his lean cheeks, and felt cold foam
Rise in his throat. He hardened his eyes to meet his father's,
They stared at each other a moment, the neurasthenic
Desire-eaten boy with the white in-door face
And the powerful coarse-fibered man, an inch less tall
And twice as broad, sunburnt and wind-bitten, dark-haired,
And the eyes paler blue, like the eyes of domestic swine, Howard thought,
    the white ones. He said "You look sick."
Howard swallowed the lump of spittle in his mouth and said "I *am* I guess.
    Let me talk to you
When you get this thing peeled." "Talk away." Howren picked up the knife
    and slit the skin
Around the wrist of the fore-leg. Jim Gomez looked up and grinned,
    tugging the inch-thick shoulder-hide. Howard said
"I'm going back to Berkeley to-day, I want to talk to you." "Go ahead:
    talk."
Howard stood in silence, watching the knives work. The valley was like a
    great swirling vortex, the luminous hills
Spun slowly around. He touched unconsciously the little amulet in his
    breast-pocket, ground his teeth and said

"Give me the knife, Jim. I'll do that work." Howren laughed: "That's the
    stuff.
Go saddle the buckskin, Jim, and your colt: let down the stirrups
Two holes for Howard." Howard took the knife and said "I'm not riding."
    Howren said "Go and saddle 'em. There's only
Two ways I can do business, liquor or horseback." Howard knelt in the dust
    and passed his left arm under
The folds of the hide, he took the bristles in his hand and tugged and
    cross-cut, panting in the odor of lard
And musky flesh. He said "I worked my way through high-school
Cleaning old Tom Birnam's slaughter house in Monterey
After school hours. You wouldn't help me, I didn't ask you to. Last year I
    worked my way in Berkeley.
I ought to 'a' got a scholarship: shabby boys from the back-country don't
    make friends, no pull, no luck.
I've worked myself to death for five years: now I've cracked up." He ceased;
    his father not answering,
He looked around the carcass to see his face.
He saw the top of his head bent to the work,
His hat was on the fence-post beyond: his hair was exactly
The pig's hair, the length and thickness, dry coarseness, rusted-black color:
    Howard's hand
Hastily let go the bristles and wiped itself
Against his clothing. Howren said: "How cracked up?"
Howard, still distracted by the sense of *what* hair
His fingers had been immersed in: "What? Ah—sunk; foundered."
—How to express what an exhausted mind feels like,
To a mind that has never worked; what screaming nerves feel like,
To one whose nerves never knew anything but the average animal
Sensualities?—"Cracked up. Foundered. Like a foundered horse.
Can't think nor work."

He was tautening the hide
By a fold of the inner surface, rather than handle
The coarse dry hair. His hand slipped as he tugged
And the knife gashed his knuckle; he felt it slightly, some blood
Slipped on the fat. Then Howren from the other side
Of the thick carcass: "Better come back to pasture then.
We shoot a foundered horse or put it to pasture." Howard, exhilarated
By the slight pain and seeing his own blood: "Ah, shoot.
Let me tell you a new riddle: Kay Conquers Napoleon.
What does that mean?" Howren was silent, whittling
The skin from the pig's left cheek. At length he said "Kay?"
Howard said "Yes. Kay." Howren said "To hell with Kay."
Howard laughed and said "How did you know it ionizes?
CN's the works." Howren with tolerant contempt:
"Is that what you learn in college," and stood erect,
Stretching cramped muscles. He had finished his side
And began to help Howard, who was still working
At the shoulder-joint. "Hell, have you nicked your finger already?
I'll finish for you." Howard whittled awhile and stood back out of his way,
Then saw the horses approaching and thought of death.
It was suddenly not refuge, not peace and easy
Annihilation, but a black fall that stopped
The heart to think of it, the horror of death. The intolerable injustice:
Pushed out of life for no crime over the precipice
To fall forever down, down, down.

Jim rode the black
And led the buckskin; both horses mad with fear of the carcass,
He had to stop at some distance. Howren and Howard
Walked twenty paces and mounted. "They can't stand pig,"
Howren said, and forced his horse toward its terror. Howard sat at distance

And watched the cruel magnificence of horsemanship, the rider making
   himself more terrible
Than the feared object. Soon the white flower of foam
Formed in the buckskin's jaws was mottled with red,
And the right flank striped with long weals. When the horse reared
A second time, and seemed toppling backward, Howard thought
"If it fell on him and killed him, mother would own
The place, and she could give me the little money
Without which I cannot live": Howren struck his horse
A stunning blow with the clenched fist on the peak of the skull
Between the ears: it fell forward and stood
Shuddering. He drove it and made it nose its terror, and returned laughing,
Saying to Jim Gomez "Get Corbett to help you quarter it,
He knows the job"; and to Howard, "Come."

                                    Howard followed him,
Thinking of the blackness of death, and that this man
Could save him from it, and almost certainly would not.
But one must try. They rode up the south hills,
Howren opened the pasture gates and left them
For Howard to close. A little squadron of steers
Deployed on the saddle of the highland and stood in line, wild beautiful
   eyes,
Faces like truncated inverted triangles, against the white lift and billow of
   the hill and blue sky beyond.
Howren said "Look, son. You may have learned God-knows-what in
   college,
But doesn't *that* say anything?" Howard said "Yes: nearly
Ripe for the butcher. D' y' think I get a clean break . . ." He changed and
   said, "This is your life.
Mine is: mine won't come off." They ran their horses on the saddle of the
   hill, walked for the steep. "What's yours?"

Howren said. "I don't think I can tell you," Howard said.
"You never could understand anything but hogs.
I want to know exactly what chemistry makes the heart beat and the brain
    burn. I want to know
What life is; how it works. I want to discover new things about it. I guess
    most of all I want to
Succeed . . . *succeed.* I want to show the scholarship boys and the damned
    snobs
That I can beat them. Life's a race I guess. I want them to know I've got a
    better mind than any of them,
And stronger will. If I can't do it I'll die in a minute."
He stopped, completely unable to bring himself
To the point of asking. Howren pulled in his horse,
Saying "How do you mean, die?" Howard stroked his buttoned
Coat with his hand, suddenly terrified,
Feeling for the little bottle in the breast-pocket:
It might have bounced out in mounting. Then he said with confidence,
"I can't support myself any longer. The oiled-hair snobs have fathers,
And the scholarship boys have scholarships: I've nothing . . .
Except t.b." Howren said "What?" "What your cows get:
Tuberculosis." "You wouldn't have got it here,"
Howren said. Howard said "I probably did," gasped and said shrilly: "This
    is not charity
But investment. Lend me thirty a month,
Any interest you want: I'll pay it all back
In seven years." He knew he was lying, it would take longer. Howren said:
"I'll give you thirty and found, if you'll stay home
And work for me." Howard said "No. Life or nothing." Howren said
    patiently
"I can't. This place is not a bank, it's a ranch.
I don't make a cent a year, I'll show you the books."

Howard felt a sudden increase of force and life in his mind, like a
    transfusion
Of strong red blood, he thought "The faithful adrenals
Have just heard how near death I am," and said "Don't lie.
Say no if you like. You bought new land last year.
You can't buy land without money." Howren said "By God I can.
Five hundred acres of redwood: that's what I'm taking you
Up the hill to see." Howard said "Down-payment borrowed
And the rest mortgage: no wonder your books . . ." The momentary
Tension of arterial blood suddenly ebbed again,
Leaving the brain darkened, sick rings of darkness
Contracted on the peripheral vision of his eyes;
But in a moment he was better. "If this is final
I will go back now." Howren said "Final, nothing's final.
I can sell the tract any time I want at forty
Percent profit. There's a boom in redwood." Howard said
"Damn you: sell it, let me live." Howren smiled at him,
"What, you're not dead yet." "To do my work," he said, "anything
Else is death. I don't want land and liquor like you,
I don't want money to buy pleasure and friends with, I don't want women, I
    hate their faces,
I'm willing to be a friendless rat all my life
And sleep in a cellar beside a urinal, but teach those people
The rat's their better: the friendless and penniless
Yellow rat has discovered what they daren't dream.
He knows how dirty sea-water under the sun
Scummed up with life. Poor starving-pale rat
Has opened a new chapter in bio-chemistry: the evolution of
Pre-cellular life. That's my work: to begin a bridge
Between broken-down rock and the virus of life.
And take my word for it: they'll read what I publish.
If I had ten years' time." Howren said "Maybe so.

What good is that?" but Howard in the shadow of another
Wave of faintness bent over the saddle-bow with both hands clinging
And could not hear; the darkness rushed over his eyes,
His head sagged forward to the black mane: then he struck the back
Of his left hand on his mouth and bit blood-deep
And pain revived him. His father said "Good God,
What's the matter?" Howard shook his head, still holding himself
With both hands on the saddle-bow, and sucking in
His lean belly, in hope to force the blood
That stagnated in the entrails back to the brain,
"Nothing. Nerves," he said faintly; and white-lipped smiling:
"I damn' near went off *that* time." "Well, you look green,"
Howren said. Howard said "Well: can I help it?"

                                              They rode on the great
     hill's whale-back
Past woman-limbed madrone-trees toward the tall crown of redwood. On
     the right a vulture's view
Of endless ridges creased with black canyons lay far below, against the long
     rim of land's-end ocean,
But Howren rather looked backward when he checked his horse, and said
     "Look around. Look at the place.
I tell you it's a good life here: what do you want with a
Tinkering unhappy life like you talk about? Call that a life?"
Howard thought of his dream of the wing-crucified dog
And said "To hell with happiness. I want to *know*." Howren said, "Look.
     Ain't it pretty here?
There's the high timber; here's range for a dozen herds when we get it
     fenced; down there's plowland and water;
The whole place rattles with game if you ride early: deer and pig, fat quail,
     mourning-doves, band-tail pigeons . . .

Coons and wild-cats and civet-cats if you want, and a mountain-lion from
    time to time . . ."
He looked at Howard's face and said "If you don't want hunting, bring
    your books and study 'em. Come on, Howard,"
He pleaded almost tenderly, "you better stay."

                                   Howard laughed and felt
The pain at the base of his skull grind like a mill.
"I won't. I'm down all right: not so deep as that.
Only grave-deep. Well: will you give me thirty a month
So that I can do my work?" "*If* you'll stay here,"
Howren said. Howard said, "Wait a minute before you answer.
This is the situation: I am your son: I'm in a noose
At my rope's end, unless you help me I'll die.
I expect you enjoyed breeding me twenty years ago.
She is still beautiful and strange and pale: her bones were not formed yet.
These pleasures imply their consequences: you get a boy
And you hate to let him die before he grows up
And does his work. I can't do my work here.
I need the laboratories. You can't understand, of course.
My mother has some intelligence, but yours is level
With a wild hog's." Howren stared and said, "On your own time then."
He rode up toward the wood, Howard toward the farmhouse.

III

But when the slope of the hill had hidden him
He turned off seaward, to cross the hill and go down
Into Mal Paso Canyon to find a search-proof
Vulture-proof place. He had pencil and paper and would post a note
In the horse's mane: "Dear mother I am going east
And try my luck in the world don't expect to hear from me

For a few years . . ." some facile message like that, and save her
From tearing her long pale hair. He crossed the hill
And rode down the steep slopes he had climbed yesterday.
The ache at the base of his skull ground like a mill, but the fainting-fits
Had ceased when he left his father . . . or when he left
His hope of living. He felt in despite of pain
Some exaltation of spirit: hope implies doubt,
That begets weakness; but certainty, even the certainty
Of death ennobles.

At the foot of a slope
Were acres of rotting thistles around an abandoned coal-mine; men had
    labored here
Sixty years ago and trampled the earth naked, and the crop was thistles.
    The mine-pit had fallen in,
Burying some Chinese laborers. No one was ever troubled to dig out their
    bodies, but they rested well
As if they had been shipped home to Asia; bones are great resters. Year
    after year the eight-foot thistles
Rot in the fall and grow up in spring.

The hollow stalks
Fell over with a sharp crackling as Howard rode through,
So that he failed to hear hoof-beats behind him
Stutter on the steep slope, but when he had passed he heard his pursuer
Plowing the dead sea of stalks. He waited and said
"Well, mother?" She made a beautiful picture of haste and fear, on a big
    bay horse without a saddle,
Her skirt caught up on the high withers, dragged up
Above her knees, and her face white as paper, pale parted lips, loops of pale
    hair
Slipping and fallen by the smooth throat. She said with a fawning smile

"Howard . . . where are you going, let me ride with you?" "To the road of
    course,
And beg rides north. I was going to tie a note to you
In the black's mane and loose him to take my love to you.
Your husband's ideas of life, and mine, don't mesh. You haven't followed us
All morning, mother?" "Oh," she answered, "no," saying something
    inaudible, and said "I happened to
Look out and see you on the hill. Howard listen to me.
Are you truly going back," she made a white smile and said "to Berkeley or
    have you perhaps dear
Some other plan?" "What? No. What kind of plan?" She sidled her horse
    close against his,
Laid hand on his and strained over to kiss his cheek, he felt her soft
Firm breast burn on his arm, he jerked the bridle
In senseless dismay and drew away from her.
She answered, "Why do you lie to me?" Her face a moment
Grew swollen and negroid with the intense grief
That looks like imbecile laughter. "I know where you" —
Through the blunt sucked-in lips of the mask — "not Berkeley I know
    where you. Exactly.
Common death that any fool finds when he wants.
There will be two." Howard said "You have extraordinary
Fantasies, mother. Death? Whose death? What do you mean?"
Her face resumed its carved pallor. "His," she answered quietly,
"*Your* life has value." Howard laughed and strained his head back and said
    "We are not exactly
At that point, mother." "No," she said, "in the dark. You lie to me and I
Daren't say what I. We are like two blind people
Feeling and reaching for each other up and down the hills
In a high wind."

                    The horses walked slowly downward
Up-slope of stunted alders toward the redwood canyon.
Howard sighed and strained his head back to ease the ache; it seemed
    localized
Between the atlas vertebra and the skull,
A factory of pain, distributing its over-production
Along the coronal suture. He thought he would study
The nerve-connections in that anatomy atlas in the library,
The beautiful plates and diagrams, "but I forgot:
I'm not going back." The future like a stopped peep-hole.
He had death in his pocket, no alternative; none but crawling
Pitiful failure. His mother was saying "I prayed to him
Last night as if he were God to help you,
Though I knew well he would not. No wonder I thought
If he were dead we'd be well. His life has no more value
Than an old range-bull's: the mind's life's value.
He is really wealthy; he could sell land, or borrow
Thousands on a moment's mortgage: if anything should happen to him
We could do that. So you'll excuse me for thinking wildly;
Because you know that I know you're not going back
To your life but to death. Would you have left the case with your books in
    it
If you meant life?" He strained his head back and said "Mother.
I have a torturing pain under the skull.
I am burnt-out and worthless. I have worked hard
And the end's . . . . this. Shall we go back now?" "Where?" she said.
    Howard said
"And be a farmhand of my father's. I did choose death instead,
But the will cracks after while."

                            She began bitter answer,
But looked at him and locked her lips; they turned and rode home.

When he dismounted by the latch-gate Howard fell
And had to be helped in-doors, helped up to bed.
The fourth day he dressed himself and went to his father:
"I'm ready to go to work now." Who stared at the raging
Eyes in the Lazarus face: "You? Get well first."

IV

Returning up-stairs Howard felt his coat for the little
Bottle of death, and marvelled it was still there.
He thought his mother would have searched his clothing while he was ill.
His books were still in the straw suit-case, and life would be simpler to
    bear
If they were put out of the way; the kitchen range
Will still have fire in it.

                         Grace Gomez washing the breakfast dishes
And France drying them spoke to him, but would not care
What he was doing. He lifted the stove-lid and laid
General Chemistry of the Proteins on the red coals,
Watched it swell and make flame. France said, "Howard.
What are you doing?" "I? Burning books, like Hitler."
"Who?" she said. "Everybody. Free life of the mind
Is the first luxury to go." She saw his face. "Oh Howard.
Don't." "What?" he said, "it's nothing. They're useless"; he laid
Physiology of the Single-Celled Organism: an Outline
On the other's flame, stuffed in a multigraphed
Manual of laboratory experiments and shut the stove-lid.
His mother came in, saying "Where is Howard?" and saw him
Standing in the smoke of paper, with books and note-books
In the crook of his arm. "What did he say to you . . . Oh
What are you . . ." He turned away from her and laid another

Book in the stove, she ran and dredged with her hand
At the red roots of fire and saved it, threw it on the floor
And shook her hand. Howard said "Oh mother." She,
White-voiced: "You'd better have killed yourself." "I know it," he said;
"Are you burnt badly?" France dipped the dish-towel in water
And was looking for baking-soda, "Where is it, Grace?" Mrs. Howren said
"Than give in to him. You will be wretched and contemptible forever
If you give up your life." France found the soda, but her mother
Refused it. Howard reached another book toward the fire,
She caught it with her left hand and they stood straining
A moment, he said slowly "Well, mother:
One of these you ought to read, really. Come outside
Where there is light." She took the wet towel from France
To cool her hand, and followed him.

                              He had laid his books
On the bench under the leafless rose-vine; the south-wind
Whipping around the house-corner opened one of them, chattered the
     pages. Howard took another
And leafed through it, his back to the wind . . . inheritance . . . somatic
     cells . . . fruit-flies . . . "Here's
Your text, mother." She read attentively, frowning in the dust-eddy, and
     said "Oh,
Because France has brown eyes?" She fixed on his face her blue ones
And saw his mouth twitching and said with mourning-dove
Pity in her voice, "Oh. Oh. Darling.
I have always been faithful to your father. The book is wrong. Oh Howard
How long have you been tormented?" "Tormented?" he said,
"I've known for years." "Dear, it's not true." France came to the door
And said with her rich brown hair blowing over her face,
"Ernie is here. He promised to take me rabbit-shooting
When they burn their hill: good-bye. Good-bye, Howard." Mrs. Howren

Nodded, and turned again to her son, touched his hand, saying
"Would you rather . . . Oh how can I know what's best for you?
Perhaps this . . . idea . . . was the spurs.
Believe whatever you need to believe, dear.
What's truth? Whatever helps us live and be strong
Is the truth." He said "My God, mother, how modern
Away off here in the mountain. Adultery's nothing,
But this amazes me."

V

Ernie Crawford and France
Rode up the hills up the ringing wind under the cloud-river
And turned west on the height, they and their horses
Leaned on the wind on the left stirrup on every summit;
At length they saw the last ridge, where a far horseman
Little and clear in the mountain distance on the dark ocean-sky
Beckoned with his arms and lifted hands to his mouth
But the wind blew away his voice. Ernie said "Quick:
I guess they've lighted it." They raced and came to the verge; Ernie's mount
    stopped,
France's went down the start of the slope, she saw the stone-gray
    foam-flawed ocean a thousand feet down
And a long smoke wind-plastered across the mountain-foot,
She brought her horse a terrifying circle on the pitch of the slope and came
    back to Ernie
Running down after her. He said "My God
I thought you were going on over, did he run away with you?"
"Ah" she answered breathlessly, her rich hair like a banner on the wind, her
    long brown eyes
Rich with delight.

They tied their horses at one of those cairns of rock
That stand along the ridges like kings' graves. Ernie stayed by to watch
    them,
And he lent France his gun. She and Paul went down
Over the verge of the height and heard the fire's roar
Devour the wind's. They hurried and stood at their vantages, north and
    south
The glen-head where brush grew highest; half way down a few trees
Stood terribly distinct against the fire-curtain. From these a great yellow
    barn-owl came up the hill's face,
Sagging down wind, drifting up from the fire; a vindictive sparrow-hawk
Dived at her and flew up and dived at her, flew up and dived at her. The
    fiery disaster
Meant nothing to that little anger if an owl flew; and France for pure
    pleasure
Twitched her finger on the trigger when the owl passed under her. The
    great pale-golden bird side-slipped and fell,
The hawk vaulted the fire and found a new field.

                          Next came the quail.
No one could hear the hawk's cry in the noise of fire, but volleys of quail
Drummed in the ears; France fired and loaded and fired again and ran to
    gather them, two birds
Out of the hundreds; and she saw a road-runner
Dive straight into the flame, and a wild-cat
Fleeing on singed pads. Then two or three jack-rabbits
Fled upward; she blasted one, but the panting fire
Came over and claimed him. It was taller than trees
And the smoke filled the west. France felt its breath
And fled to the height, seeing over her shoulder the roaring flame-surf
Reach for the sky and fall. The horses were rioting
And Paul had run to help hold them; France laid her gun

And droop-headed quail on the rock cairn by Paul's
Rabbits and gun; she reached for the reins and Ernie
Helped her up, Paul was up already.

                                  The fire crept
Languidly thwart the wind through the over-pastured
Grass of the height, sparse autumn stubble. Paul dropped the rope
From his saddle-horn and Ernie tied it to a young redwood
They had cut for its rich growth and dragged up beforehand; France held
    his horse;
He uncoiled the rope from his own saddle and tied it in the knot with
    Paul's, mounted and said
"Come along, we've got to mop up," fighting his horse
Across the ground-fire. They dragged the heavy green broom
Along the line of the fire, trotting at first, then galloping, in the wild wind
    on the mountain forehead
Above black slopes, and the ocean far down below through the spits of
    smoke; France rode beside them
Her heart flying like a bird, here was the beauty
She'd not dreamed even.

                            In the evening Ernie rode home with her.
The expected rain had not come and the wind had fallen, tender amber
    light
Poured through a great slash in the cloud-tent; the tired horses
Walked slowly. On the dome of the hill over Howren's place
France checked her horse and caught Ernie's arm. "Look.
Do you see him?" "What?" he said, "no." She said "I saw my brother
Standing there on the hill's edge with his back to us." "Well?" Ernie said.
    She said
"It disappeared, I saw it clearly." They came to the verge

And saw the house and the barn far down below them, drowned roofs in
    the lake of twilight. France said "He looked
As if he was looking down at the house. Things are sick there:
He'd better not look too long." She checked her horse
And said "I'm tired." Ernie rode on, and turned back
Seeing she had stopped, and saw past her head the young crescent
    swimming in the amber cloud-slash, thin golden skiff
Filled with a great dark pearl. He said "Look back
Over your left shoulder." She, without looking:
"I'm in earnest." "What?" he said. She said "My mother
Was married at my age; and if it's turned bad, as I think it has, that's not
From being sixteen." He said "I wish to God . . ." "Oh," she answered
    laughing,
"I know you can't marry until you're rich." He said
"Be honest France, or can't you? D' I ever say anything
That looked like that?" She said "I killed an owl, two quail and a rabbit,
    and threw them away.
I broke four shining lamps of life for no reason at all.
Or some hateful reason: have you got a hunting-
License, Ernie?" "No," he said. She said "*I* haven't.
Did you ever kill a deer out of season?" He said
"I guess you don't understand. These mountains are too big to patrol: only
    in deer-season
They watch the cars; but we that live here don't bother much
About seasons or licenses." "Only for making love," she answered,
"But not for hunting." He was silent, and she
Gazed at the mane of her horse; at length he said
"What do you mean?" "Nothing, Oh nothing.
We couldn't marry without a license you know.
I can't bear to go home for awhile, I can't breathe down there.
It's under water." She turned and rode back up hill,

He followed, he saw her head for a moment wear the young moon in her
    hair, as if it were a great jewel
And she owned it; then he rode beside her. She said: "Ernie.
Do you think mother's beautiful?" "Who," he said, "your mother?
I guess everyone does." France said "I haven't thought of her all the long
    day, I've been so happy.
I think it's a sick and twisted beauty: if I were my mother
I think my father wouldn't get drunk when he goes to town, and Howard
Wouldn't be sick. I can't understand her thoughts.
I wish . . . if I were in her place I might." She drew her horse
Close to his and laid her hand on his saddle-horn and kissed his mouth.
    "I've never known
What she has known." He instinctively wound his arm around her, the
    tired horses walked patiently, she said
"I love you and I need . . . . to know. Do we need a hunting-
License, dear love?"

VI

               The great wheel of the year shuddered and turned at
    length.
Rains fell, storms whipped the sea and red sunsets burned, deep blue-black
    and silver clouds dragged on the mountain.
Howren drove over the mountain to Monterey
With crates of turkeys and a litter of little pigs
For Christmas buyers. In the evening he had not returned.
Rain and hail scourged the windows, and every door
Rattled in the draught through the house. The lamp ran dry
After ten o'clock, then Mrs. Howren fetched another lamp
And France went up-stairs to bed. Howard said "Good-night,
Mother." She, basilisk-pale: "Stay up with me.
The road's greasy with sleet, and never a turn

Without a precipice. I can't sleep." Howard said, "How you love him."
She answered, "Hate me if you have to, I gave it to you.
And I am the one prevented you from throwing it away.
Now you must rest for a time and recover strength,
And wait on opportunity: I have dreamed twice
That he was dead. But if you prefer despair
And lie down on the farm here, it would be better
You'd eaten fire: I found your little treasure in your pocket
When you were sick. I left it there. I thought you might
Need it in the long run; or use it more wisely.
    —Or share it wi' me, ain't enough for two?" The excellently
Carved marble of her face on the last phrase
Wizened into gipsy cunning. Then Howard stood up
And walked in the room, looking away from her.
She said "Is it very painful?" "No," he said, "instant."
"Why, then," she said, "it would pass for heart-disease." He knelt on the
    hearth
And shifted the unruly oak-logs. The mountain wind
Thundered in the flue; bursts of blue smoke and ashes
Came into the room and powdered him. She said, "If you die of it
Does it leave marks?" "You'd have to see a Nevada execution.
They use it instead of hanging, out of pure kindness."
He said from a thin and disarticulated
Blade of the mind, and his gaps of ignorance, "I guess it might
Pass for some kind of heart-failure, embolism, if the peach-kernel
Smell had time to steam off, and nobody made
Chemical tests." She said "I can't myself. You know it's crazy, I fear him so.
Like a stunned rabbit when the weasel's cruel eyes. If I aimed at him
I'd miss. If I put something in his coffee I'd drop the cup. Or his thick
    shadow'd 've
Gone underground many years ago." He said "You talk like a fool.

Mother keep still." She answered, "Pure senseless terror. I couldn't touch
    him." He turned on her
Furiously: "Stop this talk." She ceased and sat rigid;
He paced the room, the wind clattered the door-latches;
Suddenly the woman moaned, saying "He can't make it.
Oh, Oh . . . he did. He must be drunk to drive
That speed in the blind rain-glitter." Howard looked and saw her
Sitting rigid on the chair, staring straight forward, he went and gripped
Her arm and she looked up at him with pure white eyes; he had heard that
    hysteria
Can roll back the eyes. "Mother?" he said quite gently. She said "He's
    driving wild at the turns and white
Rain reversing the headlights into his eyes: he's made it again.
He swooped through it like an owl, he has terrible eyes. — Oh," she said,
"He turned too wide." Howard said "What?" and thought
"I am the fool in the show, almost believing
What this hysterical woman . . ." She said quietly, "He turned too wide
And struck the bank. He was driving like a drunken man.
The wheel turned in his hands, he and the truck
Have gone down the rocks to death. Oh, when I saw his hands
Scrabble at the wheel and now his neck's broken back
On the shoulder-blades." Howard said "You are sick and dreaming mother.
    He is probably
Staying in town over night and will come home
To-morrow morning." She listened to a distant motor and said
"He has died, let me cry. I loved him terribly
When I was young."

                    Howard heard the noise of a motor across the wind's
    noise; his mother said
"I told you to wait on opportunity, something might happen. Now it has
    happened: he has died.

Now I'll find money for you, you'll be free to work: you'll do your work
    and succeed.
No more slavery, no more humiliations: pride and success,
Oh think of that.
You'll dig at the roots of life and know it like a God.
You'll understand sickness and death, you'll intervene
Like God between life and death." "Ah fine," he said, "only
Your dream fooled you. Dreams do. I hear his motor
Come down the drive." She answered "*I* heard it long ago.
He has no right to live and destroy *your* life.
His life for yours." "Steady," he said. She stood up
And gazed at the hallway door, Howard saw her lips
Twitching, and the slant shaft of her white throat
Through the blue oak-smoke. He went and touched her. "Your nerves
Are full of violence to-night, try and control them,
Forget these dreams," and suddenly pitying her
He said "Dear mother." She turned and embraced him
And pressed herself against him, shuddering like a woman in love, but with
    sidelong eyes
Watching the door, hoping Howren would come in.
Howard loosed her arms and stood back.

                       They heard the man
Stumble on the porch steps, pause long, then mount
With careful and planted feet. Wind coursing through the house
Banged the outer door. They heard him in the dark hallway
Lurch from one wall to the other, then he came in
And walked carefully across the room to the fire.
His wide shoulders were gray with sleet, and hailstones
Fell from his hat. He said "What a devil of a night. Hello Barbra.
I put the truck i' the shed, unload in the morning:
My elbow's cramped." She eyed him and looked at her son,

And said "Was the road bad?" "Hm?" he said, "hoisting drinks
All afternoon." She said "I know. Have you nothing left
For Howard and me?" He drew a half-emptied pint
From the side-pocket of his mackinaw, and from the other
A fifth, still sealed, and set them on the lamp's table.
"Fetch glasses." Howard said "No thank you," but Mrs. Howren
Said, "We were terribly worried about the road.
We're so glad you're safe home." She went to the kitchen
And brought three glasses, poured an inch into each,
Drank one of them out of hand. She gasped and said
"Howard says my nerves." Howren eyed his son and said
"Has K conquered Napoleon? Here's to K." Howard stared; then
    remembered and said
Hoarsely, "I won't." Barbara Howren unscrewed
The cap of the taller bottle and poured an inch
Into each glass, saying "What was that?" Howard said "What? An
    understanding
We have between us." She, suddenly haggard and sly:
"Have you?" Howren held up his glass and said:
"The simple joys of a cattle-man." Howard said "I think
I've fallen to that." They emptied the glasses, and Mrs. Howren
Spilled whiskey into the two glasses and raised
Her own and said, "Revolution." Howren said
"Uh? Like in Russia?" She said, "More final. More destructive, more
    destructive.
Cut *all* the throats." She sighed and smiled and stretched her white throat:
    "Like in Spain maybe.
I came not to bring peace but a sword. You know my dad was an Adventist
    and went crazy
Waiting for the end of the world: brother against brother,
The son shall rise up against his father." Howard said, "Mother.
You are talking like a fool, and this man is drunk.

We'll skip the rest." Howren said "Uh? Who's drunk?
I was drunk this afternoon, but let me go take a leak,
We'll see who's drunk." He lurched out of the room and was heard
    fumbling
Along the hallway.

Barbara Howren
Said, "That swine is your father." "I believe so," Howard said,
"But who is France's?" "Ah," she said, "his life like mud
Suffocating your clean ambition: his life for yours." Howard said, "Perhaps
He has a right to it?" "*If* you think so," she answered.
"If yours, that his kills, is valueless." He failed to answer; she said "You'll
    have
No chance like this. Fail it and forget forever
The light of the stars you aimed at. Forget discovery. Turn into not my son
    but that drunkard's:
You'll soon grow like him, ignorant and bestial, lean on the bars
In Monterey and cry about old times lost.
I love you, Howard."

"*Strangely*," he answered.
"But there's a kind of insane lucidity in it."
He dipped for the phial in the pocket of his coat,
And salted one of the glasses, but trembling so,
Jerking his hand like palsy when the deliquescent
Morsels of death stuck in the phial-throat, half of them
Rained on the face of the table: he sighed and stroked them
To the edge, and held the glass just under, and stroked them
Into the glass. He stirred the liquor with the emptied phial,
Which then he threw in the fire; and wiped his hand
Against his clothing.

He thought it was nearly certain
That nothing like this could be, there was not one needle-point
Of real in it; except his whole body shaking,
His heart bursting its rib-cage: "but as real as Europe's
Rearmament race," a jigging splinter of his mind laughed, "or Dirac's
     equations:
Nothing is real this year." He set the two glasses
Carefully side by side at the table end;
They were equally filled, they looked from a little distance perfectly alike,
One smelled no doubt of bitter almonds but a drunken man
Might hardly notice. Howard himself had forgotten
Which was the glass.

                    He stood against the wall and Howren came in,
Buttoning his trousers, tipsily straddling, saying "Old Tom Birnam
Died last week. Ed Stiles told me.
That was a good old man and a good cattle-man.
Well, he was eighty." He laid his hand for balance
On the table beside the glasses, "I guess his boys
Will now sell land. I remember old Tom . . ." He became conscious
Of a strained silence in the room, like a still pool of glassy water
Under the oak-smoke and wind's noise. He stared carefully at Howard and
     said, "By God,
You're a queer wall-hanger!" and turned, carefully balancing,
And eyed his wife. "Hm. Not a word." She moved her lips
On silence, tongued them wet and said, "Is it a lottery,
Howard?" He muttered from the white O of his mouth "What do you
     mean?
Let the dice roll."

                    Howren looked back at his son
And took one of the glasses and said "Good old

Tom Birnam, God rest him." Howard snatched the other, gasping
"Bottoms up, Ah?" and sucked in the liquor
Through chalk lips with shut eyes, staggered with shut eyes,
And breathed again. But if one could breathe . . . Oh . . .
One could breathe . . . he watched in complete helplessness his father
Tip the great head back, take the draught with its dregs
One heavy mouthful, "Don't, don't," Howard croaked, and saw the
    cartilage
Slide up and down the massive column of the throat
Between the muscles and swollen veins. Howren said "Ahhh,"
Stirring the phlegm in his throat, as one who has gulped
Neat liquor, then hoarsely: "What was that?" Howard, with his glass
In one hand, and the other like a fly's clinging
On the flat wall behind him attempted to say
"Peach-brandy," for the odor, but instead muttered "Oh
Oh Oh Oh Oh." Howren stood still, breathing difficultly, and said
"Was it that . . . white knife . . ." He jerked his emptied
Glass at her but it broke on the floor, his muscles
Without direction, jerking by themselves, even to breathe
Was nearly too difficult now, and his grim face
Grew bluish, yet he stood. Like a compact and powerfully organized state
    in the agony
Of insurrection, when strikes have blocked life-essential services, thirst,
    hunger and darkness are in the houses;
Leaders lose contact with their people, in the night of the streets under
    dead street-lamps undirected rioters,
Convulsed muscles of the great body of the state fight their own friends
    and build
Barricades against their own faction; red tongues of random fire stream up
    the sky,
The armored cars fall into traps and spit random death: still the nation
    stands, and Caesar

Or Caesar-Spartacus may capture and save and regenerate it: but this
     standing dead man
Will not be saved. He opened his mouth, wide, black and square,
As if to call judgment on his killers, through every
Hollow of the house: but there was no breath
To feed the ghastly organ: only a formed
Silence came forth. He fell to his knees and crashed
Forward, Mrs. Howren babbling "Did y' draw the black
Bean from the hat, Oh God," laughing, "I thought that Howard: he got the
     black one
Howard what a sweepstakes. Lock the door," for the dying man
Scratched on the floor with his hands, and a hard clicking
Came from his throat. Mrs. Howren walked wide around him
And locked the door; Howard could not move from the wall.

                                                                    Oh rich
Clean turbulent wind arching the house-roof,
Roaring in the creekside redwoods, tearing the mountain oaks: you living
     mountains,
Palo Corona and the ancient forest, Mount Carmel, Pico Blanco, Ventanas,
     high heads
With clear snow heavy to-night, and you sea-wall ridges and the streaming
     waters, tall granite rocks
Burly-shouldered standing watchful in pastures:
I never imagined that you can pity humanity;
You ought to pity us, perverse by nature, you are the blessed ones.
I know that you neither hear nor care, but your presence helps,
One endures extreme evil more nobly in your presence.
You are sane and stone; humanity is crafty and cruel and mad.
As for these two: heal this boy's wounds and this woman's hatred:
Their souls are worse distorted than their dead man's body:

Or offer them quickly to the eyeless night
That waits for souls.

VII

                       Mrs. Howren said "Lock the door."
Howard stared at her; she went and locked it and said
Without expression, as if it were part
Of the ceremony: "Oh God." Howard breathed, and panted like a tired
    runner, and said
"Are you satisfied?" She said "You gambled with him,
Played and won, whether you wanted to lose or not.
It's done. Be quiet." Howard said "His life was worth ten of mine.
I see that now." She pressed her hand on his mouth.
"I think that Grace is coming. Be quiet."

                        They heard Grace Gomez
Waddle barefoot along the passage from her little room
Beside the kitchen. She pressed on the door; the latch
Rattled, and the mean white knob, yellow with handling,
Rolled to and fro. Mrs. Howren watched it
And felt how venemous it looked; she sighed and said clearly:
"It's all right, Grace. Go back to bed. He's been drinking,
But I can manage." She answered through the door: "What fell?"
She answered, "He brought home liquor. It's all right, Grace." Howard
    smelled
A faint fragrance of rose-leaf soap on the hand
That pressed his mouth: she had always used that one luxury:
It stirred forgotten music in his nerves; but when Grace Gomez
Went back to her room he said: "Do you think *that*
Will pass for heart-failure? Look at his face." She looked and choked.
He said "I will write a clear confession.

You know. Where I got the stuff; and that I did it for money and so forth,
And keep you safe. There are probably four hours to dawn.
I'll write and sign it in ten minutes, and use
One of his rifles." She stared at him, with her fingers
Picking the smoky air as if it had motes in it, and whispered
"What have you done!" but smiled in a moment, through drooping
Eyelashes: "No memoirs, dear. I'll go along wi' you
Singing."

       They had still a fair chance of intact life, they preferred
  despair.
They were in fact exhausted, and the waters of their minds draining away
Left high and clear the common desire of death, that stands like a drowned
    tower in all human minds,
The waters of life cover it and hide it: now it stood dark and tall from the
    water, a forgotten tower
In a drained lake: the astonished discoverers
Wade out through mud and water to enter the door, under the lake-weed
    lintel-fringes, and climb
The ooze-choked stair.

       Howard said, "Not you: no need.
I am the one." He reached and touched her face with his fingers,
Tasting it like a blind man, delicately, the narrow oval
Outline, the high-bridged nose, the long lift of the throat.
He drew his hand back and trembled and said "I have something
Strange to ask you. Will you show me your breasts?" "What, dear?"
"Show me your beautiful breasts. I am going to die
In a few minutes, and at last understand
What all the fury was about. Slip down the cloth from your shoulders
And let me cool my face on the white snows.
My life will find all its meaning." "Do you love me," she answered,

And pressed herself against him, shuddering like a woman in love; but her
	eyes fixed
On the death on the room floor, not in
Terror but triumph, shining like knives, and said
"I love you Howard, I hope he suffered grinding ages and eternities of pain
While he was dying: or what twisted him so?
I'll do anything you want." Howard picked at the catches
That closed her dress below the beautiful throat
And said, "For you. When I starved, and worked all night
To pay the laboratory fees, and studied with burnt-out eyes in the weak
	dawns, ravenous to know
The beautiful chemistry and cells of life: it never was the chemistry of life,
	but your
Body and soul."

She had helped his helplessly twitching fingers
And stood bare to the hips, and she was more beautiful
Than he had dreamed, pale polished ivory in warm lamplight under blue
	smoke, the beautiful
Ripple of the lower ribs under breasts
Not like a mother's; and their blond eager flowers
Purer than he had hoped, pale virgin rose-color, no trace of the
	pigmentation the books
Attributed to maternity, their authors knowing perhaps
Only dark women. Howard stood away from her and sobbed, "Oh mother.
This is what my life meant."

She said "How strange to have no
to-morrows, how it sets us free. I can't
Tell what will please you: do you like me dear? Do you want . . . . all,
	dearest? Nothing's to hide nor forbidden

Among the dead." He whispered, "It's your beauty . . ." But hail was on
   the windows again, and she said "I can't
Hear you dear?" He clenched his fists and said furiously "Cover yourself."
"What, dearest? This is nothing new: why do you tremble so?
Your mouth has been on my bare breast many times before. What if you
   want me
A lovelier way? Love always wants to make gifts, and here I've nothing but
   myself to give you
On this thin strand, we have to disappear at dawn like the stars. Oh why do
   you tremble so?
Are you afraid of God? Surely if God should happen to exist he must have
   gone even farther
Beyond the tabus and tribal terrors than the rest of us. He must have been
   a long time
Laughing at the changing faiths and holy terrors of men, but now too
   bored
Even for laughter has turned away from humanity and perhaps
Enjoys the mountains. Perhaps we shall go and meet him and enjoy the
   mountains: meantime we have a four-hour
Hell and heaven of our own to live in. My life was well fulfilled in the
   poisoned dog's fall.
I wish to please you and complete yours if I could: dawn is not near." He
   answered,
"I'd rather not have known you for a whore. Cover yourself you whore.
I know now, I've been your creature all my life. The tortured ambition was
   yours, God how you worked in me—"
He remembered his dream of the wing-crucified dog
And said—"till the wires cracked and the wings broke in pieces and the
   great nailheads
Tore through my hands: I'm free of you. Go and find France's father." She
   stood quietly
Like a tall altar-candle under the pale flame of her hair, patient and white,

Saying "But we're past all that dearest. I read in the paper,
I can't remember, how do they shoot their captives in Spain for a quick
    death? In the base of the skull
Is it?" He said "And so you made me your poisoner. That was your
    voluptuousness, the man's own son
To fix him for you. I'm free of you at last,
And I'll die free." She held her clothing to her side and made her voice
Like a cool wind in June, when the flower-fragrances
Are still alive, but the homes of bees are brimming with honey and the sun
    is hot: "Darling,
All that is past. It is past. Death has us now. There is no life in this room.
    Don't you remember
That nineteen-thirty-seven will come up the calendar two weeks from now,
    and many strange things no doubt
Will be done in it, wars and peace, killings and marriages, wild hates and
    loves . . . . but we're to be absent?
Better divert our minds from it dear. Oh horses of night run slowly, give
    me time to breathe.
You might probably be hanged next year, and I should certainly go mad in
    prison, indeed the mirror's
Glittering and cracking already, long splinters crackle off and tongues of
    darkness flicker in my mind: it's easy
To keep them quiet till the great darkness." He said "Oh God,
Mother?" She answered, "I can govern myself.
I have been hateful in my life, but I loved you Howard: and apparently
That's been a curse, and has starved and tortured you.
That one good thing in my life, worse than all the evil ones."
She reached her hands toward him: "Come Howard.
Good and evil are too much mixed; but there is one supreme sweetness in
    life. I cannot bear
To let you go down into the darkness and not have known
Any sweetness at all. It's blind there, terrible: can't you hear the cats

Howling in the forest of night in the net of roots? Oh it's black underground. Even the

Moon-eyed cats bump on the root-stocks. You know what they're howling for?

Exactly: these pretties here: the poor white globes that fed you, poor handfuls of flesh

That you despise. Cat's meat." She cowered with her breasts,

And fumbled to find the sleeve-holes, draw the dress again

Over her shoulders; Howard pitied her and went to help her, but when he touched her

She screamed and screamed, many times; while a cold inner eye

That had no power to control the peripheral turbulence, and had no part in it, watched itself scream

And watched the mirror of its mind split into fragments, become a black disk of eclipsed sun, with a splintered

Corona of glass.

    At the pounding on the door

Howard went and opened it and said "Take care of my mother,

Grace"; and saw France past the others, her staring eyes

Down the dark hallway by a candle-flame. He turned from her

And said to the two men, Jim Gomez and Corbett: "Keep out of here.

My mother's sick. Come and I'll tell you something,"

He drew them toward the outer door: "Howren is dead.

I murdered him with poison because he refused

To give me money. And horror at the sight has damaged

My mother's mind. *I* did it, do you understand?

I did it. Ride for a doctor, you." He opened the door

And ran into the darkness. Neither man followed him;

They stood bewildered.

VIII

Going up the hill in the gray darkness
Howard saw a human form on the height, on the dim sky,
And recognized it for that hallucination
He had suffered before, the simulacrum of himself
That stands watching the house. He thought it would vanish
When he came near; instead it stood waiting for him,
And walked beside him in silence. Finally he clenched his fists and turned
　　on it:
"Can you talk?" It answered, "My twenty years
Of watching are at last ending. Why did you not
Complete your cycle? You returned to the breasts of infancy,
Not to the womb of birth." Howard said "I loved her.
I hate all women." It said "You are typical: your fever
And your failure from the one fountain. You wanted discovery
And then refused it, desired and yet not-desired, loved and yet hated,
The tension of the divided mind drove you on
And brought you down; that tension, the spurs and curb-bit
Of the present human world including its sciences. And now
What will you do?" "I will go down to the sea
And swim away from the earth until I go down.
I am very tired of the earth." The appearance answered,
"We'd better step down behind this thicket,
Not to be seen. Your sister is riding yonder, beating her horse
As if there were wolves behind. She is going to her lover
For consolation and help: life will continue
Though many fail." Howard sighed, "If they have to,
Let them continue." It answered again, "So you've accomplished great
　　deeds
Through divided desire and the split will . . . haven't you?
Avenged your birth on both sides. And now to cancel it

With a little drowning and escape easily.
Well, there are no tabus—did she tell you?—for modern man.
You are not required to tear your flesh with your hands,
Nor stab your eyes with her fibula." Howard stood still
And said "You're right," then turned and walked swiftly back
The way he had come. His hallucination
Walked beside him and said "The split will." He groaned and answered,
"To tell them in court that she is innocent." "She innocent!"
"But likely to accuse herself: then my sane story
Will cure her broken one." It answered, "She innocent!" Howard answered,
"She followed her twisted nature; she could not help
Being what she is." "In that sense every criminal is innocent.
And you are innocent." "In that sense," Howard answered.
It answered, "So you intend to go back, though innocent,
And confess guilt? While sweet and easy escape
Is waiting in the pale sea: you prefer prison?
It will be torture for you. You prefer the lecherous
Eyes of the court-room crowd, and a shameful death,
To clean free death?" He answered, "There are certain duties
Even for . . . . what did you say? . . . modern man. Life is not rational;
I have learned that."

He was rather glad that his phantom
Remained on the brow of the hill while he went down
To the farmhouse; and a great slow green dawn behind him
Lighted the ridges, the rolling summits patched with pale snow, the long
    dark woods and white lonely peaks.

DECAYING LAMBSKINS

After all, we also stand on a height. Our blood and our culture have passed the flood-marks of any world
Up to this time. Our engineers have nothing to learn from Rome's, Egypt's, China's, and could teach them more
Than ever their myth-makers imagined. Our science, however confused, personal and fabulous, can hardly
Lean low enough, sun-blinded eagle, to laugh at the strange astronomies of Babylon, or at Lucretius
His childish dreams of origins, or Plato's
Lunatic swan. While as for our means and mastery of warfare, at sea, on land, in the air . . .

                    So boastful?
Because we are not proud but wearily ashamed of this peak of time. What is noble in us, to kindle
The imagination of a future age? We shall seem a race of cheap Fausts, vulgar magicians.
What men have we to show them? but inventions and appliances. Not men but populations, mass-men; not life
But amusements; not health but medicines. And the odor: what is that odor? Decaying lambskins: the Christian
Ideals that for protection and warmth our naked ancestors . . . but naturally, after nineteen centuries . . .

Ô mort, vieux capitaine, est-il temps, nous levons l'ancre? It is perhaps
Time, almost time, to let our supreme inventions begin to work. The exact intelligent guns
Can almost wheel themselves into action of their own accord, and almost calculate their own trajectories.

The clever battle-ships know their objectives; the huge bombing-planes and
    meteor pursuit-planes are all poised for . . . What?
Vanity. This also is vanity; horrible too, but a vain dream.
Our civilization, the worst it can do, cannot yet destroy itself: but only
    deep-wounded drag on for centuries.

SHIVA

There is a hawk that is picking the birds out of our sky.
She killed the pigeons of peace and security,
She has taken honesty and confidence from nations and men,
She is hunting the lonely heron of liberty.
She loads the arts with nonsense, she is very cunning,
Science with dreams and the state with powers to catch them at last.
Nothing will escape her at last, flying nor running.
This is the hawk that picks out the stars' eyes.
This is the only hunter that will ever catch the wild swan;
The prey she will take last is the wild white swan of the beauty of things.
Then she will be alone, pure destruction, achieved and supreme,
Empty darkness under the death-tent wings.
She will build a nest of the swan's bones and hatch a new brood,
Hang new heavens with new birds, all be renewed.

NOW RETURNED HOME

Beyond the narrows of the Inner Hebrides
We sailed the cold angry sea toward Barra, where Heaval mountain
Lifts like a mast. There were few people on the steamer, it was late in the
    year; I noticed most an old shepherd,
Two wise-eyed dogs wove anxious circles around his feet, and a thin-armed
    girl
Who cherished what seemed a doll, wrapping it against the sea-wind. When
    it moved I said to my wife "She'll smother it."
And she to the girl: "Is your baby cold? You'd better run down out of the
    wind and uncover its face."
She raised the shawl and said "He is two weeks old. His mother died in
    Glasgow in the hospital
Where he was born. She was my sister." I looked ahead at the bleak island,
    gray stones, ruined castle,
A few gaunt houses under the high and comfortless mountain; my wife
    looked at the sickly babe,
And said "There's a good doctor in Barra? It will soon be winter." "Ah,"
    she answered, "Barra'd be heaven for him,
The poor wee thing, there's Heaval to break the wind. We live on a wee
    island yonder away,
Just the one house."

                The steamer moored, and a skiff—what they call a
    curragh, like a canvas canoe
Equipped with oars—came swiftly along the side. The dark-haired girl
    climbed down to it, with one arm holding
That doubtful slip of life to her breast; a tall young man with sea-pale eyes
    and an older man

Helped her; if a word was spoken I did not hear it. They stepped a mast
    and hoisted a henna-color
Bat's wing of sail.

            Now, returned home
After so many thousands of miles of road and ocean, all the hulls sailed in,
    the houses visited,
I remember that slender skiff with dark henna sail
Bearing off across the stormy sunset to the distant island
Most clearly; and have rather forgotten the dragging whirlpools of London,
    the screaming haste of New York.

THEORY OF TRUTH

(Reference to Chapter II, The Women at Point Sur)

I stand near Soberanes Creek, on the knoll over the sea, west of the road. I remember

This is the very place where Arthur Barclay, a priest in revolt, proposed
    three questions to himself:

First, is there a God and of what nature? Second, whether there's anything
    after we die but worm's meat?

Third, how should men live? Large time-worn questions no doubt; yet he
    touched his answers, they are not unattainable;

But presently lost them again in the glimmer of insanity.

                    How many

minds have worn these questions; old coins

Rubbed faceless, dateless. The most have despaired and accepted doctrine;
    the greatest have achieved answers, but always

With aching strands of insanity in them.

I think of Lao-tze; and the dear beauty of the Jew whom they crucified but
    he lived, he was greater than Rome;

And godless Buddha under the boh-tree, straining through his mind the
    delusions and miseries of human life.

Why does insanity always twist the great answers?

                    Because only

tormented persons want truth.

Man is an animal like other animals, wants food and success and women,
    not truth. Only if the mind

Tortured by some interior tension has despaired of happiness: then it hates
    its life-cage and seeks further,

And finds, if it is powerful enough. But instantly the private agony that
     made the search
Muddles the finding.

                    Here was a man who envied the chiefs of the
     provinces of China their power and pride,
And envied Confucius his fame for wisdom. Tortured by hardly conscious
     envy he hunted the truth of things,
Caught it, and stained it through with his private impurity. He praised
     inaction, silence, vacancy: why?
Because the princes and officers were full of business, and wise Confucius
     of words.

Here was a man who was born a bastard, and among the people
That more than any in the world valued race-purity, chastity, the prophetic
     splendors of the race of David.
Oh intolerable wound, dimly perceived. Too loving to curse his mother,
     desert-driven, devil-haunted,
The beautiful young poet found truth in the desert, but found also
Fantastic solution of hopeless anguish. The carpenter was not his father?
     Because God was his father,
Not a man sinning, but the pure holiness and power of God. His personal
     anguish and insane solution
Have stained an age; nearly two thousand years are one vast poem drunk
     with the wine of his blood.

And here was another Savior, a prince in India,
A man who loved and pitied with such intense comprehension of pain that
     he was willing to annihilate
Nature and the earth and stars, life and mankind, to annul the suffering. He
     also sought and found truth,
And mixed it with his private impurity, the pity, the denials.

Then search
for truth is foredoomed and frustrate?
Only stained fragments?

Until the mind has turned its love from itself
and man, from parts to the whole.